SECOND E

Current perspectives in
forensic psychology and
criminal behavior

CURRENT PERSPECTIVES in
FORENSIC
PSYCHOLOGY and
CRIMINAL BEHAVIOR

SECOND EDITION

CURRENT PERSPECTIVES *in*
FORENSIC
PSYCHOLOGY *and*
CRIMINAL BEHAVIOR

CURT R. BARTOL ▪ ANNE M. BARTOL

Los Angeles ▪ London ▪ New Delhi ▪ Singapore

For information:

Sage Publications, Inc.
2455 Teller Road
Thousand Oaks, California 91320
E-mail: order@sagepub.com

Sage Publications India Pvt. Ltd.
B 1/I 1 Mohan Cooperative Industrial Area
Mathura Road, New Delhi 110 044
India

Sage Publications Ltd.
1 Oliver's Yard
55 City Road
London EC1Y 1SP
United Kingdom

Sage Publications Asia-Pacific Pte. Ltd.
33 Pekin Street #02-01
Far East Square
Singapore 048763

Printed in the United States of America.

Library of Congress Cataloging-in-Publication Data

Current perspectives in forensic psychology and criminal behavior/edited by Curt R. Bartol, Anne M. Bartol.—2nd ed.
    p. cm.
Includes bibliographical references and index.
ISBN 978-1-4129-5831-8 (pbk.)
   1. Criminal psychology. 2. Forensic psychology. 3. Police psychology. 4. Correctional psychology. 5. Criminal investigation—Psychological aspects. 6. Criminal justice, Administration of—Psychological aspects. I. Bartol, Curt R., 1940- II. Bartol, Anne M.

HV6080.C87 2008
364.3—dc22   2007052834

This book is printed on acid-free paper.

08 09 10 11 12   10 9 8 7 6 5 4 3 2

Acquisitions Editor:	Jerry Westby
Editorial Assistant:	Eve Oettinger
Production Editor:	Karen Wiley
Copy Editor:	Teresa Herlinger
Typesetter:	C&M Digitals (P) Ltd.
Proofreader:	Susan Schon
Indexer:	Curt R. Bartol
Cover Designer:	Candice Harman
Marketing Manager:	Jennifer Reed Banando

CONTENTS

PREFACE

The articles in this book are offered as supplementary readings to accompany the main text in a variety of undergraduate courses, such as Introduction to Forensic Psychology, Criminology, Psychology and Criminal Justice, Psychology and Law, and similar courses. While most articles were originally published after 2000, a few were first published in the mid-1990s but are still often cited in the forensic literature. Included in the more recent articles are some that provide a different perspective on crime victims or on common or attention-getting crimes. In preparing this second edition, we deleted some of the readings that appeared in the first edition of this book. We did this reluctantly but considered it important to replace these readings with more contemporary published articles.

In the interest of space, we have taken the liberty of editing most of the original works. Ellipses indicate that phrases or sentences have been omitted; asterisks indicate that one or more paragraphs or sections have been deleted. When substantial portions of an article have been omitted, we also indicate that in an editors' note at the beginning of the article. In addition, all abstracts, notes, and many figures and tables have been removed. References now appear in a master reference list at the end of the book. Complete citations are included for those readers who wish to review the original publication, and we strongly encourage that.

The articles are introduced and are grouped in accordance with our view of forensic psychology as a specialty that has relevance to a wide range of both criminal and civil settings. Nevertheless, due to the vast amount of research on crime-related topics and the fact that this reader is a supplement to crime-related courses, the great majority of the articles relate to criminal matters.

We are grateful for the continuing encouragement and support of Acquisitions Editor Jerry Westby, Production Editor Karen Wiley, and the many individuals working behind the scenes to help us produce this book. Once again, Copy Editor Teresa Herlinger has been an invaluable asset at the eleventh hour. She does great work. Our sincere thanks to all.

UNIT I

INTRODUCTION

1

Overview of Forensic Psychology

Anne M. Bartol

Curt R. Bartol

The term "forensic" refers to matters that pertain to courts or to law, both civil and criminal. Forensic *science* involves the application of scientific knowledge to legal problems. Today, virtually all branches of the natural and social sciences have made this application. Psychology, the science of behavior, is no exception.

The forensic sciences as a whole have become popular career choices among students, and many scientific professions now have forensic specialties. In addition to forensic psychology, we have, for example, forensic engineering, forensic medicine, forensic pathology, forensic anthropology, forensic archaeology, forensic psychiatry, and forensic social work. Nonscientific professions, such as accounting and linguistics, also have forensic specialties.

The focus of each discipline is evident from the terms. Forensic anthropology, for example, refers to the identification of skeletal, badly decomposed, or otherwise unidentified human remains. Forensic linguistics is concerned with the in-depth evaluation of language-related characteristics of text, such as grammar, syntax, spelling, vocabulary, and phraseology, either to profile an offender or to determine whether specific writing samples are from the same author (Black, 1990). Forensic pathology is the branch of medicine concerned with diseases and disorders of the body that relate to questions that might come before the court. The forensic pathologist examines the bodies of crime victims for clues about the victim's demise. Popularized in a number of television shows, the work of the

Editors' Note: Adapted from Bartol, C. R., & Bartol, A. M. (2004), "Forensic Psychology: Introduction and Overview," in C. R. Bartol & A. M. Bartol, *Introduction to Forensic Psychology* (Chapter 1). Thousand Oaks, CA: Sage.

pathologist is actually quite nonglamorous, though of course crucial. "While the TV world of forensic science provides instant gratification, the real world is tedious and slow" (Hempel, 2003, p. 14). Forensic social workers, as well as other mental health practitioners, may conduct child custody evaluations, and forensic psychiatrists and psychologists evaluate juveniles and criminal defendants. These are but a few of the many tasks performed by forensic professionals.

Psychologists have long been conducting research and providing services in the legal arena. J. McKeen Cattell conducted the first experiment on the psychology of testimony in 1893, and an American psychologist testified as an expert witness in a courtroom in 1921. In 1917 and 1918, respectively, psychologists used psychological tests to screen law enforcement candidates and developed the first inmate classification system. William Marston was appointed a professor of legal psychology in 1922, and Martin Reiser became the first full-time police psychologist in 1968.

It was not until the 1970s, however, that the term "forensic psychology" emerged. In 1971, the disciplines of psychology and psychiatry each established organizations that, according to Grisso (1996, pp. 98–99), "set the stage for developments that would identify forensic assessment as a specialty and would promote the quality of mental health evaluations for the courts." These organizations were the American Psychology-Law Society (AP-LS) and the American Academy of Psychiatry and Law (AAPL). In 1974, an interdisciplinary program in psychology and law was initiated at the University of Nebraska, and in 1978 the AP-LS created the American Board of Forensic Psychology. This became the examining board for certifying diplomates in forensic psychology, under the auspices of the American Board of Professional Psychology. (Although we do not discuss them here, parallel developments occurred in the field of psychiatry.) A diplomate is a professional with extensive knowledge of and expertise in his or her area. Following this initial activity in the 1970s, forensic psychology developed very rapidly over the next two decades and embraced not only practitioners but also a large body of research literature. In 2001, the Council of Representatives of the American Psychological Association voted to recognize forensic psychology as an applied specialty within the field, joining clinical, counseling, school, and industrial/organizational psychology.

There are two major approaches to defining forensic psychology—the narrow and the broad. In the narrow sense, forensic psychology refers to the application and practice of psychology in the legal system, particularly the courts. This narrow definition focuses heavily on clinical practice. A broader conception of forensic psychology covers a wider landscape of psychology's involvement with legal matters, as will be discussed below. It is probably accurate to note that the narrow term is the more favored within psychology. For example, Ronald Roesch (cited in Brigham, 1999) notes that "most psychologists define the area more narrowly to refer to clinical psychologists who are engaged in clinical practice within the legal system" (p. 279). In addition, in recognizing forensic psychology as a specialty in 2001, the APA Council of Representatives endorsed a narrow rather than broad definition. "It was ultimately decided that the petition for specialization should define forensic psychology narrowly, to include the primarily clinical aspects of forensic assessment, treatment, and consultation" (Otto & Heilbrun, 2002, p. 8).

Nevertheless, we prefer a broader definition, and the readings in this text reflect this breadth. "We view forensic psychology broadly, as both (1) the research endeavor that examines aspects of human behavior directly related to the legal process . . . and (2) the professional practice of psychology within, or in consultation with, a legal system that embraces both civil and criminal law" (Bartol & Bartol, 1987, p. 3). This broad definition includes not only clinicians (also called practitioners) but also social, developmental, counseling, cognitive, experimental, industrial-organizational, and school psychologists, some—but not all—of whom are clinicians. The common link is their contribution to the legal system. Thus, the social psychologist who conducts research on eyewitness testimony, the psychologist who offers workshops to police on interviewing child witnesses, and the clinician who initiates a sex offender treatment program in a prison setting are all engaging in forensic psychology, broadly defined, even though they may not call themselves forensic psychologists. The field also includes research and theory building in criminology; the design and implementation of intervention, prevention, and treatment for youthful offenders; and counseling of victims of crime.

The readings in this book, then, are organized to reflect the division of a broadly conceived forensic psychology into five subspecialties: (1) police psychology, (2) psychology of crime and delinquency, (3) victimology and victim services, (4) psychology applied to the courts, and (5) psychology applied to corrections. While we separate these subspecialties for organizational purposes, it is important to note that there is considerable overlap among them. The correctional psychologist, for example, is well versed in the psychology of crime and delinquency. The police psychologist may offer services to victims as well as to police. All of the above may testify in court, and all of the above may be conducting research in more than one subspecialty area. The point here is to emphasize that the various subareas of forensic psychology are not mutually exclusive.

POLICE PSYCHOLOGY

Police psychology is the research and application of psychological principles and clinical skills to law enforcement and public safety (Bartol, 1996). Included in the term "police" is a range of primarily public agents, such as sheriffs and their deputies, fish and wildlife officers, airport security personnel, marshals, constables, and many types of other state and federal agents.

The relationship between psychology and law enforcement has waxed and waned over the years. Overall, though, we have seen an increase in the services provided by psychologists to the police community. This is partly because law enforcement agencies have become more professional and their administrators and agents better educated, and partly because the public has demanded more accountability on the part of police. However, in recent years there has been tension between psychology and some components of the law enforcement community, most particularly federal agents and military personnel involved in the interrogation of individuals suspected of being involved in terrorist activities. Psychologists do not condone techniques such as sleep deprivation, simulated drowning, sexual humiliation, or exploitation of phobias in order to obtain information. In fact, the American Psychological Association (APA) has called on the U.S. government to ban such techniques (Farberman, 2007). When these techniques are used, psychologists consulting with law enforcement must decide the most effective way of voicing their opposition.

Nevertheless, despite these tensions, psychologists today engage in many activities that are far more routine and satisfying. They perform pre-employment psychological assessment and evaluations for a variety of special situations, including fitness-for-duty, assignment to special units (e.g., SWAT teams), and deadly-force incidents. Some provide counseling or therapy to officers and their families, assist in hostage negotiations, and conduct workshops on stress management. Forensic psychologists are also increasingly asked to do investigative-type activities, such as criminal profiling, psychological autopsies, handwriting analysis, and eyewitness (or earwitness) hypnosis. Larger police departments usually hire full-time, in-house police psychologists, while the smaller departments usually use psychological consultants.

CRIMINAL AND DELINQUENT BEHAVIOR

The psychology of crime and delinquency, sometimes referred to as criminal psychology, is the *science* of the behavioral and mental processes of the adult and juvenile offender (Bartol & Bartol, 2009). It is primarily concerned with how criminal behavior is acquired, evoked, maintained, and modified. Recent research has focused on the offender's cognitive versions of the world, especially his or her thoughts, beliefs, and values and how they can be changed, if necessary. It assumes that various criminal behaviors are acquired by daily living experiences, in accordance with the principles of learning, and are perceived, coded, processed, and stored in memory in a unique fashion for each individual. Criminal psychology examines and evaluates prevention, intervention, and treatment strategies directed at reducing juvenile delinquency and criminal behavior.

Criminal psychologists also are interested in research on specific crimes as well as the perpetrators of these offenses. The focus has been on violent crimes, particularly murder, sexual assault, and aggravated assault such as that associated with hate crimes or domestic violence. For example, psychological concepts and principles associated with aggression, reinforcement, and deindividuation can help us understand causes and aid in the prevention of these violent offenses. In addition, criminal psychologists have addressed causes and prevention of drug abuse, theft, fraud, and other nonviolent crimes.

The topic that has caught considerable attention from psychologists in recent years has been criminal psychopathy. A psychopath is a person who demonstrates a discernible pattern of psychological, cognitive, interpersonal, and neurophysiological features that distinguish him or her from the general population. The term "criminal psychopath" is reserved for those psychopaths who persistently engage in a wide variety of antisocial behaviors that are harmful to others. As a group, criminal psychopaths tend to be "dominant, manipulative individuals characterized by an impulsive, risk-taking and antisocial life-style, who obtain their greatest thrill from diverse sexual gratification and target diverse victims over time" (Porter et al., 2000, p. 220). Porter and his associates go on to say that, "given its relation to crime and violence, psychopathy is arguably one of the most important psychological constructs in the criminal justice system" (p. 227).

More recently, attention has been directed at "juvenile psychopaths." There is considerable debate over whether such a label can be applied to children and adolescents, and as a result most researchers prefer to use phrases like "juveniles with psychopathic features" or with "psychopathic tendencies." Attempts at diagnosing youths as psychopaths have raised "conceptual, methodological, and practical concerns related to clinical/forensic practice and juvenile/criminal justice policy" (Edens, Skeem, Cruise, & Cauffman, 2001, p. 54). Can characteristics of adult psychopathy be applied to children in the first place? And, if it is discovered that psychopathy is a meaningful term for certain youth, what are the ethical issues of labeling a child a psychopath? A third debate centers on how accurate the assessment instrument must be before it should be used in courts. After all, a clinical diagnosis may destine the child to be considered dangerous and incorrigible throughout life. There is also concern that a diagnosis of psychopathy may be used to justify decisions to transfer juvenile offenders to the adult criminal justice system. A fourth debate examines whether psychopathy can be prevented or treated effectively. Recent research has put some of these fears to rest, however. For example, Randall Salekin and his colleagues (see, generally, Salekin & Lochman, 2008) have demonstrated that a number of instruments are now available for detecting psychopathic features in youths, and—even more important—a number of promising treatment approaches now exist. There is also little documentary evidence that the psychopathic label applied to juveniles has been misused in courts, but research in this area is still needed.

Female psychopathy and differences in psychopathic behavior due to ethnic, racial, and cultural factors have not received much research attention. These issues and the many questions concerning juvenile psychopathy will be the topics of greatest concern in future research on psychopathy.

It should be noted that developmental psychologists are becoming increasing involved in the study of crime and delinquency. Although it is generally agreed that crime and delinquency have many causes that involve both individual and environmental factors, and that they take many forms, developmental psychologists have discovered that there are many developmental pathways or trajectories to crime. Some offenders start in early childhood, while others start in early adolescence or later. Moreover, these developmental trajectories appear to differ as a function of cultures, subcultures, and sociodemographic environments. Overall, developmental psychologists have been instrumental in shifting the psychological study of crime away from personality traits as sole or even major determinants of criminal and delinquent behavior and more toward an interactive cognitive and social focus as they relate to developmental changes across the life span.

One of the most exciting developments on the criminal psychology front is the current interest in applying research and principles from *positive psychology*. Traditionally, the field of psychology has focused on mental disorders, abnormality, and maladjustment. Positive psychology—a field that has emerged over the last decade—focuses instead on human strengths and what makes individuals emotionally healthy (Seligman, 2002). A primary illustration of positive psychology is the recent interest in resilience in children and adolescents who are exposed to adversity in their lives and have been assumed to be good candidates for delinquency. Resilience research indicates, on the contrary, that many become productive, prosocial adults. Positive psychology also helps us to understand how victims of crime can become survivors and how prisoners can benefit from treatment programs. Thus, principles from positive psychology are highly relevant to clinical work in corrections.

VICTIMOLOGY AND VICTIM SERVICES

Victimology is the study of persons who have experienced either actual or threatened physical, psychological, social, or financial harm as the result of the commission or attempted commission of crime against them. The harm may be direct or primary (against those who experience it and its consequences firsthand) or indirect or secondary (against family members, relatives, survivors, or friends who experience the harm because of their closeness to the victim) (Karmen, 2001). This latter group is often referred to as the *covictims* of the crime. Interestingly, some researchers are also beginning to look at the effects of crime on relatives and close friends of the perpetrator (Eschholz, Reed, Beck, & Blume Leonard, 2003; reprinted in this text).

Violent victimization of children, such as terrifying abductions, school shootings, and sexual attacks, can disrupt the course of child development in very fundamental ways and can be associated with emotional and cognitive problems over the course of the life span (Boney-McCoy & Finkelhor, 1995). In adults, there is strong evidence that the effects of criminal victimization—such as assault, robbery, and burglary—are both pervasive and persistent (Norris & Kaniasty, 1994). Until recently, psychological services were received by a very small fraction of crime victims (2 to 7%) (Norris, Kaniasty, & Scheer, 1990). Today, psychologists counsel victims, perform psychological assessments, and testify in courts about the effects of victimization, such as in the case of victims who experience post-traumatic stress disorder (PTSD) as a result of their experiences. Some practicing psychologists accompany police officers who must notify persons of the sudden death of a loved one, and others serve as consulting psychologists in domestic abuse situations, including elder abuse. Increasingly, forensic psychologists are beginning to play major roles in the research, evaluation, and treatment of crime victims from diverse cultural contexts and age groups.

Psychologists also provide victim-related services in civil cases. A plaintiff in a civil suit who alleges emotional distress as a result of employment discrimination or sexual harassment may require a psychological assessment to document that distress. Likewise, the specialized assessment conducted by a forensic neuropsychologist may be warranted when brain disorder is alleged or suspected.

PSYCHOLOGY AND THE COURTS

Psychologists in this area conduct research on a very wide assortment of topics that have relevance to the judicial system, such as eyewitness testimony or the effects of prejudicial publicity on juries. Some psychologists who primarily conduct research on legal topics prefer to call themselves legal psychologists, and the terms "legal psychology" and "forensic psychology" are sometimes used interchangeably in the literature.

Psychologists also consult with judges and lawyers, perform assessments, and testify in both criminal and civil courts on such matters as competency to stand trial, criminal responsibility (insanity defense), involuntary civil commitment of the mentally disordered, child custody determinations, and criminal sentencing. This expert testimony based on clinical activities is the essence of the narrow definition of forensic psychology.

Expert testimony is perhaps the most visible function within this subspecialty area, but it is not always required. For example, many psychologists perform pretrial evaluations of criminal defendants and assess juveniles with respect to their amenability for rehabilitation—i.e., are they good candidates for certain treatment programs? Reports of the results of these assessments are often entered into the official record of judicial proceedings, even when the direct courtroom testimony of the psychologist is not needed. Finally, psychologists provide many services behind the scenes, such as advising lawyers on selecting jurors or preparing witnesses for trial.

CORRECTIONAL PSYCHOLOGY

Correctional psychology is arguably the fastest growing branch of forensic psychology, broadly defined. We must keep in mind, though, that many—perhaps most—psychologists providing clinical services to corrections do not refer to themselves as forensic psychologists (Magaletta, Patry, Dietz, & Ax, 2007; reprinted in this text). The number of persons incarcerated in the United States has passed the 2 million mark. Although only a portion (7–10%) of these individuals qualify as "chronic offenders," it is estimated that each chronic offender costs society about $1.3 million over the course of the offender's lifetime (Crawford, 2002). In addition, over 4 million persons are under correctional supervision in the community, such as on probation or parole. Clearly, there is a great need for the services of correctional psychologists, who make substantial contributions to corrections, particularly pertaining to inmate classification systems, psychological assessments, program/treatment evaluation, crisis intervention strategies, and substance abuse treatment approaches.

Psychologists in correctional settings give direct services to inmates, including crisis intervention and individual and group therapy, particularly in such areas as substance abuse treatment, sex offender treatment, and violence prevention or anger management. They also administer a wide variety of psychological assessments (intellectual, personality, aptitude, vocational and educational), interpret results, and prepare comprehensive reports. Their recommendations are often considered in decisions to release prisoners, change their security levels, or assign them to a variety of programs. The above services also are offered to offenders who are serving their sentences, or the end of their sentences, in the community, specifically on probation or parole. Finally, correctional psychologists also offer consultative services relating to corrections staff, which may include screening and selection, employee assistance counseling, and mental health consultation with hostage negotiation or crisis support teams.

Like the legal psychologists discussed above, whose research can be applied to the court process, correctional psychologists also conduct research that has relevance to corrections. For example, what is the effect of imprisonment on special populations of offenders, such as the mentally disordered or the elderly? What are the effects of crowding and isolation on those who are not mentally disordered or elderly? Evaluation of rehabilitation programs and the development of offender classification systems are other professional activities uniquely associated with correctional psychology.

The foregoing sections indicate that the field of forensic psychology, as we define it broadly, provides ample opportunities for psychologists interested in interacting with some aspect of the law. The rapid expansion of the field has been accompanied by calls for specialized graduate programs, increased training, and guidelines and standards to achieve more standardization of practice. Some psychologists also support the certification of individuals, particularly clinicians, who specialize in forensic psychology.

EDUCATIONAL AND TRAINING REQUIREMENTS IN FORENSIC PSYCHOLOGY

The growth in the field of forensic psychology is demonstrated by the recent development of several graduate programs (both at the master's and doctoral level) throughout the world, particularly in Canada, the United States, the United Kingdom, and Australia. There has also been considerable growth in *training* opportunities in forensic psychology at the predoctoral, internship, and postdoctoral levels (Otto & Heilbrun, 2002). In recent years, a discernable expansion has also occurred in the number of doctoral programs in clinical and counseling psychology that offer one or more courses or internships in forensic psychology. Many colleges and universities offer courses in forensic psychology, legal psychology, or psychology and law at the undergraduate level.

Most of the graduate programs in the United States either concentrate on clinical or counseling psychology as they relate to corrections, or social psychology at it relates to legal psychology or psychology and law. Some universities offer a combined JD and PhD as part of the academic package. Formal programs offering specific degrees in police psychology are virtually nonexistent in the United States and Canada, although there are several programs called "investigative psychology" in the United Kingdom. Canada leads the world in research in correctional psychology, and the curricula in Canadian forensic programs reflect this strong research or empirical attention. Students graduating from any of the worldwide graduate programs are expected to be able to analyze, organize, apply, and transmit existing knowledge in the field of forensic psychology, broadly defined.

Standards and Guidelines

Psychologists who specialize in forensic psychology are assisted in their work by standards or by guidelines that inform their professional practice. All psychologists who belong to the American Psychological Association—regardless of their specialization—are expected to comply with the standards of their profession as outlined by the *Ethical Principles of Psychologists and Code of Conduct* (APA, 2003). A violation can result in a complaint to the APA's Professional Conduct Board and a variety of sanctions that include expulsion from the association itself.

The APA or its subdivisions also put forth guidelines, which are suggestions for practice and—unlike the APA standards—are usually not accompanied by an enforcement mechanism. Guidelines are offered in a number of areas associated with research and clinical practice. A good example is the *Specialty Guidelines for Forensic Psychologists* (Committee on Ethical Guidelines for Forensic Psychologists, 1991). "The primary goal of the SGFP is to improve the quality of forensic psychological services by providing guidance to psychologists delivering services to courts, members of the bar, litigants, and persons housed in forensic, delinquency, or correctional facilities" (Otto & Heilbrun, 2002, p. 7). In addition, there are guidelines for the very specialized and complex custody evaluations conducted by psychologists (e.g., in divorce situations).

Another set of APA guidelines addresses issues of cultural diversity. In clinical and counseling practice throughout the United States, psychologists are finding that their clients are often from cultural backgrounds different from their own (Morris, 2001): "The majority of service providers are European Americans with middle-class values and orientation; a sizeable portion of the diverse client populations are African-Americans and under-served with mixed values and orientations" (p. 563). It is interesting to note that only half of the doctoral-level clinicians in one survey felt competent to provide services to African Americans despite their training exposure and diverse clientele (Morris, 2001; Allison, Crawford, Echemendia, Robinson, & Kemp, 1994). In addition, psychologists are encountering in their practices more persons of Latino, Asian, Native American, Persian, and Arabic heritage.

It is extremely crucial for practicing psychologists to be sensitive to the cultural values and norms held by persons to whom they are providing service, just as it is crucial to expand the racial and ethnic representation within the profession itself. This may be especially important for forensic psychologists, who are often called upon to assist in making decisions that may drastically affect the life of someone they are evaluating or treating. The APA (1993) took notice of this important issue by publishing its *Guidelines for Providers of Psychological Services to Ethnic, Linguistic, and Culturally Diverse Populations*. The *Guidelines* emphasize, for example, that psychologists "consider the validity of a given instrument or procedure and interpret resulting data, keeping in mind the cultural and linguistic characteristics of the person being assessed" (p. 46). In addition, the *Guidelines* further recommend that "Psychologists who do not possess knowledge or training about an ethnic group seek consultation with, and/or make referrals to, appropriate experts as necessary" (p. 46).

Psychologists working in correctional facilities are guided by a series of standards developed by the American Association for Correctional Psychology (Standards Committee, 2000), which has recently changed its name to the American Association for Correctional and Forensic Psychology. (Note that, although they are called standards, they really are guidelines, since there is no enforcement mechanism associated with them. However, they do incorporate many of the principles outlined in the APA Standards.) The AACP Standards provide the minimum acceptable levels for psychological services offered to offenders, whether they are adults or juveniles; held in local, state, or federal facilities; or supervised in the community. They cover such topics as licensure, staffing requirements, confidentiality issues, duty to warn, professional development, informed consent, segregation, and a host of other areas relating to this work.

Licensing and Certification

The rapid development of the field of forensic psychology has been accompanied by calls for certification or accreditation of those who practice it. In any profession, certification or accreditation is usually a sign that an individual possesses the requisite knowledge and competence to qualify as an expert in the field. In forensic psychology, some movement toward certification can be observed, but primarily for those psychologists who provide services to the courts, such as by conducting pretrial evaluations or testifying as expert witnesses. It should be noted that all states and all Canadian provinces require a *license* to practice psychology (Tucillo, DeFilippis, Denny, & Dsurney, 2002), with one of the chief criteria—in almost all states—being possession of the doctoral degree. Thus, anyone who offers clinical services as a forensic psychologist must be licensed. However, someone who conducts research on matters related to the law (or even offers seminars) need not be licensed. Moreover, few states require specific certification as a forensic psychologist.

Although there are few formal doctoral programs in the discipline, a variety of national and state certification boards have emerged. For example, as noted earlier, the American Board of Professional Psychology has awarded diplomate status in forensic psychology since 1978. Diplomate certification in forensic psychology attests to the fact that an established organization of peers has examined and accepted the psychologist as being at the highest level of excellence in his or her field of forensic practice. The psychologist must be licensed in order to qualify for diplomate status. The American Board of Psychological Specialties (ABPS), which is affiliated with the American College and Board of Forensic Examiners, also issues certifications to forensic psychologists. Criteria used by the various boards and organizations to grant credentials or titles vary widely, though (Otto & Heilbrun, 2002).

Several authors (e.g., Grisso, 1996; Otto & Heilbrun, 2002) posit that if forensic psychology is to continue to grow and develop, some oversight of both the certification process and the practice is necessary. Currently, they note, a relatively small group of forensic specialists devote themselves full time to this field, while a much larger group of psychologists provide occasional forensic services or provide such services only within a circumscribed area, such as child custody evaluations. Otto and Heilbrun argue that forensic psychology, as a field, must acknowledge the fact that forensic practice is occurring at a variety of levels and for different reasons. The field must develop a plan to ensure that forensic practice overall is well-informed and competent. This plan is especially needed in the area of forensic testing and assessment.

Otto and Heilbrun (2002) and Donald Bersoff and his colleagues (1997) suggest that forensic psychology should recognize three levels of psychologists or clinicians who provide services in the field. First, there would be the "legally informed clinician" who has a basic education in law relevant to professional practice, "including information about confidentiality, privileged communication, and response to subpoenas for clinical records or personal notes" (Otto & Heilbrun, p. 15). Second, there would be the "proficient clinician" who has a mid-level expertise gained from academic coursework, professional training, and a supervised experience in forensic psychology. This professional's knowledge should consist of relevant law, procedures, and ethics applicable to the kinds of forensic practice in which the individual engages. The third category would be the "specialist clinician" who would demonstrate the highest level of expertise obtained through formal training in forensic psychology at the graduate and postgraduate levels. Training in this category should include intensive and in-depth understanding of the relevant law and legal procedures as well as knowledge about a range of relevant psychological procedures and issues. Whether these three levels of expertise eventually become recognized remains to be seen.

Summary and Conclusions

As recently as 25 years ago, the term forensic psychology had barely been introduced into psychological or legal literature. Today, as we have seen, it is a commonly encountered term, but it still defies definition. While the consensus might seem to favor a narrow definition limiting it to clinical practice, the contributions of research psychologists may be undermined by such an approach. In addition, it is important to consider the context in which forensic psychology is practiced. Limiting forensic psychology to work with civil and criminal courts—which seems to be the consequence of a narrow definition—does not recognize well enough the law-related functions performed by psychologists working with law enforcement, corrections, or victims. Finally, the many contributions of psychologists who study the psychology of crime and delinquency deserve to be included in this field. As we noted in this chapter, recent concepts and research in developmental psychology and positive psychology, for example, have direct relevance to the interests of forensic psychologists.

The readings included in this book reflect the broader definition. While the majority deals with criminal justice, we must emphasize that forensic psychologists also do much of their work in the civil arena. Neuropsychological assessments, child custody evaluations, and mental status evaluations in discrimination suits are just a few examples. In fact, when we include the many ways in which forensic psychologists interact with juveniles under the "civil" rubric, the distribution of forensic psychology services between criminal and civil contexts may be equal.

UNIT II

POLICE AND INVESTIGATIVE PSYCHOLOGY

INTRODUCTION AND COMMENTARY

Police enforce and uphold the law, are gatekeepers to the criminal court process, and gather evidence that is used in courtroom settings. Nevertheless, psychologists that consult with police have not traditionally been considered forensic psychologists. In the narrow definition discussed in Chapter 1, it is chiefly services directly associated with courts—and typically clinical services—that are included under the rubric forensic psychology. If we adopt a broader definition, however, it is difficult to justify excluding police psychology, as well as the investigative psychology that is a subset of law enforcement consultation.

The article by **Curt R. Bartol** was written for a special issue of the journal *Criminal Justice and Behavior* dedicated to assessing the state of forensic psychology, broadly defined. Of particular interest are the four overlapping historical trends in police psychology that the author identifies: cognitive assessment, the search for personality attributes, counseling and stress management, and organizational consultation.

The author's predictions for the future of the field, though offered reluctantly, are interesting to review in light of the years after 1996, when this article was first published. Bartol could not have predicted the events of September 11, 2001, or the subsequent deployment of troops to the Middle East, which had unanticipated effects on law enforcement nationwide. Vocabulary and resources, for example, shifted from phrases like "community policing" and "war on drugs" to "terrorist profile" and "war on terror." With the invasion of Iraq and the call-up of National Guard units, numerous law enforcement agencies across the United States lost officers, both temporarily and permanently as a result of casualties.

Nevertheless, the author's predictions should prompt examination and discussion. Do women now make up close to 25% of police departments? Have police psychologists become more involved in rural and semirural communities? Has preemployment screening increased? Is there yet a graduate program specifically designed to prepare police psychologists? Have police psychologists addressed diversity, multiculturalism, and discrimination issues? This last is a crucial question, considering the curtailment of civil liberties associated with surveillance activities and interrogations in recent years.

The article by **Robert E. Cochrane et al.** provides answers to at least one of these questions; specifically, whether preemployment screening has increased. The authors mailed a 20-item survey to a random sample of 355 municipal departments in the United States and received responses from 155 (43%). Ninety percent of the responding departments required psychological evaluation of all candidates, a figure considerably higher than indicated in an earlier survey of a comparable number of respondents. Furthermore, the typical department utilized three or four psychological measures, with the MMPI-2, the clinical interview, the Personal History Questionnaire, and the California Psychological Inventory (CPI) being the most frequently used. Very few applicants were rejected solely on the basis of results of psychological measures, however.

The Cochrane et al. article is informative in its review of the multiple instruments—nonpsychological as well as psychological—used by police agencies in selecting candidates for employment. Finally, while the authors conclude that the law enforcement agencies in their sample were on the whole very professional in their approach to evaluating candidates for hire, a minority did not always follow public policy guidelines. For example, 17.4% of the responding departments used pathology-based psychological tests prior to a conditional offer of employment, which violates provisions of the Americans with Disabilities Act (ADA). Similarly, slightly over 13% used different norms (though not different cutoff scores) on some measures for various racial groups or genders.

The reading by **Kamala London** provides an excellent illustration of psychological research informing police practices, in this instance the interviewing of children. In most jurisdictions, children today are presumed to be competent witnesses unless proven otherwise. Nonetheless, during investigations of a crime, some children are influenced by leading questions posed by an authority figure, such as a police officer. London's article is replete with practical suggestions for investigating officers, based on the rapidly developing psychological research. Avoiding anatomically-detailed dolls, yes/no questions, and repeated questions are just three examples. A frequent theme in the article is the need to take a hypothesis-*testing* approach rather than a hypothesis-*confirming* approach. That is, investigators should seek to *determine whether* a child was a victim of a crime, rather than to *document that* he or she was. The latter approach is significantly more likely to result in false information.

The next two articles, both on criminal or offender profiling, should be read in tandem. Even an initial, cursory review should introduce readers to the many terms that are used interchangeably to denote this endeavor. As both articles indicate, criminal profiling has increased significantly, despite the absence of a well-defined profiling framework or empirical evidence in strong support of its use.

The article by **Brent Snook et al.** summarizes—through narrative reviews and two meta-analyses—a good portion of the research literature on criminal profiling. The authors suggest that much profiling is based on common sense rather than empirical evidence. The available data indicate that profilers as a group are no more accurate than nonprofilers at pinpointing criminal suspects. In reading Snook et al.'s article, readers should take note of differences among experienced investigators, profilers, and self-designated profilers. Interestingly, not all profilers designate themselves thus; some who call themselves profilers are not scientifically based; and experienced investigators may or may not be good profilers.

Damon A. Muller is a bit more favorably disposed toward criminal profiling than Snook and his colleagues. Muller's article focuses on two models of criminal profiling: crime scene analysis (CSA)—as developed predominantly in the United States—and investigative psychology (IP)—developed in the work of David Canter in England. Muller describes CSA as a methodology whose scientific validity is questionable because it cannot be falsified. IP, on the other hand, represents a variety of approaches based on theory and holds much promise of scientific validity. The article includes numerous illustrations of the two models of profiling in action, which should help the reader gain a better understanding of the profiling process.

The final article in this section deals with the comprehension of *Miranda* rights and with false confessions, topics that have gained considerable attention in recent years. Researchers have been especially concerned about the ability of juveniles to understand their right to be protected against self-incrimination and their right to legal representation. **Naomi E. Sevin Goldstein** and her colleagues review key U.S. Supreme Court cases and the legal and psychological research in this area, and they report the results of their own study of 55 delinquent boys. Using a tool designed to assess *Miranda* comprehension, Goldstein et al. found significant misconceptions among these juveniles about their *Miranda* rights and the roles of defense lawyers. Furthermore, the study suggests that juveniles are susceptible to making false confessions, either because of their suggestibility or their need to acquiesce to authority.

As a group, the readings in this section provide a sampling of what police psychologists do and how psychological research can be applied to police work. Many areas, though, are not represented in the readings. For example, psychologists conduct research on police line-ups, offer stress management workshops to officers and their spouses, accompany police on domestic violence calls, perform fitness-for-duty evaluations, and screen detainees held in police lockups for mental illness. The extent to which interested psychologists work directly with police—either consistently or "as needed"—is limited primarily by the willingness of the police to call upon them for service. Particularly in recent years, it has also been limited by the unwillingness of psychologists to participate in activities that they consider unethical or antithetical to their professional and personal values.

2

POLICE PSYCHOLOGY

Then, Now, and Beyond

CURT R. BARTOL

M y involvement in psychological services to law enforcement began in 1973 when I was asked to teach a course in abnormal psychology at a police academy. Shortly thereafter, law enforcement agencies began seeking my help in dealing with various psychological issues, such as job stress, interactions with the mentally disordered, and preemployment screening. I soon found myself sliding into longer and longer hours consulting and training. I became a certified academy instructor in crisis intervention, interviewing and interrogation, hostage negotiation, and criminal psychology. I was appointed to a statewide Criminal Justice Training Council, where I helped establish standards for the screening and selection of law enforcement officers. It wasn't long before I was asked to evaluate and make recommendations concerning the police academy curriculum, with the idea of moving it from a paramilitary format to a human relations one. I also was asked by agencies nationwide to offer workshops on screening and selection or to participate in the training of police recruits.

At this point, I began to believe I was quite good and that I even possessed a tinge of charisma. It did not dawn on me then that it was more a case of being in the right place at the right time. The Law Enforcement Assistance Administration (LEAA), created by Congress in 1965, was in full swing, disbursing substantial funds to encourage law enforcement agencies to become more human sensitive. I began to realize that I simply happened to be one of the few psychologists in the area willing to work with law enforcement. Since this early propitious beginning, I have continued to provide many psychological services to a variety of law enforcement

Editors' Note: This article first appeared in *Criminal Justice and Behavior,* Vol. 23, No. 1, March 1996, pp. 70–89. Reprinted with permission of Sage Publications.

agencies. I also have conducted large-scale, longitudinal research projects by following the careers of officers in small-town police and sheriff's departments in an effort to identify potential predictors of success. Not surprisingly, I follow avidly any developments in the emergence of police psychology.

The term *police psychology* is discomfiting, however, because it appears to preclude other law enforcement agents, such as deputy sheriffs, marshals, or constables. Blau (1994), a psychologist and deputy sheriff in the Manatee County (Florida) Sheriff's Department, may have felt the same way when he called his book *Psychological Services for Law Enforcement.* The term *law enforcement* also has its critics, however, particularly those who argue that police enforce the law selectively and minimally. The real work of police is maintaining order, keeping the peace, or being coproducers, with citizens, of public safety. Rather than weigh in heavily in favor of one or the other term, I will opt for the less cumbersome. Police psychology here will encompass all law enforcement agencies and agents, with the caveat that they do much more than—and sometimes much less than—enforce the law. In the remainder of the article, I shall sketch the development of police psychology, describe its current status, and try to predict its future.

THEN: 20 YEARS AGO AND EARLIER

When did police psychology begin? Some have said that the profession was launched formally at the National Symposium on Police Psychological Services (NSPPS) held at the FBI Academy on September 17, 1984 (Chandler, 1990; McKenzie, 1986). The proceedings of this meeting were published in a monograph (Reese & Goldstein, 1986) titled, like Blau's work, *Psychological Services for Law Enforcement.* The NSPPS was [predated] by a number of symposia, conferences, and workshops on police psychology, however. The Society of Police and Criminal Psychology, for example, has had annual conferences and symposia on topics pertaining to police psychology since 1971.

To set 1984 as the date for the origin of police psychology seems unjustified, given the amount of conference activity over a decade before that. Another important date in the history of police psychology was December 1968, when Martin Reiser was hired by the Los Angeles Police Department [LAPD] as a full-time psychologist. Soon afterward, in 1969, Reiser (1972) presented a paper at the Western Psychological Association Convention, Vancouver, titled "The Police Department Psychologist." Chandler referred to this presentation as the informal birth of the profession of police psychology. Here, too, my own opinion differs. There is no doubt that Reiser's contributions to the field have been invaluable. In the early 1970s, he was clearly the most prolific writer on police psychology. In 1972, in cooperation with the California School of Professional Psychology, he helped establish an internship in police psychology in the Los Angeles Police Department. To conclude, as Chandler did, that Reiser's paper marked the informal beginning of the profession is problematic, however. Psychologists were working in various capacities in law enforcement settings long before the 1970s. Reiser (1982) himself, in a collection of published papers, noted that he was not at all sure he was the first full-time police psychologist in the country. Reese (1986, 1987), a historian on psychological services to law enforcement, estimated that only six police agencies in the United States had full-time psychologists by 1977.

Before we become too myopic in our proclamations of historical firsts, we should realize that our international colleagues may have been ahead of us. Viteles (1929) reported that police departments in Germany were using psychologists in a variety of capacities as early as 1919. Chandler (1990) noted that, in 1966, the Munich (Germany) police were employing a full-time, in-house psychologist to train officers to deal with various patrol problems, such as crowd control. The informal origin of police psychology probably goes back more than 50 years, but I leave it to others to propose a more specific date. I much prefer to discuss the developmental stages of police psychology. A review of the literature suggests that police psychologists have pursued four distinct, although overlapping, trends, beginning with an affinity for cognitive assessment and proceeding through personality assessment, a clinical focus, and an organizational approach.

The first trend was concerned with the cognitive functioning of police officers, specifically intelligence and aptitude. This track probably began in this country with Terman's (1917) testing (using the Stanford-Binet) of applicants for several firefighter and police officer positions for the city of San Jose, California, in 1916. His results, which suggested police applicants were not a very intelligent lot, appeared in the first issue of the *Journal of Applied Psychology.* Five years after the Terman report, the intelligence of police officers still was being debated, particularly in the work of Thurstone (1922, 1924) and Telford and Moss (1924).

The cognitive approach, although never wholeheartedly subscribed to, had very little competition until the mid-1960s. Moreover, involving psychologists in policing seems to have been the exception rather than the rule. In a survey of 90 police departments (Oglesby, 1957), only 14 reported that they used some type of psychiatric or psychological input in their screening procedures. Only two departments said that they used a psychologist for the screening, with the rest preferring to use a psychiatrist. Interestingly, one department reported dropping the services of its psychiatrist because he rejected none of the 1,500 applicants. A subsequent survey by Narrol and Levitt (1963) to discover the extent of selection testing used by major police departments in the United States found an increase in the use of psychological testing. Specifically, they found that 100% of the departments used some kind of selection test, usually a standardized intelligence test (40%) or nonstandardized aptitude test (87%) that usually was developed by the department itself. Only 22% were using any kind of personality inventory or psychiatric interview. [In addition], only 6 of the 55 cities surveyed indicated that they employed qualified psychologists in connection with their selection procedures.

In the mid-1960s, interest shifted to assessing the personality attributes of police officers. Some of the shift from cognitive appraisal to personality assessment was probably due to widespread concerns directed at "IQ tests" and the danger of [their] adverse impact on minority groups. The major impetus, however, was the report by the President's Commission on Law Enforcement and the Administration of Justice (1967) recommending widespread use of psychological tests to determine the emotional stability of all potential officers. Specifically, the commission asserted,

> Screening out candidates whose emotional stability makes them clearly unfit for police work—through psychological tests and psychiatric interviews—should also improve the capacity of police forces to improve community relations. . . . While there is no one psychological test which can reliably identify all candidates who are emotionally unfit for police service, a combination of tests and oral psychiatric interviews can pinpoint many serious character defects. (pp. 164–165)

The commission hoped that departments would reject police candidates who demonstrated racial and ethnic prejudice prior to being hired. Similarly, the 1968 National Advisory Commission on Civil Disorder called for screening methods that would improve the quality of the law enforcement officers hired (Scrivner, 1994).

In keeping with commission recommendations, Congress provided LEAA funds for law enforcement agencies to retain the services of mental health professionals. Many of us currently working in some capacity in law enforcement started our work with the help of some variant of LEAA funding. LEAA, which became President Johnson's centerpiece in his war on crime, also funded technical assistance, materials, training, college education (through LEEP, the Law Enforcement Education Program), and research, including searches for selection procedures that would identify emotionally suitable police officers. Because the funding was intended to identify the emotional stability and prejudices of law enforcement officers, psychologists were required to become more clinical and personality/psychopathology-based in their work with law enforcement organizations. In 1973, the Police Task Force Report of the National Commission on Criminal Justice Standards and Goals encouraged the establishment of a behavioral sciences resource unit or consultant for all law enforcement agencies.

By the early 1970s, personality assessment had increased, but it certainly was not the norm. In a survey, Murphy (1972) found that only 44% of large municipal police departments used some kind of psychological test or inventory in evaluating applicants, most commonly the Minnesota Multiphasic Personality Inventory (MMPI). Murphy also found that only 13% of state agencies used psychological instruments for screening purposes.

Murphy (1972) concluded that general psychological testing for screening had not changed significantly over the 8 years since the Narrol and Levitt (1963) survey. However, he did notice an increase in the use of personality assessment. For example, the MMPI was the instrument of choice for nearly 50% of the agencies indicating that they used psychological testing in their screening and selection procedures.

The personality assessment trend had two research offshoots, the first being a search for the "police personality" (Lefkowitz, 1975). Agencies began to ask, Does law enforcement draw a certain type of person? Some psychologists obliged them by trying to answer. The question has yet to be answered satisfactorily, however, and researchers today have shifted their interests to other issues.

The second research offshoot involved an effort to identify instruments that could select in, as well as screen out. Selecting-in procedures are intended to identify those attributes (almost invariably personality) that distinguish one candidate over another as being a potentially more effective officer. Implicit in this assessment is the ability to rank order applicants, allowing agencies to select the top candidates from a pool [of those] who passed the initial screening

procedures. This approach assumes that there are traits, habits, reactions, and attitudes that distinguish an outstanding cop from a satisfactory one. To the best of my knowledge, there is little evidence that psychologists can accomplish this goal in any satisfactory manner. For more than 20 years, I have tried, unsuccessfully, to develop an instrument or instruments that would help identify applicants who would become above-average or superior officers in the field.

Screening-*out* procedures, on the other hand, try to eliminate those who demonstrate significant signs of psychopathology or emotional instability, or who lack the basic ability or mental acuity to perform the job in a safe and responsible manner (R. D. Meier, Farmer, & Maxwell, 1987). On average, about 15% of candidates are screened out through personality assessment. We have been far more successful in our screening-out than in our screening-in determinations. Research on officers who did not succeed in law enforcement, for example, has suggested that warning signs were present on MMPI measures (Bartol, 1991), rendering them "true negatives." The "false negative" picture is much more difficult to obtain, however, because agencies generally heed the MMPI warning signs pointed out by the police psychologist.

The third trend is best represented by the word stress, which became the overriding theme from the mid-1970s to the early 1980s. More than ever before, clinicians were called upon to identify and dissipate stress, which presumably—if left unmanaged or untreated—would result in an array of psychological and physical health problems for the officer and potentially put the public at risk. *Stressors, burnout, posttraumatic stress disorder,* and *critical incident trauma* became standard terms in the police psychologist's vocabulary. Whether police officers actually experienced more stress than people in other high-risk occupations (e.g., air traffic controller) remained highly debatable, however (Yarmey, 1990). Nevertheless, there was little doubt that stress played a major role in the lives of law enforcement officers at all levels within the organization. The focus on stress was significant because it propelled police psychologists away from their traditional testing functions and into a much larger realm of opportunity and services. Consequently, psychologists began to offer not only stress management, but also crisis intervention training, hostage negotiation training, domestic violence workshops, and substance abuse treatment.

The fourth trend reflects a discernible move into industrial/organizational kinds of issues and a drift away from exclusively clinical and mental health ones. During the mid-1970s, a trend developed toward looking more closely at the law enforcement organization rather than emphasizing—sometimes to the exclusion of other factors—the person. There were moves, of course, in that direction earlier. Bard's work (1969; Bard & Berkowitz, 1969) promoted a closer look at training and the police organization from a psychological perspective, for example. We will examine this organizational trend in more detail later in the article, when the future of psychological services to law enforcement is discussed.

During the 1980s, the development of police psychology seemed to reach a plateau. Federal funding to state, municipal, and county agencies became limited, and law enforcement agencies were inclined not to require or seek additional psychological services unless absolutely necessary. Although psychologists continued to consult with law enforcement agencies, give workshops, provide screening services, and offer therapy and counseling, there is no indication that the decade of the 1980s was one of significant growth. However, police psychologists did continue to refine their profession through conferences, professional meetings, and publications.

NOW: WHO, WHAT, AND HOW MUCH?

Perhaps the best way to describe the present work of police psychologists is to ask police psychologists themselves what they are doing. The following data are taken from an unpublished nationwide survey of 152 police psychologists conducted by the author during the spring of 1994. Respondents were members of the Police and Public Safety section of the American Psychological Association's Division of Psychologists in Public Service, the Council on Police Psychological Services (COPPS), the police psychology section of the International Association of Chiefs of Police, and the Society of Police and Criminal Psychology. The survey had a return rate of 74%, representing a good cross-section of the psychologists engaged in providing services to law enforcement. The respondents were asked to indicate whether they were a full-time in-house police psychologist, a full-time consultant to law enforcement, or a service provider to law enforcement as part of their professional activity. Therefore, much of the discussion will be based on these three major professional groupings. Forty respondents were full-time in-house psychologists, 36 were full-time consultants, and the remainder ($N = 76$) indicated that they worked with law enforcement as psychologists in some part-time capacity.

The respondents tended to be a rather senior group, with an average age of 48.7 (SD = 5.5) and an average experience of 11.8 years (SD = 4.8) in services to law enforcement. The age and experience data were highly similar to Scrivner's (1994) data on 65 psychologists employed in large-city police departments. No significant age differences were found between in-house psychologists and consultants, or between those employed full- and part-time. The average age of psychologists working in law enforcement underscores the point made above about the influence of LEAA funds on careers in police psychology [in the 1960s and 1970s].

Most (89%) of the respondents had PhD degrees, followed by EdD degrees (4.5%), master's degrees (3.6%), and PsyD degrees (2.7%). Most obtained their terminal degrees in clinical (60.7%), counseling (17%), or industrial/ organizational (8%) psychology. Interestingly, the terminal degree-granting institution most frequently mentioned by the respondents was the California School of Professional Psychology (CSPP) (6.3%), probably reflecting the LAPD internship program started by Reiser. All but one of the CSPP graduates were working full-time in providing psychological services to law enforcement.

The average salary for psychologists employed full-time in psychological services to law enforcement was $77,412 (median = $64,000). However, psychologists who considered themselves full-time consultants in law enforcement made considerably more than individuals employed as full-time, in-house police psychologists (mean = $102,192, compared to $57,133; median = $80,000, compared to $53,000). About 25% of the respondents (N = 36) were women. However, only 3 were employed as in-house psychologists. On the other hand, 14 of the 36 full-time police consultants were women. There were no significant differences in salary or age between the men and women.

Participants in the nationwide survey were requested to indicate the type of services they provided specifically to law enforcement during a typical month, as well as the amount of time they usually spent on each activity. As expected, the respondents, as a whole, indicated that preemployment screening consumed the largest percentage (34.3%) of their time. However, psychologists who engaged in full-time police services, particularly in-house psychologists, spent less time at this activity. In-house psychologists reported that only about 15% of their time involved preemployment screening. A greater portion (28.7%) of their time was occupied working directly with the officers in such services as counseling and treatment. Full-time consultants, on the other hand, spent about 27.5% of their professional time in preemployment screening and 23.2% in the counseling of officers.

Interestingly, full-time consultants were more involved in providing various services to the family members of police personnel and were more engaged in fitness-for-duty evaluations. This pattern probably reflects a tendency for departments to contract out sensitive issues for more objective appraisals, thereby avoiding criticism about conflict of interest.

Unfortunately, little time in a typical month was spent dealing with victims. It is interesting to note, however, that Delprino and Bahn (1988) reported that police departments saw a great need for this service. Apparently, few departments are able to provide it because of the more immediate, pressing demands of agency personnel.

One surprising finding of the survey was the amount of time consumed by criminal or psychological profiling of offenders. Criminal profiling refers to the process of identifying personality traits, behavioral tendencies, and demographic variables of an offender, based on characteristics of the crime (Bartol & Bartol, 1994). On average, 2% of the total monthly work time of in-house psychologists and 3.4% of the monthly workload of part-time consulting psychologists were directed at criminal profiling. Although this may not seem to be a dramatically high percentage, the finding is surprising, considering that a majority of the surveyed police psychologists (70%) did not feel comfortable profiling and seriously questioned its validity and usefulness. This skepticism was especially pronounced for the in-house psychologists (78%). One well-known police psychologist, with more than 20 years of experience in the field, considered criminal profiling "virtually useless and potentially dangerous." Many of the respondents wrote that much more research needs to be done before the process can become a useful tool.

Several of the questions on the survey focused on the best way to prepare for police psychology as a career. Although 61% of the respondents had doctorates in clinical psychology, most indicated that, because of the rapid expansion of the psychological services requested by law enforcement agencies, a broad graduate education in psychology with a strong research focus was critical. Nearly 20% of the respondents felt that course work or background in industrial/organization psychology was highly desirable. Specific graduate course work most recommended by all respondents was assessment (38%), testing (37%), counseling (33%), and crisis intervention (23%).

The psychologists appeared to be extremely satisfied with their careers. About 54% indicated that they were extremely satisfied, and 39% were moderately satisfied; only 3% were neutral or dissatisfied. Women were especially satisfied with the profession, with all female respondents indicating they were either extremely (65%) or moderately satisfied (35%).

The police psychologists also were asked about their perceptions of the current, as well as the future, job market in police psychology. Full-time and part-time police psychologists perceived the market similarly. About two thirds of both groups saw both the current and future job market as either *good* (defined as a balance between available positions and qualified psychologists), *very good* (more positions available than qualified psychologists), or *excellent* (many more positions than qualified psychologists). These data suggest that police psychologists, as a whole, perceive good opportunities in the field and see room for expansion in the future.

BEYOND: SANGUINE PREDICTIONS

I am usually as cautious predicting trends in the field as I am predicting human behavior. Some of what follows . . . falls into the category of what *should* happen without being optimistic that it *will*. Psychologists should, for example, address issues of diversity, multiculturalism, and discrimination. I am not so sure we will.

In reality, police psychology in the United States depends greatly on political, economic, and social pressures, ultimately reflected in executive, legislative, and, to a lesser extent, judicial decision making. The LEAA and a variety of presidential commissions had enormous influence on policing and police psychology during the late 1960s and 1970s. The media also have played a prominent role. Televised events focus public attention on police behavior, as they did during the 1968 Democratic Convention in Chicago [when police on horseback were seen beating demonstrators with clubs]. More recently, the videotape documenting Rodney King's beating by Los Angeles police officers, as well as the conviction of two officers by a federal jury, created a nationwide concern about the use of excessive force. As a result, Scrivner (1994), a police psychologist, was encouraged to conduct

an extremely useful study examining the many psychological factors involved in excessive force and suggesting strategies for monitoring and preventing it. The recently completed Mollen Commission Report (July of 1994), detailing widespread police corruption in New York City, should prompt police psychologists to address this disturbing behavior. In the relationship among crime, fear of crime, and the public perceptions of policing, the media are exerting a more powerful influence than ever before (Manning, 1994).

In an attempt to control police deviance, pre-employment screening (of the screening-out variety) will continue to be an important service provided by police psychologists. Although organizational factors are relevant to explaining police behavior, the effort to identify potentially problematic officers should and will continue. Preemployment screening, however, will be affected increasingly by legislation and judicial decision making. It is quite clear to me, for example, that police psychologists who continue to resist using the MMPI-2 in favor of the MMPI do so at their own risk, in light of *Soroka et al. v. Dayton Hudson Corporation* (1991).

Target Stores (owned and operated by the Dayton Hudson Corporation) administered a battery of psychological tests to candidates for security officer positions. The battery, called *Psychscreen,* was a combination of the MMPI and the California Psychological Inventory (CPI). Plaintiff Soroka argued, among other things, that MMPI questions probing religious attitudes and sexual orientation were invasive and offensive. The California Court of Appeals ultimately ruled that invasive psychological tests violated both the constitutional right to privacy and statutory prohibitions against improper inquiries into a person's sexual orientation and religious beliefs. Although the defendants could have attempted to justify continued use of the test, they chose instead to settle out of court and to stop using the test.

I have been disturbed by the reactions of some of my colleagues to this case. First, they believe that the case does not relate to them because the plaintiff was applying to a private security firm rather than a public police agency. This observation misses the point, because the court's decision struck a fatal blow to the content of the test, regardless of the context. Second, some colleagues believe that this case should have been played out in the courts, rather than settled. They argue that, despite the appeals court's objections to the MMPI items, a case could be made for continued usage of the test if it could be shown to be job validated. Why the insistence on retaining an instrument that has so often made us uncomfortable and alienated professionals in other disciplines? As one who has been faced for many years with the task of justifying offensive items on the original MMPI to students, police chiefs, and candidates, I am very happy that the court in this case forced the issue.

The MMPI-2 is a vast improvement over its predecessor and addresses many of the legal concerns about standardization and item content. Again, my opinion is not shared; some colleagues, even workshop presenters, proclaim that the revised test is nothing but a marketing gimmick. Those psychologists who wish to reduce their potential time in court, however, should use the MMPI-2 in place of the MMPI and validate it the best way possible on the population being evaluated. Screening instruments—including the MMPI-2—will continue to be tested in the courts on validation issues. Just as surely will they be tested on offensive item content, however.

One piece of recent legislation that may affect the work we do is the Americans with Disabilities Act (ADA), which became fully effective in July 1992. The ADA is the most far-reaching public law since the Civil Rights Act of 1964, affecting all levels of state and local governments, about 5 million private businesses, and some 43 million people defined by law as physically or mentally disabled (Bartol & Bartol, 1994, 2004b). The law prohibits employers from discriminating against any people with disabilities who can perform the essential functions of the jobs they hold or desire to hold. It specifically prohibits oral questions or questionnaire items pertaining to past medical history or otherwise eliciting information about disabilities. It is unclear at this time how the law will affect screening and selection procedures, but if police psychologists validate their methods in relation to effective performance measures, the overall effect of the ADA on police psychology is apt to be minimal.

Psychologists seeking to expand their contributions beyond the traditional screening, therapy, training, and crisis intervention areas may be drawn to the current zeitgeist of community policing. Its primary philosophy is straightforward: It attempts to form a coalition between the community and the police to solve community problems. In application, the concept is not that clear, however.

Moreover, proponents of community policing sometimes ignore segments of communities that do not feel that the police represent them. This current interest in community policing, then, challenges social and community psychology to give valuable input concerning attitudes and attitude change, as well as neighborhood and group dynamics. It should be an exciting area for police psychologists; at this point, however, I see little indication that these contributions are being made.

One area needing far more attention, by both practitioners and researchers, is the rural and semi-rural community. Police psychologists—at least those with high visibility—have studied and consulted with large metropolitan police departments or state police agencies, to the neglect of small-town and rural law enforcement. Approximately 80% of the 17,000 local police agencies in this country are located in small towns (i.e., having fewer than 50,000 people) and rural communities. The current interest in community policing may shift some attention to small-town and rural policing, but it would be optimistic to think that they ever will be the center of research focus. Nevertheless, the need for psychological services is great. Small-town policing generates its own unique stress, for example, and some crimes, such as domestic violence, are believed to be more hidden. Therefore, psychologists involved in police training programs in small towns and rural areas are faced with challenging tasks.

The composition of police forces will continue to change significantly in the future, which, in turn, will affect the nature of police psychology.

The two decades ahead will see greater attention to gender issues in policing, an important trend that is beginning to emerge. Research demonstrates that women and men are equally capable—cognitively, emotionally, and behaviorally—of doing law enforcement work (Bartol, Bergen, Volckens, & Knoras, 1992). There are some indications that women may have a more "gentling effect" on law enforcement, using communication and interpersonal skills more effectively. This may be a crucial variable for policing in the future, especially as policing evolves into increased community involvement.

Women going into law enforcement still encounter sexual harassment and attitudinal resistance, primarily from their male supervisors. However, I anticipate a growing and substantial influx of women into both law enforcement and police psychology in the near future. In 1972, for instance, women constituted 4.2% of police officers employed in urban departments. By 1988, the figure had more than doubled to 8.8% (Manning, 1994; Martin, 1990). I fully expect that women will comprise at least 25% of the police forces within the next two decades. If these predictions are borne out, they will produce significant changes in police training and the prioritization of services. The needs of victims, for example, are more likely to be attended to with a better gender balance, both on police forces and among police psychologists.

The percentages of African Americans and members of other minorities will continue to increase, especially in the large metropolitan departments. At this writing, 58% of the officers in the Detroit Police Department are African American, and it is anticipated that the percentages in other major cities will begin to approximate that of the minorities within their community. It also is highly likely that the [ethnic] composition of police psychology will change. One glaring aspect of the police psychology survey described above is that only 3 of the 152 respondents were from minority groups.

The future also should see a shift from the counseling/clinical orientation to more non–mental health-oriented psychological services. This shift will be consistent with and accompany the overall changes occurring in policing. For example, there are clear indications that policing is moving away from the professional crime fighting model to a more corporate strategy model, where policing resembles a corporate business rather than a public service agency (Manning, 1994; Moore & Trojanowicz, 1988). Manning observed, "The currently fashionable language of economics and management used by command personnel to describe police functions, command obligations, and planning creates a picture of policing as a business" (p. 2). Problem-solving strategies and strategic decision-making models are likely to predominate in the near future. Industrial/organization, community, and social psychology will be called upon to make many major theoretical and practical contributions to police psychology. These contributions will be especially notable in human resource management, police management skills, mediation, organizational psychology, community policing, human factors, and operations research. Psychological research on how to deal effectively with turnover rates, personnel dissatisfaction, and lowered morale in reactions to budget cuts and cycles of hiring blitzes and freezes will become critical.

During the personality trend of police psychology, a group of political and social scientists argued that police behavior was not the result of some personality characteristic that existed prior to entry into law enforcement, but rather of the culture found within each department. Presumably, the rough edges of individual differences were sanded and polished by the social and political forces of the organization. J. Q. Wilson (1968), for example, developed a departmental typology consisting of various policing styles. He argued that the preexisting personality of the individual really did not matter. The department promoted specific policing styles, with differences in policing being explainable by differences among organizations. Wilson's perspective has merit. As I have found in my own consulting work, it is not uncommon for an individual to be regarded as a failure in one agency but a success in another. Nevertheless, individual attributes of some officers preclude them from being a success in any law enforcement setting. It is becoming increasingly apparent, therefore, that the study of police behavior requires a careful examination of all the systems involved, such as the individual or *infrasystem,* the organization, the family, the culture, and the community. We need to be more sensitive to the interactions among these systems rather than to assume that one law enforcement organization is like any other.

Police psychology increasingly will become international in scope, with psychologists across the globe sharing ideas, research, and programs. Although this exchange takes place now, it will increase substantially within the next decade.

Traditionally, law enforcement has used psychologists on an "as needed" basis rather than for systematic human resource development and prevention (Scrivner, 1994). The growing array of available psychological services, therefore, has not been integrated systematically into law enforcement. For this to be accomplished, psychologists themselves must articulate what it is they have to offer; we cannot expect the police community to know how we can help. Psychological services directed toward prevention and proaction will, in the long run, bring more benefit to policing than the reactive activity that has been expected in the past.

More than anything else, police psychologists need to become better and more skillful researchers and evaluators of programs, including their own. One of the things that was most emphasized by practicing police psychologists in our survey was that aspiring police psychologists must be better equipped with research skills. In her survey, Gettys (1990) also found an unfortunate lack of research involvement by police psychologists. Chandler (1990) strongly recommended that future police psychologists become well versed and much more active in conducting research. He said this within the context of acknowledging that law enforcement agencies are highly prone to act on "hot" issues without the benefit of good research and evaluation. These hot issues have included missing children campaigns, voice stress analysis, use of psychics, ritualistic crimes, and satanic cults. Good

research, he stated, eventually brings fad-like behavior in check.

***

Finally, we need a broad-based graduate program in police psychology that will encompass not only clinical areas but also will prepare aspiring police psychologists in the many areas described here. . . . With the exception of a master's degree in forensic psychology offered by the John Jay College of Criminal Justice and various internships sponsored by some universities, I know of no academic graduate programs that prepare future police psychologists for the enormously diverse demands that they will encounter in the future. . . . A majority of the respondents in our survey thought that a graduate program in police psychology was an excellent idea, but they also strongly recommended that the program be diverse and academically broad. Several of the respondents believed that most traditional graduate programs are too narrow and circumscribed for training police psychologists. Therefore, with confidence, I predict that police psychology will have several graduate programs exclusively devoted to the field within the next decade.

In conclusion, police psychology has an extremely promising future. Professions rarely develop along a continuum of steady growth but usually expand and contract in a cyclical fashion. Police psychology is about to experience another upward swing, perhaps equal to the growth seen during the 1970s. Legislatures and much of the public continue to be convinced that the best way to deal with the crime problem is by improved and expanded policing, as demonstrated by the Crime Control Act of 1994. Although the law provides for preventive programs, it [also] gives more support to law enforcement efforts, particularly those of the community policing variety. It is highly likely that this prioritization of policing will welcome the skills and knowledge of police psychologists. This anticipated growth in police psychology will be sustained, however, only if we engage in high-quality research designed to test the effectiveness of various programs, policies, methods, and innovations.

3

PSYCHOLOGICAL TESTING AND THE SELECTION OF POLICE OFFICERS

A National Survey

ROBERT E. COCHRANE

ROBERT P. TETT

LEON VANDECREEK

Personnel selection practices have become more widely used over the years, particularly with law enforcement candidates. This increased use has included more sophisticated methods of evaluating potential police officers. One reason for greater emphasis on selection procedures is the negative impact of having unqualified employees. Financial costs are one way police agencies are affected. For example, the Los Angeles Police Department spends approximately $100,000 to train each new police officer. Furthermore, it was estimated that the average new police recruit was required to undergo nearly 1,000 hours of training (U.S. Department of Justice, 1996). Obviously, if hires later prove unable to perform their duties, substantial resources have been wasted. Although several factors influence the potential success or failure of police recruits, agencies are largely concerned about the emotional or psychological adequacy of recruits. Hibler and Kurke (1995) defined this as "psychological suitability," or the

Editors' Note: This article was originally published in *Criminal Justice and Behavior*, Vol. 30, No. 5, October 2003, pp. 511–537. Reprinted with permission of Sage Publications. We have deleted findings related to differences on the basis of department size.

presence of personal factors that contribute to human reliability and the absence of those that create unreliability.

Shusman, Inwald, and Landa (1984) reported several purposes for preemployment screening of police officers. First, employers want to weed out lateness and absenteeism, which result in understaffing, excessive overtime pay, and a breakdown in trust among officers. Second, disciplinary interviews increase department expenses and use up valuable administrative time. Third, screening helps to avoid potential harm to citizens or fellow officers. Last, poor publicity and court litigation may result from reckless or irresponsible officer behavior. In at least one case, a plaintiff won a large settlement due to a department's negligence in conducting psychological evaluations of its officers (*Bonsignore v. City of New York,* 1981). Considering the duties of a police officer, there is little room for error. Besides the military, there is perhaps no other profession that has the authority to use force on others if necessary and invade the privacy of citizens. The consequences of officers' behavior can result in negative effects for the department, individuals, and the community.

The purpose of properly selecting a candidate is rather obvious. However, employee selection is more difficult to conduct than other personnel decisions (e.g., promotion) because little is known about the individual and there is no in-house record of previous performance for the candidate. Because recruiters cannot evaluate applicants based exclusively on their observed performance, other measures must be utilized. Determining persons' abilities from their past performance and behavior would probably be ideal. Unfortunately, this information is often unavailable for a new recruit. Lester (1983) argued that the most valuable information comes from observing officers in training and during a probationary period. This may be true, but many resources (e.g., money, time) will be depleted if all applicants go through the training process. Furthermore, not all determinants of job performance, such as cognitive ability and personality variables, can be acquired or altered via training

(Reiss, Ones, & Viswesvaran, 1996). Also, if well-designed selection is used during the recruitment phase, less socialization will be needed in terms of social control, disciplinary procedures, and ongoing supervision (Hancock & McClung, 1984).

THE SELECTION AND ASSESSMENT PROCESS

In 1973, the National Advisory Commission on Criminal Justice Standards and Goals recommended that every police agency follow a formal selection process that includes (a) a written test of mental ability or aptitude, (b) an oral interview, (c) a psychological examination, and (d) a background investigation. Even earlier, the President's Commission on Law Enforcement and the Administration of Justice (1967) recommended the screening of all potential officers. It was believed that introducing greater screening and standardization to the selection process would result in a more qualified police force. More recently, the International Association of Chiefs of Police (1998) developed several guidelines for preemployment psychological evaluations. These recommendations address such issues as validation of testing instruments, compliance with legislation (e.g., Americans with Disabilities Act [ADA]), using qualified psychologists who are familiar with the relevant research, and content of the written reports.

Over the years, countless measures for screening candidates have been used to predict officer performance; these have shown varying levels of success. One of the best predictors of future work performance has been ability to perform duties similar to those required on a job (Guion & Gibson, 1988). For example, Schmidt, Hunter, McKenzie, and Muldrow (1979) compared job performance for employees selected with an ability test (e.g., situational exercise) and those without the test and found on average that those selected with the test were 0.487 standard deviation units better in job performance. Hunter and Hunter's (1984) meta-analysis showed that when artifacts such as statistical error and small sample size were removed from research studies for entry-level jobs, the best predictor of job performance was ability, which had a mean validity of .53. Assessment centers have a long history of evaluating candidates based on how well they perform job-related activities in simulated settings. These centers are typically private agencies that design evaluation instruments and assess candidates on numerous variables before providing feedback to the employers. However, as of 1990, less than one fourth of police departments reported using assessment centers (Ash, Slora, & Britton, 1990). Although still controversial, the polygraph is frequently cited as a tool used in selection (e.g., Ben-Shakhar & Furedy, 1990; Lykken, 1981; Saxe, 1994). Of the municipal agencies responding to the Ash et al. survey, 73% indicated using the polygraph in preemployment screening. The Civil Service Examination (CSE) is a multiple-choice exam designed for the selection of civil servant employees, including police officers (Cortina, Doherty, Schmitt, Kaufman, & Smith, 1992). However, there is no indication as to how extensively the CSE is used. The National Police Officer Selection Test (POST), a less well-known skills-based instrument, has also shown decent reliability and criterion-related validity in several studies (Henry & Rafilson, 1997; Rafilson & Sison, 1996). The POST assesses mathematics, reading, grammar, and incident report writing. Certain information derived from the interview, application blank, and background investigation has also been used to select police officers, even though much of this data is not subject to predictive validity studies like other variables. For example, many departments will deny an applicant further consideration if he or she has a history of a reckless driving conviction. In this case it would be impossible to validate the predictive or concurrent validity of this measure without danger to the public. Cognitive measures have also been used to predict job performance across various occupations. However, intelligence and cognitive ability are not highly predictive of on-the-job performance, despite showing some promise in predicting police academy performance

(Aylward, 1985; Henderson, 1979; Spielberger, Ward, & Spaulding, 1979).

Two large meta-analytic studies have demonstrated the usefulness of personality measures in predicting job performance using the "big five" personality dimensions (conscientiousness, agreeableness, extraversion, neuroticism, and openness to experience) (Barrick & Mount, 1991; Tett, Jackson, & Rothstein, 1991). Other studies have also established the ability of personality tests and inventories to predict job performance (e.g., Inwald, 1988; . . . McDaniel & Frei, 1994; . . .). Traits from the Neuroticism, Extraversion, and Openness (NEO) Personality Inventory–Revised, which was based on the five-factor model of personality, have also shown to be predictive of police performance. In fact, conscientiousness added incremental validity to cognitive testing in one study with 284 police recruits (H. C. Black, 2000).

The Minnesota Multiphasic Personality Inventory–2 (MMPI-2) and the Inwald Personality Inventory (IPI) have been shown to be effective in predicting several job criteria for police officers, as well (e.g., Bartol, 1991; Inwald & Knatz, 1988; Scogin, Schumacher, Howland, & McGee, 1989; . . .). Various inventories and psychological measures have also been used to assess the degree to which applicants present excessive socially desirable responses, because applicants may have a tendency to minimize their flaws or weaknesses (e.g., Borum & Stock, 1993; Grossman, Haywood, Ostrov, Wasyliw, & Cavanaugh, 1990).

Between 1979 and 1988, there was enormous growth in the use of psychological services in police departments, assessment being the primary service used (Delprino & Bahn, 1988). In their 1988 nationwide survey, Delprino and Bahn found that 52% of responding police agencies were conducting psychological screening on police recruits and 90% perceived a need for its use in their department. Similarly, Behrens (1985) found that 50% of police agencies responding to a nationwide survey were doing psychological screening. Bartol (1996) surveyed 152 police psychologists and found that preemployment screening consumed the largest percentage of their time

(34.3%), again suggesting this activity's importance to police departments.

The psychological tests most frequently used in departments throughout the United States are personality measures (Hancock & McClung, 1984). Hartman (1987) reported that most agencies use the MMPI and the clinical interview along with one or more of the following: the California Psychological Inventory (CPI), the Sixteen Personality Factor Questionnaire (16PF), Edwards Personal Preference Schedule, and the Inwald Personality Inventory. An earlier survey found the most commonly used personality instruments were the Rorschach, MMPI, CPI, and Eysenck Personality Questionnaire (EPQ) (Spielberger, 1979). However, a more recent finding (Ash et al., 1990) suggested that Rorschach use has declined among police departments (only 4.4% using it).

Clearly, numerous different psychological tests are used to screen officers, yet little is known about the degree of variability among departments in the United States. Understanding the psychological tests and procedures used today to select officers may help us understand whether departments are using those instruments shown to be most effective in selecting police officers. This information will also allow us to take a look at possible reasons why different departments use different measuring devices. Examining selection practices will also inform us about how police agencies use collected data to make decisions and how much attention they give to various measures and outcomes.

Other important questions that have not been adequately addressed to date are the extent to which police departments are following public policy guidelines regarding selection procedures and the extent to which selection practices have been affected by policy changes. Various agencies have put in place several policies and guidelines including *Standards for Educational and Psychological Tests* (American Psychological Association [APA], 1985), *Principles for the Validation and Use of Personnel Selection Procedures* (Society for Industrial and Organizational Psychology, 1987), *Enforcement Guidance: Preemployment Disability–Related Inquiries and Medical Examinations Under the Americans with Disabilities Act of 1990* (Equal Employment Opportunity Commission, 1995), and the *Civil Rights Act of 1991*. These guidelines address such issues as inappropriate inquiries during selection, cutoff scores on standardized tests, and the use of norms. Also, the Equal Employment Opportunity Commission focuses much attention on selection procedures that may discriminate or have an adverse impact on certain racial and gender groups.

In addition to examining current selection practices and adherence to guidelines, this study examines how police departments differ based on their size and degree of selectivity of applicants. Knowledge gained from this study will help determine if changes are needed in how police officers are selected as well as provide important feedback to police agencies regarding how well they are performing their selections relative to accepted standards and normative practices. We gathered information to help answer these questions via a survey developed specifically for this study.

Although this study was intended to primarily be exploratory in nature, the following hypotheses are offered: (a) Police departments would use psychological evaluations to a higher degree than has been found in prior studies (Behrens, 1985; Delprino & Bahn, 1988); (b) larger police departments (those that served larger areas and had more employees) and more selective departments (those with higher applicant-to-selection ratios) would use a greater number of selection devices as well as more sophisticated procedures because these agencies tend to have more options and greater resources (sophistication was defined as the use of psychological assessment, development of norms, conducting a job analysis, using a greater number of selection procedures, and making conditional offers of employment); and (c) larger departments would use a pass–fail approach to psychological assessment and a minimum cutoff score approach to the selection process, based on the belief these approaches require less judgment and lend themselves to quicker decision making, which is especially important for larger and busier departments.

METHOD

Participants

We mailed the survey to personnel departments of municipal police agencies located throughout the United States. We chose municipal police departments because they are the most widely recognized law enforcement agencies and they represent the largest number of police or safety personnel in the United States. Currently, more than 12,000 municipal agencies exist in this country. Of the 355 departments randomly selected based on geography and population size served (stratified random sample), 155 agencies returned completed surveys (43%). To facilitate the analyses and illustration of the data, we categorized each department into one of three groups based on the size of the population served. Departments were considered *large* if population size served was greater than 100,000, *medium* if between 25,000 and 100,000, and *small* if less than 25,000. The source used to select departments and determine population size was *The National Directory of Law Enforcement Administrators and Correctional Agencies* (National Police Chiefs and Sheriffs Information Bureau, 1996).

SURVEY

We developed 20 survey questions that were intended to cover the content relevant for this study. . . . These questions encompassed several topics such as background about the department, selection procedures utilized, the selection process, public policy issues, and use of norms and job analyses.

Procedure

We asked four reviewers (psychologists) with experience in the criminal justice system,

police selection, or test construction to review the survey questions for clarity, content, and ease of response. We revised item content based on feedback from these sources. Then we showed the revised survey to two personnel managers at local police departments. They reported no difficulties in reading or understanding the questions on the survey and invested approximately 10 to 15 minutes in completing the survey.

We analyzed survey results to identify selection practices and procedures among police departments. In the first sets of analyses, descriptive statistics were computed (i.e., percentages) comparing the procedures and psychological tests used among small, medium, and large departments. We then utilized chi-square analyses to discern statistically significant differences among these departments.

We implemented further analysis to compare departments based on their number of employees, population size, and degree of selectivity in hiring. We completed Pearson correlation coefficients to show relationships between these continuous variables and several procedures related to sophisticated methods utilized by departments (e.g., use of job analysis, use of norms).

RESULTS

Selection Procedures

Table 3.1 lists the diverse procedures used by departments serving different population sizes as well as the percentage of departments that use each procedure. Results show that the median number of procedures reported by departments to select officer candidates was nine, indicating that respondents use a package of tools to select employees.

More than 90% of departments use the background investigation along with a medical exam, interview, application, and psychological assessment. More than half of the agencies also reported utilizing drug testing, measures of physical fitness, and the polygraph.

Table 3.1   Percentage of Departments That Use Selection Procedures

| Procedure | Department Size | | | |
	Small (n = 35)	Medium (n = 53)	Large (n = 67)	Combined (N= 155)
Background investigation	100.0	98.1	100.0	99.4
Medical exam	97.0	98.1	100.0	98.7
Interview	100.0	98.1	97.0	98.1
Application blank	97.0	90.5	98.5	95.5
Psychological assessment	73.5[a]	94.3[b]	98.5[b]	91.6
Drug testing	70.5[a]	90.5	95.5[b]	88.4
Physical fitness	64.7	81.1	86.5	80.0
Polygraph	26.4[a]	69.8[b]	82.0[b]	65.8
Civil Service Exam	32.3	50.9	56.7	49.7
Recommendation letters	50.0	35.8	53.7	46.5
Knowledge, skills, abilities	47.0	49.0	44.7	46.5
Other	20.5	26.4	31.3	27.7

NOTE: Figures within a row that do not share subscripts differ at $p < .001$ by the chi-square test.

One interesting finding is that more than 27% of police departments use procedures other than those listed. Also, 36 different procedures were reported by responding agencies. Of these 36 procedures, not one was utilized by more than six departments. Clearly, a wide variety of selection tools is used by police agencies. Although there is conformity among agencies in using the major selection procedures, departments also utilize many unique methods.

Additionally, there were a few differences in selection procedures used by departments of different sizes. Small departments reported using psychological assessment less frequently than medium . . . and large departments. . . . Small agencies also reported less use of drug testing than large departments . . . and they used the polygraph less than medium . . . and large departments. . . .

Psychological Assessment

Survey results indicate that approximately 91% of respondents reported they required psychological assessment for all new police recruits. This figure compares with 52% in 1988 (Delprino & Bahn, 1988) from a study that used a fairly similar sample (287 municipal agencies and 49 state police agencies). Although a large percentage of departments require a psychological evaluation, the amount of weight or consideration reportedly given to the evaluation in the overall selection process is modest. Almost one third (31.9%, $n = 44$) of the 155 agencies in our final sample reported they weighted the evaluation in comparison to other selection procedures used, whereas the remaining 68.1% of agencies ($n = 94$) viewed data from the psychological evaluation in terms of passing or failing for the candidate. In other words, the majority of respondents see candidates as either passing or failing the psychological evaluation with those who fail no longer being considered for a position. However, of these departments, psychological assessment is given a median weight of 30.0% (range = 15 to 100), a fair degree of emphasis. The percentage of applicants ultimately rejected solely on the basis of psychological assessment is small (median = 5.0%, $n = 111$, range = 0 to 75).

Table 3.2 lists the psychological tests most frequently used by police departments. Consistent

Table 3.2   Percentage of Departments That Use Psychological Tests

	Department Size			
Psychological Test	*Small* (n = 35)	*Medium* (n = 53)	*Large* (n= 67)	*Combined* (N = 155)
Minnesota Multiphasic Personality Inventory-2	52.9[a]	67.9	83.5[b]	71.6
Clinical interview	50.0	52.8	64.1	57.4
Personal History Questionnaire	50.0	49.0	56.7	52.9
California Psychological Inventory	17.6	20.7	29.8	24.5
Other	5.8	20.7	31.3	21.9
16 Personality Factor Questionnaire	14.7	13.2	23.8	18.7
Inwald Personality Inventory	2.9	13.2	14.9	11.6
Mental status exam	11.7	16.9	4.4	10.3
Rorschach/inkblot	2.9	7.5	5.9	5.8
Hilson Safety/Security	2.9	9.4	1.4	4.5
Eysenck Personality Questionnaire	5.8	0.0	1.4	1.9

SOURCE: Cochrane et al.

NOTE: Figures within a row that do not share subscripts differ at $p < .001$ by the chi-square test.

with results from the late 1980s (Hartman, 1987), the most widely used testing instrument is the MMPI-2. The clinical interview and the CPI also continue to be used by a large number of agencies (57.4% and 24.5%, respectively), whereas the EPQ and the Rorschach have decreased in use. The Personal History Questionnaire was used by a large number of departments (52.9%). This tool is useful for collecting information that can be used to rule out job candidates and to verify information obtained through other means (e.g., background check).

The only significant difference in psychological tests used by departments of different sizes was with the MMPI-2. Small departments reported less use of the MMPI-2 . . . than large agencies.

PUBLIC POLICY ISSUES

Conditionally offering employment to potential employees is one way for departments to avoid soliciting medical information prior to hiring, which would violate public policy guidelines

(i.e., ADA, 1990). In this study, 87% of municipal police departments reported using conditional offers in their selection process. The median year these departments began this procedure was 1992. This may be a response to the 1990 ADA, which prohibited medical inquiries prior to job offers. Medical information can include information from such sources as medical examinations, psychological tests that measure psychopathology, drug testing, and physical fitness tests. . . .

Overall, most departments resist medical inquiries until after offers of employment have been made. However, medical exams are conducted prior to offers in 12.3% of departments, whereas pathology-based psychological testing (testing to assess mental illnesses or disorders) is done prior to offers in 17.4% of departments.

Municipal police departments also appear to comply fairly well with other mandates regarding selection of potential employees. However, a small portion of police departments utilize different norms for racial groups or genders (13.3%, n = 113). This practice violates guidelines in *Standards for Educational and*

Psychological Testing (APA, 1985). However, virtually all departments that use cutoff scores on various procedures do not use different cutoff scores when selecting members of different races or genders (95.0%, n = 61), suggesting a very high level of compliance in this area.

LEVEL OF SOPHISTICATION OF SELECTION PROCEDURES

Several authors have made suggestions regarding the procedures and processes of selecting police officers (e.g., Beutler, Storm, Kirksih, Scogini, & Gaines, 1985; Hiatt & Hargrave, 1988; Meier et al., 1987). However, police agencies are under no obligation to follow these recommendations and there may be times or circumstances when a department should follow other procedures not suggested. Nonetheless, one point this study was designed to address is the level of sophistication of police departments' selection procedures and the extent to which agencies follow recommendations offered by available research.

Conducting job analyses to determine the essential job functions, duties, and work skills needed for police officers involves a great endeavor and investment by police departments. Performance of job analyses suggests a high level of sophistication in the selection process. Prior to this study, it was not expected that many agencies would utilize job analyses, given this high degree of investment. Surprisingly, 74.5% of departments surveyed reported having completed a job analysis or systematic evaluation of essential job functions at their agencies. Furthermore, an additional 7.4% of departments reported using job analysis information from other sources. Results show that the median year agencies last conducted a job analysis was 1995 (*N* = 98), and on average a job analysis is updated every 2.8 years (*SD* = 2.4).

For the evaluator to properly determine whether an applicant will be capable of performing the required duties of an officer, the evaluator needs to know what those duties are and the kind of environment in which the officer will be working. Agencies that request psychological assessment to cover more than just "rule outs" for mental disorders should provide or make sure the evaluator has access to job analysis results. When asked whether job analysis or job description information was provided to the evaluator(s), 78.8% (*n* = 108) of police departments reported providing this material. This suggests the majority of evaluators are aware of job requirements and duties of officers when conducting the evaluations.

Another question examined was whether police departments review applicant results on a procedure-by-procedure basis or with a more global outlook where performance on all selection procedures is considered together. The majority of agencies used a minimum cutoff score approach (62.9%, *n* = 83) where applicants who do not achieve a certain predetermined score on a particular measure are no longer considered for a position. A more global approach where performance is evaluated together for all measures was reported by 15.9% of departments, whereas 21.2% used both a minimum cutoff score and a global approach.

In terms of procedures used to select officers, it was of interest to determine how frequently formal assessment centers were used by police departments. Assessment centers can be a costly means of assessing police candidates, and the benefits they reap may or may not outweigh the costs. In response to the survey, only 8.1% of the police departments reported using a formal assessment center. The low use of this selection procedure may reflect the belief by police personnel that the costs do indeed outweigh the gains, or they may simply not know how to use them. Whatever the reasons, many authors (e.g., Ash et al., 1990; Coulton & Field, 1995; Dunnette & Motowidlo, 1976) would argue that assessment centers are currently being underutilized.

***

DISCUSSION

Municipal police departments throughout the country have given increasing attention to procedures for selection of police officers. One reason for greater emphasis on selection of new recruits is the high costs associated with poor officer performance. These costs are incurred through such means as greater supervision, dismissals, lawsuits, and low morale. The primary purpose of this study was to identify the selection procedures used by municipal police departments, paying particular attention to the psychological assessment process. It appears that greater emphasis on selection can be seen in the increased use of selection procedures, particularly psychological assessment procedures. In fact, comparing this study's results with that of prior research (Delprino & Bahn, 1988), psychological assessment of police candidates has increased dramatically over the past 10 years, with 52% of agencies using psychological screening in 1988 compared to more than 90% in this study.

The Selection Process and Psychological Assessment

Large attention given to selection is also reflected in the high number of procedures used by departments to evaluate candidates. On average, police agencies use nine different procedures when selecting new recruits. And although most departments reported using similar procedures (i.e., background investigation, medical exam, interview, application, and psychological assessment), great variability existed. This diversity among departments may reflect an appropriate application of selection techniques because departments differ to some degree in terms of specific duties and the amount of time invested in performing different tasks. These wide differences could also be the result of a lack of awareness by municipal agencies or their consulting psychologists regarding the most effective selection procedures. The high degree of variability found in this study may also be due to each department utilizing different selection criteria. The measures used and the conclusions drawn depend to a large degree on the police department's criteria. For example, some departments

may consider abuse of an officer's power and early termination as highly important, whereas other agencies may place greater emphasis on tardiness and poor supervisory evaluations.

Despite the fact that no unified criteria or selection procedures exist at this time and there is great variability in procedures used, many agencies use a core set of similar selection measures. In fact, the typical department reported using the following measures when selecting officers: an application, background investigation, medical exam, oral interview, psychological assessment, drug test, physical fitness measures, and polygraph test. It also makes conditional offers of employment to those candidates [it is] interested in and then conducts the medically related tests following this offer. The typical department also uses approximately three or four different psychological tests or procedures, with the MMPI-2, clinical interview, Personal History Questionnaire, and the CPI being the most common.

Although psychological assessment appears to be valued in the selection process (median weight = 30.0%), very few individuals are rejected based solely on the results (median = 5%). This contrasts with a previous finding reported by Meier et al. (1987) that approximately 15% of candidates were screened out through personality assessment. The reason for this difference is not clear. One possible explanation could be that, more recently, qualified candidates are pre-selected through other procedures prior to the psychological evaluation. Therefore, once the psychological evaluation is completed, few individuals are found to be outright unqualified. At a first glance, this would seem to make psychological assessment essentially irrelevant. However, although a 5% rejection rate based on psychological assessment results does not appear high, if only half of these candidates (2.5%) would eventually prove to be problematic, this could cost a police department a tremendous amount of difficulty including loss of money, potential harm to others, and negative publicity.

Whereas the typical agency did not report using norms for most of their procedures (many of which are not conducive to developing normative data), a large percentage did use norms for psychological testing. Also, the average agency conducted its own job analysis and provided this information to the person(s) conducting the psychological evaluation. Overall, the average municipal police department appears to have a relatively thorough and professional selection process. Almost 25 years ago, the National Advisory Commission on Criminal Justice Standards and Goals (1973) recommended that police agencies use written tests of mental abilities (i.e., tests of Knowledge, Skills, and Abilities [KSAs]), an interview, psychological assessment, and a background check on all police officer candidates. With the exception of KSAs, this study found that police departments are following these suggestions at a relatively high rate.

PUBLIC POLICY ISSUES AND TESTING RECOMMENDATIONS

A significant minority of agencies failed to follow public policy guidelines and other recommendations. For example, respondents reported making medical inquiries prior to conditional offers of employment at a fairly high rate (medical exams = 12.3%, pathology-based psychological tests = 17.4%). These are somewhat alarming numbers considering that a plaintiff may have grounds to file a lawsuit if he or she discovered that not being hired was due to a medical condition or disability. It is not clear why these agencies neglect to adhere to these regulations and suggestions. Many agencies may not be aware of the guidelines and just simply continue old practices that have worked in the past. Others may be aware of guidelines but are willing to take the risk of using certain procedures (e.g., medical inquiries prior to conditional offers), believing they are exempt from such policies due to the nature of the job of police officer. In many ways, departments may be justified in this position, given that certain criteria are unique to that of a police officer and are job-related. For example, individuals with severe emotional or psychological problems should be excluded from consideration for a police officer position, given the nature of the job. One would think this could be justified in a court of law if necessary, but it is still a risk departments may not wish to take.

Departments appear to consider the psychological assessment component of the selection process as a procedure that has an all-or-none value. In other words, the majority of agencies use a pass–fail approach to psychological assessment results, keeping candidates who pass and rejecting those who fail. This is consistent with Ho's (1999) study on the effects of test results and demographic factors on 420 police candidates in a North Carolina police department. Ho found the decision-making process in selection of officers was primarily testing oriented, whereby candidates who failed to achieve a satisfactory rating on any of the tests were less likely to be recruited.

These results indicate police agencies may be underutilizing the usefulness of a psychological evaluation. Many authors have argued that psychological assessment has incremental validity beyond simply screening out candidates with psychopathology. For example, certain personality instruments (e.g., IPI) have shown strong predictive power in determining those candidates who will likely have problems with absenteeism or poor supervisor ratings. The departments that use a pass–fail approach may be the same departments that only request assessments to rule out psychopathology. Conversely, agencies that weight the assessment results may be those that request a greater degree of input from the psychological assessment referral. Each approach could be justified based on the information they were seeking to obtain. However, it seems many departments may not consider the psychological results very useful beyond informing them of obvious problem candidates.

***

LIMITATIONS AND RECOMMENDATIONS

Results from this survey need to be considered in light of the fact that only 155 municipal police departments participated in the study. Although this size is not small, generalizability may be of concern because more than 12,000 municipal agencies exist in this country. Also, as previously mentioned, the survey was completed by police department personnel managers, not psychologists or other persons directly assessing the candidates.

One area that deserves greater attention is the validation of various selection methods and procedures within particular departments. Although every procedure utilized by departments cannot be validated, many tests and procedures can be appropriately validated, particularly psychological tests. Given the predictive validity demonstrated with the MMPI-2, IPI, and CPI, departments may want to specifically request that these tests be used in the assessment process. And until norms are developed for a department with these tests, results can be interpreted with the aid of broader normative data that are available through various testing companies (e.g., Caldwell Reports).

Examining whether a multiple-hurdle selection strategy is superior to a global evaluation process (where all candidates receive all measures) may be of great interest to police departments, as well. Economically speaking, departments would likely save considerable money if they employed a multiple-hurdle strategy. Each candidate could be rated at each stage or hurdle, and those not meeting a minimum standard could be disqualified. Those candidates who completed all the hurdles could then be given a total rating, allowing comparisons and selections to be made based on the number of available positions. And in terms of psychological evaluation, departments may wish to request that the psychological evaluators rate or rank candidates. Ratings could include broad categories (e.g., highly acceptable, acceptable, marginally acceptable, unacceptable) that could then be incorporated into the overall selection rating process. This would broaden the usefulness of the psychological evaluation beyond simply ruling out obviously poor or problematic candidates.

Lastly, although various psychological tests have shown predictive validity, studies are lacking in the value of other selection procedures (e.g., Civil Service Examination). It would be prudent for police departments to solicit and promote greater research into other procedures and tests that are both cost effective and predictive of important outcome criteria. This will likely occur with the assistance and expertise of diligent psychologists in the field.

4

INVESTIGATIVE INTERVIEWS OF CHILDREN

A Review of Psychological Research and Implications for Police Practices

KAMALA LONDON

In the 1970s, there was a shift in societal and legal views toward family issues. Whereas events that occurred among family members were once considered private affairs, the 1974 Federal Child Abuse Prevention and Treatment Act mandated that professionals such as physicians, teachers, police, and social workers report suspected cases of child maltreatment. As reporting and public awareness of child abuse increased, child welfare agencies and police were flooded with suspected cases of abuse.

As a response to children's increasing presence in the legal system, researchers began to empirically study children's ability to give accurate testimony. The purpose of this article is to review the psychological research pertaining to interviewing child victims/witnesses. Interview guidelines based on psychological research are reviewed. Furthermore, implications for police practices are discussed in light of the psychological empirical work.

Until the 1980s, children were generally required to pass extended *voir dires,* or tests of their competency, before being allowed to give courtroom testimony (Ceci & Bruck, 1993). For instance, children were once required to demonstrate an understanding of "truth versus lie." Children under certain ages were sometimes forbidden from giving testimony, because their autobiographic memories were considered questionable.

Editors' Note: This article was originally published in *Police Quarterly*, Vol. 4, No. 1, March 2001, pp. 123–144. Reprinted with permission of Sage Publications.

The courts no longer require that children undergo competency hearings but rather let the jury decide how much weight to give children's testimony. Also, in the 1980s, all states dropped former requirements that children's allegations of sexual assault be corroborated by either physical evidence or by adult witnesses (Ceci & Bruck, 1993). In sum, many legal barriers that once discouraged or prevented children from being the sole complainant to a crime were largely removed.

***

INVESTIGATIVE INTERVIEW TECHNIQUES AND FALSE ALLEGATIONS OF ABUSE

In the past 20 years, there has been a flood of research that has examined children's competency to act as court witnesses. Research suggests that children can often give accurate accounts of past events (e.g., Geiselman & Padilla, 1988; Poole & Lamb, 1998). However, research has also revealed that children may give inaccurate or blatantly false accounts when interviewed with certain techniques (for reviews, see Ceci & Bruck, 1993; Poole & Lamb, 1998). Children's competency to give accurate testimony is dependent on the quality of the investigative interview techniques.

Although memory skills certainly improve with age, young children have demonstrated accurate recall of past events, particularly with regard to action-related salient events (G. M. Davis, Tarrant, & Flin, 1989). For instance, Poole and Lindsay (1995) found that 3- to 4-year-olds and 5- to 7-year-olds accurately recalled a recent event. Children in their study interacted with "Mr. Science," who did various demonstrations. For instance, "Mr. Science" showed the children how to lift newspaper print with Silly Putty. Children were interviewed with nonsuggestive techniques immediately following their interactions. Even 3- and 4-year-olds were highly accurate in their recall of the events.

Goodman and Reed (1986) provided further support of children's competency to accurately report on past events. They staged an event and questioned adults and 6-year-olds about the event after a 4- to 5-day delay. They found few age differences in testimony when children were asked objective questions. Although the 6-year-olds were more likely than the adults to be misled about periphery events, they generally were not misled regarding central events.

Although research suggests that children can give accurate accounts of past events, a sizable literature also reveals that children sometimes give inaccurate or blatantly false accounts when interviewed (for review, see Ceci, Bruck, & Battin, 2000). For instance, Poole and Lindsay (1995) conducted a follow-up interview with some of the children who participated in the "Mr. Science" project. The second interview was conducted after a 3-month delay. For 3 consecutive days prior to the second interview, children's parents read them stories about experienced and nonexperienced events pertaining to the "Mr. Science" project. The researchers then interviewed children with leading and nonleading questions. In the second interview, 41% of 3- to 4-year-olds reported having experienced fictitious events.

The now well-known case of Kelly Michaels raised researchers' attention to false allegations that may arise from suggestive interview techniques. Michaels, a 26-year-old nursery care worker at the Wee Care Nursery School in New Jersey, was charged with 115 counts of child sexual assault (CSA). Over a 7-month period of interviews, twenty 3- to 5-year-old children accused Michaels of sexual assault. Their accusations included bizarre claims that certainly would have produced physical evidence. For instance, children accused Michaels of putting peanut butter on their genitals and of sodomizing them with knives, forks, and Lego blocks. Despite the lack of physical evidence to corroborate these claims, Michaels was convicted and sentenced to 47 years in prison. After serving 5 years in prison, the case was overturned by appeals, in part based on an amicus brief that was filed by numerous child witness researchers on Michaels's behalf.

Examinations of interview records clearly show that investigators in the Michaels case used highly suggestive questions, combined with bribery and intimidation of the children (Ceci & Bruck, 1993). Children were repeatedly interviewed until they were "good boys or girls" and provided the interviewer with abuse information. For instance, during one interview, a child was told, "You told us everything once before. Do you want to undress my dolly? Let's get done with this real quick so we could go to Kings to get Popsicles" (*State v. Michaels,* 1993). Following high-profile cases such as the Michaels case, researchers turned their focus to examining how different questioning techniques affect children's accounts. The results from these studies reveal a variety of ways that interviewers can taint children's testimony.

Suggestive Questions

The Kelly Michaels case and the "Mr. Science" project conducted by Poole and Lindsay (1995) suggest that children sometimes make false allegations. The true proportion of criminal allegations that are false is difficult to establish in actual abuse cases, particularly cases such as sexual assault in which physical evidence may be lacking. A frequently cited rate of false reports in the psychological literature is 5% to 8% of [child sexual abuse (CSA)] cases. Moreover, false allegations of sexual abuse are estimated to be as high as 50% when the alleged victim is from a family currently undergoing a divorce and custody battle (Raskin & Yuille, 1989). Considering that around 200,000 new abuse allegations arise each year (Finkelhor, 1984), if 8% of abuse allegations are false, then an astounding 16,000 people would be falsely charged with CSA each year.

Sometimes false allegations may unintentionally result from conversations with well-intentioned adults. Parents, teachers, and child care workers seem to hold certain assumptions about behaviors that are indicative of abuse. For instance, if a teacher witnessed a preschool-aged child masturbating, such behavior might be brought to the attention of authorities (remember, teachers are mandated to report suspected cases of child abuse). Indeed, researchers have found that sexual acting out is more common in sexually abused than nonabused children (Koocher et al., 1995). However, nonabused children may also display sexual behavior. Nonabused children may learn about sexual activity through a variety of modes, including peers, siblings, parents, or television. Sexual play is rather common among children, with around half of 2- to 5-year-olds estimated to engage in genital manipulation (Chess & Hassibi, 1986). Despite the long history of investigators, therapists, and parents assuming that abuse occurred based on behavior such as phallic drawings, there is not adequate validity in such behavior to be diagnostic of abuse (Buros, 1989). In sum, sexual knowledge may originate from a variety of sources, and sexual activity is relatively common among children.

Parents or teachers may become alarmed at a child's behavior and report their suspicions to social welfare agencies or police. However, some children may simply be displaying normal childhood behavior. Even in cases in which the child seems to clearly make an abuse allegation (e.g., "My bottom was licked at daddy's"), alternative explanations are possible (e.g., the family dog licked the child). However, investigators have traditionally assumed a priori that children who came to their attention were abused. Traditionally, investigators saw their role as collecting information to confirm the abuse (Ceci & Bruck, 1993).

Some investigators have used suggestive, leading questions to satisfy their perhaps well-meaning intentions of corroborating abuse (Ceci & Bruck, 1993; Warren, Woodall, Hunt, & Perry, 1996). Unfortunately, this hypothesis-confirming approach to conducting abuse investigations may elicit false statements from the child. Suggestive, leading questions may cause some nonabused children to assent to abuse. Numerous studies have found that children may succumb to suggestive questions (for a review, see Bruck & Ceci, 1999). Once false statements emerge, it is difficult to reliably distinguish between true and false reports, as false statements are often rich in detail (Bruck, Hembrooke, & Ceci, 1997).

***

Interestingly, children [tend] not to succumb to misleading questions when interviewed by a 7-year-old child (Ceci, Ross, & Toglia, 1987, Experiment 2). Ceci et al. suggest that children see adults as authority figures and attempt to please the adult by agreeing with their questions. Therefore, children may be particularly susceptible to leading questions from authority figures such as police officers (Walker-Perry & Wrightsman, 1991).

On the other hand, Goodman and colleagues (e.g., Goodman, Aman, & Hirschman, 1987; Goodman, Hirschman, Hepps, & Rudy, 1991) have conducted numerous studies that suggest children may sometimes be resistant to suggestive questions. For instance, Goodman, Rudy, Bottoms, and Aman (1990) conducted a project in which 4- to 7-year-olds played with a clown and were interviewed about the event 10 to 12 days later. They found that children generally were resistant to misleading questions about the event. However, in this study, children were only questioned once by a nonintimidating adult. Even so, some children in the study did agree to suggestive questions that might be construed as indicative of abuse.

***

Once children agree to suggestive events, Ceci and colleagues (Ceci & Bruck, 1995; Ceci, Huffman, Smith, & Loftus, 1994) suggest that they may actually come to believe that the suggested events occurred. Young children sometimes have difficulties with memory-source monitoring (Ceci & Bruck, 1995; Taylor, Esbensen, & Bennett, 1994). Therefore, children may continue to report such nonexperienced events as having actually occurred when subsequently questioned.

In sum, using suggestive, leading questions during investigative interviews heightens the risk of eliciting inaccurate or erroneous reports from children—reports that may persist during subsequent interviews. Leading questions seem to emerge when the investigators seek to confirm rather than test the hypothesis that a child was abused. Leading questions are also quite likely to be challenged in court, potentially ruining the child's credibility.

The main implication for interviewing child witnesses that emerges from the suggestibility literature is that interviewers should take a hypothesis-testing rather than a hypothesis-confirming approach. With the hypothesis-testing approach, interviewers should consider whether factors other than abuse might explain some of the child's behavior. Interviewers should consider who first came forward with the abuse charges and any potential motivation that parents might have to encourage a child to make false allegations. Investigators should also consider base rate behavior of sexual play rather than viewing sexual play as a confirmation of abuse. Clearly, leading questions should be avoided.

Repeated Questions

Repeated questioning may also lead children to report false allegations of abuse. The effect of repeated interviews on children's statements depends on factors such as the timing of the repetition and the types of repeated questions (Poole & Lamb, 1998). If repeated interviews are conducted, then interviewers must be particularly careful to avoid leading questions.

Ceci and colleagues (Ceci & Bruck, 1995; Ceci et al., 1994) found that preschool children are especially prone to agree with repeated leading questions. In their study, preschoolers selected cards with statements such as "Got finger caught in mousetrap and had to go to the hospital." The cards were read to children who were then asked if the event ever occurred. Initially, most children disagreed with the statements. However, after 12 weeks of being interviewed once a week, more than half of the children gave false narratives of at least one event. [Twenty-five percent gave] false narratives to a majority of the nonexperienced events. Children's reports tended to be rich in detail. Furthermore, following debriefing, 27% of children refused to believe that the suggested event did not actually occur.

On the other hand, repeated interviews may sometimes help children provide new details of a past event (Howe, Kelland, Bryant-Brown, & Clark, 1992). Multiple interviews may help a confused but cooperative witness by helping him or her learn to talk about the event. Bradley and Wood (1996) examined 234 cases of corroborated CSA and found that 6% originally denied abuse. Thus, repeated interviews may sometimes be necessary for children to disclose abuse information.

However, investigators must use caution during repeated interviews. If asked repeated specific questions, children may change their responses, thinking the adult is repeating the question because the child provided the wrong answer.

***

In the actual legal setting, children are interviewed an average of 11 times before reaching court (McGough, 1994). Police administrators may help lessen the number of times children are interviewed by coordinating with other agencies (e.g., protective services) involved. By coordinating in advance with other social service agencies, interviews could be conducted by a team of professionals. If children are repeatedly interviewed by different professionals (e.g., a social worker and then a police officer), the interviewers should be careful to explain that they are not aware of the information that the children have already told others and would like to learn about it. Children are less likely to be misled if they are told in advance that the interviewer has no prior knowledge of the events in question (Toglia, Ross, Ceci, & Hembrooke, 1992).

Language Development

False allegations of abuse may also arise from linguistic confusion. Research suggests that it is necessary for investigative interviewers to have a rather sophisticated understanding of language development. Adults, including interviewers, often ask questions that are confusing to children

(Brennan & Brennan, 1988; Warren et al., 1996). To complicate matters further, children who have experienced abuse may display delayed language development (Beeghly & Cicchetti, 1994).

Typical conversations with adults and children are quite different from proper interview conversations. Adults typically converse with children in a highly structured manner. Gleason (1977) suggests that adults are directive during their conversations with children to promote language development. Adults often make leading and reinforcing statements during normal conversations.

Understanding children's language development is a complex task for interviewers. Interviewers must learn and practice a proactive linguistic style with young children. There is little evidence to suggest that interviewers automatically conduct interviews with these linguistic principles in mind. Rather, investigative interviews with children appear to be conducted in a linguistic manner similar to typical adult–child conversations. Hence, police administrators should encourage specialized training in interviewing child witnesses.

Subtle variations in interviewers' talk with children can have a tremendous impact on their reports. Both children and interviewers may be confused at the other's communicative intent. Research indicates that children often misunderstand seemingly simple words and concepts. For instance, children are often confused by words related to "touch" (Warren, 1992). Children may state that "He put his fingers inside me," but say no to the question, "Did he touch you?" A. G. Walker (1994) notes that children may have a different understanding of commonly used words than adults. For instance, children may think that to remember something, it must first be forgotten. Thus, if asked whether they remember a particular event, children may say no simply because they have remembered it all along.

Investigators should also avoid questions about emotional concepts (e.g., "How did that make you feel?"). J. Aldridge and Wood (1997) found that until around age 8, children easily become confused by words such as fear, anxiety, and anger. Even until age 14, children's understanding of the concept of emotion may differ from that of adults.

Children may also not fully understand or be able to report concepts of time (Friedman, 1991). Instead of trying to get a specific date and time of an alleged abusive event, investigators should ask more general questions. For instance, investigators could inquire as to whether the alleged victim was on break from school, whether the abuse allegation occurred following a school day, and so forth. Asking children about specific times and dates may only serve to discredit the child in the courtroom.

Investigators must also pay attention to syntactical development. Research suggests that investigators should avoid using passive tenses during questioning. Passive-tense questions have been shown to confuse children until around ages 10 to 13. Furthermore, investigators should avoid multiple and negatively phrased questions, as these may also confuse children (A.G. Walker, 1994).

Children may also display confusion toward adult language pragmatics. For instance, children sometimes fail to realize or indicate topic transitions (Fivush & Shukat, 1995; Poole & Lindsay, 1995). Poole and Lindsay found that when children were asked final open-ended questions about the "Mr. Science" project, the requests often led to off-topic responses. They found that even 8- to 10-year-olds would stray from the relevant topic when asked such questions. If children make frequent topic shifts, then interviewers must be sure to clarify the information.

In sum, it is important for interviewers to work toward minimizing and recognizing linguistic confusion. Children may not tell adults that they are confused but rather attempt to answer the questions. M. Hughes and Grieve (1980) found that 5- to 7-year-olds often gave answers of yes or no to bizarre questions such as "Is milk bigger than water?" Warren and McCloskey (1997) found that when children were confused about a topic, they often either agreed with or paraphrased interviewers' prior statements. Such statements could lead investigators to superfluous conclusions.

The main implication for investigative interviews based on the child witness-language literature is that investigators must have a general understanding of language development. Investigators should be sensitive to the children's developmental level, allowing them to set the language level of the interview (Poole & Lamb, 1998). Awareness and sensitivity to language development can minimize interviewer–child miscommunication.

***

INTERVIEWING THE CHILD WITNESS

General Recommendations

There is no single structured interview that can be used to question all children. Interviewers must remain flexible to accommodate the varying characteristics of criminal cases. The interviewers should "consider life circumstances of individual children and adapt their methods accordingly" (Poole & Lamb, 1998, p. 8). The general interview techniques recommended below are flexible in that they focus on how to gather information rather than on what specific information to gather.

Pre-Interview Preparation

Research is lacking to address whether the quality of the interview is affected according to the amount of information collected prior to the interview. Prominent child-investigation researchers Poole and Lamb (1998) suggest gathering some information about the allegations and learning some personal information about the children to use in rapport building. Having some prior knowledge regarding the allegations or the children's family may help interviewers clarify details of the children's report. For instance, knowing whether children recently took sex education or whether the family is undergoing a divorce may be useful in considering alternative hypotheses to the abuse allegations.

Rapport Building

First, interviewers should introduce themselves to children. They should allow the children to become familiar with the interview environment and ask any questions. Interviewers should begin building rapport with children by asking open-ended questions about non-abuse-related topics such as school. Research suggests that building rapport may increase the accuracy of the children's statements. For instance, Saywitz, Geiselman, and Bornstein (1992) had detectives from a sheriff's department interview third and sixth graders about staged events. They found that children who participated in interviews that began with open-ended rapport building made the fewest mistakes in their accounts. Furthermore, Sternberg et al. (1997) found that interviews that began with open-ended rapport building produced twice as many details and words than did brief rapport building with closed questions. See Sternberg et al. for an example of an open-ended rapport-building protocol.

Interviewers should explain to children the goals and the general rules of the interview, including that they have the right to say, "no," "I don't remember," and "I don't understand" (Poole & Lamb, 1998). Children often think that they must answer every question adults ask, regardless of whether they know the answer (Moston, 1990). Interviewers should explain to children that they have the right to express confusion and to correct any false interpretations. In Warren, Hulse-Trotter, and Tubbs (1991), the researchers warned 7-year-olds, 12-year-olds, and adults that they may be asked some tricky, confusing questions during an interview. They found that all age groups were more resistant to suggestion when given such a warning.

Rapport building also allows children practice in being informative (Sternberg et al., 1997). Not only does this allow children to become relaxed and familiar with the interviewers, but it also establishes the tone of the interviews. Interviewers should be encouraging and supportive to children (Goodman et al., 1990). However, interviewers should avoid comments such as "good boy" to specific disclosure responses, as such encouragement could be leading. Children should be encouraged to be active participants in the interviews (Goodman et al., 1991; Poole & Lamb, 1998). As children begin to communicate, interviewers can partially assess the children's language abilities.

To foster rapport, it is best for one person to interview the child. Although a team approach of police/social worker interviews is highly recommended, a single person should do the interviews (Poole & Lamb, 1998). One-way mirrors and microphones ideally would be available to allow others to add questions to the interview. If this is not feasible, then a second investigator can sit in the room and take notes. Additional questions could be written and passed to the primary interviewer.

Interview Environment

Interviews should take place in environments that contain minimal distractions to children. Investigators should avoid wearing a police uniform or a gun, inasmuch as this likely will be distracting. To maximize children's concentration, the room should be simple, cheerful, uncluttered, and nonthreatening (Poole & Lamb, 1998).

The investigative environment should allow audio and video recordings of children's statements. Recorded interviews seem useful for several reasons. First, recordings allow investigators to counter claims of poor investigation techniques. In turn, recordings may also encourage proper interview techniques. Second, videotapes allow investigators to look back through children's accounts to review and clarify their communicative intent. Third, videotaped testimony may reduce the number of times that children are interviewed.

On the other hand, investigators must be prepared to have their interview methods challenged by the defense. Furthermore, inconsistencies between the videotaped interviews and the children's courtroom testimony may cast doubt on their reliability. Regardless, a general consensus appears to be emerging among researchers that the potential advantages of recording the interview outweigh the potential disadvantages. Interviews should be audiotaped and videotaped (e.g., Ceci & Bruck, 1995; Lamb, 1994; McGough, 1994, 1995; Poole & Lamb, 1998; Raskin & Yuille, 1989; Walker-Perry & Wrightsman, 1991).

Truth Versus Lie Ceremony

Investigators should avoid asking children to provide a narrative description of "truth versus lie." Such a question is abstract and confusing even to school-aged children (Pipe & Wilson, 1994; A.G. Walker, 1994). Furthermore, researchers have found that children's ability to explain "truth versus lie" does not predict the accuracy of their statements (Goodman et al., 1987; Pipe & Wilson, 1994). Researchers have only recently begun to examine the efficacy of different types of truth-lie discussions in increasing the veracity of children's reports (e.g., Huffman, Warren, & Larson, 1999; London & Nunez, 2002). Currently, there is inadequate evidence to direct the practice of truth-lie discussions with children. However, if a truth-lie ceremony is conducted, then interviewers should use concrete questions (Poole & Lamb, 1998).

Open-Ended Questions

Open-ended questions should be used as much as possible during investigative interviews. Open-ended questions allow children to respond to questions in a variety of ways. Children tend to be more accurate on their free recall than in response to forced-choice questions. Poole and Lamb (1998) emphatically state, *"Regardless of the experimental procedures, the ages studied, the cognitive capacity of the subject, or the length of the delay between events and the interview, open-ended questions are more likely to elicit accurate accounts"* (p. 53, emphasis in original).

Although open-ended questions produce more accurate recall, children tend not to report events in great detail during narrative reports (Poole & Lamb, 1998). For instance, in a study

in which children were told secrets and later asked about the secrets from a second interviewer, children were much more likely to reveal their secrets when directly asked (J. C. Wilson & Pipe, 1995). Open-ended questions generally did not lead to commensurate disclosure.

Although specific questions may be necessary to gather more information, such questions increase the risk of inaccuracy (Poole & Lamb, 1998). Dent and Stephenson (1979) found that 19% of children's reports were inaccurate when asked specific questions compared with 9% when asked open-ended questions.

***

In sum, specific questions may be necessary to allow interviewers to gather more information and to clarify the information that children have already reported. Hence, interviewers should begin the interview with open-ended questions to be followed by a series of specific questions. When specific questions are used, care should be taken to phrase questions differently to explore whether children are simply agreeing to all questions. Yes-no questions should be avoided whenever possible. When using specific questions, children should be allowed to further describe their account.

Interview Aids

Anatomically detailed or anatomically correct dolls (AD dolls) became widely popular in the 1980s, despite the lack of standardized procedures or empirical support (Poole & Lamb, 1998). Even in the early 1990s, Conte, Sorenson, Fogarty, and Rosa (1991) found in a U.S. survey of more than 200 professionals that 92% reported using AD dolls in child abuse investigations. Kendall-Tackett and Watson (1992) found in a Boston survey that 62% of police officers and 80% of mental health workers reported using AD dolls.

AD dolls were assumed to help children describe abuse for a variety of reasons. Interview aids such as dolls were speculated to act as memory aids and to lessen children's embarrassment caused by verbally describing sexually explicit information. Dolls were thought especially to help younger children overcome language deficits. Some investigators even tried to infer abuse based on children's play with AD dolls (assuming abused children would display more sexual play than nonabused children).

The efficacy of interview aids such as AD dolls was based solely on intuition. Empirical studies now cast serious doubt on the utility of AD dolls. First, abuse cannot be reliably inferred based on children's play because nonabused children may also display sexual play (Realmuto, Jensen, & Wescoe, 1990). Second, studies show that the use of AD dolls does not lead children to recall more information than interviews with no aids (Bruck, Ceci, & Francoeur, 2000; DeLoache & Marzolf, 1995). Third, the dolls likely do not help younger children overcome language deficits because younger children probably do not understand the purpose of the dolls. That is, younger children have difficulties understanding the symbol-referent nature of AD dolls (DeLoache, 1995). Finally, if dolls are used to encourage children to first disclose abuse, then the dolls can be leading (Bruck & Ceci, 1996).

In general, police administrators should discourage the use of investigation aids such as AD dolls and drawings for interviewing children (Yuille, Hunter, Jeffe, & Zaparniuk, 1993). Dolls should not be used as a diagnostic tool (Everson & Boat, 1990). If dolls or drawings are used, then it should only be in helping children clarify information that they have already disclosed (e.g., names of body parts).

Closing the Interview

Investigators should close the interview by asking children if they have anything further they would like to add about the events that were discussed. Children should be allowed to ask any final questions. Children or their parents should be given contact information in case they want to further discuss something (Poole & Lamb, 1998).

***

The Necessity of Training Investigating Officers in Interviewing Child Witnesses

It is difficult to assess whether and to what extent psychologically based interview techniques are applied in actual interviews. Ethical considerations in police interviews often prevent controlled police studies. Police interviews can obviously have serious consequences, so experimental studies with actual victims of crime may not be conducted. Furthermore, resource limitations (e.g., time and money) may prevent well-intentioned police departments from utilizing new investigative procedures. Thus, for police departments, economy and efficiency are also practical concerns regarding investigative procedures.

Police have traditionally seen their role as one of simply gathering the facts from cooperative witnesses (Ainsworth, 1995). That is, traditionally, police officers have lists of the information that they should gather but are left untrained regarding how to gather it. Fisher, Geiselman, Raymond, Jurkevich, and Warhaftig (1987, p. 178) cited one police officer as stating, "Basically, you just ask them who, what, when, where, why, and how."

Even with proper training and policies, officers may not apply proper interview techniques (Geiselman et al., 1987). Questioning children is very complex; it may be difficult for officers to change their communication styles. Aldridge and Cameron (1999) administered a 1-week intensive training course to police and social workers on interviewing children. An examination of subsequent videotaped interviews revealed that there were no differences in performance between trained and untrained interviewers.

Role-playing and feedback may be important for officers first learning the psychologically based interview methods (Geiselman et al., 1987). New recruits should be trained in the methods before they learn maladaptive interview habits.

***

CONCLUSION

The role of police officers traditionally has been to serve and protect the community. This role is inherently ambiguous, as officers encounter a variety of tasks on a daily basis. Police are expected to be experts in a wide variety of domains, including interrogating suspects, interviewing victims and witnesses, gathering physical evidence, and operating equipment such as police vehicles and firearms. Considering the tremendous range of duties for which the police officers are responsible, it seems questionable to expect them to also gain the expertise necessary to interview child witnesses. A better alternative may be to train selected officers who will be responsible for taking the initial reports and subsequently investigating the case.

Interviewing children is a complicated endeavor. Recent psychological research has found that the quality of children's reports is dependent on the quality of the investigative interview. This article reviewed some of the steps that investigating officers can take to increase the reliability of children's reports. In addition, police administrators can help investigators reach this goal by endorsing specialized training and by ensuring that the appropriate interview environment is provided.

The nature of investigative interviews does not allow for a simple recipe that can be applied when questioning all children. Interviewers need special skills and training. A variety of interview protocols that maximize children's accuracy and minimize distortion are now available. However, research is unclear as to whether or to what extent these interview protocols are being applied in actual forensic settings. Future research should work toward further improving investigative techniques. Researchers also must consider the feasibility of law enforcement officers or child welfare workers applying these techniques.

5

TAKING STOCK OF CRIMINAL PROFILING

A Narrative Review and Meta-Analysis

BRENT SNOOK

JOSEPH EASTWOOD

PAUL GENDREAU

CLAIRE GOGGIN

RICHARD M. CULLEN

Criminal profiling (CP) is the practice of inferring personality, behavioral, and demographic characteristics of criminals based on crime scene evidence (Douglas, Ressler, Burgess, & Hartman, 1986). The frequency with which CP has been used in criminal investigations, as well as the volume of literature addressing this topic, has grown steadily over the past 30 years (Copson, 1995; Egger, 1999; P. Wilson, Lincoln, & Kocsis, 1997; Witkin, 1996), and profiling techniques are now commonplace within police investigations worldwide

Editors' Note: This article first appeared in *Criminal Justice and Behavior,* Vol. 34, No. 4, April 2007, pp. 437–453. Reprinted with permission of Sage Publications. We have shortened it considerably, deleting large sections of the methodology and results, preserving primarily the literature review and discussion. Readers are encouraged to review the original article.

(Homant & Kennedy, 1998). This upward trend has occurred in the absence of a well-defined profiling framework and cumulated empirical knowledge in support of CP. Some researchers (e.g., Grubin, 1995; Hicks & Sales, 2006; Muller, 2000; Wilson et al., 1997) have cautioned that CP is growing in popularity in the absence of compelling scientific evidence that it "works" (i.e., is a reliable, valid, or useful tool for assisting with the identification and apprehension of criminals). Given that the effect of profiling on criminal investigations is unknown, the goal of the current article is to conduct a systematic review of the literature to determine the scientific credibility of CP, which in turn will inform the utility of this particular investigative technique for practitioners.

Constructing a profile of an unknown perpetrator typically involves three stages (Annon, 1995; Ault & Reese, 1980; Douglas et al., 1986; Homant & Kennedy, 1998). First, police officers collect crime scene data and forward it to a profiler; second, the profiler conducts an analysis of the crime scene data; and third, the profiler provides predictions about the type of individual likely to have committed the crime in question. The processes that profilers use in analyzing crime scene data can be classified as either "clinical" or "statistical" in nature. Clinically oriented techniques incorporate aspects of the profilers' intuition, knowledge, experience, and training to generate predictions (e.g., Douglas & Olshaker, 1995, 1997; Ressler & Schachtman, 1992; Turvey, 1999; West, 2000). By contrast, statistically oriented predictions are based upon descriptive and inferential statistical models derived from an analysis of characteristics of offenders who have previously committed similar types of crime (e.g., D. V. Canter, 2004; Farrington & Lambert, 1997; Keppel & Weis, 1993; Salfati, 2000).

Published accounts testify to the prolific growth in the utilization of CP techniques. Between 1971 and 1981, the FBI provided profiling assistance on 192 occasions (Pinizzotto, 1984). Just a few years later, Douglas and Burgess (1986) indicated that FBI profilers had been asked to assist with 600 criminal investigations per year. More recent accounts indicate that CP was applied by 12 FBI profilers in approximately 1,000 cases per year (Witkin, 1996). Police officers in the United Kingdom have also incorporated CP into their investigations with greater frequency. Copson (1995), for instance, reported that 29 profilers were responsible for providing 242 instances of profiling advice between 1981 and 1994, with the use of CP increasing steadily during that period. Although we do not have an exact estimate of CP prevalence elsewhere, the use of CP has been documented in a variety of countries including Sweden, Finland, Germany, Canada, and The Netherlands (see Åsgard, 1998; Case Analysis Unit, 1998; Clark, 2002; Jackson, Herbrink, & van Koppen, 1997).

As the prevalence of CP has grown over the past three decades, there has been a concomitant increase in the volume of published literature on the topic. Reviews of the CP literature have most often outlined its developmental history, described the various theoretical approaches that profilers use, and commented on the need for future research (Egger, 1999; Grubin, 1995; Homant & Kennedy, 1998; Muller, 2000; Wilson et al., 1997). The authors of these reviews appear to have reached the consensus that, notwithstanding deficiencies in the empirical literature regarding its predictive accuracy, profiling works or, at least, has the potential to work. As a consequence, readers of this literature may be inclined to believe that CP is a valuable addition to the standardized investigative repertoire. The sheer volume of scholarly and media attention accorded to CP might also contribute to this belief. Thus, a critical examination of the current status of CP is timely. As a first step toward that end, we conducted a systematic narrative review of the published CP literature and a meta-analysis of the extant experimental studies of profiler accuracy. Using a classification framework adapted from Gendreau, Goggin, Cullen, and Paparozzi (2002), the narrative review classified CP articles according to whether the authors used commonsense or empirical-based arguments.

The genesis of the Gendreau et al. model was based on an analysis of how practical, or "bad," common sense (as opposed to "good" common sense and as outlined on the left-hand side of Table 5.1) can lead to serious errors in judgment in the field of criminal justice policy (see also Latessa, Cullen, & Gendreau, 2002). For the remainder of the article, we avoid the pejorative label and refer to it simply as common sense. The application of this model to the narrative review was particularly relevant to an evaluation of the criminal profiling literature because it was hoped that the conclusions of such an analysis would make a useful contribution to the ongoing debate regarding the status of CP as "art" (based on experience and intuition) or "science" (based on empirical research that generates falsifiable hypotheses), and, ultimately, speak to its utility as a criminal investigative tool. Given the acknowledgment by some researchers that there is a shortage of empirical evidence substantiating profiling techniques (e.g., Kocsis, 2004; Kocsis, Irwin, Hayes, & Nunn, 2000), it was anticipated that the CP literature contained a considerable volume of commonsense rationales.

***

STUDY 1: NARRATIVE REVIEW

Method

Sample articles. Potential studies for inclusion in the narrative review were located through an electronic search of PsycINFO and Criminal Justice Abstracts databases using the keywords *criminal profiling, psychological profiling,* and *offender profiling.* Citations in the reference sections of the obtained articles were also checked for possible inclusion in the review. Eligible articles in the narrative review were peer-reviewed journal articles, book chapters, magazine articles, research reports, and published conference papers, all of which had CP as their primary focus.

Procedure. Studies that met the inclusion criteria were first coded along the following dimensions: article characteristics (e.g., year of publication and location of research), principal author characteristics (e.g., gender, qualifications, discipline, whether a criminal profiler, theoretical approach, and number of CP publications), and author perspective on CP (e.g., opinion of CP, whether CP is an art or science, and beliefs regarding profiler accuracy/usefulness).

Table 5.1   Summary of the Commonsense and Empirical Rationales Used in Coding Criminal Profiling Articles

Commonsense	Empirical
Sources of knowledge	
Qualitative: Based on authority, testimonials, evidence from anecdotes, and intuition	Quantitative: Based on scientific literature
Analytical process	
Post hoc propter hoc, availability heuristic, hindsight bias, self-serving bias, and illusory correlates	Data collection from case histories, surveys, quasi- and experimental studies
Integration of evidence	
Simply "tell it like it is" and "what everybody knows" statements, explanation by naming, exceptions prove the rule, and idiographic focus	Causality is complex, results described in probalistic terms, expectations that the theory will be revised, acknowledgment of covariation consequences, and nomothetic focus

NOTE: Adapted from Gendreau et al. (2002).

Using the classification framework adapted from Gendreau et al. (2002), sample CP articles were classified as to whether authors used commonsense or empirically based arguments in interpreting phenomena. Articles were evaluated along the following criteria: (a) sources of knowledge (e.g., qualitative vs. quantitative), (b) analytical processes (e.g., hindsight bias vs. experimental), and (c) integration of evidence (e.g., idiographic vs. nomothetic focus). Gendreau et al.'s original classification framework included 25 specific categories of commonsense ($k = 14$) and empirical ($k = 11$) rationales, the majority of which were suitable for inclusion in the present review (see Table 5.1; see also Kimble, 1994; Matlin, 1998; D. G. Myers, 1996). One addition and one deletion were made to the classification scheme for the current research purpose. For the narrative review, and in light of the first author's familiarity with the CP literature, it was deemed appropriate to add post hoc ergo propter hoc reasoning as a supplemental item to the analytical process criterion in the commonsense category. The anchoring heuristic was not included as a commonsense rationale for the criminal profiling literature as it could not be operationally defined to facilitate coding. Table 5.1 contains the final list of rationales used in the narrative review.

***

DISCUSSION

The evidence generated in this study indicated that commonsense rationales have flourished in the CP literature. Even if one were to view the glass as half full in this regard, and focus on the lower limits of the CIs [confidence intervals] (keeping in mind their distance from the mean), the percentage estimates of the frequency of some of the commonsense rationales for sources of knowledge and analytical processes are of concern if CP is to be considered a scientific domain.

Those who would promote CP as a scientific practice may point to the reality that commonsense rationales are those that are most available

to the authors, as the research literature is in its infancy from an empirical perspective, which makes it difficult to substantiate validity arguments with empirical sources. These individuals might also draw attention to the fact that authors appear to have recognized the importance of empirical rationales in attempting to integrate evidence. Admittedly, endorsement of causality is complex and expectation that theory will be revised were noted by authors as components of the process of integrating evidence in slightly more than half of the reviewed articles. Nevertheless, commonsense ways of integrating evidence (e.g., "tell it like it is," exceptions prove the rule, and idiographic focus) appear, in our opinion, disconcertingly frequently (percentages ranged from 8% to 41%).

The use of commonsense and empirical rationales varied strikingly according to the article characteristics and the author's perspective. Articles with a clinical orientation, and those that were authored by law enforcement officers, were more likely to contain commonsense rationales and less likely to contain scientific rationales than those that had a statistical orientation and were written by academics, respectively. Similarly, articles in which the authors were more favorable toward profiling contained more commonsense and less empirical rationales than those that were less favorable. It was intriguing to discover a greater proliferation of commonsense rationales in articles coming from the United States (> 70% vs. the United Kingdom and other countries). Regardless of the reasons underlying this overemphasis on common sense and the relative shortage of empirical support in the CP literature, there is a notable incongruity between CP's lack of empirical foundation and the degree of support for the field, as expressed by the authors of CP articles.

***

CONCLUSION

The evidence generated from this research confirms the perceptions of those who have concluded that the CP field relies on weak standards of proof and that profilers do not decisively outperform other groups when predicting the characteristics of an unknown criminal (e.g., Alison, Bennell, Mokros, & Ormerod, 2002; Muller, 2000). Based on the results of narrative review and meta-analytic reviews presented herein, profiling appears at this juncture to be an extraneous and redundant technique for use in criminal investigations. CP will persist as a pseudoscientific technique until such time as empirical and reproducible studies are conducted on the abilities of large groups of active profilers to predict, with more precision and greater magnitude, the characteristics of offenders.

6

CRIMINAL PROFILING

Real Science or Just Wishful Thinking?

DAMON A. MULLER

The subject of criminal profiling has caught the public's imagination in recent times, with references to it appearing in all forms of media. The most well-known example of criminal profiling in the popular media is in the film *Silence of the Lambs,* based on the Thomas Harris novel of the same name. Several television shows have also recently been based around the premise of criminal profiling, including *Millennium, Profiler,* and even *The X-Files*. It is interesting to note that all of these popular portrayals of profiling are somewhat inaccurate because they suggest that profiling is a magical skill somewhat analogous to a precognitive psychic ability.

Those who practice criminal profiling have claimed that it is alternatively a science or an art, depending on whom you listen to. Even those who confess that it is more an art than a science (e.g., Ressler & Shachtman, 1992) still point to supposedly scientific studies to support their claims that it is in fact worth using. Yet one of the biggest hurdles standing in the way of acceptance of criminal profiling is that there is very little authoritative material on it, and almost nothing in the way of scientific studies to support the claims of the profilers.

Many of the law enforcement agencies around the world are still quite skeptical of the work of criminal profilers. Holmes and Holmes (1996) observe that an offender profiler is usually only called in when the police have exhausted all other leads, sometimes including psychics and astrologers. Techniques such as forensic DNA

Editors' Note: This article was originally published in *Homicide Studies*, Vol. 4, No. 3, August 2000, pp. 234–264. Reprinted with permission of Sage Publications. Here, it has been shortened considerably, with sections on defining science and some of the conclusions removed. The emphasis here is on describing profiling and highlighting available research.

analysis have become essential to modern criminal investigation, possibly because one can point to the strong scientific basis on which they are founded. Yet most people have no idea how effective profiling is, let alone how it works, apart from what they have picked up from the media.

The aim of this article is to look beyond the ubiquitous media hype that surrounds profiling and critically examine the reality. Initially, the two main approaches to profiling will be examined in some detail, highlighting the differences and similarities of the approaches. Profiling is usually conducted on serial offenders, which will also be examined, along with some of the research findings and controversies surrounding serial offenders. The approaches to criminal profiling will then be examined in light of two criteria for a science: the need for a paradigm and the requirement of falsifiability. The empirical support and problems with each of the approaches will be discussed, as will the studies that have empirically examined profiling. It is concluded that the current approaches to profiling do not yet have any substantial empirical support, but that they do have the potential to be scientific if they are worked on.

WHAT IS CRIMINAL PROFILING?

Definitions

Criminal profiling is the process of using available information about a crime and crime scene to compose a psychological portrait of the unknown perpetrator of the crime. The information that the criminal profiler uses is often taken from the scene of the crime, and takes into account factors such as the state of the crime scene, what weapons (if any) were used in the crime, and what was done and said to the victim. Other information used in criminal profiling can include the geographic pattern of the crimes, how the offender got to and from the crime scene, and where the offender lives. The actual process of profiling differs from one profiler to another (depending on the training of the

profiler), but the aim remains the same: to deduce enough about the behavioral, personality, and physical characteristics of the perpetrator to catch him.

According to Holmes and Holmes (1996), psychological profiling has three major goals, to provide the criminal justice system with the following information: a social and psychological assessment of the offender(s), a psychological evaluation of relevant possessions found with suspected offenders, and consultation with law enforcement officials on the strategies that should be used when interviewing offenders. Not all profiles involve all of these three aspects, with the role of the profiler usually being dictated largely by the needs of the law enforcement officials for whom they are consulting. Also, not all crimes are suitable for profiling. Holmes and Holmes state that profiling is only appropriate in cases in which the unknown offender shows signs of psychopathology or the crime is particularly violent or ritualistic. Rape and arson are also considered by Holmes and Holmes to be good candidates for profiling.

A profile will rarely by itself solve a crime or catch a criminal, but is designed to be an aid to the investigating police (P. Wilson & Soothill, 1996). The profile will rarely be so accurate as to suggest a certain individual as being responsible for the crime, but should point the police in the right direction and help reduce the possible number of subjects. When the police have no leads, a profile might suggest some potentially helpful area that the police might have overlooked. Despite what the movies might suggest, profilers do not go running around the countryside solving crimes for hapless local police or rescuing hostages from dangerous psychopaths.

It is important to note that criminal profiling is not just one technique and that there are several distinct approaches to profiling. P. Wilson, Lincoln, and Kocsis (1997) list three main paradigms of offender profiling: diagnostic evaluation (DE), crime scene analysis (CSA), and investigative psychology (IP). Other approaches to profiling exist, such as geographic profiling (Holmes & Holmes, 1996), but these will not be discussed in this article. The two latter approaches, both of which have been adapted and modified somewhat by various practitioners depending on their needs, will be discussed in the current report. The first method, DE, is not so much a discipline as the adaptation of psychotherapeutic (largely Freudian psychoanalytic) theory to crime by individual practitioners. As the DE approach relies mainly on clinical judgment, and as it is approached by each practitioner in a different way, there is no one body of work that can be examined to determine whether it is scientific, and as such will not be discussed here. . . . The more widely known of the remaining two approaches, CSA, was developed by the Behavioral Science Unit (BSU) of the American Federal Bureau of Investigation (FBI). It is the FBI approach to profiling that has been popularized by films such as *Silence of the Lambs* and television shows such as *Profiler.* The other, less publicly well-known, approach was developed by Professor David Canter, a British academic psychologist. Canter's theories are IP and owe more to environmental psychology than to traditional criminal investigation. Although these methods have similarities, they are different enough to warrant separate treatment.

CSA

As mentioned above, the FBI approach is the more popular approach to criminal profiling. Although it is true that many people will have heard of criminal profiling and will associate it with the FBI, until recently there has been very little publicly available information as to what it actually is and how it works. Within the past few years, however, those who developed profiling with the FBI have written several popular books. Former BSU agents Ressler (Ressler & Shachtman, 1992) and Douglas (Douglas & Olshaker, 1995, 1997) have written books with journalists describing their experiences as profilers. Yet despite these books, which are more biographical than anything else, there is little authoritative information on the actual mechanics of the FBI profiling process.

Holmes and Holmes (1996) provide what is probably the best description of the underlying rationale that the FBI uses to profile offenders. The CSA approach, which is primarily applicable to serial murderers, places offenders into two broad categories on the basis of their crime and the crime scene. The two types of offenders are the disorganized asocial offender and the organized nonsocial offender, although in recent times the FBI tends to refer to these as simply disorganized and organized offenders, respectively (e.g., Ressler, Burgess, & Douglas, 1988). Ressler states that the simplistic dichotomy was to enable police who had little or no knowledge of psychological jargon to understand what the BSU thought was a basic differentiation between two distinct groups of offenders (Ressler & Shachtman, 1992). Holmes and Holmes note that this categorization is particularly applicable to crimes such as rape, sexual assault, mutilation, and necrophilia.

The disorganized offender will usually be of low intelligence, often demonstrating some sort of severe psychiatric disturbance, and will have probably had contact with the mental health system. He will often be socially inept with few interpersonal relationships outside his immediate family, and will be sexually incompetent if he has any sexual experience at all. The crime scene of the disorganized offender will often show little or no premeditation, with whatever is at hand used for a weapon and usually left at the crime scene. The victim (selected more or less at random) will have been quickly overpowered and killed, with the killing often showing extreme overkill and brutality (what the FBI refers to as a "blitz" attack; see Douglas & Olshaker, 1995). The victim's face will often be severely beaten in an attempt to dehumanize her, or she will be forced to wear a mask or blindfold. If the victim is sexually assaulted, it will often be postmortem, with mutilation to the face, genitals, and breasts not uncommon. The body will often be left at the murder scene, but if it is removed, it is more likely that the offender wants to keep it as a souvenir than to hide evidence (Holmes & Holmes, 1996; Ressler et al., 1988; Ressler & Shachtman, 1992).

The types of offenders who make up the organized and disorganized dichotomies are relatively straightforward and are, as the names suggest, organized and disorganized personalities. The organized offender is usually reasonably intelligent but an underachiever with a sporadic education and employment history. He is often married and socially adept, at least at face value, but usually has an antisocial or psychopathic personality. The crime scene left behind by an organized offender will show signs of planning and control. The offender will often bring his own weapons and restraints, which he will then take with him after the crime. The victim will be a targeted stranger, very often female, with the offender searching for either a particular sort of victim or merely a victim of convenience. The victim will often be raped, and the offender will control the victim by using threats and restraints. The offender will usually torture the victim, killing in a slow, painful manner, which the killer will have fantasized about extensively beforehand. The body will also usually be hidden, often transported from the place where the killing occurred, and may be dismembered by more forensically aware killers to delay identification.

From the analysis of the crime scene, the investigator should then be able to determine some characteristics of the perpetrator, which will be of use to the investigating police.

According to Ressler et al. (1988), criminal profiling is a six-stage process. The first stage is referred to as Profiling Inputs, and concerns the collection of all of the information that might be pertinent to solving the crime. This includes photos of the crime scene, the preliminary police report, information about the victim, and all of the collected forensic information. The second stage is the Decision Process Models, in which the information is organized and a preliminary analysis is conducted. In this stage, the homicide type and style are determined (e.g., whether it is a single, mass, spree, or serial murder). Several other important factors are determined in this stage, such as the intent of the offender (e.g., whether homicide was the primary objective or whether it was secondary to another crime), the

risk status of the victim (a prostitute would be an example of a high-risk victim, whereas a married woman who lived in a middle-class area would probably be a fairly low-risk victim), and the risk the offender would have been putting himself in to commit the crime. The length of time that was taken to commit the offense is determined and information about the locations (such as where the victim was abducted and where the killing was actually performed) is also investigated.

The third stage of the profiling process, Crime Assessment, is presumably the inspiration for the title of Douglas's book, *Journey Into Darkness* (Douglas & Olshaker, 1997), as it is where the profiler attempts to reconstruct the crime in his or her head. This is where the profiler attempts to "walk in the shoes" of both the victim and the offender, or what the media likes to refer to as "getting into the mind of the killer." It is at this stage that the crime is categorized as organized or disorganized, as the profiler tries to determine how things happened, how people behaved, and how the offender planned and executed the crime. Also considered is the offender's motivation for the crime, such as what the offender hoped to achieve with the crime. The selection of a victim is considered, as is whether the offender staged the scene (modified the crime scene to confuse police). Common elements of the crime scene that are thought to have significance for identifying certain types of offenders, such as types and locations of wounds and the positioning of the body, are also examined.

It is not until the fourth stage, the Criminal Profile, that the profiler ties all of the above information together and the profile is actually constructed. The profiler attempts to describe the person who committed the crime and proposes strategies that might be most effective in apprehending that particular offender. The profiler constructs the profile by examining all of the information pertinent to the crime in the light of his or her experiences with other similar crimes. The finished profile will contain anywhere between a few paragraphs and several pages of information about the unknown offender, depending on how much material about the crime was forwarded to the profiler. The following elements are commonly found in a profile: the age, race, gender, and general appearance of the offender; the offender's relationship status and any notable points about his relationship history; his likely occupation; and any notable features of his employment, education, or military record. The profiler also includes whether the offender lived in or was familiar with the area; the behavior of the offender both before and after the crime; some basic features about the offender's personality (including whether he has an organized or disorganized personality); and significant belongings that the offender may own, such as pornography. It also contains suggested strategies for interrogating, identifying, and apprehending the [offender].

The fifth stage, the Investigation, is where the profiler submits a written report to the agency investigating the crime, which is added to their investigative efforts. If a suspect is identified and a confession is obtained, then the profile is judged to have been successful. If any additional information becomes available (e.g., new evidence or another connected murder), the new information is given to the profilers so that the profile can be re-evaluated. . . . The sixth stage is the Apprehension, and assumes that the correct offender has been caught. The profile and the profiling process are evaluated in terms of the actual offender so that future profiles might be even more accurate.

IP

Unlike CSA, IP is more a collection of related theories and hypotheses than a comprehensive methodology. As mentioned previously, IP originated in Britain, mainly due to the work of David Canter, an environmental psychologist who was then the head of the psychology department at the University of Surrey (Canter, 1989). Canter (1994) reports that he was first approached in 1985 by British police who were interested in determining whether psychology had anything to offer police to help them apprehend criminals. Although he observes that police are often very

resistant to anything new or to any outsiders telling them how they should do their jobs, Canter's advice proved very helpful to the police in catching John Duffy. Duffy, who was dubbed the "Railway Rapist" by the media, committed approximately 25 rapes and three murders in London between 1982 and 1986 (Nowikowski, 1995). Since that case, Canter has worked on over 60 murder and rape cases in the United Kingdom (Casey, 1993).

Canter (1989) claims that psychology is directly applicable to crime, as crime can be seen as an interpersonal transaction in which criminals are performing actions in a social context (often just between themselves and their victims). He argues that our methods of psychological interaction are ingrained into our personalities, and reasons that the actions the criminal performs while engaging in a crime are direct reflections of the way [the individual] will act in other, more normal, circumstances. He postulated five broad approaches with which psychology can be used to profile offenders.

The first is interpersonal coherence, which proposes that actions performed by criminals make sense within the criminals' own psychology. For instance, the offender will select victims that are consistent with the important characteristics of people who are important to the offender. For example, there is some anecdotal evidence that serial killers only attack those of the same ethnicity as themselves in the United States (Canter, 1989). Therefore, the psychologist should be able to determine something about the offender from the victim and the way the offender interacted with the victim (where this can be determined, such as with rape). The second approach is the significance of place and time. The locations the offender chooses in which to commit the offenses will usually have some sort of significance to the offender. People are unlikely to murder or rape in locations that are unfamiliar to them, as these are crimes of control, and the offender will not be able to feel completely in control in a strange environment. Therefore, if all of the crimes are committed in a certain geographic location, there is a high chance that the offender lives or works around the area. The third approach, criminal characteristics, involves looking at crimes and offenders and seeing if differences can lead to classifications of offenders into categories and subcategories. Canter does not actually provide an example of such as classification, but one attempt to do this has been the FBI Crimes Classification Manual (Douglas, Burgess, Burgess, & Ressler, 1992). Douglas and Olshaker (1995) state that "we set about to organize and classify serious crimes by their behavioral characteristics and explain them in a way that a strictly psychological approach such as *DSM [Diagnostic and Statistical Manual of Mental Disorders]* has never been able to do" (p. 346). Canter (1994), however, is quite critical of the FBI approach—especially the organized–disorganized dichotomy used by the FBI—arguing that there is too much overlap between the two categories for it to be helpful and that they have no theoretical backing. It will be interesting to see an attempt to derive a system like this by the proponents of IP and see what similarities and differences [compared] to the CSA system they come up with.

The fourth approach, criminal career, seeks to take advantage of the observation that criminals do not change the way they commit crimes throughout their criminal career, although they may escalate the crimes. Even escalation, though, may be a result of what has happened to the offender while committing earlier crimes, and it may be possible to negatively extrapolate back to earlier crimes committed by the offender where more evidence might be available. The fifth and final approach is forensic awareness. When a serial offender takes steps to cover his tracks, such as forcing his rape victim to take a bath or combing her pubic hair to remove any of his own hair, it is a clear sign that he has had some previous contact with police. The particular type of forensic awareness displayed by the offender should be a direct indication of the offender's previous police contact, and should help narrow the range of offenders to those with records for particular prior offenses.

Although this has been a fairly brief overview of some of Canter's suggestions, one particular area, that of space and time, has received a reasonable amount of attention and has been empirically tested. P. Wilson et al. (1997) report that the "circle hypothesis" (as it is referred to in Canter, 1994) is one of the more prominent of the IP theories. This approach is built on the hypothesis that serial offenders will tend to operate within an area where they feel comfortable (e.g., close to their own homes) and has many similarities to the independently developed field of geographic profiling (Holmes & Holmes, 1996). In a recent paper, Godwin and Canter (1997) investigated the spatial behavior of 54 U.S. serial killers, each of whom had killed at least 10 times. They investigated the relationship of the offender's home to the locations at which he encountered and then dumped the bodies of his victims and the changes over time. Godwin and Canter found that the serial killers in the sample were likely to encounter and abduct nearly all of their victims close to their own home. The offender would then travel some distance, usually in a different direction for each offense, to dump the body. They also found, however, as the number of offenses progressed, the offender was more likely to dump the bodies close to home, reflecting perhaps a growing confidence [in] his ability to remain undetected.

The study by Godwin and Canter (1997) clearly demonstrates that experimental psychology, and IP in particular, does have something to offer police investigating serial crimes. Although psychological profiling alone will not catch an offender, the aim is to supplement police investigative efforts and give the police additional information that might focus their investigation.

Serial Murderers

One of the concepts most frequently associated with criminal profiling is that of the serial offender. This is partly due to some of the conditions under which profiling is most useful, but more to do with the fact that whenever profiling is mentioned in the popular media, it is usually in the context of profiling a serial killer. As [will be] discussed later, serial offenders have had considerable input into the development of profiling, and any discussion of profiling would be amiss if it were not to discuss serial offenders.

In addition to making good newspaper headlines, serial killers are excellent candidates for criminal profiling. Unlike most offenders, serial killers often spend a great deal of time fantasizing about and executing their crime. The fact that they kill multiple times, generally mutilating their victims, and often demonstrate some sort of psychopathology means that there is frequently a lot of material for profilers to work with (P. Wilson et al., 1997). These killers generally have no obvious motive for the killing, are the hardest offenders to apprehend, and their crimes are the ones that profiles are most often sought for (Holmes & Holmes, 1996).

Although serial murder has recently captured public attention, it is by no means a new phenomenon. The most well-known serial killer, who has been extensively profiled in recent times, was probably Jack the Ripper, who killed at least five women in the Whitechapel area of London in 1888 (Jenkins, 1994). Yet the term serial killer, popularized by Ressler (Ressler & Shachtman, 1992), is a relatively recent one and the definition is still the subject of some debate. We might think of a serial murderer as an individual who commits a series of homicides over an extended period of time, with at least a few days in between at least some of the killings. This distinction of time between the killings is important to distinguish serial killing from mass murder, in which one person kills many people in a spree, such as the recent Port Arthur massacre in Tasmania.

One of the initial hurdles in defining serial murder is how many people need to be killed before an individual is classified as a serial murderer. This has important implications for research and for the development of profiling. Some believe that two murders are enough to justify the label of serial murder (Holmes & Holmes, 1996), whereas others would argue that [at least] four murders are necessary (Jenkins, 1994). Whatever cutoff point is chosen, the

important question should be whether serial murder (and by extension, serial murderers) is qualitatively and quantitatively different from other murders. Is it simply the number of people that are killed that defines an offender as a serial killer, or is there some fundamental difference between serial killers and all other murderers?

The motive of the serial killer is a subject that is still open to some debate. As mentioned above, many serial killings appear to lack a clear motive, with the victims often not known to the offender and seemingly chosen at random. Ressler et al. (1988) suggest that almost all serial murders are sexual in nature, although their use of the term sexual in this case seems to be inspired by the Freudian notion of psychosexual development. A more current view of both serial murder and serial rape is that it is not about sexual gratification per se, but rather about the exercise of power and control over the victim (Canter, 1994; Egger, 1997). In fact, it seems that there is little difference between serial rape and serial murder, with Egger observing that it does not take much to turn a violent rape into a murder. Thus, the term sexual might be interpreted in the context of the killer's attempt to sexually control and dominate his victim.

It is important to know the extent of the problem that serial killers pose because they generally require a great deal of effort to apprehend. If serial killers are really a rare phenomenon, then it may not be worth focusing all these resources into profiling them. The problem is, it is not even known with any confidence how many serial killers there are or how many people are the victims of serial killers. In Australia, for example, it seems that serial murderers are reasonably rare, but then there are not that many murders in Australia of any sort. For example, in Australia from 1991–1992 there were 312 murders, with 309 identified suspects/offenders and 42 incidents for which an offender was not identified (Strang, 1993). This is relatively low when we consider that Washington, D.C., a single North American city, has over 500 reported homicides each year (Chappell, 1995). To confuse matters, when serial killers are suspected, they attract much more attention than any other murder. One of the more infamous of the Australian serial killers was John Wayne Glover, the "Granny Killer" who killed six elderly women in 1989 and 1990 in Sydney's North Shore district. According to Hagan (1992), these killings prompted one of the most extensive police investigations in Australia's history.

Serial murder usually involves the killing of a stranger and is therefore hidden somewhere in the crime statistics under the category of stranger homicide. The question is, [w]hat proportion of the stranger homicides can be attributed to serial murder? Egger (1990) notes that it is very difficult to tell, but the FBI often tends to take the pessimistic view that most of the stranger homicides are due to serial killers (Ressler et al., 1988). The FBI is probably not a very impartial judge in these matters, because as Jenkins (1996) notes, they have a vested interest in making serial offending seem to be much worse than it is. A more reasonable explanation might be to use the suggestion of Polk (1994) that the majority of these stranger homicides are so-called "honor contests" in which fights between mainly young men, often over a trivial incident, lead to death. Kapardis (1992) also notes that there are at least five separate categories of stranger homicide, and that serial and mass murder only makes up an extremely small proportion of stranger killings in Victoria, Australia.

**

Is Profiling Scientific?

CSA

CSA relies heavily on the experience and intuition of the profiler, both of which are difficult to empirically test. One of the main problems with a scientific analysis of CSA is that its proponents have never felt the need to have it scientifically verified. Yet . . . there are various aspects of this technique that may be amenable to investigation.

**

CSA does have the potential to be scientific (with some work), but the main problem seems to be that it does not want to be scientific. Douglas, the FBI agent who was responsible for hiring profilers for the BSU, states that in a profiler, "degrees and academic knowledge [are not] nearly as important as experience and certain subjective qualities" (Douglas & Olshaker, 1997, p. 30). Jenkins (1996) states that criminal profiling is the FBI's special area of expertise, something that they believe they do better than anyone else in the world. In essence, in the United States at least, the FBI has a monopoly on criminal profiling and it does not look like they are about to endanger that by telling anyone else how it works—or even if it works.

Although there might be some validity to the argument that revealing too much about how profiling is done might reveal to offenders ways in which they can avoid being apprehended (assuming, of course, that serial offenders read psychology or criminology journals), the dangers of not having the techniques open to investigation are even more serious. Canter (1994) states quite succinctly that "a doctor is not expected to operate on hunch and intuition, to learn his trade merely from hearing how others have treated patients in the past, to have no firmly established principles to operate on" (p. 275). Although the experience of police officers is certainly valuable and should not be overlooked, if we have no way of measuring the effectiveness of this approach we may be missing something important.

IP

Unlike CSA, IP was designed from the beginning with science in mind, but this does not mean that it is a science in itself. Canter and his colleagues have attempted to use established psychological principles and research methodology to create a discipline that is empirically sound and open to peer review. IP has a great deal of potential to become a science, but it still has a long way to go before it will be recognized as a discipline in itself.

**

P. Wilson et al. (1997) claim that one of the main problems with the IP approach to profiling is that it does not actually tell us anything new, except to propose new avenues to explore. This is probably a somewhat extreme view, as . . . the application of . . . psychological knowledge to criminal investigation potentially has great value. Canter has shown that the application of psychological principles and methodologies can, for example, help identify where the offender might live and what his job might be (e.g., Godwin & Canter, 1997). It is very easy for those in academia to remain aloof and remote from the real world, yet this is an attempt to make some practical use of psychology by applying it to genuine social problems.

Even within Great Britain, Canter is not without his critics. Copson, Badcock, Boon, and Britton (1997) state that "it seems to have been assumed by some observers that Canter's is the only systematic approach to profiling in use in Britain, not least because he says so" (p. 13). Copson and his colleagues, proponents of the DE model of profiling, claim that statistical approaches to profiling (such as those used in IP) are only reliable so long as the data set that they are based on is reliable. As has been mentioned previously, it is extremely difficult to determine even how many serial killers there are, let alone get reliable statistics on their activities and characteristics. They argue that until a more reliable database is built up, the clinical judgment of practitioners is a more reliable way to construct a criminal profile. Although it is true that there is lack of reliable data on serial offenders, criminologists have spent years collecting data on "normal" (i.e., nonserial) rapes and murders, which may be able to contribute to profiling. What is not known, however, is how applicable these data are to serial offenders.

STUDIES CONDUCTED ON PROFILING

CSA

If profiling is to be thought of as a science, and a science is defined by the studies that examine its theories, then the defining study for the FBI approach would be that published under the title of *Sexual Homicide: Patterns and Motives* (Ressler et al., 1988). This study is basically the foundation on which the scientific basis of the FBI approach to profiling rests. The fact that there have been so few published studies on the FBI approach means that the scientific credibility of the FBI approach rests solely on this study. The study, which attempts to determine the antecedents of serial murder, presents both qualitative and quantitative data. In the sample examined, the researchers find a large amount of support for their hypothesis that the serial offender is the result of a developmental process, with most of the subjects reporting that they had troubled childhoods. For example, 69% of the respondents reported a history of alcohol abuse in their families while growing up, and 74% reported that they were psychologically abused. The authors also provide quotes from the offenders that seem to support their hypothesis that most serial homicides are sexual in nature. Unfortunately, this study does have some fundamental flaws, which call into question the legitimacy of the approach.

One of the first things that any social science researcher learns is the danger of using retrospective self-report studies. . . . This research methodology is open to considerable abuse and can be very inaccurate. For example, using the present topic, if you are talking to a person who was a neighbor of a serial killer when he was young, then the subject will be quite likely to selectively recall information that [he or she] think[s] will be of interest to the researcher. There is also a very real danger of subjects' lying (e.g., to impress the researcher), and there is often no way to verify the veracity of the data.

The study conducted by Ressler et al. (1988) consisted mainly of interviews with 36 convicted serial killers who were in prison. Most, if not all, serial killers would be classified under *DSM-IV* (American Psychiatric Association, 1994) as suffering from antisocial personality disorder (Egger, 1997). In the mass media, this usually translates into their being referred to as psychopaths or sociopaths. According to Davison and Neale (1994),

> the adult antisocial personality shows irresponsible and antisocial behaviour by not working consistently, breaking laws, being irritable and physically aggressive, defaulting on debts and being reckless. He or she is impulsive and fails to plan ahead. In addition, he or she shows *no regard for truth* [italics added] nor remorse for misdeeds. (p. 271)

Surely the psychopathic serial killer is the least suitable person on whom to conduct retrospective self-report research. Furthermore, the study included only convicted and imprisoned serial offenders who were willing to participate in the study, which most criminologists would consider to be an unacceptably biased sampling procedure (P. Wilson et al., 1997). For example, there may be some fundamental difference between those serial offenders who get caught and those who are able to evade capture. Thus, the profiling based on the imprisoned serial offender may not be appropriate for catching all serial offenders.

One of the most important factors of the CSA model of criminal profiling is the dichotomous categorization of offenders as organized or disorganized offenders, but how useful is this distinction? Holmes and Holmes (1996), for example, state that these categories are more useful in "lust killings" than in other sorts of serial murder that do not show evidence of sexual motives. Although the concepts of the organized and disorganized offenders are discussed at length in Ressler et al. (1988), they do not attempt to use the data from the offenders in their sample to support or explain this typology. Ressler and Shachtman (1992) hypothesize that about one third of all serial killers are disorganized offenders and the remaining two thirds are organized offenders, but offer no data to support the claims. P. Wilson et al. (1997) claim that it is actually more of a continuum between organized and disorganized than two distinct types, with many offenders falling into the mixed category that displays features of both the organized and disorganized offenders.

The real truth is that we simply do not know. As far as this author knows, there have never been any published empirical studies on the differences [among] various subtypes of serial offenders. The organized/disorganized typology is the brainchild of the BSU, and although they have published information about it, they have never actually articulated any theoretical basis for the typology on which a study might be based.

Ressler et al. (1988) provide an excellent example of how politics and ideology may influence one's objectivity. The FBI, as North America's premier law enforcement organization, is a bastion of White, middle-class, conservative views, a fact admitted by many of the agents themselves (e.g., Douglas & Olshaker, 1995; Ressler & Shachtman, 1992). Is it then surprising that the FBI experts believe that serial killers often come from broken homes (where they are often raised by a single mother) and report daydreaming, masturbation, confusion about sexual preference, and an interest in pornography as features of their childhood?

It is also important to remember that the only thing that has been determined so far is a correlation between factors such as abuse or neglect in childhood and serial killers. This does not imply that serial offending is causally related to an individual's having a difficult childhood or an obsession with pornography. Egger (1997) describes one serial killer, Arthur Shawcross, who did not show any evidence of coming from a dysfunctional or violent family. Rather than the antecedents of Shawcross's offending being environmental, as CSA might argue, they appeared more to be biological with Shawcross being involved in a number of serious accidents, some of which involved cerebral concussion. Examples such as this tend to cast doubt on the validity of the CSA paradigm of the development of serial offending.

IP

The most obvious of the studies conducted on IP, in which Godwin and Canter (1997) investigated the spatial patterns of serial murderers in the United States, has been described in some detail previously. Professor Canter and many of his colleagues have a history in experimental psychology, and several other studies have been published in the psychological and criminological literature. As yet there has not been a great deal of experimental work on the core features of IP, that of the narrative of the offender and how it is reflected in the crimes. Some of the other research that the IP department at the University of Liverpool [is] working on includes the decision-making process of detectives, psychological autopsies (investigating the course of actions that leads to an assault), and investigative interviewing ("What Is Investigative Psychology?" 1997).

Although the overall paradigm itself has not been experimentally tested, some of the theories that contribute to IP have. In one example, Canter and Kirby (1995) look at the conviction history of child molesters. This study investigated the validity of the common assumption that child molesters will have a history of sexually deviant behavior and assaults on children, and that these men will escalate their offending from minor to more serious sexual offenses. Interestingly, they found that these assumptions, which are often held by police officers, had no empirical basis. They found that these offenders were more likely to have had a history of convictions for theft, burglary, and violent offenses than for prior minor sexual offenses. They also found that there was little evidence to suggest escalation from less serious offenses. For example, very few of the men who were child molesters had any history of indecent exposure.

The Canter and Kirby (1995) study has very obvious implications for profiling sexual offenders, as it suggests strategies for narrowing the range of potential suspects by suggesting the offenses that the offender is more likely to have been convicted of in his past. A less obvious implication of this study is for CSA, where the assumptions and preconceptions that the profilers have about certain offenders greatly influence the profile. This study suggests that, in the case of child molesters, these assumptions are likely to lead the profile astray.

An interesting point to note about the Canter and Kirby (1995) study is that it does not seem to fit within the paradigm of the criminal narrative. This could be taken as evidence that IP is not scientific, as the paradigm is not broad or thorough enough to cover all of the work in the area. Another way to look at it, however, is as providing a less direct support for the paradigm. Canter (1994) does not just believe that criminals have narratives but that all people do, and that these narratives are developed by the individual's experiences of interacting with the world. Canter notes that police officers also tend to have rather limited narratives, with their explanations of how criminals operate formed mainly from their experience of police work and by what they observe in the courts. What Canter and Kirby have demonstrated is that, at least in regard to sex offenders, the narratives that the police have to explain the behavior of sex offenders may be too limited and are in some cases misleading. Although this does not directly support the idea of criminal narratives, it does provide some support for the narrative per se, and thus does fit within the paradigm of IP.

Other Related Studies

***

In probably the most comprehensive experimental study on profiling conducted to date, Pinizzotto and Finkel (1990) examined profiles conducted by professional profilers, detectives, psychologists, and students for a series of cases. The study was looking at whether the accuracy of the profiles differed between the groups and whether there was a qualitative difference between the profilers and the nonprofilers in the process in which the profile was constructed. The accuracy of the profilers varied depending on the case, with the profilers more accurate than all of the other groups combined in the sex offender case, but these same profilers not especially accurate for the homicide. With regard to the sex offender case, the profilers were significantly more accurate for items such as the gender, age, and education of the offender. In the homicide case, however, the detectives were significantly more accurate than the profilers in regard to the offender's employment and the relationship of the offender's residence to the crime scene. It was also found that the profilers wrote richer, more detailed reports than the non-profilers and that the profilers recalled more details that were necessary to generate the profile. There are, of course, some problems with the study. The psychologists and students used, for instance, had no special interest in policing or profiling, so it would be expected that those who have to construct profiles for a living were both better prepared and more invested in the process, and thus tried harder than the nonprofilers.

Does It Actually Work?

In asking profiling to be scientific, we are trying to establish with some reliability whether profiling is of any use to us. Many police officers have shown a great deal of skepticism about profiling, partly due to the fact that they see apprehending offenders as their particular area of expertise, but also because it is still such a poorly developed field (e.g., A. Davies, 1994). As has been discussed above, the experimental evidence is still not overwhelming, but studies such as those conducted by Pinizzotto and Finkel (1990) suggest that profiling might have some validity. Experimental verification is not what will win the police over, however. Police still persist in using psychics to help them solve difficult cases, although Wiseman and West (1997) have shown experimentally that there is absolutely no validity to the claims made by psychics in regard to criminal investigations.

The real test of profiling is not experimental studies in the laboratory, but evaluations on how well profiling actually performs in practice. P. Wilson et al. (1997) suggest, somewhat naively, that after looking at the track record of profiling so far, the suggestion is that it works. They base this claim on a case study of selected high-profile crimes, but do not give any references or source for the data. The main problem with this claim is that it is purely anecdotal. Related to that is the problem of reporting bias, as we are only likely to hear about cases in which profiling has been used if the case was successfully resolved and the profile was accurate.

Organizations such as the FBI are, understandably, reluctant to release figures on the successes and failures of the profiles that they provide. Although figures such as an 80% success rate have been circulated (e.g., Ressler & Shachtman, 1992), there has yet to be any data put forward to substantiate this claim. According to Ressler et al. (1988), the accuracy of each profile is looked at after an offender has been apprehended so that the profilers may learn from their errors. The evaluation is not performed in public, and most people have no knowledge of how accurate profiles actually are. This is becoming increasingly important, as more private individuals are commissioning profiles themselves (or requesting that the investigating police do) for cases in which they have an interest. We would not tolerate other participants in criminal investigations (such as forensic DNA analysts) withholding data on the effectiveness of their techniques, so why do we tolerate it with psychological profiling?

There is also the question as to how accurate a profile actually has to be to be of help to the investigating authorities. Obviously, an incorrect profile has the potential to mislead the investigation, but this may only be a problem if the police place a greater amount of faith in the profile than they do in their own investigative skills. Pinizzotto (cited in P. Wilson et al., 1997), for example, found that from 192 requests for profiles, only 17% actually were used to help identify the suspect. More positively, 77% of the respondents reported that the profile had helped them to focus their investigation. Overall, however, if profiles are consistently found to be incorrect in at least some aspects, police will quickly lose faith in their worth.

CONCLUSIONS

Offender profiling, in all its various guises, is still very much a discipline that is yet to be proved. Unlike much of psychology or criminology, the accuracy of an offender profile may have profound implications. If a profile of an offender is wrong or even slightly inadequate, police may be misled, allowing the offender to escape detection for a little while longer—and innocent people may be dead as a result. This is not to say that we should ignore profiles or that police should not use them, but that we should approach profiling with caution. We should not blindly accept or rely on something that may not have any relationship to the truth. This article has demonstrated that, of the two main approaches to offender profiling, IP is easily more scientific than CSA. Whereas IP has produced testable hypotheses and has several empirical studies to back up its claims, CSA is based mainly on experience and intuition of police officers and is not particularly amenable to testing. We cannot say which approach is more successful (defining successful as providing information that results in more arrests) as there is no reliable published information on the effectiveness of the various approaches. There is a great deal of anecdotal evidence supporting CSA and it is more widely depicted in the press than IP; yet this is not enough to indicate that it is significantly more successful than IP. Clearly, the effectiveness of the approaches is a subject [on] which more investigation is needed.

***

7

Juvenile Offenders' Miranda Rights Comprehension and Self-Reported Likelihood of Offering False Confessions

Naomi E. Sevin Goldstein

Lois Oberlander Condie

Rachel Kalbeitzer

Douglas Osman

Jessica L. Geier

The procedural safeguards established by *Miranda v. Arizona* (1966) protect defendants against self-incrimination and police intimidation. The U.S. Supreme Court established the content of the *Miranda* warnings, but the specific wording varies across jurisdictions. A typical *Miranda* warning informs suspects, "You have the right to remain silent. Anything you say can be used against you in court. You have the right to a lawyer. If you cannot afford one, one will be appointed for you before questioning if you wish. If you choose to answer questions, you may stop at any time to consult your lawyer" (Oberlander & Goldstein, 2001).

Prior to the *Miranda* decision, courts recognized coerced confessions as inherently untrustworthy and used a "totality of the circumstances" test to determine admissibility of a waiver of

Editors' Note: This article was published in *Assessment,* Vol. 10, No. 4, December 2003, pp. 359–369. Reprinted with permission of Sage Publications. We have deleted sections on psychometric properties, figures, and most results, but have kept most of the introductory material and discussion intact. Readers wishing more information about the study's results are encouraged to review the original article.

rights against self-incrimination (Oberlander & Goldstein, 2001). This voluntariness test allowed courts to consider the influence of factors such as a suspect's age, intelligence, custody status at the time of confession, background, and prior history with the criminal justice system (*Coyote v. U.S.,* 1967; *Johnson v. Zerbst,* 1938). In 1964, the U.S. Supreme Court decided in *Malloy v. Hogan* that the constitutional bases for the voluntariness requirement (i.e., the Fifth Amendment right against self incrimination and the Fourteenth Amendment right to due process) applied to states. Two years later, *Miranda* affirmed and expanded this decision, providing clearer guidelines for informing suspects of their rights prior to and during police interrogations. Over time, the basis of the *Miranda* decision has been challenged, and attempts have been made to eliminate the presumption that a confession is invalid unless suspects in custodial interrogation are informed of their rights prior to interrogation (*Dickerson v. U.S.,* 2000). However, in *Dickerson v. U.S.,* the court reaffirmed the constitutional underpinnings and implications inherent in *Miranda,* allowing it to assert authority over and uphold *Miranda.* The court also pointed out the importance of *Miranda,* stating that it had "become embedded in routine police practice".

The juvenile justice system was founded on the notion that youthful offenders require special protections because of their developmental vulnerabilities (Oberlander, Goldstein, & Ho, 2001). Historically, there was an underlying belief that troubled children and adolescents could be reformed to become productive members of society, and, therefore, sentences were intended to rehabilitate rather than provide retribution (Grisso, Miller, & Sales, 1997). Because of the belief that children were not criminals, juvenile trials were carried out in the manner of civil proceedings. Therefore, protections that were provided to adults, such as *Miranda* warnings, did not apply to youth. In the landmark rulings of *Kent v. U.S.* (1966) and *In re Gault* (1967), the due process rights and procedural protections that serve as the basis of *Miranda* warnings were extended to juveniles. In *Kent,* the court found that "the right

to representation by counsel is not a formality. It is not a grudging gesture to a ritualistic requirement." In *Gault,* the court stated that "admissions and confessions of juveniles require special caution" because juveniles are at a disadvantage when dealing with police because of their vulnerability and immaturity.

As juveniles increasingly are tried as adults and juvenile sentences become more punitive, adequate understanding of *Miranda* rights is a particularly important issue to safeguard valid confessions and fair sentencing. The *Miranda* court established that a waiver is only valid if it is given knowingly, intelligently, and voluntarily (1966). In other words, the suspect must understand the vocabulary in the warning and the basic meaning of the rights, appreciate the consequences of waiving the rights, and provide the waiver without coercion or police intimidation (Grisso, 1981).

Because of juveniles' intellectual and emotional immaturity, they are at increased risk for poor comprehension and false confessions (i.e., admitting to the commission of crimes they did not commit) (Oberlander & Goldstein, 2001). In *Gallegos v. Colorado* (1962), the court recognized this risk and held that an "interested adult" would provide additional protection to help ensure the validity of a youth's confession. In addition, in *People v. Lara* (1967), the court decided that adolescent defendants might not fully comprehend the meaning of the effect of the waiver and, thus, may have difficulty meeting the "intelligent" requirement for a valid waiver. In 1979, in *Fare v. Michael C.,* the Supreme Court affirmed the "totality of the circumstances" approach as the federal constitutional standard and applied it to juvenile as well as adult proceedings. Similar to the "totality" test used to determine adult waiver validity, factors typically considered for validity of juveniles' waivers include a defendant's age, intelligence, maturity, and prior experience with criminal proceedings as well as details of the interrogation, such as the amount of time elapsed between arrest and confession, when the confession was given, and whether the defendant was advised of the *Miranda* rights (Grisso, 1981; Oberlander & Goldstein, 2001).

MIRANDA COMPREHENSION ASSESSMENT TOOLS

Instruments for Assessing Understanding and Appreciation of *Miranda* Rights

Researchers have developed instruments to assess defendants' capacities to provide knowing, intelligent, and voluntary waivers. Grisso's (1998) *Instruments for Assessing Understanding and Appreciation of Miranda Rights* is among the recommended tools for forensic psychologists conducting evaluations of youth or adult defendants' capacities to waive *Miranda* rights (Oberlander & Goldstein, 2001). Although these instruments are widely used and well respected among attorneys, judges, and psychologists, they were created and normed in the 1970s using now-outdated language of the *Miranda* warnings from St. Louis County, Missouri. Since the creation of the original instruments, a fifth prong has been added to many jurisdictions' *Miranda* warnings that explicitly informs suspects that they can choose to stop questioning and consult an attorney at any time. The language used in Grisso's instruments is more complicated than modern versions of the *Miranda* warnings currently used in most jurisdictions across the United States, thereby potentially limiting the utility of the instruments. Furthermore, it is unclear whether adolescent norms from the 1970s are generalizable to youth in the 21st century.

To maintain the validity and applicability of these instruments, Condie, Goldstein, and Grisso (2003) revised the assessment tools in several ways. The language was generalized to reflect typical *Miranda* warnings used in jurisdictions across the United States. Additionally, the newly introduced fifth prong was added to each of the relevant *Miranda* instruments. A fifth instrument, Perceptions of Coercion during Holding and Interrogation Process (PCHIP), was added to assess juveniles' self-reported likelihood of offering true and false confessions in response to specific police behaviors during interrogation. Finally, the generation of new norms reflects juveniles' comprehension of *Miranda* rights during the first decade of the twenty first century. The revised instruments, the *Miranda* Rights Comprehension Instruments–II (MRCI-II), are described in the Method section of this article.

RESEARCH ON JUVENILES' COMPREHENSION OF *MIRANDA* RIGHTS

Although used clinically today, Grisso initially developed his instruments in the 1970s to study juveniles' capacities to waive rights, and he conducted much of the existing research in this area. Comparing male and female youth and adults from offending and nonoffending populations, results of his studies suggested that juveniles under the age of 15, as a class, do not understand the nature and significance of the rights to remain silent and to counsel. Therefore, they are likely incapable of validly waiving these rights. Specifically, as a class, juveniles younger than 15 years of age failed to meet both the absolute and relative standards of comprehension. However, the interaction between age and IQ seemed to be a better predictor of *Miranda* comprehension for older youth than did age alone. For instance, 15- and 16-year-olds with IQ scores below 80 also failed to meet both absolute and relative standards. Fifteen- to 16-year-olds with average intelligence were able to understand their rights as well as 17- to 22-year-old adults of comparable intelligence, but one third to one half of these adolescents exhibited inadequate comprehension using the absolute criteria (Grisso, 1981).

Grisso (1981) also found that, overall, gender and socioeconomic status were not significantly related to *Miranda* rights comprehension. However, among juveniles with low IQ scores (i.e., below 80), African American juveniles exhibited poorer comprehension than did White youth. This interaction was found across the three *Miranda* comprehension measures, including the Comprehension of *Miranda* Rights–Recognition Instrument (CMR–R), which required no verbal expressive abilities. Prior court experience was unrelated to understanding the words and phrases in the *Miranda* warning, overall, but ethnicity significantly moderated the relationship between the number of prior felony referrals and *Miranda* comprehension scores. Scores were higher among White juvenile offenders with three or more felony charges. Conversely, African Americans with three or more felony referrals demonstrated lower comprehension scores.

A number of American (e.g., Ferguson & Douglas, 1970; Grisso, 1981; Lawrence, 1983; Shepherd & Zaremba, 1995; Wall & Furlong, 1985) and Canadian (Abramovitch, Higgins-Biss, & Biss, 1993; Abramovitch, Peterson-Badali, & Rohan, 1995) studies have explored young people's understanding of the rights to legal counsel and to silence. Some of these studies have examined offender populations, whereas others have focused on nonoffender populations, such as students. Results suggested that simplified versions of warnings did not improve understanding (Ferguson & Douglas, 1970), that education improved surface knowledge but not deeper understanding of rights (Wall & Furlong, 1985), and that adolescents who understood their rights were more likely to assert them (Abramovitch et al., 1993). Studies have also supported Grisso's findings that age (Abramovitch et al., 1995) predicted understanding of rights.

In addition to diminished comprehension of rights, juveniles are more suggestible than adults are (Richardson, Gudjonsson, & Kelly, 1995) and, therefore, may be more easily persuaded or coerced by police during interrogations. Because confessions are one of the most powerful sources of evidence in determining guilt (Kassin & Neumann, 1997), it is important to investigate whether juveniles involved with the justice system are particularly likely to offer false confessions.

Research focusing on the suggestibility of juvenile offenders revealed that when performance was subjected to criticism and negative feedback, male youth in custody were more likely than nonoffending adults to concede to suggestive questions (Gudjonsson & Singh, 1984). Gudjonsson and Singh concluded that delinquent adolescents may be particularly

responsive to interpersonal pressure during interrogation and that delinquent adolescent boys may be more prone to offer untrustworthy testimony when they have been criticized and pressured by interrogators. Similarly, compared to adults, adolescent suspects with lower intellectual abilities are likely to be more suggestible and may be more vulnerable to offering false confessions (Richardson et al., 1995). This is a particularly relevant finding, as, based on a sample of more than 6,000 youth involved with the juvenile justice system, the average IQ was 81 (Bove, Goldstein, Appleton, & Thomson, 2003).

METHOD

Participants

As part of a larger, ongoing study to develop norms for and establish psychometric properties of the MRCI-II (Condie et al., 2003), the revised version of the *Instruments for Assessing Understanding and Appreciation of Miranda Rights* (Grisso, 1998), data were collected from 57 boys in a residential postadjudication facility in Massachusetts between October 1999 and August 2000. Ages ranged from 13 to 18 years ($M = 16.3$, $SD = 1.3$). The ethnicity breakdown was 34.5% White, 21.8% Latino, 14.5% African American, and 5.5% Asian; 21.8% identified as another ethnicity, and one youth did not provide information about his ethnicity. All youth were fluent in English; one adolescent spoke Spanish as his primary language. Juveniles' self-reported delinquent offenses ranged from curfew violations to attempted murder. Other crimes for which juveniles frequently reported they were arrested included armed robbery, breaking and entering, and drug possession.

The Massachusetts Department of Youth Services provided participation consent for all youth in the postadjudication facility at which the research was conducted. Parents were also contacted by mail and invited to deny participation. Furthermore, assent was obtained from all youth participants. No parents denied participation, and all youth agreed to participate. Youth were thanked for their participation with a $20 gift certificate to a music store that could be used postre-lease. Two youth were withdrawn from the study because they were transferred out of the facility before data collection was completed. Thus, results of this study are based on data from the 55 youth that completed all measures.

Measures

The five instruments included in the MRCI-II (Condie et al., 2003) are as follows:

Comprehension of Miranda Rights–II (CMR-II). This instrument assesses adolescents' understanding of a standard *Miranda* warning by asking them to explain the meaning of each specified right in their own words. Total CMR-II scores range from 0 to 10 points. Responses are rated according to standardized scoring criteria to determine if youths' responses are *adequate, questionable,* or *inadequate,* with corresponding scores of 2, 1, or 0, respectively. Scoring criteria were developed for the original instruments by a national panel of lawyers and psychologists (Grisso, 1998). CMR-II scoring for the additional prong of the *Miranda* warning paralleled the original, and attorneys and psychologists specializing in *Miranda* warnings reviewed the updated scoring criteria. A Pearson correlation established a test-retest reliability of .61 (Mesiarik, Goldstein, & Thomson, 2002).

Comprehension of Miranda Rights–Recognition–II (CMR-R-II). This instrument assesses adolescents' understanding of each *Miranda* warning without reliance on verbal expression skills. The examinee is presented with a series of three preconstructed sentences for each of the five *Miranda* warnings. The examinee is then asked to determine whether each sentence is semantically identical to the corresponding sentence of the *Miranda* warning. Correct responses are awarded 1 point each, and incorrect responses are awarded 0 points. Total CMR-R-II scores range from 0 to 15 (a possible 3 points per warning). Test-retest reliability was established, $r = .75$ (Mesiarik et al., 2002).

Function of Rights in Interrogation (FRI). This instrument remains identical to that included in Grisso's *Instruments for Assessing Understanding and Appreciation of Miranda Rights.* The FRI assesses the examinee's appreciation of the significance of *Miranda* rights in interrogation situations and legal proceedings. The examinee is presented with four drawn pictures and corresponding scenarios related to legal processes (e.g., a picture of a boy in a room with two police officers is accompanied by a story about a suspect being questioned about a recent crime). The examinee is then asked 15 standardized questions to assess appreciation of the significance of the warnings in three areas: recognition of the nature of interrogation (NI subscale), significance of the right to counsel (RC subscale), and significance of the right to silence (RS subscale). Scoring procedures are identical to those of the CMR-II, and total scores range from 0 to 30. A Pearson correlation of .58 was found for test-retest reliability (Mesiarik et al., 2002).

Comprehension of Miranda Vocabulary–II (CMV-II). This instrument assesses adolescents' understanding of legally relevant vocabulary words frequently used in *Miranda* warnings across U.S. jurisdictions. While the examinee views a list of words, the examiner reads each word aloud, uses it in a sentence, and reads it aloud again. The examinee is then asked to define the term. For the MRCI-II, 12 words were added to Grisso's original 6 to promote the utility of the instruments throughout the United States. Scores range from 0 to 36. Methods of scoring each item are identical to those of the CMR-II and FRI. As with the CMR-II, scoring of new items paralleled Grisso's original, and the scoring criteria were reviewed by a panel of experts prior to use. A test-retest correlation coefficient of .77 was found for this instrument (Mesiarik et al., 2002).

Perceptions of Coercion During Holding and Interrogation Process (P-CHIP). Designed to supplement the revised instruments, the P-CHIP assesses examinees' self-reported likelihood of offering true and false confessions during

hypothetical holding and interrogation procedures. The examiner reads a scenario aloud to the
individual about a boy who reports to the police
that he was mugged by an individual of the examinee's age and gender; the examinee is asked to
pretend that he is the suspect. The examiner then
adds hypothetical situations about police behavior to the original scenario. Following each hypothetical situation, the examiner asks for ratings
about the youth's probable discussions with police
if he did commit the alleged offense, his stress
level if he is guilty, and his probability of offering
a confession if he did not commit the crimes of
which he is accused. The scenarios that are presented to the examinee are based on guidelines
for interrogation tactics recommended in the
police training manual, *Criminal Interrogation
and Confessions* (Inbau, Reid, & Buckley, 1986).
These scenarios include positive pressure items
(e.g., police officers express sympathy and understanding to elicit a confession), negative pressure
items (e.g., police officers use intimidating tactics
to persuade the youth to confess), and parental
pressure items (e.g., police persuade the youth
that his parents will be proud if he confesses).

The scoring criteria for the P-CHIP are composed of three subscales. For each subscale, a
scenario is read aloud by the examiner, and the
examinee is asked to choose a response to each
of the 26 items describing police behaviors. The
first subscale is designed to assess the response
to police questioning if the suspect is guilty of
the alleged offense. Three options are provided:
Say nothing to the police (0 points), talk to the
police but not about the crime (1 point), or talk to
the police about the crime (2 points). Total scores
range from 0 to 52. For the second subscale,
scoring is based on a rating of stress level in
response to the 26 specified police behaviors.
Item scores range from 1 (*very stressed*) to
6 (*very relaxed*), and total scores range from
26 to 156. For the third subscale, scores are
based on the examinee's self-reported likelihood
of offering false confessions in a variety of
police interrogation situations. Scores for each
item range from 1 (*will definitely falsely confess*)
to 6 (*will definitely not offer a false confession*),

and total scores range from 26 to 156. For the
purposes of data analysis, the stress and false
confession subscores were reverse scored so that
higher scores represent more stress and greater
self-reported likelihood of false confessing.

Stability of the P-CHIP was established using
Pearson correlations for test-retest for each subscale. The subscale measuring responses to
police questioning if the suspect is guilty had a
correlation of .76, the stress subscale had a correlation of .71, and the false confession subscale
had a correlation of .77 (Mesiarik et al., 2002).

***

EVALUATION OF MRCI-II SCORES

For clinical purposes, scores on the five MRCI-II
instruments should be evaluated separately
as each instrument is designed to measure a different facet of understanding and appreciation.
Youths' scores on each scale can be judged
against either an absolute standard or a relative
standard to determine the level of understanding
and appreciation of *Miranda* rights.

As described by Grisso (1981), to meet a minimal absolute standard of understanding, juveniles
may not have inadequate understanding of any
prongs of the *Miranda* warning (i.e., no zero-point
responses on a particular measure, such as the
CMR-II). To meet a somewhat higher absolute
standard of understanding, juveniles must have
adequate understanding of each *Miranda* warning
prong (i.e., 2-point responses on each item of a
particular measure, such as the CMR-II). In contrast to the absolute standards that assume a requisite level of basic comprehension, the relative
standard compares juveniles' scores to the adult
level of understanding of *Miranda* rights, which,
frequently, is less than perfect (Grisso, 1981).

Procedure

Adolescents completed a demographics
survey and the following three instruments:
(a) verbal scales of the Wechsler Abbreviated

Scale of Intelligence (WASI) (Psychological Corporation, 1999), (b) verbal scales of the Wechsler Individual Achievement Test (WIAT) (Psychological Corporation, 1992), and (c) the MRCI-II. Verbal scales were used because verbal IQ tends to be a good representation of overall IQ (Wechsler, 1997), and IQ and verbal skills are theoretically more relevant to *Miranda* comprehension and false confessions than are performance abilities and math achievement.

***

RESULTS

Miranda Comprehension

Male juvenile offenders in this study produced a mean verbal IQ score of 83 ($SD = 13.57$) and an average overall *Miranda* comprehension score of 1.6 ($SD = .29$), with *Miranda* comprehension ranging from 0 (*no understanding*) to 2 (*full understanding*).

***

Controlling for age, higher IQ predicted better *Miranda* comprehension among adolescent delinquent boys.

Although analysis of variance (ANOVA) revealed no overall significant differences in *Miranda* comprehension among the various ethnic groups in the study ($F[4, 49] = 2.40$, $p = .06$), planned comparison results revealed that the overall *Miranda* rights comprehension scores were significantly higher for African American youth ($M = 1.73$, $SD = .07$) than they were for Latino youth ($M = 1.38$, $SD = .35$; $t[12.4] = 3.33$ [homogeneity of variance not assumed], $p < .01$). No significant differences were found among the other ethnic groups.

***

Self-Reported Likelihood of Offering False Confessions

Rates of self-reported likelihood of false confessions revealed that 42% of male juvenile

offenders reported they were leaning toward giving a false confession in at least 1 of the 26 hypothetical police interrogation situations. Twenty-five percent reported they would definitely give a false confession in at least one hypothetical situation. For this male juvenile offender sample, confession scores ranged from 36 to 156 (higher scores represent greater self-reported likelihood of falsely confessing).

Miranda comprehension correlated negatively with false confessions—the better the comprehension, the less likely youth were to report they would falsely confess ($r = .34$, $p = .01$).

***

DISCUSSION

Results of this study suggest that adolescent male offenders' *Miranda* comprehension in the early 21st century is similar to the levels of understanding of delinquent boys in the 1970s. Despite speculation that youth are more knowledgeable about police interactions and *Miranda* rights than children were three decades ago, this research suggests that adolescents' *Miranda* comprehension has not significantly improved over time. This continuity across generations suggests that *Miranda* comprehension may be a developmental skill beyond the capacity of young adolescents. In addition, consistent with earlier findings, age and IQ are still the primary predictors of *Miranda* comprehension; older youths were generally better able to understand the *Miranda* warnings than were younger youths, and juveniles with higher IQ scores demonstrated better comprehension than those with lower IQs. Special education enrollment also was related to *Miranda* comprehension.

Compared with Grisso's (1981) findings, youth continue to exhibit similar misunderstandings of their rights. Like adolescents three decades ago, juveniles frequently misunderstood that they were entitled to consult with an attorney before interrogation and to have an attorney present during interrogation. Furthermore, similar percentages of youth mistakenly believed that lawyers only protect the innocent and that the right to silence can be revoked at a later date by a judge. The two most commonly misunderstood vocabulary words at both time points were "interrogation" and "consult." Juveniles understood the former to be analogous with a court hearing, and youth often failed to understand the advisory purpose of "consultation," describing it as a simple conversation instead. Thus, despite increased exposure to the *Miranda* warnings from depictions in television and movies, juvenile offenders today understand their rights in much the same way adolescents did generations ago. Therefore, mere exposure to the rights appears to be an inadequate method of promoting the legal protections of youth. It should be noted, however, that those most frequently misunderstood words appeared in the more complicated versions of the *Miranda* warning, so their relationship to overall comprehension might not be relevant in some jurisdictions. The updated version of the vocabulary test includes a span of simple and complex words appearing in warnings to increase the likelihood that words in the instruments are relevant to a broad range of jurisdictions.

The P-CHIP does not assess a suspect's actual likelihood of falsely confessing to a crime, but results suggest that there is considerable danger of youth offering false confessions to police during hypothetical holding and interrogation procedures. Interestingly, only age was found to be a significant predictor of self-reported likelihood of falsely confessing; *Miranda* comprehension was not independently related. One explanation for this finding may be that younger children are more prone to suggestibility (Gudjonsson & Singh, 1984), but there may be a more general developmental feature of acquiescence to authority that would increase the probability of offering a false confession.

Original Versus Revised Instruments

Similar findings from the research conducted in the 1970s and the current study suggest that until the MRCI-II is released, the original

Instruments for Assessing Understanding and Appreciation of Miranda Rights continues to offer critical insight into juvenile defendants' capacity to waive rights. However, revisions made to the original instruments in the MRCI-II have increased their utility with today's warnings and their generalizability across jurisdictions.

The simplification of the language of the *Miranda* warnings in the revised instruments and the addition of the fifth *Miranda* prong to all of the relevant instruments provide norms that are appropriate for a broader range of jurisdictions. Likewise, because the warnings in the MRCI-II are more similar to the actual warnings administered in most jurisdictions, forensic evaluators should find better generalization of the test results to true capacity to waive rights.

Considering that juvenile offenders are at increased risk of offering false confessions (Richardson et al., 1995), the newly added P-CHIP is an essential component of the assessment instruments. This study represents the first published research on this instrument. Should further research establish its validity, the P-CHIP would serve as the first assessment tool to directly assess youths' likelihood of offering false confessions. Furthermore, as Grisso's instruments assessed the knowing and intelligent requirements for a valid waiver, the P-CHIP would be the first instrument to directly tap into the voluntariness construct.

Limitations of Research Findings

Although results of this study may contribute valuable information to forensic evaluators and policy makers interested in juveniles' capacity to waive *Miranda* rights, there are several limitations of this study. First, participants were juvenile offenders in a postadjudication facility and, therefore, had already been through legal hearings and experienced the serious consequences of being sent to a secure facility. As a result, participants may have learned about their rights during their talks with attorneys or during their hearings. In addition, youth who confessed to crimes and were adjudicated delinquent and sent to the facility may have learned that information they provided to police was used against them in court. Thus, data from this study may represent an overestimate of preadjudicated youths' *Miranda* rights comprehension, the population for which *Miranda* evaluations are most critical. For the same reasons, the data may represent an underestimate of preadjudicated youths' likelihood of falsely confessing to a crime. However, results of Grisso's (1981) studies and the current study consistently demonstrated that, overall, juveniles' *Miranda* comprehension does not improve as youths acquire greater experience with the justice system. Similarly, we found that juveniles' self-reported likelihood of offering a false confession did not decrease with an increase in the number of occasions on which they said police read them the *Miranda* warnings. Thus, the findings from this study probably apply to preadjudicated youth. The additional testing that is part of the ongoing multistate study will confirm that assumption, as the majority of participants are preadjudicated youth.

Another potential limitation of the current study is that only male juvenile offenders served as participants in this study. Consequently, results may not be generalizable to adolescent girls in the juvenile justice system. Grisso (1981), in his original research, however, found no gender differences in juveniles' *Miranda* comprehension. Again, the ongoing, multistate study involves female juvenile offender participants, and results should reveal whether the lack of gender difference is consistent across three decades. We speculate that although a gender difference will not exist for *Miranda* comprehension, female delinquents will be more suggestible than male delinquents and will, therefore, be more likely to say they would falsely confess to a crime under police pressure.

Another limitation of the study is the use of verbal IQ as a measure of overall IQ. Certainly, there are many aspects of intelligence other than verbal IQ that may be necessary for understanding, appreciating, and asserting *Miranda* rights, such as problem-solving abilities and memory. Such skills were not assessed during this study

because of time limitations for administering instruments. However, future studies should assess other aspects of intelligence as well as other skills that may affect *Miranda* decision making, such as ability to inhibit responses. Because the P-CHIP is a new instrument, its validity has not been established. It is unclear whether youth behave as they say they would in actual interrogation situations. Consequently, assessment data on self-reported likelihood of offering false confessions should be interpreted with caution until further data are collected. Research also has suggested that stressful situations may heighten suggestibility and increase a youthful offender's likelihood of falsely confessing to a crime (Gudjonsson & Singh, 1984; Richardson et al., 1995). Given that a research study is far less stressful than a true police interrogation, juveniles' P-CHIP scores may underestimate their actual likelihood of offering false confessions.

***

Research and Policy Implications

The results of this study have implications for courts determining juveniles' capacities to waive *Miranda* rights and offer valid and admissible confessions. Age and IQ are two of the most common factors courts use in weighing the "totality of the circumstances," and this research supports the continued use of these factors in decision making. Similarly, courts consider academic history as part of the totality of the circumstances surrounding the validity of a *Miranda* waiver. The current study provides the first findings that examination of special education status is important when evaluating *Miranda* comprehension.

If the results of the multistate extension of this study are consistent with the results obtained from this sample of male juvenile offenders, public policy reform may be needed to obtain valid confessions from adolescents, particularly those below age 16 with low IQs. To promote the validity of waivers, many states have introduced an "interested adult" rule, requiring that a suspect below a specified age have an opportunity to consult a parent, guardian, or other interested adult party prior to or during interrogation. However, research suggested that this policy has failed to fulfill its goal, as parents present during interrogations rarely helped their children understand or assert their rights. Furthermore, parents who did guide their children during interrogations, frequently persuaded them to confess to crimes (Grisso, 1981). Should policy makers truly wish to guarantee that juveniles' confessions are valid, it would be ideal for all youth under the age of 15 or 16 to have an attorney present during interrogation. However, many police departments might object to this policy recommendation because of their goal of crime solving. Consequently, a potential alternative that would decrease the likelihood of invalid waivers and promote the probability of confessions' admissibility involves the brief, structured assessment of *Miranda* comprehension prior to interrogation.

***

UNIT III

CRIMINAL AND DELINQUENT BEHAVIOR

INTRODUCTION AND COMMENTARY

Criminologists' explanations (or theories) of juvenile delinquency and criminal behavior range from those that are individually based to those that indict the broad society in which the individual is imbedded. At one pole are biologically based explanations—such as those related to psychopathy. At the midpoint of the continuum we find those theories that consider multiple individual and social influences on a person's behavior, such as the theories focusing on resilience. At the other pole are theories that reject individual differences and place the blame for crime on society at large, such as those that suggest that a capitalist society encourages those who hold power to commit crimes (e.g., political crimes or corporate crimes).

Most of the readings in this section were selected to represent psychologically based theories or crimes that have received considerable attention in the psychological research. The **Curt R. Bartol** selection, written specifically for this book of readings, summarizes literature on resilience, a concept that began to appear in the delinquency literature in the 1980s. Resilience helps us understand why some children and adolescents, even if imbedded in a neighborhood with high rates of antisocial behavior, are able to take a different path. Bartol first summarizes the "risk" factors that have traditionally occupied theorists and researchers (e.g., poverty, low intelligence, deviant peer groups), then moves on to the protective factors that allow the child to overcome adversity. He ends by addressing promising approaches to developing resilience in children often considered at risk of committing serious antisocial behavior.

At-risk children and adolescents as well as those not typically considered at risk may be susceptible to illegal drug use. Furthermore, some adolescents and young adults, in particular, have taken advantage of drugs to facilitate sexual assault. In the next selection, **Elena Pope** and **Michelle Shouldice** discuss substance use and abuse in the context of acquaintance rape. The authors, both physicians, have written an up-to-date, informative review of the properties and effects of these "date-rape drugs," which not only decrease resistance but also impair the victim's memory of the event. However, their presence in the victim is difficult to detect, and specific tests must be requested. The authors thus provide helpful information, not only for potential victims but also for investigators.

Like acquaintance rape, a crime that has received considerable recent attention is stalking. Defining this illegal behavior presents unique challenges, however. In addition, the perceptions of the stalking target are crucial. The selection by **Lorraine Phillips et al.** focuses on this important aspect. The researchers conducted two experiments that examined how college students, male and female, perceived the behavior described in a variety of vignettes. They wondered whether the perception of stalking was affected by such variables as the gender of the perpetrator and the target, past experiences with stalking, and the relationship between the stalker and the target. Some gender effects were found, with women in one study being somewhat more likely than men to perceive certain behavior as stalking. However, there were several unanticipated findings as well.

In the next selection, we move from discussion of specific crimes to characteristics of some perpetrators, specifically criminal psychopaths. **Robert D. Hare,** a widely cited contemporary researcher and expert on psychopathy, reviews what psychology has learned about this rare phenomenon. Psychopaths—who are believed to comprise between 11 and 25% of the prison population, depending upon the study—are extremely resistant to treatment, but they often play the treatment game quite well. Hare's article is part literature review and part personal recollection of a struggle to have psychopathy recognized, accepted, accurately diagnosed, and understood.

Those who offend against children are the topic of the next article by **Robert A. Prentky and his colleagues.** Prentky et al. summarize research findings on child sexual molestation, including its frequency and characteristics of the offenders, such as their social competence and the developmental influences on their adult behavior. For example, research has found that caregiver inconstancy—frequent changes in a child's primary caregiver—is a powerful predictor of sexual violence as well as attachment disorder in adulthood.

All sex offenders are not alike, a finding made very clear in this reading. Even within a category of these offenders, there are important differences. Thus, the article outlines systems for the classification of child molesters, including the *DSM-IV* classification and the heavily researched model developed by the Massachusetts Treatment Center, the MTC:CM3. There is also discussion of the various approaches to sex offender treatment and the methods of assessing risk of future offending.

As a group, the above readings represent either cutting-edge theory in criminal psychology (e.g., resilience, psychopathy, classification of sex offenders) or deal with crimes that are serious, widespread, and often resistant to efforts at prevention and prosecution (e.g., acquaintance rape, stalking, child sexual assault). They will likely continue to capture the research attention and theory-building efforts of criminal psychologists.

8

RESILIENCE AND ANTISOCIAL BEHAVIOR

CURT R. BARTOL

Over the past quarter century, the literature of juvenile delinquency has experienced an interesting paradigm shift. Until that time, references to "children at risk" or to "risk factors" for delinquency or serious antisocial behavior predominated. Depending on the writer's theoretical orientation, children were seen to be at risk if they were poor; lacked good cognitive skills; were undernourished; had attention deficits; came from one-parent families; associated with delinquents peers; were physically or sexually abused; or experienced a multitude of other individual, family-based, or educational problems.

It has now become apparent, though, that a significant number of children who are considered at risk do not engage in serious, persistent antisocial behavior but rather develop into prosocial and productive adults (Doll & Lyon, 1998). That is, despite experiencing a stressful, disadvantaged, or abusive childhood, many children do not engage in serious delinquency and, indeed, mature successfully. Researchers began to refer to this as *resilience* and to search for factors that might account for it (Garmezy, 1991; Werner, 1987). Thus, while risk factors remain a major concern, their conceptual opposites—protective factors—are now considered equally important. Knowledge about the personal attributes of resilient children and the environmental influences they experience will help greatly in the prevention and treatment of delinquent and antisocial behavior among at-risk populations.

We should note at the outset that the term *juvenile delinquent* is troublesome in several aspects. It is a legal classification assigned by the juvenile or family court after it has been determined that a juvenile has committed a criminal act. Accordingly, delinquency is behavior against the criminal code committed by an individual who has not reached adulthood, as defined by state or federal law. However, many juveniles commit crimes but are never formally declared delinquents. Others are informally called delinquents by adults without being arrested by police or processed by the courts. Still others—who meet the age criterion for delinquency—are tried in criminal courts rather than juvenile courts and consequently are never adjudicated delinquent.

Psychologists prefer the term *antisocial behavior* to refer to the more serious habitual actions that violate personal rights, laws, or widely held social norms. Included in this definition is a wide assortment of behaviors ranging from homicide and sexual assault to verbal assault and vandalism. Though self-destructive behaviors such as substance abuse or suicide are also often called antisocial behaviors, we restrict our definition here to "recurrent problem behaviors that lead to injury to others or arrest" (Dodge & Pettit, 2003, p. 350). Arrest and subsequent court processing cannot be the only indicators of antisocial behavior because, as indicated above, many of these actions go undetected or escape the attention of law enforcement. They are, of course, still problematic. Consequently, the concepts in this chapter are relevant to both juvenile delinquency, as legally defined, and more generally to antisocial behavior. Although the terms will be used interchangeably, the focus will be on antisocial behavior. We will begin the chapter with a brief discussion of the risk factors that have long been identified in the research before moving on to discuss the concept of resilience and summarize its accompanying protective factors.

RISK FACTORS

Risks can be defined as "processes that predispose individuals to specific negative or unwanted outcomes" (McKnight & Loper, 2002, p. 188). Risk factors refer to individual attributes and developmental experiences that are believed to increase the probability that a person will engage in persistent antisocial or delinquent behavior. Researchers have identified a host of risk factors, often dividing them into four somewhat overlapping categories: (1) individual attributes, (2) family characteristics, (3) extrafamilial influences, and (4) psychobiological and health factors.

Individual risk factors include inadequate cognitive and language ability, a troublesome temperament (Bates, Pettit, Dodge, & Ridge, 1998; Dodge, 2002; Kochanska, 1998), poor self-regulation skills and impulsivity (Patterson, DeGarmo, & Knutson, 2000; Stoolmiller, 2001), low motivation, inadequate interpersonal and social skills, low self-esteem, and a negative self-concept. Family risk factors include faulty or inept parenting, parental psychopathology (especially depression), antisocial siblings, and various kinds of maltreatment and abuse. Examples of extrafamilial risk factors are antisocial peers, inadequate schools, inadequate social networks and support systems, and the stress of living in dangerous and violent neighborhoods. Extrafamilial developmental factors may also include poverty and its concomitants of malnutrition, lead poisoning, low birth weight, living under conditions of chronic violence, and the many other effects of socioeconomic disadvantage. Examples of psychobiological and health factors include risk factors that involve hereditary influences, prenatal influences, postnatal diseases, and inadequate nutrition and medical care.

Most risk factors by themselves probably do not directly engender serious antisocial or delinquent behavior. Even parental psychopathology or a poor self-concept does not necessarily produce it. Rather, the research evidence suggests that it takes some combination of risks over a period of time to encourage criminal or delinquent behavior (Lösel & Bender, 2003).

Although a considerable amount of research on the relationship between risk factors and juvenile delinquency has been conducted over the years, until recently very little attention has been directed at those dispositions and influences that enable children to cope, adjust, and overcome adverse circumstances. These attributes and events—which are collectively called protective factors—are now believed to play significant roles in encouraging many children to avoid participation in serious antisocial or delinquent behavior. For many psychologists, studying the influence of protective factors on the developmental trajectories of nondelinquent children is a much more positive approach. It is clear that many children have a variety of protective factors, and that it is easier for adults in their environment to provide such factors for them than to overcome the negative effects of risk factors. Furthermore, by emphasizing strengths rather than limitations, we have more hope for dealing effectively with children and adolescents who otherwise might follow the path of serious antisocial behavior. The study of resilience also helps us formulate effective strategies and policies for the prevention and treatment of antisocial behavior.

PROTECTIVE FACTORS

As we have seen, risk factors place an individual at elevated risk for involvement in antisocial behavior. Protective factors, on the other hand, insulate or shield the individual from the adverse effects of risk factors (Walters, 2002). Children who are exposed to many risk factors but are able to overcome their effects because of the presence of protective factors are called "resilient." Put another way, protective factors help build resilience in children and adolescents.

Resilience is generally defined as "successful coping with or overcoming risk and adversity, the development of competence in the face of severe stress and hardship, and success in developmental tasks or meeting societal expectations" (McKnight & Loper, 2002, p. 188). Resilience, then, is the ability to bounce back quickly and adaptively from negative emotional experiences (Tugade & Fredrickson, 2004). In an effort to emphasize the ongoing and changing developmental aspects of resilience, a few researchers define the concept as "a dynamic process encompassing positive adaptation within the context of significant adversity" (Luthar, Cicchetti, & Becker, 2000, p. 543). Some researchers also distinguish between the terms "resilience" and "resiliency." For them, resilience refers to a dynamic developmental process, while resiliency refers to a personality trait or attribute that is relatively stable over the course of a lifetime

(Masten, 1994). However, there is increasing evidence that, although resilience may be subjected to developmental fluctuations, at-risk children who show resilience at one stage of their lives tend to show resilience across their entire life span (Luthar et al., 2000). Consequently, it becomes difficult to make the fine distinction between resilience and resiliency with any kind of precision. Therefore, to avoid confusion, the term resilience will be used broadly here to encompass both the process and the personality trait.

At a minimum, two critical conditions must be met before a child can be called resilient. First, the child must have been exposed to significant threats or severe adversity, ranging from a single stressful event such as the death of a sibling to an accumulation of ongoing negative experiences, such as abuse. Second, the child must demonstrate the achievement of positive adaptation despite major assaults on the developmental process (Luthar et al., 2000). It should also be noted that resilience has been conceptualized as an outcome or process that does not eradicate risk, but allows an individual to compensate for it successfully. Resilient children do not simply evade the negative outcomes associated with risk, but are able to take risk head-on and adapt in the face of such adversity.

Research on resilience also underscores the perspective that children have different vulnerabilities and protective systems at different ages and points during their development. For example, infants, because of their total dependence on parents or caregivers, are highly vulnerable to the consequences of mistreatment by these adult figures. Adolescents, on the other hand, tend to be more vulnerable to the experiences they have with friends and school, which would be well beyond the understanding of young children (Masten & Coatsworth, 1998).

The study of resilience arose from the study of risk, as pioneering investigators realized that there were many children who flourish in the midst of extreme adversity (Masten & Coatsworth, 1998). Prior to the current resilience research, the conventional wisdom was that growing up in oppressive and adverse conditions inevitably damages children and thwarts normal development (Waller, 2001). It was assumed, also, that children who survived and emerged psychologically healthy from severe adversity were very unusual or special. However, systematic research on resilience in children soon revealed that the original assumptions about the dire and irrevocable effects of growing up under adverse conditions were wrong or misleading (Masten, 2001) and that resilience in children is far more common than originally supposed (Bonanno, 2004). In essence, most children are far more adaptive and resilient than we might expect. According to Ann Masten (2001), "Resilience does not come from rare and special qualities, but from the everyday magic of ordinary, normative human resources in the minds, brains, and bodies of children" (p. 235).

In recent years, developmental research has been able to identify some common characteristics of resilient children and adolescents. In general, the accumulating evidence reveals that resilient children exhibit positive social, interpersonal, and cognitive competencies that help them survive and succeed while living in high-stress and adverse environments. They are often described as having an optimistic, zestful, and energetic approach to life; are curious and open to new experiences; and demonstrate a strong tendency for laughter and positive emotionality (Tugade & Fredrickson, 2004). Another repetitive theme that emerges from the research literature is that resilience is developed from close relations with supportive, loving caregivers, effective schools, and connections with competent, caring adults in the wider community (Luthar et al., 2000). Children and adolescents who participate in serious, violent behaviors or chronic delinquency rarely display these qualities or these experiences. In fact, research suggests that resilient youth not only do not engage in serious or violent delinquency, they usually do not participate in delinquent gangs or use illegal drugs, either (Tiêt & Huizinga, 2002).

RESEARCH ON RESILIENCE

The study of resilience in children at risk began in earnest during the 1970s (Masten, 2001). Having originated in the disciplines of psychiatry and developmental psychology, it has tended to focus on the individual, often to the exclusion of the psychosocial environment (Waller, 2001). Thus, resilience was initially conceptualized as the result of personality traits or coping styles that allowed some children to progress along a developmental trajectory even when confronted with considerable adversity.

One of the earliest studies on resilience was Emmy Werner's (1987) longitudinal research in what is known as the Kauai study. Werner and her collaborators (Werner, Bierman & French, 1971; Werner & Smith, 1977, 1982; Werner, 1987, 1993) followed a cohort of 698 children, living on the Hawaiian Island of Kauai, from birth to adulthood. This longitudinal study spanned the years 1954–1986 and included data from pediatricians, psychologists, public health personnel, and social workers. The project identified a number of personality, constitutional, and environmental variables that presumably distinguished children who became delinquent from those who did not.

We should note that Werner's measure of delinquency raises problems, although it is not unusual in delinquency research. Of the 698 children, 102 were labeled "delinquent" based solely on official records or police and family court files. A vast majority of these 102 "juvenile offenders" (both males and females) had committed relatively minor offense violations, such as traffic violations or running away. This word of caution should be kept in mind as we review the findings of the study.

Nevertheless, Werner (1987) stated that a combination of about a dozen variables provided the best prediction for eventual delinquency. For example, children with a history of a difficult temperament, hyperactivity, substandard living conditions, low IQ, and unstable conflictful home life were more likely to be delinquent than children without these background variables.

However, a significant number of these children (total of 72) with four or more of these features in their background did not become delinquent, indicating that predicting delinquency on the basis of background variables is unwarranted.

Werner divided those children with four or more high risk variables into a "resilient" group (those who did not become delinquent) and a "vulnerable" group (those who became delinquent). She reports that one of the strongest differences between the two groups was the mother's perception concerning the child's temperament. Mothers of the resilient children perceived them as affectionate, cuddly, good-natured, and easy to handle. Resilient children also demonstrated a positive social orientation toward others. They were more skilled at engaging others and recruiting care, help, and support from siblings, peers, grandparents, neighborhood adults, and teachers. As the children got older, they were described as active, sociable, easy-tempered, independent, and self-confident. They did better in school, communicated well, and had considerable curiosity about things in their world. As young adults, many continued their education beyond high school, were achievement oriented, and had a stable employment history. The families of the resilient children also had fairly extensive social support systems. That is, they had many supportive adults and caretakers available to them when problems arose.

Children in the vulnerable group were far different. Mothers of these vulnerable children perceived them as being difficult to handle. They believed their children exhibited more temper tantrums, as well as eating and sleeping problems. The children's orientation toward others was negative and aggressive. Overall, the families of vulnerable children seemed to have meager support systems.

Following the Kauai study, research has continually discovered that resilient and adaptive children and adolescents do not usually engage in serious, chronic delinquency or antisocial behavior (Coie, 2004; Conduct Problems Prevention Research Group, 2004; Lösel & Bender, 2003; Masten & Coatsworth, 1998). Resilient children and adolescents, in spite of heavy exposure to risk factors, are accepted by peers; have excellent interpersonal and social skills; do well in school; and are usually good-natured, active, independent, self-confident, and have a very positive self-concept. They develop and sustain strong connections to competent and caring adults in the family and community, and they demonstrate strong cognitive abilities and self-regulation skills that help them control their impulses, frustrations, and anger.

Some research has focused on youth resilience after being away from institutional rearing characterized by extreme deprivation. Studies of Romanian adoptees provide dramatic documentation of "developmental catch-up" in many of the children, both physically and cognitively (Masten, 2001). The degree of catch-up by the age of 4 was spectacular (Rutter & English and Romanian Adoptees [ERA] Study Team, 1998). "As observed in many other situations of extraordinary adversity, the capacity for developmental recovery when normative rearing conditions are restored is amazing" (Masten, 2001, p. 233). However, this does not mean that all children exposed to deprivation recover well. Some develop serious and chronic problems, including antisocial behavior, partly as a result of their earlier experiences with adversity. Systematic investigations of why some children respond adaptively while others do not should offer a promising framework for intervention and treatment.

Clearly, then, it is in society's interest to encourage and provide conditions that promote the development of resilience in children and adolescents at risk. It is also clear that many children—even if immersed in numerous risk factors—can overcome their effects. As articulated by Masten (2001), "Attention to human capabilities and adaptive systems that promote healthy development and functioning have the potential to inform policy and programs that foster competence and human capital and aim to improve the health of communities and nations while also preventing problems" (p. 235). The following sections will review those protective factors most conducive to the development of resilience in youth exposed to high risk.

ENVIRONMENTAL FACTORS

Although much of the theoretical and research work has tended to view resilience as a quality of the individual, a strong argument can be made that it also reflects the quality of the social context in which the child develops. Many developmental theorists have argued that resilience to aversive childhood contexts results from a cumulative and interactive mix of genetic (e.g., temperament), personal (e.g., cognitive ability), and environmental (e.g., family, community support systems) risk and protective factors (Rutter, 1999; Werner, 1995). Therefore, resilience is not only a quality of individuals but is also reflective of the social contexts in which they are embedded.

Family Influences

A majority of experts would agree that the family is the single most important social environment in any child's development. Protective factors within the family include such characteristics as warmth, cohesion, enlightened discipline, and cultural and ethnic identification (Barbarin, 1993). For many decades, research has shown that good parental functioning in at least one parent or at least one adequate and stable caregiver is crucial to the development of resilience and healthy functioning (G. Smith, 1999; Waaktaar, Christie, Borge, & Torgerson, 2004). Research has also consistently shown that effective parenting generally prevents serious antisocial behavior or delinquency (Dubow, Edwards, & Ippolito, 1997; Masten 2001). Emotionally attentive, supportive, and interested parents promote nondelinquency and prevent serious, persistent antisocial behavior from developing in their children (Lösel & Bender, 2003; Stouthamer-Loeber et al., 1993).

Parental attributions about child misbehavior and the discipline styles parents use to reduce such behavior also powerfully influence the development and persistence of antisocial behavior in children (Snyder, Cramer, Afrank, & Patterson, 2005). For example, researchers have found that when parents make negative or hostile attributions about their children prior to school entry, the children are likely to be disruptive and exhibit other antisocial behavior at school (Nix et al., 1999; Snyder et al., 2005). Parental "hostile" attributions refer to descriptions of a child's behavior as careless, selfish, defiant, inconsiderate, bad, or hostile. Moreover, many of these parents tend to blame the misconduct on the basic traits of the child. Interestingly, negative parental attribution also has a strong link to harsh punishment and disciplinary tactics by parents (Snyder et al., 2005).

Peer Influences

Recent studies have discovered that supportive, prosocial peers are among the most important network factors contributing to resilience in children and adolescents and to the prevention of antisocial behavior (Waaktaar et al., 2004). Children seek out other children who are fun to be with and who share common interests. In addition, resilient children appear to be skillful at sustaining peer relations that are mutually beneficial. That is, resilient children have interpersonal and social skills that facilitate and enhance, rather than undermine, the goals and interests of their peers. Recent research indicates that sibling support is also a strong protective factor in the development of resilience (Ozer, 2005).

One of the strongest predictors of later involvement in antisocial behavior is early rejection by peers (Dodge, 2003; Laird, Jordan, Dodge, Pettit, & Bates, 2001; Parker & Asher, 1987). More specifically, those children who were rejected for at least 2 or 3 years by second grade had a 50% chance of displaying significant antisocial behavior later in adolescence, in contrast with just a 9% chance for those children who managed to avoid early peer rejection (Dodge & Pettit, 2003). Aggressive behavior appears to be a key factor that promotes peer rejection. Children tend to reject those children who frequently use forms of physical aggression as their preferred way of dealing with others. Moreover, children who are both physically aggressive and socially rejected by their peers have a high probability of becoming serious delinquents during adolescence. Researchers Coie and Miller-Johnson (2001), for example, conclude from their review of the literature that "those aggressive children who are rejected by peers are at significantly greater risk for chronic antisocial behavior than those who are not rejected" (p. 201).

On the other hand, positive peer relations have been thought to contribute to the development of empathy, and also reinforce and model self-regulation and prosocial behavior (Eisenberg, 1998; Waaktaar et al., 2004). Studies find that peer-rejected and aggressive children are deficient in being able to emotionally and cognitively put themselves in the place of others (Pepler, Byrd, & King, 1991). They are deficient in role-taking skills and they lack the ability to empathize. As a result, these youths, with increasing age, become less concerned about the consequences of violence, including the suffering of the victim or the amount of peer rejection they receive.

Positive peer relations are also believed to reduce significantly the tendency to display hostile attribution bias. According to Nigg and Huang-Pollock (2003), the term "hostile attribution bias" was first used by Nasby, Hayden, and Depaulo (1979) to describe the tendency of some aggressive children to routinely attribute hostile intent to other children, even if the other children have no such intentions. Hostile attribution bias begins to develop during the preschool years in most children who display it. Highly aggressive children, for instance, repeatedly fail to respond adaptively to minor provocations from others. In ambiguous situations, they are inclined to perceive even slight transgressions of others as threatening. Therefore, unclear intentions from peers are often met with aggressive overreactions. If a classmate accidentally spills a drink near his belongings, the highly aggressive boy believes this was a deliberate attempt to damage his possessions and he responds with physical aggression. Peer-rejected and aggressive children appear to be less equipped cognitively for dealing with ambiguous or conflict situations.

Resilient youth also appear to place themselves in healthier contexts, generating opportunities for success or raising the odds of connecting with prosocial mentors in a manner consistent with the concept of niche seeking. In other words, resilient children have a knack for selecting and creating social environments that enable them to grow and thrive. Even infants have considerable power to elicit assistance from parents and caregivers, especially from adults that are sensitive to their needs. The quality of this relationship has predictive significance for success in later developmental tasks, such as better problem solving in toddlers and better peer relations in middle childhood. Youngsters who are persistently antisocial either have abandoned this strategy or do not have the necessary judgment for negotiating socially acceptable ways of getting their needs met.

Community and Neighborhood Social Support

The research associating resilience with neighborhood factors is sparse, but it does indicate that neighborhoods supplement the other environmental and individual-level factors associated with resilience by providing a context in which children can be exposed to positive influences (Wandersman & Nation, 1998). Several studies have demonstrated the positive effects of social network factors such as dense adult friendship networks and the adult monitoring and supervision of youth in reducing serious delinquency. These data support the position that youth are mentally and physically healthier in neighborhoods where adults talk to each other and get along (Wandersman & Nation, 1998). A strong social network in which adults are connected to each other produces healthy outcomes. Several studies (e.g., Garbarino & Kostelny, 1992; Garbarino, Kostelny, & Dubrow, 1991) support this hypothesis, and clearly demonstrate the importance of good social networks in preventing child abuse, child antisocial behavior, and violence, even in areas of concentrated poverty (Wandersman & Nation, 1998).

Supportive extrafamilial relationships can be found in church affiliations, neighborhood organizations, and schools that effectively promote competence in social and cognitive domains (Barbarin, 1993). These social interactions play an important role in the development of resilience. Based on their extensive review of the relevant literature, Lösel and Bender (2003) conclude, "The availability and use of social support from family members, relatives, teachers, educators, ministers of religion, and friends . . . contribute to resilience" (p. 164).

INDIVIDUAL FACTORS

Cognitive Skills

According to Nigg and Huang-Pollock (2003), "cognitive problems in the child usually contribute to difficult interactions with [the] caretaker, interfere with socialization, and leave the child unprepared to adapt to the greater diversity he or she faces within a high-risk environment" (p. 237). Good cognitive functioning, on the other hand, provides protection from the many negative influences of risk factors. The specific cognitive skills and abilities that contribute to resilience are intelligence; language skills; self-regulation skills; and other cognitive perceptions of self, such as self-efficacy and talent (Olsson, Bond, Burns, Vella-Broderick, & Sawyer, 2003).

It is clear that intelligence exists in multiple forms and relates to a wide assortment of abilities. Howard Gardner (2000), for example, describes nine different types of intelligences or cognitive styles. They are linguistic (or language intelligence), logical-mathematical, spatial (used in getting from one place to another), musical, body-kinesthetic (such as what good athletes and dancers have), existential (ability to ponder meaning of life), naturalistic (ability to see beauty and patterns in nature), insight into oneself, and understanding of others. There are probably many more types as well, such as wisdom, spirituality, synthesizing ability, intuition, metaphoric capacities, humor, and good judgment (Gardner, 1986, 1993, 1998). Gardner considered the last two of the primary nine—insight into oneself and the understanding of others—features of "emotional intelligence." A deficiency in this form of intelligence may play a prominent role in human violence. Individuals who continually engage in violence may lack significant insight into their own behavior and possess little sensitivity or empathy toward others.

For our purposes, intelligence will be defined as the ability to adapt, learn, and engage in abstract thought (Nigg & Huang-Pollock, 2003). It is usually measured by various intelligence tests or scales. A nearly universal finding in the research literature is that children with a higher level of measured intelligence are more likely to be more resilient (Aldwin, 1994: Lösel & Bender, 2003). While a large amount of research links cognitive deficits to antisocial behavior in children and adolescents (Nigg & Huang-Pollock, 2003, p. 227), considerable research has also shown that youth with high or above-average intelligence are far less likely to participate in serious or chronic delinquency: "Intelligent children may be more capable of planning their behaviour, anticipating negative outcomes, settling conflicts verbally, developing alternatives to aggressive reactions, and making better decisions" (Lösel & Bender, 2003, p. 155). Intelligent children are more likely to develop better and more realistic coping strategies, and because of their cognitive skills are more likely to learn nonaggressive problem-solving capabilities at an early age. Furthermore, intelligent children usually perform well at school, a behavioral pattern that provides them with a powerful source of achievement and self-esteem that can buffer other stressors. More broadly, intelligent children receive greater levels of social reinforcement from the general social environment (e.g., teachers and other significant adults) than less intelligent children (Born, Chevalier & Humblet, 1997). Inversely, "children with worse than average intellectual skills may find it difficult to negotiate threatening situations, disengage from school because of feelings of failure, or fail to learn as much from their experiences" (Masten & Coatsworth, 1998, p. 213).

Good intelligence may also reflect the central importance of cognition and language to adaptation during early development, and it appears to have specific and very important protective functions (Masten & Coatsworth, 1998). Interestingly, the verbal and language aspects of intelligence seem to be one of the more important components of the relationship between intelligence and delinquency. Nigg and Huang-Pollock (2003) affirm,

> Early specific weakness in verbal-learning and verbal-reasoning modestly but reliably predicts later persistent offending, conduct disorder, and antisocial outcomes, whereas nonverbal intelligence does not do so. . . . Weakness in verbal intelligence is associated with the subgroup of delinquent youth with early onset and chronic patterns of antisocial behavior . . . even though not all of those youth [with poor verbal skills] have antisocial outcomes. (p. 231)

Perhaps more importantly, good verbal intelligence contributes substantially to language development.

Language Development

Language is a powerful tool for parents and other socializing adults to use in transmitting and expressing social expectations and values. It is also the primary means by which children can communicate their needs, frustrations, and concerns. Therefore, language serves both as a form of external communication and the basic internal ingredient for thinking and self-regulation. In essence, language plays a major constructive role in the growth of all cognitive processes. According to Keenan and Shaw (2003), language is the "primary means by which children learn to solve problems nonaggressively and effectively decrease negative emotions such as anger, fear, and sadness" (p. 163). Toddlers with better communication skills are easier to socialize. This is because they comprehend parental instructions better, are more able to develop internal controls of their emotions and behaviors,

and can communicate their wishes better (Lahey & Waldman, 2003). Hence, these children are less likely to become highly frustrated during interactions with their parents.

On average, children utter their first word at between 8 and 14 months of age. During this time, they add words to their repertoire at a relatively slow rate. By age 24 months, children have an average vocabulary level of 300 words (Ganger & Brent, 2004). For the average child, there is a substantial amount of growth in language during the second year of life (Keenan & Shaw, 2003). In addition, it is widely held that children's rate of vocabulary acquisition does not simply increase but undergoes a discrete transition at approximately 50 words. During this stage, children presumably switch from an initial stage of slow vocabulary growth to a subsequent stage of faster growth (Ganger & Brent, 2004). Although the reasons for this transition remain debatable, it is often called the vocabulary spurt, the vocabulary burst, or the naming explosion in the developmental research literature.

By the end of the preschool period, the average child has internalized—primarily through the use of language—rules that are linked to the ability to inhibit behavior, follow orders, and manage negative emotions (Keenan & Shaw, 2003; Kochanska, Murray, & Coy, 1997). In addition, the child demonstrates more empathy and prosocial behavior toward others as a result of language development (Keenan & Shaw, 2003).

Delayed language development, on the other hand, is believed to increase stress and frustration for many children and impede normal socialization (Keenan & Shaw, 2003). Toddler language development at ages 6 months, 18 months, and 24 months predicts later delinquency and antisocial behavior for boys, even when socioeconomic status (SES) and test motivation is controlled (Nigg & Huang-Pollock, 2003; Stattin & Klackenberg-Larson, 1993). A higher incidence of expressive language delay also has been observed among male children who display disruptive behaviors during the preschool years and antisocial behavior during the school years (Dionne, Tremblay, Boivin, Laplante, &

Pérusse, 2003). A similar finding was reported by Stowe, Arnold, and Ortiz (2000), who found that delayed language functioning was associated with observed disruptive behaviors in male preschoolers. Interestingly, although early delays in language attainment may be a powerful predictor of highly aggressive and antisocial behavior in boys, the current research pertaining to girls is sparse and inconclusive.

What might explain this association between language and delinquency or antisocial behavior? Researchers theorize that, when language deficits limit general communication, the child may use disruptive behavior to compensate for limited communication skills (Dionne et al., 2003). Basically, early language delay and limited communication skills may predispose a child to employ more physically aggressive tactics for dealing with the social environment. Frustrated about not getting his needs met through normal communication and social strategies, the child is drawn to more physical, demonstrative behavior to get his way. There is a circular effect, however, since aggressive and disruptive behaviors interfere with creating a conducive social or academic learning environment. Therefore, antisocial behavioral patterns may, in turn, curtail language development. In contrast to children with language deficits, verbally advantaged children may benefit from their verbal skills by developing prosocial behaviors and may thus steer away from the antisocial trajectories (Dionne et al., 2003).

Executive Functions

Closely related to intelligence and language development is the concept of *executive functions.* The concept is largely based on complex neuropsychological functions and includes such technical terms as set shifting, interference control, inhibition planning, and working memory (Nigg & Huang-Pollock, 2003). Executive functions more simply refers to deliberate problem solving and the regulation of one's thoughts and actions (Tremblay, 2003; Zelazo, Carter, Reznick, & Frye, 1997). For example, given the problem of being unable to open a container, what might a

typical 6-year-old boy do? Several tactics are available: keep trying, ask the teacher for help, or have a temper tantrum. The child with poor self-regulation is likely to do the last of these.

Several studies of school-age children and adolescents have demonstrated a strong relationship between different aspects of executive functions and aggressive and antisocial behavior (A. B. Morgan & Lilienfeld, 2000; Nigg, Quamma, Greenberg, & Kusche, 1999; Séguin, Tremblay, Boulerice, Pihl, & Harden, 1999; Tremblay, 2003). Deficits in executive function have also been shown for disruptive and "problem" preschoolers (Hughes, Dunn, & White, 1998; Hughes, White, Sharpen, & Dunn, 2000; Speltz, DeKlyen, Calderon, Greenberg, & Fisher, 1999; Tremblay, 2003). According to Nigg and Huan-Pollock (2003), youngsters with executive function deficiencies, in addition to having self-regulation problems, probably have difficulty in foreseeing consequences of behavior and in the development of empathy.

Self-Regulation Skills

In their relationships with adults, children begin to acquire tools that enable them to control their behavior in numerous ways. They gain increasing control over their attention, emotions, and behavior. Together, this set of skills is known as self-regulation. Difficulty regulating negative emotions is strongly related to aggression and violence. For the average child, self-control begins to emerge in the second year, as does the concern and empathetic feelings for others. Children are expected to become reasonably compliant with parent requests and to internalize the family and cultural standards for behavior. This aspect of self-control begins to emerge in the third year of life, or between 2 and 3 years of age.

Self-regulation also involves children being able to direct their attention, "enabling them to shift or focus their attention more readily or to persist in attending, skills that will help them function in [a] classroom or a play activity with peers" (Masten & Coatsworth, 1998, p. 208). As the child gets older, good attention regulation is associated with prosocial behavior and peer popularity. Conversely, poor self-regulation and noncompliance to the wishes of caretakers and teachers set the stage for aggressive, disruptive behavior in the classroom; academic problems; and peer rejection.

The research on self-regulation as a whole strongly suggests that these skills are extremely important for the development of resilience. They begin to emerge in early childhood and are shaped in part by a child's experiences. Thus, sensitive and consistent caregiving and warm but firm parenting styles all have been associated with the development of self-control and compliance with social rules. However, research also suggests that a child's own disposition or temperament may have an effect.

Temperament refers specifically to persistent individual differences in social and emotional responding that are believed to constitute the foundation for many personality traits later in life. As it is currently used in the research, "temperament" is assumed to (1) have a constitutional or biological basis; (2) appear in infancy and continue throughout life; and (3) be influenced by the social environment. Researchers also often refer to three broad types of child temperaments: the easy child, the slow-to-warm-up child, and the difficult child (e.g., Thomas & Chess, 1977). As noted earlier, resilient children are often described as having "sunny" temperaments or are perceived by their parents as being "easy babies," even under the most trying conditions (Aldwin, 1994). On the other hand, many chronically antisocial children tend to demonstrate "difficult" temperaments (e.g., emotional lability, restlessness, short attention span, negativism, roughness) as young children (Lösel & Bender, 2003; Moffitt, Caspi, Dickson, Silva, & Stanton, 1996). "An easy temperament makes interaction with caregivers smooth, and is also reinforced. In contrast, children with a difficult temperament are more frequently targets of parental criticism, irritability, and hostility" (Lösel & Bender, 2003, p. 152). A difficult temperament becomes particularly problematic when parents lack financial and social resources,

are under stress or pressure, and lack the knowledge or skill for dealing with the difficult child.

Although temperament is present at birth, it must be emphasized that its manifestations can be quickly modified by the social environment, especially by parents and significant caregivers. Difficult temperaments can be challenging, but a nurturing and warm caregiver environment in which rules are firmly laid out can prevent, change, or eliminate antisocial behavior in children.

Positive Emotions

Emotions influence how children perceive and respond to others and events. Emotions can inspire the child or discourage him or her from taking action, and they contribute to or disrupt our interpersonal relationships (Lagattuta & Wellman, 2002). Positive emotions—which include joy, interest, contentment, pride, and love—all share the ability to build a child's enduring personal resources (Fredrickson, 2001). Negative emotions include hostility, anger, anxiety, sadness, and despair. Positive emotions and positive beliefs are important ingredients for building psychological resilience. Even though highly resilient children and adolescents may experience high levels of anxiety and frustration under stressful or pressure situations, their reliance on positive emotions to adapt to these conditions is very effective in their long-term coping (Tugade & Frederickson, 2004).

One way children and adolescents may experience positive emotions in the face of adversity is by finding positive meaning in ordinary events and within the adversity itself (Folkman & Moskowitz, 2000; Fredrickson, 2001). The belief and the emotion are reciprocal. Not only does finding positive meaning trigger positive emotion, but also positive emotions, because they broaden thinking, should increase the likelihood of finding positive meaning in subsequent events, even highly negative ones (Fredrickson, 2001). Youths who experience more positive emotions than others, become more resilient to adversity over time.

Motivational Factors

Psychologists have long distinguished between intrinsic and extrinsic motivation. Intrinsic motivation refers to behavior provoked by pleasure and enjoyment, whereas extrinsic motivation is behavior encouraged by external pressures or constraints (Henderlong & Lepper, 2002). Intrinsic motivation is doing something because it is enjoyed for its own sake, such as doing a puzzle or creating a painting. Extrinsic motivation is doing something in order to receive rewards from others, such as in hopes of receiving a gift or money. Resilient children tend to demonstrate significant amounts of intrinsic motivation. Although it is well-known that praise encourages intrinsic motivation, the kind and quality of the praise is very important. Specifically, intrinsic motivation is most effectively encouraged and developed through praise that encourages competence and self-efficacy. In other words, the child is praised for attempts at mastery over something, such as puzzle-solving ability, language development, or reading activity. On the other hand, praise that is based primarily on social comparisons—ranking the child or making comparisons to the performance or abilities of others—is problematic. Not surprisingly, schools and what transpires within them are often targeted by resilience researchers. For example, in the classroom an emphasis on social comparison necessitates that some children receive positive feedback while others receive negative feedback. As Henderlong and Lepper note, "After all, not everyone can be at the top of the class" (p. 785). Thus, praise based solely on social comparison may, in the long run, not be helpful. It may leave children unprepared for the eventual and inevitable negative feedback they are bound to experience as they progress through school.

PREVENTION AND INTERVENTION

With increasing awareness of the protective factors that promote resilience in children and adolescence, theorists, researchers, and policy makers are now attempting to apply this knowledge toward the prevention and intervention of antisocial behavior. Prevention programs that promote cognitive and social competencies in the child or adolescent and improve childrearing practices in the family, and the development and maintenance of effective social support systems are most likely to be effective in the long run. As Ann Masten (2001) writes, "The great threats to human development are those that jeopardize the systems underlying these adaptive processes, including brain development and cognition, caregiver–child relationships, regulation of emotion and behavior, and the motivation for learning and engaging in the environment" (p. 234).

Strategies include the enhancement of a child's strengths and interests, as well as the reduction of risk or stressors, and the facilitation of protective processes. Overall, the rallying cry for many programs focusing on enhancing resilience has become, "Every child has talents, strengths, and interests that offer the child potential for a bright future" (Damon, 2004, p. 13). These attitudes reflect a major transformation in the conceptualization of prevention of antisocial behavior and other childhood problems over the past decades.

There is little doubt that living conditions in the poorest inner city neighborhoods are extremely harsh and the daily onslaught of violence, substance abuse, racism, child abuse, and hopelessness are highly disruptive to a child's normal development. For many children who are exposed to an adverse family life and inadequate living arrangements, with little opportunity to develop even the rudiments of social and interpersonal skills for dealing effectively with others, the damage may be irreparable. Clearly, the longer a child is exposed to this adverse environment, the more difficult it may be to modify his or her life course away from crime and delinquency. Hence, successive intervention programs must not only begin as early as possible, but also must be intensively directed at as many causes and negative influences as possible. Nancy Guerra and her colleagues (Guerra, Huesmann, Tolan, Van Acker, & Eron, 1995) recommend that interventions begin no later in life than the first grade (before age 8). In addition, there is evidence to suggest that the earlier the signs of antisocial behavior, the more serious or violent the antisocial behavior or delinquency will be later (Tolan & Thomas, 1995).

As we have seen, for any program to be truly effective it must go beyond merely affecting the child him- or herself, but must affect the whole social context within which he or she is developing. Research has continually shown that the most successful interventions concentrate on the family—including all members (e.g., siblings, grandparents, uncles and aunts) if possible. As discussed earlier, certain family relationships and parenting practices are strongly related to serious antisocial behavior. More important, these family characteristics seem to be linked to delinquency regardless of ethnic or socioeconomic status (Gorman-Smith, Tolan, Zelli, & Huesmann, 1996). The family characteristics most closely associated with serious delinquency are poor parental monitoring of the child's activities, poor and inconsistent discipline, and a lack of family closeness or cohesion. Research indicates that emotional closeness and family cohesion, where the child receives emotional support, adequate communication, and love, are essential in the prevention of antisocial behavior and serious delinquency (Gorman-Smith et al., 1996).

There is no single means of maintaining equilibrium following highly aversive events, but rather there are multiple pathways to resilience (Bonanno, 2004). For example, McKnight and Loper (2002) found that the most prominent resilience factors in adolescent girls at risk for delinquency were an academic motivation and a desire to go to college, absence of substance abuse, feeling loved and wanted, belief that teachers treat students fairly, parents trusting adolescent children, and religiosity.

Waaktaar et al. (2004) conducted a study to explore how resilience or protective factors could be used to help at-risk youths. The youth averaged 12.3 years of age, and a little over a third were girls. They represented a medley of cultural and ethnic backgrounds, including the

West Indies, Far East, Central Asia, the Arab world, and northeast Africa. All the participants had experienced serious or multiple life stresses and, at the time of the study, were not receiving "satisfactory help" through "psychiatric" intervention.

The researchers targeted four resilience factors for therapeutic intervention: positive peer relations, self-efficacy, creativity, and coherence. Positive peer relations were defined as prosocial interactions, peer acceptance, and support. Self-efficacy is the belief that one can achieve desired goals through one's own actions (Bandura, 1989, 1997). Creativity in this context refers to individual talent to create an artistic or other communicative product, such as a song, dance, film, play, poem, or short story. This approach requires that children be encouraged to express themselves and their experiences symbolically. Coherence refers to the ways in which people cognitively and emotionally appraise themselves and their circumstances. It involves "helping young people to find a coherent meaning to their past, present, and future life through positive thinking, accepting the reality of their bad experiences, avoiding self-blame for uncontrollable circumstances and finding adaptive paths forward" (Waaktaar et al., 2004, p. 173). The researchers discovered that child therapy that focuses on these four concepts has the potential to enhance resilience significantly.

A deeper understanding of resilience can be greatly facilitated by consideration of cultural and ethnic factors (Barbarin, 1993). Ethnic group identity, both within the family and neighborhood, are essential components of any explanatory model or prevention program. Factors and characteristics delineated with one population of children cannot be attributed directly to another culturally and ethnically different population of children (Hampson, Rahman, Brown, Taylor, & Donaldson, 1998). Programs that have shown long-term success have utilized multipronged approaches concentrating on treating children through their broad social environment, and with particular sensitivity to the family's cultural background and heritage. Intervention programs that neglect the gender, ethnicity, socioeconomic status, and other demographic markers that affect the development of antisocial behavior are destined to fail. Even poverty may affect individuals differently on the basis of their ethnicity and the meaning of poverty within a given cultural context (Guerra et al., 1995).

An excellent illustration of a culturally sensitive program developed for resilience development is Project SELF, a school curriculum designed to promote self-esteem, self-efficacy, and improved problem-solving skills in inner city fourth-grade black children through a culturally based curriculum (Hampson et al., 1998). The researchers write, "Using a pre/post evaluation design with a control group, we demonstrated that students who received the program exhibited greater improved knowledge of the curriculum, elevated self-esteem, a greater sense of self-efficacy, and improved long-term consequential thinking skills as compared to controls" (p. 24). What really made the difference, the researchers concluded, was the program's focus on "the students' own ancestral history, biology, beliefs and values, choices and potential" throughout the curriculum (p. 27). In order to improve resilience, the researchers reasoned, a minority child must touch base with his or her cultural or ethnic identity.

Notably lacking in existing research on resilience is the role played by biology and genetic factors (Luthar et al., 2000). It is clear that biological factors affect psychological processes, and psychological processes in turn affect biological factors. It may be that resilience is strongly affected by genetic or biological predispositions, whereas resilience may be more strongly affected by the social environment. Therefore, effective intervention programs should also include prenatal and perinatal medical care, and intensive health education for pregnant women and mothers with young children. These services reduce the delinquency risk factors of head and neurological injuries, exposure to toxins, maternal substance abuse, nutritional deficiencies, and perinatal difficulties.

Problems

Over the past few years, research has shifted away from simply identifying protective factors and has focused more on trying to understand the underlying protective processes (Luthar et al., 2000). Consequently, rather than studying which child, family, or environmental factors are involved in resilience, the recent emphasis has been attempts to understand how such factors may contribute to it. As researchers have identified the characteristics of resilience and determined the forces of the social environment that contribute to resilience, there has also been a discernible shift to build and strengthen programs that enhance and foster the development of protective mechanisms. However, although resilience studies have been able to indicate clear risk and protective factors in human development, the knowledge of exactly how these factors work is still lacking (Waaktaar et al., 2004). Perhaps even more challenging is how these systems can be most effectively implemented in working with at-risk children.

One of the many questions that need to be answered revolves around the multidimensional nature of resilience. Can we expect, for instance, at-risk children who demonstrate resilience in one area to show a comparable resilience in other areas? If an at-risk child does well in school, can we expect that same child to demonstrate positive outcomes in his or her social or emotional life to the same degree? So far, the research suggests a tentative "yes" to both questions. A very promising feature of effective intervention, for example, seems to be that improvement in one resilience characteristic of a child is likely to also affect other resilience factors in that child, creating what are called "positive chain reactions" by clinicians (Waaktaar et al., 2004).

A sobering problem, however, is reflected in a recent report summing up several decades of resource-enhancing preventive interventions, such as the Head Start project. Intervention effects tend to persist only as long as the intervention continues, "and only 'magic' will help if the intervention does not address the basic problems of poverty, illness, parental dysfunction, high-risk neighborhoods and unemployment" (Waaktaar et al., 2004, p. 179).

SUMMARY AND CONCLUSIONS

This overview examined why some children and adolescents do not engage in serious, violent antisocial behavior—despite being exposed to a multitude of risk factors—while other youths begin their persistent criminal careers after being exposed to similar risk conditions. The article focused on the numerous protective factors that may shield at-risk youngsters from the onset of antisocial behavior, and how these factors can contribute to the development of prevention and intervention programs. This review also suggested ways to enhance these protective factors through the development of resilience in children and adolescents.

The number of intervention, prevention, and treatment programs that have been tried on children at risk for delinquency and antisocial behavior is overwhelming. For many years, very few were shown to be effective or have long-term, lasting effects. Part of the problem is that so many of them concentrated on reducing risk factors, to the exclusion of building on protective factors and resilience. Risk factors (e.g., poverty, poor health services, violent neighborhoods) are often societal problems that cannot be easily rectified without considerable political clout, influence, and enormous financial resources.

However, there is mounting evidence that prevention programs that are carefully designed and implemented can be effective in preventing antisocial behavior in children and adolescents (Nation et al., 2003). The research indicates that most effective programs for dealing with at-risk children and preadolescents should focus on the development of resilience (Lösel & Bender, 2003).

Programs that are most successful for dealing with at-risk children are appropriately timed, socioculturally relevant, comprehensive, and use varied teaching methods (Nation et al., 2003). Programs that are "appropriately timed" provide interventions that occur in a child's life when they will have maximal impact. In most cases, interventions should begin early, usually before preschool or at school entry. Successful programs are also not based on "one size fits all" but

are sensitive to cultural, ethnic, and geographical differences and needs (Castro, 2005). Each child has his or her unique way of viewing the world through the lens of cultural and linguistic experiences. For any intervention program to be successful, it must build on these differences (Bartol & Bartol, 2004a). Programs that are comprehensive target the development of cognitive, language, and social skills. Varied teaching methods involve interactive instruction designed to provide active, hands-on experiences that increase the child's skills and self-confidence. Providing opportunities for children to develop strong, positive relationships is consistently associated with positive outcomes and resilience building.

We have much knowledge about what needs to be done, but often this knowledge is not implemented into programs across the country. One of the more prominent problems in implementation is that there is a gap between the science-based prevention programs and what is provided by practitioners to families and children (Gendreau, 1996; Morrissey et al., 1997; Nation et al., 2003). Practitioners cannot afford to implement research-based programs that were developed on well-funded, university-based research grants (Nation et al., 2003). Some innovative way to bridge this gap is necessary if we are to move forward on prevention and intervention for those children at risk to become delinquent.

The resilience factors and the intervention programs that were reviewed in this chapter indicate that focusing exclusively on risk factors alone is not enough, nor is it realistic. Enhancing protective factors and developing resilience in at-risk children while reducing risk factors is far more likely to produce long-lasting, positive results. More importantly, this is a far more optimistic and hopeful approach. As noted by Lösel & Bender (2003), "being aware of protective processes and resilience may help practitioners or policymakers to counter the pessimism and resignation associated with a 'nothing-works' ideology" (p. 180). This awareness also helps policy makers decide how the limited resources should be allocated.

9

DRUGS AND SEXUAL ASSAULT

A Review

ELENA POPE

MICHELLE SHOULDICE

Recent statistical figures illustrate an alarming trend in sexual assault. According to a U.S. study, 25% of women have been sexually assaulted during their lifetime (Schwartz, 1991). In 75% of the cases, the assailant was known to the victim (National Victim Center and Crime Victims Research and Treatment, 1992). The incidence is even higher in adolescents and young women. One study estimated the lifetime prevalence of date rape among adolescents to be between 20% and 68% (Rickert & Wiemann, 1998). Apart from younger age, there are other demographic characteristics that have been reported to increase vulnerability to date rape, including early sexual activity, earlier age of menarche, past history of sexual abuse or prior victimization, and higher acceptance of rape myths and violence toward women. An independent risk

factor seems to be the use of alcohol and drugs (Rickert & Wiemann, 1998). According to the American Academy of Forensic Sciences, one third of cases of sexual assault occurred in the context of alcohol use (Li, 1999). Other studies quote that more than 75% of the perpetrators and more than 50% of the victims had been consuming alcohol before the assault (Koss, 1984; Koss & Dinero, 1989; LeBeau et al., 1999). The effects of alcohol may contribute to misinterpretation of friendly cues as sexual invitation, decreased coping mechanisms, and inability to defend against an attack (Rickert & Wiemann, 1998).

But alcohol is not the only substance associated with sexual assault. Various drugs have recently been reported to be used in association with sexual assault by an acquaintance (LeBeau et al., 1999). All of these drugs have a similar clinical profile:

Editors' Note: This article first appeared in *Trauma, Violence, & Abuse*, Vol. 2, No. 1, January 2001, pp. 51–55. Reprinted with permission of Sage Publications.

rapid onset of action and ability to induce sedation and anterograde amnesia (inability to recall events after ingestion). Moreover, their formulation is such that they can be added to drinks without the victim's knowledge (K. M. Smith, 1999). When used in combination with alcohol, potential for central nervous system (CNS) depression (sedation) increases and so does the risk of sexual assault (Le Beau et al., 1999).

FLUNITRAZEPAM (ROHYPNOL)

Rohypnol is a fast acting benzodiazepine, 10 times more potent than diazepam (Valium) (Matilla & Larni, 1980). Its effects consist of rapid induction of sleep (hypnotic effect), sedation, and muscle relaxation (Simmons & Cupp, 1998). These effects, coupled with anterograde amnesia and relatively low cost, make Rohypnol very attractive for a potential perpetrator (Calhoun, Wesson, Galloway, & Smith, 1996). The drug is not legal in Canada or the United States but is marketed in South America, Asia, and Australia by Hoffman-La Roche Pharmaceuticals. It is supplied as 0.5 mg, 1 mg, and 2 mg tablets in bubble packaging, which gives the appearance of a prescribed medication. Rohypnol is tasteless, odorless, and soluble in alcohol. Because of reports of its use as a date rape drug, a new formulation has been produced that dissolves more slowly, changes clear drinks into a bright blue color, and clouds dark beverages.

Once absorbed, Rohypnol quickly distributes into body tissues from plasma, then is metabolized and excreted mainly by the kidneys. Its half-life (time at which 50% of the drug is eliminated from the body) is about 20 hours. However, because it is readily distributed into various tissues, its clinical effects are much shorter than its half-life. Typically, Rohypnol's effects begin approximately 20 to 30 minutes post-ingestion and peak at 2 hours. Psychomotor impairment, such as delayed reaction time, muscle relaxation, and amnesia, can last up to 12 hours (Simmons & Cupp, 1998). The severity and duration of sedative effects may be accentuated by use of alcohol, carbonated beverages, and coffee (Calhoun et al., 1996).

The detection of Rohypnol is difficult. Urinary metabolites are present in very low concentration, and detection can be accomplished only within 72 hours of ingestion (K. M. Smith, 1999). Various laboratory methods have been tried to enhance the ability of detection. Recently, a sensitive assay using a gas chromatography/mass spectrometry (GC-MS) technique was developed with a limit of detection of 2 ng/mL (LeBeau et al., 1999; Simmons & Cupp, 1998). When submitting a victim's urine sample, one has to be familiar with the capabilities of the laboratory used or, ideally, submit specimens to specialized laboratories.

GHB

GHB is also known as gamma-hydroxybutyrateor sodium oxylate. It is currently available legally only as an investigational drug for the treatment of narcolepsy. Between 1996 and 1999, the Drug Enforcement Administration (DEA) received 22 reports of sexual assaults committed under the influence of GHB (K. M. Smith, 1999).

GHB causes CNS depression (sedation) secondary to direct action at the brain receptor level (GABAb). The initial symptoms, occurring 15 to 30 minutes after ingestion, consist of drowsiness, confusion, and dizziness. Rapid decrease in level of consciousness (even coma), vomiting, and respiratory depression may follow (K. M. Smith, 1999). Occasionally, patients experience terrifying hallucinations and paranoia. As with Rohypnol, anterograde amnesia is common, which may limit the victim's ability to provide detailed recall of the assault. The spectrum of clinical symptoms is dose dependent. Doses of 10 mg/kg induce amnesia and somnolence, whereas doses exceeding 50 mg/kg can lead to coma and severe respiratory depression ("Gamma-Hydroxy Butyrate Use," 1997). The sedative effects may be enhanced by the use of alcohol or other drugs.

The usual formulation of GHB is a white powder that can be added to any liquid. The resultant solution is colorless and odorless with a mild salty or soapy taste. The onset of action is short (15 to 30 minutes). Sedation may last a few hours, with full recovery approximately 8 hours after ingestion. Occasionally, dizziness may last up to 2 weeks (K. M. Smith, 1999).

Given the short half-life (20 minutes to 1 hour) of GHB, detection is very difficult. Urine assays using GC-MS can detect GHB in certain laboratories if done within 12 hours of ingestion of the drug (LeBeau et al., 1999; K. M. Smith, 1999).

KETAMINE

Ketamine is a general anesthetic used widely in medicine. Its illicit use has been reported, and DEA received at least one case report in which Ketamine was used to facilitate sexual assault (K. M. Smith, 1999).

The major effects of Ketamine consist of analgesia (decreased pain) and amnesia, with an onset approximately 20 minutes after ingestion. Higher doses may lead to a feeling of detachment from the surroundings and floating. Hallucinations and rapid eye movements (nystagmus) have also been reported (K. M. Smith, 1999). Intravenous as well as oral preparations are available. The standard anesthetic dose is 2mg/kg intravenously or 5 to 10 mg/kg intramuscularly. The dosage used for illicit purposes is unknown. Ketamine undergoes extensive hepatic (liver) metabolism and elimination by the kidneys.

Currently, there is no available detection test.

MDMA (ECSTASY)

Ecstasy is a synthetic chemical derived from an essential oil of the sassafras tree. Merck first synthesized this chemical in 1912. Given the psychotherapeutic effects and its growing popularity, Ecstasy became illegal in the United States in 1985. Currently, it is a very popular drug, particularly at rave parties. Because of the big demand,

anything can be sold as Ecstasy, with potentially serious results.

Ecstasy's effects consist of euphoria, disinhibition, and dizziness. Other symptoms described in association with Ecstasy are nystagmus (involuntary eye movements) and hallucinations (Morland, 2000). Dangerous effects associated with it derive from hyperthermia (increased body temperature) leading to dehydration, hyponatremia (decreased body salt), seizures, and irregular cardiac rhythm (Ajaelo, Koenig, & Snoey, 1998).

MDMA (Ecstasy) is readily absorbed and starts acting approximately 30 to 60 minutes after its ingestion. The peak effects tend to occur at around 1 to 5 hours, with symptoms lasting up to 8 hours depending on the ingested amount. It is metabolized in the liver and eliminated by the kidneys as an active metabolite usually within 24 hours after intake. The hallucinogenic effects are typically seen in doses ranging from 50 to 150 mg.

The presence of the drug can qualitatively be detected in blood and urine by using methods such as thin layer chromatography and gas or gas-liquid chromatography (Jurado, Gimenez, Soriano, Menendez, & Repetto, 2000). However, because various labs have different detectable concentration limits, consultation with laboratory staff should occur.

CONCLUSION

Date rape is a common occurrence, especially among young women and adolescents. Drugs and/or alcohol may be used with the intention of decreasing resistance to the assault by causing sedation as well as by decreasing detailed recollection of the events by the victim because of induced amnesia.

The most common substances reported in association with sexual assault are alcohol, cocaine, and marijuana. This is not surprising because they make up a great majority of street drugs. However, other drugs such as Rohypnol, GHB, Ketamine, and Ecstasy have recently been associated with sexual assault, probably because of their amnesic potential. All of these drugs share several features: CNS depression (sedation), impaired judgment, impaired memory, decreased motor control, and decreased inhibition. Depending on the dose of the drug and/or use of other substances (especially alcohol), clinical effects can be significant enough to lead to respiratory depression, irregular heart rhythm, and coma.

The possession, sale, or use of most of these drugs is a criminal offense in most of the United States and in Canada. Hence, the detection of these drugs is of paramount importance, particularly given the victim's frequent difficulty recollecting the events surrounding the assault or the details about the perpetrator. Detection of these drugs may be problematic because of limitations in laboratory testing methods. The short half-life of these drugs, in combination with a victim who may not seek medical attention immediately due to an inability to recall events, may make detection of these drugs even more problematic. A recent review suggested

a standard protocol for specimen collection in rape victims (LeBeau et al., 1999). This includes a specimen collection as soon as possible after the event. Urine specimens should be obtained within 72 to 96 hours after ingestion and kept refrigerated. Blood specimens are less useful. It is important to know that, with the exception of Ecstasy, standard toxicology screening rarely detects substances potentially used in sexual assault, and specific testing must be requested. A high index of suspicion is therefore recommended, particularly in sexual assault cases when the victim reports sedation or an inability to recall events clearly. Blood analysis is possible if collection is obtained within 24 hours of the assault and the specimen is collected in a tube with sodium fluoride or potassium oxalate preservative. The testing request should specify what substance is suspected. Knowledge about a laboratory's ability to detect these substances is very important.

10

Is It Stalking?

Perceptions of Stalking Among College Undergraduates

Lorraine Phillips

Ryan Quirk

Barry Rosenfeld

Maureen O'Connor

As public interest in stalking crimes grew during the past decade, critics have increasingly pointed to the ambiguity ("vagueness") present in most legal definitions of stalking (e.g., Jordan, Quinn, Jordan, & Daileader, 2000; Mullen, Pathé, & Purcell, 2000). For example, California's anti-stalking law specifies that the behavior must "be such as would cause a reasonable person to suffer substantial emotional consequence" (California Penal Code, Section § 646.9, 1990). Even New York's recent anti-stalking law, developed long after concerns regarding definitional ambiguity had been raised and

litigated, requires that the victim must experience a "reasonable fear of material harm" from the stalker for the behaviors to qualify as "stalking" (New York Criminal Procedure Law, Section § 120.45, 1999; Pappas, 2000). But despite attempts to define the contours of stalking, these laws offer little, if any, guidance as to what behaviors would qualify as inducing a "reasonable fear" or engendering "substantial emotional harm." Indeed, the same behaviors could be interpreted as frightening by one individual yet seem flattering or absurd to another (Jordan et al., 2000). How, then, does one determine whether a stalker's actions meet the

Editors' Note: This article was originally published in *Criminal Justice and Behavior*, Vol. 31, No. 1, February 2004, pp. 73–96. Reprinted with permission of Sage Publications. We have omitted portions of the literature review and the results sections of both studies discussed herein.

legal requirement for criminal prosecution or even constitute stalking in lay terms?

Despite the importance of understanding individual differences in perceptions of stalking, research has rarely focused on understanding the factors that influence these perceptions. At one extreme of this continuum are the occasional reports, although largely anecdotal, of false accusations of stalking, often termed "false victimization syndrome" (Mohandie, Hatcher, & Raymond, 1996; Pathé, Mullen, & Purcell, 1999; Sheridan & Blaauw, 2004). On the other hand, many stalking victims fail to recognize or interpret the harassment they are subjected to as "stalking," and therefore, they neglect to seek appropriate help or take protective measures that might be necessary. More critically, third-party observers, such as police officers or coworkers, may find it particularly difficult to perceive the behavior as sufficiently threatening to the target to constitute stalking. Even when stalking or harassment is accurately recognized, individual reactions vary tremendously, with some stalking victims moving to another state and changing their identity and others continuing their lives seemingly without significant interference. Clearly, perceptions of the risk posed by a stalker play a central role in determining how an individual should react. These same perceptions will also determine the efficacy of stalking laws as law enforcement officials, prosecutors, judges, and, ultimately, jurors must also evaluate whether particular behaviors rise to the level of unlawful stalking.

Although early attention to stalking focused largely on celebrity victims and gradually expanded to the general public, stalking has only recently been identified as a significant problem plaguing college students. Several studies have observed high rates of stalking among college students that far exceed the prevalence rates found in the general population (e.g., Bjerregaard, 2000; Fremouw, Westrup, & Pennypacker, 1997; Haugaard & Seri, 2000). For example, Fremouw and his colleagues reported that 27% of the women and 15% of men in their sample of West Virginia University students had been stalked. Bjerregaard found a comparable rate of stalking among college students; 25% of the women in her sample and 11% of the men reported this experience. Not surprisingly, female victims in Bjerregaard's sample were more likely than males to be threatened by their stalker and were also more likely to express fear for their physical safety. In fact, female stalking victims reported twice the level of fear compared to male victims, even when they had received similar threatening communications.

Despite the importance of victim perceptions in both defining and reacting to stalking, very little research has attempted to identify factors that influence these perceptions. Hills and Taplin (1998) studied the perceptions of Australian adults in response to a stalking vignette that varied across two dimensions, the nature of the perpetrator–target relationship . . . and the presence or absence of an implicit threat. . . . Interestingly, despite a growing body of research demonstrating that stalkers who were previously involved in an intimate relationship with the target of their harassment (i.e., "former intimates") are more likely to be violent than are offenders who target strangers (e.g., Rosenfeld, 2003), both categories of targets reported fear, but the likelihood of calling the police was significantly greater in response to the "stranger" vignette. The presence of a threat, on the other hand, had no impact on perceived fear, but it did correspond to an increased likelihood of calling the police. . . .

Dennison and Thomson (2000) also studied a large sample of Australian adults ($N = 540$) in their investigation of the influence of situational variables on determinations of stalking and perceptions of the perpetrator's intentions. They, too, studied perpetrator–target relationship (strangers, acquaintances, or former intimates), the intent of the perpetrator (whether there was explicit evidence of actions that would instill fear or cause emotional harm), and the impact this behavior had on the victim (extreme fear, moderate fear, or no fear). . . .

In a subsequent study, Dennison and Thomson (2002) expanded this methodology in a study of 1,080 Australian adults by adding an additional variable—that is, perpetrator persistence. Because their previous study utilized a vignette in which perpetrators were highly persistent, they added two additional conditions describing perpetrators whose actions reflected either moderate or low levels of persistence. As in their previous study, the vast majority of respondents (83%) characterized the behavior described in the vignette as stalking, but they found a significant difference across gender, with 86% of women labeling the vignette as stalking compared to 78% of men. Not surprisingly, degree of persistence and the presence of specific intent were significantly associated with the determination that stalking had occurred. They also found that women were more likely than men to perceive the perpetrator as intending to inflict fear and cause physical or mental harm to the target. Although they also observed a number of effects for perpetrator–target relationship, these associations were more complex (often taking the form of interaction effects). However, because their vignettes only depicted a male perpetrator and a female victim, the extent to which these gender effects reflect a greater concern or awareness of stalking on the part of women in general versus a greater concern for the potential violence inflicted by males is unknown. Moreover, in many analyses, the magnitude of the gender effects they observed was relatively modest. Nevertheless, the authors concluded that the factors that influence perceptions of stalking might be more complex than had been previously thought.

Interestingly, analogous research literature focusing on sexual harassment perceptions has evolved over the past decade that has examined the influence of individual- and situational-level variables on determinations of whether behaviors were perceived as sexual harassment. Fairly consistently, gender of the participant plays a small but significant role in explaining sexual harassment judgments (e.g., Gutek et al., 1999; Rotundo, Nguyen, & Sackett, 2001; . . .). But this gender effect may also be explained by sexist attitudes and perceptions of the target's credibility (see Wiener & Hurt, 1999). Interestingly, a target's prior personal experience with sexual harassment does not appear to influence sexual

harassment perceptions (Stockdale, O'Connor, Gutek, & Geer, 2002).

The sexual harassment literature shares many similarities [with] the emerging research on perceptions of stalking and provides a context for understanding the gender effects found in both literatures. In an effort to supplement this small but growing body of research, the current investigations focused on whether behaviors would be more or less likely to be considered stalking depending on situational factors . . . and participant characteristics. . . . In the first of these studies, the behavior of the perpetrator was described in a relatively ambiguous manner to increase the variability of subjective perceptions as to whether the vignette described stalking and whether a risk of harm existed, whereas the second study systematically manipulated the seriousness of the behavior.

Specifically, it was hypothesized that female participants and those who report having previously been the target of stalking would be more likely to label the vignettes as "stalking" and would associate greater risks to the perpetrators' behavior. In addition, the impact of terminology (i.e., use of the term stalking versus a description of repetitive harassment behaviors) on reports of whether one has been stalked was explored. In the second study, similar effects regarding participant gender were hypothesized (i.e., female participants would be more likely than men to label the vignettes as stalking), although it was anticipated that the proportion of participants labeling the vignettes as stalking would increase as the severity of the behaviors increased. Both studies also hypothesized that vignettes describing a male perpetrator and a female target would be readily classified as stalking and would generate higher levels of safety concerns.

EXPERIMENT 1

Method

Participants were students in introductory psychology classes at a large private university in the northeast United States; the students volunteered for this study as a method of fulfilling the course research requirement. Participants were informed that they would be participating in a study of perceptions of behavior in which they would read a series of vignettes and answer several questions that pertained to each. Each participant received a questionnaire packet that contained one of six stalking vignettes, all of which described interactions between a male and a female using a 2×3 design to vary gender of the perpetrator and target (male perpetrator pursuing a female target and female perpetrator pursuing a male target) and the relationship between these individuals (stranger, acquaintance, and a previous romantic relationship or former intimate). Table 10.1 presents examples of these vignettes. Participants also completed a brief demographic questionnaire, and they read and responded to two additional vignettes with accompanying questions that served as a filler to distract attention from the stalking vignette.

After reading the vignette, participants indicated their reactions to a series of questions using a Likert-type scale from 1 *(definitely)* to 5 *(definitely not)*. These questions included whether the behavior described in the vignette constituted stalking . . . , whether the target should be worried about his or her safety, whether the target should meet with the perpetrator, whether the perpetrator would become violent, whether the target should seek help from the police or security, and whether the perpetrator needs psychiatric treatment. To ease interpretation of the data, responses to several of these questions were reversed so that a higher score on all variables reflected a greater degree of concern over the perpetrator's behavior.

Participants were also asked several questions that pertained to their personal experiences with stalking. The wording in the primary question used to assess prior stalking victimization was also varied to ascertain whether the term *stalking* influenced perceptions of one's own experiences. Toward this end, half of the participants were asked whether they had "ever been stalked," and the remainder were asked whether they had "ever been repeatedly followed (i.e., more than once) and/or harassed by another person." Participants who responded affirmatively to this question

Table 10.1   Sample Stalking Vignettes: Experiment 1

Prior intimate relationship. Jane and Joe, both of whom are doctors, had been dating for several months. Joe realized that things were not working out in the relationship and decided that it would be best to break up with Jane. Jane, however, wanted to continue the relationship. Since the breakup, Jane has called Joe several times, but he no longer answers her phone calls. Jane has also sent flowers and other gifts to Joe's house along with personal letters. Lately, Joe thinks that he has seen Jane outside his house.

Acquaintance. Jane is a doctor in a large hospital where Joe, another doctor, was recently hired. Shortly after meeting Jane, Joe became interested in pursuing a relationship with her. Joe called Jane on the telephone, but she indicated that she was not interested in a relationship. Since then, Joe has called Jane several times, but she no longer answers his phone calls. Joe has also sent flowers and other gifts to Jane's house along with personal letters. Lately, Jane thinks that she has seen Joe outside her house.

Stranger (no prior relationship). Joe, a doctor, was interviewed by the local news after his hospital announced that it would be laying off employees. Jane, a doctor too, saw Joe on television being interviewed. Jane found Joe to be very attractive and was interested in pursuing a relationship with him. Jane called Joe on the telephone, but he indicated that he was not interested in a relationship. Since then, Jane has called Joe several times, but he no longer answers her phone calls. Jane has also sent flowers and other gifts to Joe's house along with personal letters. Lately, Joe thinks that he has seen a woman outside his house.

were asked to provide details regarding the stalking experience, including the number of times they have been stalked . . . , the length of time this behavior continued, and the occurrence of several specific stalking behaviors (e.g., receiving unwanted gifts, waiting outside of work or school, etc.).

***

DISCUSSION

The results of this study contradicted our hypothesis that female participants would be more likely to label the vignettes as stalking compared to male participants. Moreover, there was no difference in perceptions of whether the behavior described constituted stalking between vignettes describing a male perpetrator and female target versus a female perpetrator and male target (although the three-way interaction effect suggests that some complex relationships between character gender and perpetrator–target relationship may exist). This interaction clearly requires further analysis before any conclusions can be drawn. Finally, there was no relationship between prior experience as a target of stalking and perceptions of stalking, again contradicting commonsense assumptions regarding the influence of past experience on perceptions of behavior. This null finding, however, is consistent with the emerging literature on perceptions of sexual harassment, which demonstrate that prior sexual harassment victimization does not influence perceptions of whether behaviors constitute sexual harassment (Stockdale et al., 2002).

Despite the compelling findings observed in this study, a number of questions arose, such as whether young, predominantly Caucasian undergraduates are an appropriate reference group against which to base conclusions regarding stalking perceptions. In addition, because the behaviors described in these vignettes were deliberately vague, it is unclear whether similar findings would emerge if the behaviors described were more strongly suggestive of stalking. These

limitations were addressed in the subsequent study in which vignettes varied according to the severity of the stalking behaviors described (rather than the relationship between perpetrator and target). This study also included a substantially larger sample with considerably greater diversity in terms of ethnicity, age, and socioeconomic levels.

EXPERIMENT 2

Method

Participants in the second study consisted of 376 undergraduate and graduate students in an urban, public college that has the primary mission to provide undergraduate and graduate training in criminal justice and related fields. Participants were recruited through undergraduate and graduate classes. Each participant was given one of six possible vignettes that described an interaction between a man and a woman (Tom and Mary) who met at a party. Based on the New York State anti-stalking law, three scenarios depicting potential stalking behavior were developed. One scenario depicted behaviors that did not meet the definition of stalking under New York State law, while a second scenario depicted behaviors that were consistent with stalking in the fourth degree (misdemeanor stalking), and the third scenario depicted behaviors that were consistent with stalking in the third degree (felony stalking). Each of these scenarios was built on the previous one such that the length of each scenario became slightly longer as the criminality of the perpetrator's behaviors increased (Table 10.2). Finally, two versions of each of these three scenarios were created—one describing a male perpetrator and a female victim and a second describing the reverse scenario, thus resulting in a total of six conditions.

After reading the vignette, participants indicated their reactions to a series of questions using a 5-point, Likert-type scale where 1 = *definitely* and 5 = *definitely not*. These questions included whether the behavior described in the vignette constituted stalking . . ., whether the behavior would be considered a crime (specifically, stalking under New York law), whether the perpetrator has a legitimate purpose for contacting the target, whether the target should be worried about his or her safety, whether the perpetrator would become violent, and whether the perpetrator suffered from mental illness. Participants were also asked about their own familiarity level with New York anti-stalking law along with a series of demographic questions.

DISCUSSION

This study further supported the earlier findings regarding the lack of any influence of either participant or perpetrator/target gender on perceptions of whether stalking has occurred. On the other hand, these data supported the previous finding that vignettes describing a male perpetrator and female target elicited greater concerns regarding safety than vignettes describing a female perpetrator and a male target. Contrary to the expectations, female participants were no more likely than male participants to label the vignettes as stalking. However, these results support the distinctions made by New York State's anti-stalking law, as participants were more likely to correctly identify both of the vignettes describing fourth-degree stalking and third-degree stalking as stalking as compared to the no-stalking condition (but no significant differences existed between the two stalking vignettes). Interestingly, although few differences in perceptions were observed across ethnic groups, there was no identifiable pattern to these findings, and the relatively small number of participants in some categories limits the ability to interpret these findings.

Table 10.2   Study Two: Sample Vignettes With Conditions Embedded—Tom Pursuing Mary

(Paragraph 1) *All conditions.* Tom met Mary at a party that a mutual friend hosted. They talked for a while at the party before going their separate ways. Mary worked at the local bank as a teller. Mary noticed that Tom began coming into the bank to make transactions.

(Paragraph 2) *No stalking condition.* Usually he would wave at Mary if he saw her, and a few times, he waited specifically for Mary to help him with his transaction. After a few weeks of the same pattern, Mary was beginning to question Tom's intentions. She didn't think that anyone could possibly have as much banking to do as Tom seemed to have.

(Added to Paragraph 2) *Third- and fourth-degree stalking conditions.* Within a few weeks, Tom started calling the bank to make sure Mary was working before he came in. Mary took a week off from work and went out of town. When she came back to work her manager was very angry with her. "Some guy named Tom keeps calling at least 6 or 7 times a day to see where you are at. I told him not to call here anymore." The bank manager warned Mary that if this continued he would have to fire Mary.

(Paragraph 3) *No stalking condition.* Mary, not sure of how to reach Tom, called their mutual friend. Mary was informed that Tom is very shy but found her very easy to talk to and would like to take her out on a date. Mary called Tom and thanked him for his interest in her. She then explained that she was not interested in dating anyone but would like to remain friends with Tom. Tom agreed and told Mary that if she changed her mind to just call him.

(Added to Paragraph 3) *Third- and fourth-degree stalking conditions.* Mary also told Tom that the bank that she works for does not like its employees to receive too many personal phone calls. Mary told Tom that if it is an emergency, he is welcome to call her at the bank, but she does not want to lose her job. Tom agreed.

(Paragraph 4) *No stalking condition.* Mary still saw Tom at the bank, but now she was seeing him when she went to the market, and he was on the same bus that Mary takes to and from work. When Tom would see Mary, he would wave or smile. Mary decided to tell Tom to stop following her. When she did, Tom told her that she was nuts. "This is a small town. What market would you like me to shop in? Where do you think I should do my banking?" Mary just shrugged her shoulders and told Tom that she didn't care where he shopped or banked as long as she wasn't around. Despite confronting Tom, Mary would still see Tom when she was working or running errands, but he would not acknowledge Mary.

(Added to Paragraph 4) *Fourth-degree stalking condition.* The next day Mary came to work to find a teddy bear holding a red rose with a card signed "your special friend Tom." Later that morning. Tom called her to see if she received the gift. Mary thanked him and reiterated that she could not receive phone calls. Later that day Tom called just to say "Hi" and then called to find out if she would like to go to dinner. Mary turned Tom down and asked him to stop calling her. The next day Tom called Mary at the bank to apologize for his behavior and promised never to call again.

(Added to Paragraph 4) *Third-degree stalking condition.* The following week when Mary was leaving work, Tom was waiting in the bank parking lot. Mary ignored Tom when he said hello to her and just walked [away]. Tom became very angry and began to yell at Mary. "I don't understand you, Mary. . . . I am a really nice guy and would make you happy if you only let me. I only came here to apologize to you. Why won't you go out with me? Do you really think that you are so much better than me?. . . . Just wait. . . . It is only going to be a matter of time before you go out with me." Tom then walked away. The next day Tom called Mary at the bank to apologize for his behavior.

***

GENERAL DISCUSSION

With a growing number of anti-stalking laws defining stalking in terms of whether the individual had a "reasonable fear" of harm, the need to understand how individuals perceive stalking behaviors has become increasingly evident. These studies addressed several important aspects related to perceptions of stalking in complementary ways. In particular, these studies represent some of the first attempts to systematically analyze the extent to which stalking behaviors, victim–perpetrator relationships, and gender (of both the parties and the respondents) influence determinations of whether stalking has occurred and the potential risk posed to victims.

The first study utilized a vignette in which the determination of whether stalking had actually occurred was ambiguous. In this context, the relationship between target and perpetrator (i.e., strangers, coworker acquaintances, or former dating partners) and the gender of these actors (i.e., male perpetrator/female target vs. female perpetrator/male target) significantly influenced responses to the stalking vignettes. Specifically, participants were significantly less likely to characterize the vignette as stalking when the actors were described as having previously been involved in an intimate relationship compared to the vignette describing the two characters as having been merely acquaintances or having had no prior relationship (strangers). Interestingly, this apparent reluctance to characterize harassing behaviors as stalking when a prior relationship exists stands in contrast to the growing body of epidemiological data demonstrating that stalking is far more common among prior intimates compared to acquaintances or strangers (e.g., Budd & Mattinson, 2000; Tjaden & Thoennes, 1998).

On the other hand, although gender of the vignette characters did not influence determinations of whether stalking had occurred, it did influence perceptions of safety for the target of the behaviors. Several indicators of concern for safety differed significantly depending on the perpetrator/target gender, including whether the target should be concerned for his or her safety, should seek help from the police or hospital security, and should meet with the perpetrator. Interestingly, a question directly targeting the risk of violence (i.e., "How likely is it that Joe/Jane will be violent toward Jane/Joe?") did not differ by perpetrator/target gender, suggesting that the influence of gender on perceived risk may be somewhat subtle. Alternatively, participants may be more sensitive to fear-inducing behaviors when the target is a woman, even though they do not fear explicit assault or violence per se.

The perception of male stalkers as more dangerous than female stalkers, although clearly logical, is not consistent with the existing empirical data. Rates of violence among female stalkers have been comparable to those for males in several studies (Purcell, Pathé, & Mullen, 2001; Rosenfeld, [2003]; Rosenfeld & Harmon, 2002), and there is no evidence that the severity of violence inflicted by women stalkers is substantially less than [by] males. Yet the finding that male stalkers engender more concern than female stalkers echoes the data presented by Sinclair and Frieze (2000), who observed that men generate more fear in those individuals whom they pursue than women do, even when they do not display overt indications of aggression.

The second study utilized a similar methodology, but instead of comparing responses to an ambiguous vignette, vignettes were systematically varied in terms of the severity of stalking behavior (i.e., vignettes that did not fulfill the New York State definition of stalking vs. vignettes characterizing misdemeanor and felonious stalking). In these analyses, in which gender of the perpetrator and target were varied in a similar manner to the first study (male perpetrator/female target vs. female perpetrator/male target), severity of stalking clearly influenced determinations of whether stalking had occurred (supporting the validity of the experimental manipulation). Participants were significantly more likely to consider the behaviors described to be criminal (i.e., reflecting stalking) in the vignettes describing third- and fourth-degree stalking (felony and misdemeanor, respectively)

compared to the no-stalking vignette. There were no differences between the third- and fourth-degree stalking vignettes regarding criminality. As in the first study, perpetrator/target gender did not influence determinations of stalking but did influence safety concerns, as participants considered the stalker to be significantly more likely to harm the target when the perpetrator was male and the target was female versus the reverse scenario (female perpetrator/male target).

Gender of the participant, however, appears to have a more complex effect on stalking perceptions. In the second study, women participants were somewhat more likely to perceive the vignettes as indicative of stalking than were men, regardless of the perpetrator/target gender. This finding is similar to the gender effect found by Dennison and Thomson (2002). Yet, in the first study, no such main effect emerged. Instead, a significant three-way interaction effect between participant gender, gender of the vignette characters, and relationship of the vignette characters was found. Both men and women appeared more likely to identify the behavior described in the stranger vignette as stalking when the perpetrator was of the same gender as the participant, whereas they rated the acquaintances vignettes as more indicative of stalking when the target was of their same gender. This pattern may reflect a tendency to identify with the behavior of the perpetrator in the stranger vignettes and the target in the acquaintance vignettes, decreasing the likelihood that participants would identify the behavior described in the vignette as inappropriate (i.e., stalking). Because perpetrator–target relationship was not varied in the second study, it is unclear whether these effects would have remained consistent in cases where the stalking behaviors were more clear-cut. Thus, although there may be some differences in how men and women perceive certain aspects of stalking, these differences are quite modest and inconsistent. Also observed in the second study was an unexpected influence of ethnicity on safety concerns and attributions for the stalking behavior. Because there was no consistent pattern to these findings, their implications are unclear. Furthermore, the first study was almost entirely composed of Caucasian participants, precluding the analysis of any ethnicity effects. Clearly, these findings, which have not emerged in any of the published research to date, require further exploration.

[In the first study,] contrary to the expectations, participants who reported personal prior experience of having been stalked did not differ from those who reported no such experience in relation to perceptions of stalking or risk of harm. (These data were not available in the second study.) Although it was anticipated that participants who had been previously stalked would be more attuned to this behavior—and therefore be more likely to identify harassing behaviors as stalking—this pattern did not emerge. This null finding might reflect sample limitations, as stalking victimization among college students may be different in nature, intensity, and impact from stalking victimization among the general population (hence, the substantially higher rates of stalking victimization reported by college students compared to the general population). Individuals who have experienced more severe types of stalking than that of typical college students might have more readily identified the vignettes as indicative of stalking, whereas the college students studied in this investigation did not reveal this pattern. Alternatively, this null finding may reflect a limitation of the study methodology, as more striking differences might emerge with different vignette characteristics (e.g., more overt or potentially dangerous stalking behaviors). Yet, similar null findings regarding the lack of influence of past experience on harassment perceptions have been reported in the context of sexual harassment (Stockdale et al., 2002). Thus, although commonsense assumptions often foster the belief that past experience with harassment may sensitize targets to future harassment, these null findings call such assumptions into question.

Despite the consistency across these two studies with regard to many aspects of stalking perceptions, several methodological limitations are noteworthy. First, although there is no doubt that stalking occurs among college undergraduates,

the nature of these experiences may be quite different [from that] among the general population. However, this criticism is substantially less valid for the data reported in the second study, in which participants ranged in age from 18 to 60 and reflected a broad diversity of ethnic and socioeconomic backgrounds. Moreover, many of these findings supported and extended those of previous researchers who used samples drawn from the general public (i.e., Dennison & Thomson, 2000, 2002; Hills & Taplin, 1998), suggesting that sample differences may not have dramatically influenced the study results.

Also, although ecological validity concerns may apply to the analysis of ambiguous vignettes in the first study (i.e., the behaviors described were not indisputably reflective of stalking), this criticism does not apply to the second study, and yet similar results regarding gender effects emerged. The second study, however, utilized vignettes of varying lengths, as each vignette built on the previous one by adding additional stalking behaviors (to be consistent with the legal standards for stalking offenses in New York). Thus, the finding that increasing levels of stalking severity were associated with increased likelihood of labeling the behaviors as stalking is confounded by the amount of information presented in the vignettes. Future research should evaluate the possibility that vignette length influences perceptions of stalking.

The analysis of the perpetrator–target relationship is also necessarily limited. First, this variable was included only in the first study, and in [these vignettes], the actors were described as physicians. The characterization of the actors as credible authority figures may have decreased the likelihood that some respondents would identify the behaviors as indicative of stalking, particularly among a college student sample in which respect for authority figures may be heightened. Because this variable was not included in the second study, it is unclear whether similar relationship influences would occur in a scenario in which stalking was less ambiguous, although the results of previous research (e.g., Dennison & Thomson, 2002) suggests that the influence of situational variables may be less pronounced as the ambiguity of the behaviors decreases. Nevertheless, by varying the perceived credibility and/or prestige of the vignette characters, this potentially important determinant of participant stalking perceptions may emerge as a significant factor, either in isolation (i.e., a main effect) or in conjunction with other variables (i.e., interaction effects).

Despite these limitations, the present investigations represent one of the few attempts to analyze the interrelationships between characteristics of the harassment and characteristics of the respondents in terms of perceived stalking and risk of harm. These findings demonstrate that both participant gender and the characteristics of the perpetrator and target influence perceptions of stalking and the risks associated with this behavior. The implications of these findings for the legal system are multiple, including the possibility that jurors' perceptions may differ in a systematic manner [regarding] whether a stalking victim's claims of reasonable fear are justified. Also, the relatively lesser concern paid to female stalkers in these studies suggests an important avenue for clinical intervention, as male stalking victims may underestimate the risk of harm posed by a female stalker. Clearly, further attention is needed to better understand the perceptions and stereotypes that influence behavior in response to stalking.

11

PSYCHOPATHY

A Clinical Construct Whose Time Has Come

ROBERT D. HARE

Psychopathy is a socially devastating disorder defined by a constellation of affective, interpersonal, and behavioral
characteristics, including egocentricity; impulsivity; irresponsibility; shallow emotions; lack of
empathy, guilt, or remorse; pathological lying;
manipulativeness; and the persistent violation of
social norms and expectations. This article is a
personal, selective view of some major changes
and trends in the empirical research on psychopathy from 1974 to 1994. The focus is on the
assessment and diagnosis of psychopathy and its
implications for the mental health and criminal
justice systems, with brief reference made to several recent trends in the application of cognitive
neuroscience to the study of the disorder.

Let me begin with a framework that helps me to
make sense of what often appears to be senseless

behavior (Hare, 1993, 1995). Psychopaths can
be described as intraspecies predators who use
charm, manipulation, intimidation, and violence to
control others and to satisfy their own selfish
needs. Lacking in conscience and in feelings for
others, they cold-bloodedly take what they want
and do as they please, violating social norms and
expectations without the slightest sense of guilt or
regret. Viewed in this way, it is not surprising that
in spite of their small numbers—perhaps 1% of the
general population—they make up from 15% to
25% of our prison population and are responsible
for a markedly disproportionate amount of the serious crime, violence, and social distress in every
society. Furthermore, their depredations affect
virtually everyone at one time or another, because
they form a significant proportion of persistent criminals, drug dealers, spouse and child

Editors' Note: This article was originally published in *Criminal Justice and Behavior*, Vol. 23, No. 1, March 1996, pp. 25–54.
Reprinted with permission of Sage Publications. Some background information about the *DSM* and some recidivism research
have been omitted.

abusers . . . corrupt politicians, unethical lawyers, terrorists. . . . They are well represented in the business and corporate world, particularly during chaotic restructuring, where the rules and their enforcement are lax and accountability is difficult to determine (Babiak, 1995). It is not uncommon for psychopaths to emerge as "patriots" and "saviors" in societies experiencing social, economic, and political upheaval (e.g., Rwanda, the former Yugoslavia, and the former Soviet Union). Wrapped in the flag, they enrich themselves by callously exploiting ethnic, cultural, or racial tensions and grievances.

***

THE CONSTRUCT OF PSYCHOPATHY

Psychopathy began to emerge as a formal clinical construct in the last century, but references to individuals we now readily recognize as having been psychopathic can be found in biblical, classical, medieval, and other historical sources (Cleckley, 1976; Rotenberg & Diamond, 1971). Like most clinical constructs, psychopathy has been, and continues to be, the subject of considerable debate, scientific and otherwise. Some commentators, no doubt influenced by the inconsistent, fuzzy, and legalistic ways in which the term has been used, have suggested that the disorder is mythological, a view that appeals to those who feel uncomfortable about psychiatric labels or the role of individual differences in abnormal and antisocial behavior. Clinical and empirical evidence, however, clearly indicates that the construct, whatever we label it— psychopathy, sociopathy, antisocial personality disorder, dyssocial personality disorder—is anything but mythological. It is true that the etiology, dynamics, and conceptual boundaries of the disorder are the subject of much speculation, but at the same time, there is a reasonably consistent clinical tradition concerning its core affective, interpersonal, and behavioral attributes. Interestingly, this traditional view of psychopathy cuts across a broad spectrum of groups, including

psychiatrists, psychologists, criminal justice personnel, and experimental psychopathologists, as well as the lay public (. . . Cleckley, 1976; W. Davies & Feldman, 1981; . . . Livesley, Jackson, & Schroeder, 1992; . . .).

Of course, agreement on the descriptive features of a disorder means little unless it can be shown that the features define a valid clinical construct capable of reliable identification. That they do, in my opinion, is beyond question. Descriptively, the clinicians "got it right," and my own research efforts are firmly grounded in their work. However, translating their keen insights into solid empirical research has long been hampered by inadequate measurement of the construct.

THE ASSESSMENT OF PSYCHOPATHY

Progress in any discipline is difficult without psychometrically sound procedures for measuring key constructs. Psychopathy is no exception, and the lack of such procedures has hindered not only the development of a body of replicable, theoretically meaningful research findings but also society's acceptance of psychopathy as an important clinical construct with practical implications.

DSM-II

The second edition of the American Psychiatric Association's *Diagnostic and Statistical Manual of Mental Disorders (DSM-II)* appeared in 1968. In line with clinical tradition, it described psychopaths (referred to as people exhibiting an antisocial personality) as unsocialized, impulsive, guiltless, selfish, and callous individuals who rationalize their behavior and fail to learn from experience. However, *DSM-II* did not provide explicit diagnostic criteria for the disorder, and in the 1970s, many researchers attempted to operationalize the disorder in other ways (see review by Hare & Cox, 1978). For example, my colleagues and I made global ratings of psychopathy based on clinical accounts of the disorder (especially those by Cleckley, 1976). Other researchers used scales derived from self-report inventories, such as the Minnesota Multiphasic Personality Inventory (Dahlstrom & Welsh, 1960) and the California Psychological Inventory (Gough, 1969). The psychometric properties of most of these procedures, as indicants of psychopathy, were unclear, and the tenuous relationships they bore to one another made it difficult or impossible to generate a solid body of replicable research findings (Hare, 1985). I might add that although self-report and other personality tests play an important role in clinical assessment, their use as reliable indicants of psychopathy for clinical or research purposes cannot be recommended.

DSM-III

With the publication of *DSM-III* (American Psychiatric Association, 1980), the diagnostic situation improved in one respect but worsened in another. The improvement was the introduction of a list of explicit criteria for psychopathy, now referred to as antisocial personality disorder (APD). Unfortunately, these criteria consisted almost entirely of persistent violations of social norms, including lying, stealing, truancy, inconsistent work behavior, and traffic arrests. Among the main reasons given for this dramatic shift away from the use of clinical inferences were that personality traits are difficult to measure reliably and that it is easier to agree on the behaviors that typify a disorder than on the reasons why they occur. The result was a diagnostic category with good reliability but dubious validity, a category that lacked congruence with traditional conceptions of psychopathy. . . .

THE PSYCHOPATHY CHECKLIST AND ITS REVISION

In 1980, I first described a research tool for operationalizing the construct of psychopathy (Hare,

1980). Later referred to as the Psychopathy Checklist (PCL), it was revised in 1985 and formally published several years later (Hare, 1991; see also Hart, Hare, & Harpur, 1992). Recently described as "state of the art" (Fulero, 1995, p. 454), the PCL-R is a 20-item clinical rating scale completed on the basis of a semistructured interview and detailed collateral or file information. Each item is scored on a 3-point scale according to specific criteria. The total score, which can range from 0 to 40, provides an estimate of the extent to which a given individual matches the prototypical psychopath, as exemplified, for example, in the work of Cleckley (1976). The PCL-R's psychometric properties are well established with male offenders and forensic patients and, to an increasing extent, with female (Strachan, 1994) and adolescent (Forth, Hart, & Hare, 1990) offenders. Indices of internal consistency (alpha coefficient, mean interitem correlation) and interrater reliability are high, and evidence for all aspects of validity is substantial. Mean PCL-R scores in male and female offender populations typically range from about 22 to 24, with a standard deviation of from 6 to 8. Mean scores in forensic psychiatric populations are somewhat lower, about 20, with about the same standard deviation. For research purposes, a score of 30 generally is considered indicative of psychopathy, although some investigators have obtained good results with cutoff scores as low as 25.

The high internal consistency of the PCL and PCL-R indicates that they measure a unitary construct, yet factor analyses of each version consistently reveal a stable two-factor structure (Hare et al., 1990; Harpur, Hakstian, & Hare, 1988). Factor 1 consists of items having to do with the affective/interpersonal features of psychopathy, such as egocentricity, manipulativeness, callousness, and lack of remorse, characteristics that many clinicians consider central to psychopathy. Factor 2 reflects those features of psychopathy associated with an impulsive, antisocial, and unstable lifestyle, or social deviance. The two factors are correlated about .5 but have different patterns of correlations with external variables. These patterns make theoretical and clinical sense. For example, Factor 1 is correlated positively with prototypicality ratings of narcissistic and histrionic personality disorder, self-report measures of narcissism and Machiavellianism, risk for recidivism and violence, and unusual processing of affective material (see below). It is correlated negatively with self-report measures of empathy and anxiety. Factor 2 is most strongly correlated with diagnoses of APD, criminal and antisocial behaviors, substance abuse, and various self-report measures of psychopathy. It is also correlated negatively with socioeconomic level, education, and IQ. The PCL-R factors appear to measure two facets of a higher-order construct, namely, psychopathy.

Comparisons between the PCL-R and the *DSM-III-R* category of APD are illuminating. . . . Although PCL-R scores are significantly correlated with diagnoses of APD in forensic populations, the association is an asymmetric one. This is because in these populations, the base rate for PCL-R–defined psychopathy is much lower (15% to 25%) than the base rate for APD (50% to 75%). Most of the psychopaths also meet the criteria for APD, but most of those with APD are not psychopaths. That is because APD is defined largely by antisocial behaviors and consequently taps the social deviance components of psychopathy (Factor 2) much better than it does the affective/interpersonal components of the disorder (Factor 1). APD more or less leaves out the personality traits necessary to differentiate between psychopathic and other criminals.

Although my colleagues and I have taken great pains to differentiate between psychopathy and APD, some clinicians and investigators use the labels as if the constructs they measure were interchangeable. They are not, and the failure to recognize this simple fact results in confusion and misleading conclusions (see Hare, [1998]; Mealey, 1995).

The Psychopathy Checklist: Screening Version

The PCL-R takes several hours to complete, too long for the average clinician working in acute psychiatric and mental health facilities. Several years ago, John Monahan asked if it would be possible to develop a brief version of the PCL-R for use in the John D. and Catherine T. MacArthur Foundation project on the prediction of violence in the mentally disordered. With generous support from the foundation, we began development of the 12-item Psychopathy Checklist: Screening Version (PCL:SV; Hart, Cox, & Hare, 1995; Hart, Hare, & Forth, 1993). The PCL:SV is conceptually and empirically related to the PCL-R and can be used as a screen for psychopathy in forensic populations or as a stand-alone instrument for research with noncriminals, including civil psychiatric patients (as in the MacArthur Foundation project). It has the same factor structure as the PCL-R, with the affective/interpersonal and socially deviant components of psychopathy each being measured by six items.

PSYCHOPATHY IN CHILDREN

Most clinicians and researchers are reluctant to speak of psychopathic children, yet it is likely that the personality traits and behaviors that define adult psychopathy begin to manifest themselves in childhood (Lahey & Kazdin, 1990; Robins, 1966; Robins & Rutter, 1990). If so, early intervention is essential if we are ever to have any hope of influencing the development and behavioral expression of the disorder. The problem, however, is complicated by general failure to differentiate the budding psychopath from other children who exhibit serious emotional and behavioral problems, particularly those children diagnosed with conduct disorder, attention-deficit hyperactivity disorder, or oppositional defiant disorder.

Recently, Frick, O'Brien, Wootton, and McBurnett (1994) modified the PCL-R items so that they were suitable for children and could be rated by parents and teachers. In a sample of clinic-referred children between the ages of 6 and 13 years, the items identified much the same two-factor structure (although in reverse order) as that found with adults (Harpur, Hare, & Hakstian,

1989). One dimension was associated with impulsivity and conduct problems (similar to PCL-R Factor 2) and the other with the interpersonal and motivational aspects of psychopathy, such as lack of guilt, lack of empathy, and superficial charm (similar to PCL-R Factor 1). These two dimensions had different patterns of associations with a variety of external variables, including conduct disorder. An important implication of their findings is that children with conduct disorder constitute a small subset with, and a larger subset without, psychopathic features. Presumably, each subset has a different developmental history and requires different treatment strategies.

DSM-IV

In preparation for *DSM-IV* (American Psychiatric Association, 1994), the American Psychiatric Association carried out a multisite APD Field Trial (Hare, Hart, & Harpur, 1991; Widiger & Corbitt, 1995). Stated goals of the Field Trial were to shorten the criteria set and to improve coverage of the traditional symptoms of psychopathy. These symptoms were represented by a 10-item psychopathic personality disorder (PPD) criteria set derived from the PCL:SV and by the ICD-10 criteria for dyssocial personality disorder (World Health Organization, 1990). The PPD items were as follows: lacks remorse, lacks empathy, deceitful and manipulative, glib and superficial, inflated and arrogant self-appraisal, early behavior problems, adult antisocial problems, poor behavioral controls, impulsive, and irresponsible. The results of the Field Trial were described in detail by Widiger et al. ([1996]).

Many researchers and clinicians hoped that the Field Trial would bring the diagnosis of APD back on track, but it did so only in a limited sense, and certainly not explicitly or formally. The *DSM-IV* criteria for APD remain problematical (see Hare & Hart, 1995). . . .

***

DSM-IV presents clinicians working in the criminal justice system with an additional problem. The term *psychopathy* was absent in *DSM-III-R*. The *DSM-IV* text (American Psychiatric Association, 1994) now says that antisocial personality disorder "has also been referred to as psychopathy, sociopathy, or dyssocial personality disorder" (p. 645), thereby making it easier for forensic clinicians to use the construct of psychopathy in their reports or court testimony. Indeed, the text makes many references to the personality traits traditionally associated with psychopathy. However, the listed diagnostic criteria for APD actually identify individuals who are persistently antisocial, most of whom are not psychopaths. . . .

It seems that *DSM-IV*—perhaps inadvertently—has established two different sets of diagnostic criteria for APD, one for the general public and one for forensic settings. Individuals diagnosed as APD outside of forensic settings might not be so diagnosed once they find themselves in prisons or forensic hospitals, unless they also exhibit personality traits indicative of psychopathy. The inclusion of such traits in the forensic diagnosis of APD apparently is a matter of judgment for the individual clinician; as a result, a given offender or defendant might be diagnosed as APD by a clinician who chooses to use only the listed criteria and as *not* APD by one who chooses to include psychopathic personality traits in the diagnosis. In each case, the diagnostic strategy would be consistent with *DSM-IV* guidelines, a situation that should provide some interesting courtroom debates.

***

. . . [A]n unfortunate consequence of the approach adopted in *DSM-IV* is that, now more than ever, researchers and clinicians will be confused about the relationship between APD and psychopathy, sometimes using them interchangeably and other times treating them as separate clinical constructs. Perhaps most serious will be situations in which a clinician diagnoses an offender or forensic patient as APD according to the formal *DSM-IV* criteria, and then uses the research literature on psychopathy to make statements about treatability, likelihood of reoffending, and risk for violence. As I indicate below, the predictive validity of psychopathy, as measured by the PCL-R, is impressive but has little direct relevance to APD.

PSYCHOPATHY: CONTINUUM OR DISCRETE CATEGORY?

One of the questions often raised by clinicians, researchers, and the public is this: Do psychopaths differ from the rest of us in degree or in kind? Many researchers (e.g., Blackburn, 1993; Livesley & Schroeder, 1991) prefer dimensional conceptualizations of personality disorders, whereas formal diagnostic systems, such as *DSM-IV,* make it difficult to adopt anything other than a categorical view (i.e., that an individual is either APD or not APD).

Recently, Harris, Rice, and Quinsey (1994) used extensive file information to obtain PCL-R scores for 653 male forensic patients, in order to determine if the . . . PCL-R reflected a dimensional or a categorical construct. Using four different taxonometric methods, they obtained results consistent with the hypothesis that psychopathy is a discrete category, or taxon. Their procedures allowed for the emergence of only two groups or classes of patients, those in the psychopathy taxon and those not in the taxon. They concluded that the optimal PCL-R score for inclusion in the psychopathy taxon was about 25, somewhat lower than the cutoff score of 30 recommended for research purposes (Hare, 1991). More recently, David Cooke (personal communication, November 21, 1994) analyzed two large sets of PCL-R scores, one from male offenders who had taken part in research conducted by my laboratory and the other from his own stratified random sample of the Scottish prison population. Cooke's analyses differed from those of Harris et al. (1994) in two important ways: His PCL-R scores were based on both semistructured interviews and file information, and his taxonometric procedures allowed for the emergence of more than two classes of offenders. Each of his two samples yielded three classes, one clearly being a

psychopathy taxon. The optimal PCL-R score for inclusion in this taxon was between 28 and 32, in line with the recommended cutoffs for the diagnosis of psychopathy.

The results of these studies are certainly suggestive, but more research is needed, in part because of problems with taxonometric methods, but also to determine the generalizability of the findings, not only in different samples and cultures but [also] with different procedures for the assessment of psychopathy.

PSYCHOPATHY AND THE CRIMINAL JUSTICE SYSTEM

Over the past two decades, one of the more dramatic changes in our view of psychopathy has been in its significance to the criminal justice system, particularly with respect to the assessment of risk for recidivism and violence. Guze (1976), for example, noted that once a person had been convicted of a felony, psychiatric diagnoses, including sociopathy, were not very helpful in predicting criminal activities. This view, however, was compromised by the use of diagnostic criteria at that time that permitted almost 80% of felons to receive a diagnosis of sociopathy. By way of contrast, there is now an extensive literature indicating that current assessments of psychopathy, either by themselves or as part of risk equations, are highly predictive of treatability, recidivism, and violence. This literature is based almost entirely on research involving the use of the PCL-R. For this reason, each of the studies referred to in the rest of this article used the PCL-R for the assessment of psychopathy, unless otherwise indicated.

PSYCHOPATHY AND CRIME

Although some psychopaths manage to ply their trade with few formal contacts with the criminal justice system, their personality clearly is compatible with a propensity to violate many of society's rules and expectations. The crimes of those who do break the law run the gamut from petty theft and fraud to cold-blooded violence (Hare & McPherson, 1984; Kosson, Smith, & Newman, 1990; Wong, 1984). However, it is primarily the violence of psychopaths that captures the headlines, particularly when it ends in an apparently senseless death.

The ease with which psychopaths engage in instrumental and dispassionate violence (Cornell et al., 1993; Serin, 1991; Williamson, Hare, & Wong, 1987) has very real significance for society in general and for law enforcement personnel in particular. For example, a recent study by the Federal Bureau of Investigation (1992) found that almost half of the law enforcement officers who died in the line of duty were killed by individuals who closely matched the personality profile of the psychopath.

Although the typical criminal career is relatively short, there are individuals who devote most of their adolescent and adult life to delinquent and criminal enterprises (Blumstein, Cohen, Roth, & Visher, 1986). Many of these career criminals become less grossly antisocial in middle age (Blumstein et al., 1986; Robins, 1966). About half of the criminal psychopaths we study show a relatively sharp reduction in criminality around age 35 or 40, primarily with respect to nonviolent offenses (Hare, McPherson, & Forth, 1988). Their propensity for violence and aggression appears to be rather persistent across much of the life span, a finding also reported by Harris, Rice, and Cormier (1991). I should note that age-related reductions in overt criminality do not necessarily mean that the individual has become a warm, loving, and moral citizen. Robins (1966) observed that many psychopaths become less grossly antisocial with age but remain thoroughly disagreeable individuals. My own experience with several "reformed" or "resocialized" psychopaths can certainly attest to the folk validity of her observation (Hare, 1993).

The question I would ask is this: Are age-related reductions in the criminality of psychopaths paralleled by changes in core personality traits, or have these individuals simply learned new ways of staying out of prison? Although I share the view of many clinicians that

the personality structure of psychopaths is too stable to account for the behavioral changes that sometimes occur in middle age, empirical, longitudinal evidence is needed to resolve the issue. Meanwhile, a recent cross-sectional study of 889 male offenders provides a clue to what we might expect (Harpur & Hare, 1994). The offenders ranged in age from 16 to 70 at the time they were assessed with the PCL or the PCL-R. Scores on Factor 2 (socially deviant features) decreased sharply with age, whereas scores on Factor I (affective/interpersonal features) remained stable with age. These results are consistent with the view that age-related changes in the psychopath's antisocial behavior are not necessarily paralleled by changes in the egocentric, manipulative, and callous traits fundamental to psychopathy....

RECIDIVISM AND RISK FOR VIOLENCE

Perhaps the most dramatic change over the past 20 years in the perceived—and actual—importance of psychopathy to the criminal justice system has been in its predictive validity. Various actuarial systems generally did a fairly good job in predicting criminal behavior, and the use of personality traits resulted in little or no incremental validity. As a psychopathy researcher, I always found this situation perplexing. I could never understand, for example, why two individuals with much the same scores on some actuarial device—based on similar criminal and demographic characteristics—but one egocentric, cold-blooded, and remorseless and the other not, could possibly present the same risk. That they do not is clearly indicated by the results of a score of recent studies....

***

RECIDIVISM FOLLOWING TREATMENT

In my home city of Vancouver, it is not uncommon for a trial judge to accept expert testimony that a defendant convicted of a serious crime is a psychopath and then to sentence him to a prison where "he can receive treatment." Much the same scenario probably is played out in many other jurisdictions. The uninformed views of the judge and the protestations and anecdotes of those who run prison programs notwithstanding, there is no known treatment for psychopathy. This does not necessarily mean that the egocentric and callous attitudes and behaviors of psychopaths are immutable, only that there are no methodologically sound treatments or "resocialization" programs that have been shown to work with psychopaths. Unfortunately, both the criminal justice system and the public routinely are fooled into believing otherwise. As a result, many psychopaths take part in all sorts of prison treatment programs, put on a good show, make "remarkable progress," convince the therapists and parole board of their reformed character, are released, and pick up where they left off when they entered prison.

Several . . . studies illustrate the point. For example, Ogloff, Wong, and Greenwood (1990) reported that psychopaths, defined by a PCL-R score of at least 30, derived little benefit from a therapeutic community program designed to treat personality-disordered offenders. The psychopaths stayed in the program for a shorter time, were less motivated, and showed less clinical improvement than did other offenders. It might be argued that even though the psychopaths did not do well in this program, some residual benefits could conceivably show up following their release from prison. However, in a survival analysis, Hemphill (1991) found that the estimated reconviction rate in the first year following release was twice as high for the psychopaths (83%) as for the other offenders (42%).

Some of the most popular prison treatment and resocialization programs may actually make psychopaths worse than they were before. Rice, Harris, and Cormier (1992) retrospectively scored the PCL-R from the institutional files of patients of a maximum-security psychiatric facility. They defined psychopaths by a PCL-R score of 25 or more, and nonpsychopaths by a score

below 25. They then compared the violent recidivism rate of 166 patients who had been treated in an intensive and lengthy therapeutic community program with 119 patients who had not taken part in the program. For nonpsychopaths, the violent recidivism rate was 22% for treated patients and 39% for untreated patients. However, the violent recidivism rate for treated psychopaths was *higher* (77%) than was that for untreated psychopaths (55%). How could therapy make someone worse? The answer may be that group therapy and insight-oriented programs help psychopaths to develop better ways of manipulating, deceiving, and using people but do little to help them understand themselves.

***

Sex Offenders

The past few years have seen a sharp increase in public and professional attention paid to sex offenders, particularly those who commit a new offense following release from a treatment program or prison. It has long been recognized that psychopathic sex offenders present special problems for therapists and the criminal justice system. Indeed, some jurisdictions make provision for designating convicted sex offenders as psychopaths and for sentencing them to indefinite terms of detention. . . .

The prevalence of psychopathy—defined by a PCL-R score of at least 30—appears to be relatively high among convicted rapists. Forth and Kroner (1994) reported that in a federal prison, 26.1% of 211 rapists, 18.3% of 163 mixed sex offenders (including child molesters), and 5.4% of 82 incest offenders were psychopaths. Forth and Kroner's sample of sex offenders included 60 who were either serial rapists or rapists who killed their victims; 35% of these offenders were psychopaths. The prevalence of the disorder seems to be particularly high among offenders adjudicated by the courts as "sexually dangerous." For example, Prentky and Knight (1991) found that 45.3% of 95 rapists and 30.5% of 59 child molesters in the Massachusetts Treatment Center for

Sexually Dangerous Persons at Bridgewater met the PCL criteria for psychopathy.

Sex offenders generally are resistant to treatment (Quinsey, Harris, Rice, & Lalumiere, 1993), but it is the psychopaths among them who are most likely to recidivate early and often. For example, Quinsey, Rice, and Harris (1995), in a follow-up of 178 treated rapists and child molesters, concluded that psychopathy functions as a general predictor of sexual and violent recidivism. In a survival analysis, they found that within 6 years of release from prison, more than 80% of the psychopaths, but only about 20% of the nonpsychopaths, had violently recidivated. Many, but not all, of their offenses were sexual in nature. Most dangerous of all were psychopaths sexually "turned on" by violence (Rice, Harris, & Quinsey, 1990).

The implications of psychopathy are just as serious among adolescent sex offenders as among their adult counterparts. Preliminary results from a longitudinal study of adolescent sex offenders (ages 13 to 18) released after treatment at a forensic facility in Vancouver revealed that the mean PCL-R score for 193 male sex offenders was 21.4 (*SD* = 7.0), with about 18% meeting our criteria for psychopathy (O'Shaughnessy, Hare, Gretton, & McBride, 1994). Survival analyses indicated that the reconviction rate for sexual offenses in the first 36 months following release was low (i.e., less than 10%) and unrelated to psychopathy. However, the pattern for other types of offenses was quite different. Thus, within 36 months of release, about 70% of the psychopaths and 40% of all other offenders had been convicted of a nonsexual offense. The results were most striking within the first 12 months of release; the reconviction rate for nonsexual crimes was about 55% for psychopaths, but only about 15% for all other offenders. About 31% of the psychopaths and only 14% of the other offenders had been convicted for a nonsexual violent offense within 12 months of release. One conclusion is that, following release, many of our adolescent sex offenders, and most of the psychopathic ones, were more likely to be convicted of a nonsexual

than a sexual offense. Many of these individuals were not so much specialized sex offenders as they were offenders, and their misbehavior—sexual and otherwise—presumably was a reflection of a generalized propensity to violate social and legal expectations. If so, it may be as important to target antisocial tendencies and behaviors as it is to treat sexual deviancy.

COGNITIVE NEUROSCIENCE AND THE CRIMINAL JUSTICE SYSTEM

Twenty years ago, much of the theory and research on psychopathy was influenced by prevailing theories of learning, emotion, and motivation (Hare, 1978; Hare & Schalling, 1978). We learned much about the biological (especially the autonomic) correlates of psychopathy and about the role of rewards and punishments in establishing and maintaining psychopathic behavior. Although scientifically valuable, much of this work had little practical impact on the general public or on forensic and mental health workers. The situation is beginning to change dramatically, primarily because of the increasing use of procedures and paradigms from cognitive psychology and neuroscience (see Newman & Wallace, 1993). Research on cognition and emotion is particularly interesting because of its potential implications for the issue of criminal responsibility.

Clinicians have long maintained that the cognitions, language, and life experiences of psychopaths lack depth and affect. Recent laboratory research provides neurophysiological support for this view. Space prevents anything more than brief reference to some of this work. Perhaps the most interesting findings are that psychopaths seem unable or unwilling to process or use the deep semantic meanings of language; their linguistic processes appear to be relatively superficial, and the subtle, more abstract meanings and nuances of language escape them (Gillstrom, 1994; . . . Williamson, Harpur, & Hare, 1991). Furthermore, behavioral, electrocortical, and brain imaging research adds weight to the clinical belief that psychopaths fail to appreciate the emotional significance of an event or experience (Larbig, Veit, Rau, Schlottke, & Birbaumer, 1992; Patrick, 1994; Williamson et al., 1991).

In short, psychopaths appear to be semantically and affectively shallow individuals. Presumably, the deep semantic and affective networks that tie cognitions together are not well developed in these individuals (Hare, 1993). Perhaps this is why psychopaths show, on close examination, signs of what seems to be a subtle form of thought disorder. For example, Williamson et al. (1991) scored the audiotaped narratives of male offenders for cohesion and coherence in discourse. She found that the narratives of the psychopaths contained more than a normal amount of logical inconsistencies, contradictions, and neologisms and showed a tendency to derail or "go off track." In some respects, it is as if psychopaths lack a central organizer to plan and keep track of what they think and say (Gillstrom & Hare, 1988).

Why do these cognitive and linguistic problems typically go undetected? For one thing, psychopaths use their own attributes to put on a good show. Intense eye contact, distracting body language, charm, and a knowledge of the listener's vulnerabilities are all part of the psychopath's armamentarium for dominating, controlling, and manipulating others. We pay less attention to what they say than to how they say it—style over substance. Because it is so easy to become sucked in by psychopaths, my research group routinely videotapes all of our interviews for later, more detached, analysis. We advise others to do likewise.

The cognitive, linguistic, and behavioral attributes of psychopaths (Hare, 1993; Newman & Wallace, 1993) may be related to cerebral dysfunction, particularly in the orbito/ventromedial frontal cortex (Gorenstein & Newman, 1980; Lapierre, Braun, & Hodgins, 1995). This dysfunction need not actually involve organic damage (Hart, Forth, & Hare, 1990), but could reflect structural or functional anomalies in the brain mechanisms and circuitry—including the orbito/ventromedial frontal cortex, medial temporal

cortex, and amygdala—responsible for the coordination of cognitive and affective processes (Intrator et al., [1997]).

Behavioral and neuroimaging studies indicate that damage to these regions can produce a dissociation of the logical/cognitive and affective components of thought (H. Damasio, Grabowski, Frank, Galaburda, & Damasio, 1994), or even what A. Damasio, Tranel, and Damasio (1987) refer to as "acquired sociopathy."

The relevance of this to the criminal justice system is that very little of what we do is based solely on logical appraisals of situations and their potential ramifications for us and others. In most cases, our cognitions and behaviors are heavily laden with emotional elements. As A. Damasio (1994) recently put it, "emotion is integral to the process of reasoning" (p. 144). I would argue that it is also an essential part of "conscience." However, it is this very element that is missing or seriously impaired in psychopaths; their conscience is only half formed, consisting merely of an intellectual awareness of the rules of the game. The powerful motivating, guiding, and inhibiting effects of emotion play little role in their lives, presumably not so much by choice as because of what they are. In effect, their internalized rule books are pale, abridged versions of those that direct the conduct of other individuals.

In most jurisdictions, psychopathy is considered to be an aggravating rather than a mitigating factor in determining criminal responsibility. However, I've been asked if research evidence of the sort presented above—affective deficit, thought disorder, brain dysfunction—might lead some to view psychopathy as a mitigating factor in a criminal case. As one psychiatrist put it, perhaps psychopathy will become "the kiss of life rather than the kiss of death" in first-degree murder cases. This would be appalling, because psychopaths are calculating predators whose behavior must be judged by the rules of the society in which they live. However, the issue is really one for the judicial system to settle. If psychopathy is used as a defense for a criminal act, the flip side of the coin is that the disorder currently is untreatable, and any civil commitment likely would be permanent.

BAD, MAD, OR BOTH?

There is a related issue that complicates matters even further. Psychopaths typically are judged legally and psychiatrically sane. Many clinicians and investigators believe that psychopathy is incompatible with psychoticism, and there is some evidence to support their position (Hart & Hare, 1989). Not everyone agrees with this view, though. Some argue that psychopathy and schizophrenia are part of a common spectrum of disorders. Cleckley (1976) himself considered psychopathy to be closer to psychosis than to normality; after all, he titled his book *The Mask of Sanity* for a reason. Also, some forensic psychiatrists say that they occasionally see a mentally disordered offender who is both a psychopath and a schizophrenic. A recent study by Rasmussen and Levander (1994) suggests that diagnostic comorbidity of this sort is not uncommon in maximum security psychiatric units housing severely violent or dangerous patients. They evaluated 94 consecutive admissions to such a unit in Norway and found that 22 patients met the PCL-R criteria for psychopathy. Of these, 12 (55%) also satisfied the *DSM-III-R* criteria for schizophrenia. They suggested that in such patients, schizophrenia may be superimposed on an underlying syndrome of psychopathy and, conversely, that psychopathy may be a vulnerability factor for schizophrenia. In any case, the combination would seem to be a particularly dangerous one, assuming that [the] diagnoses are valid.

I suspect that genuine cases of psychosis-psychopathy comorbidity are rare. More common are psychopaths who malinger, that is, fake psychotic symptoms in order to avoid prison. They present a particularly difficult problem for the mental health and criminal justice systems, typically bouncing back and forth between prisons and forensic psychiatric facilities (Gacono, Meloy, Sheppard, Speth, & Roske, 1995). Criminal psychopaths are more likely to be bad than mad.

THE FUTURE

Psychopathy has long been a poor relative of experimental psychopathology, even though it has no equal in terms of the amount and degree of social, economic, physical, and emotional distress generated. The number of dedicated researchers is small and the research funding miniscule in comparison with the manpower and funding devoted to schizophrenia, the affective disorders, and even antisocial personality disorder. The nature of psychopathy, however, provides just as much of a challenge as does any other clinical disorder. Of course, it is easier and more convenient to study psychiatric patients than psychopaths. The former manifestly are impaired and either seek or are sent for treatment, where they provide a steady pool of readily available research subjects for well-funded programs designed to understand and help them. Psychopaths, on the other hand, suffer little personal distress; seek treatment only when it is in their best interests to do so, such as when seeking probation or parole; and elicit little sympathy from those who study them. Furthermore, studying them in a prison environment is fraught with so many institutional and political problems, inmate boycotts, staff roadblocks, and red tape that most researchers simply give up after a few projects. In addition, and unfortunately, in my view, resources have been targeted primarily at programs and projects that eschew the politically incorrect idea that individual differences in personality are as important . . . determinants of crime as are social forces.

As the title of this article implies, the situation is changing rapidly. Even those opposed to the very idea of psychopathy cannot ignore its potent explanatory and predictive power, if not as a formal construct then as a static risk factor. In the next few years, indices of psychopathy almost certainly will become a routine part of the assessment batteries used to make decisions about competency, sentencing, diversion, placement, suitability for treatment, and risk for recidivism and violence. Because psychopaths with a history of violence are a poor risk for early release, more and more will be kept in prison for their full sentence, whereas many other offenders will be released early with little risk to society. However, unless we are content simply to warehouse high-risk offenders, we must develop innovative programs aimed at making their attitudes and behaviors less self-serving and more acceptable to the society in which most eventually must function.

Following publication of a book written for the general public (Hare, 1993), scores of people called or wrote to ask why I devoted so much space to psychopathic criminals and so little to the psychopaths with whom they daily lived and worked and who somehow always managed to stay out of prison. Many of these correspondents seemed caught up in emotionally damaging and dangerous situations from which there apparently was no escape (see Meloy, 1992). Their plight raises an issue that urgently needs to be addressed and researched: the prevalence of psychopathy in the general population and its expression in ways that are personally, socially, or economically damaging but that are not necessarily illegal or that do not result in criminal

prosecution. We study incarcerated offenders for two reasons: the base rate for psychopathy is high, and we have access to enough solid information to make reliable assessments. However, we must find ways of studying psychopaths in the community if we are ever to provide some relief for their victims, which is to say, all of us.

Prognostications are always risky, but the next decade will certainly see dramatic advances in our understanding of psychopathy, in large part because of increasing cross-cultural and interdisciplinary collaborations. Family and twin studies will combine with developmental investigations to provide the first solid data on the interactive roles of heredity and environment. Neuroimaging and neurophysiological protocols will lead to new insights into brain structure and function and may set the stage for effective intervention programs. Finally, there will be a continuation of the recent trend toward integration of pure research and practical application, for example, the conceptual linkage between the neurophysiological evidence of abnormal affective processes in psychopaths and their penchant for callous, cold-blooded behavior.

12

CHILD SEXUAL MOLESTATION

Research Issues

ROBERT A. PRENTKY

RAYMOND A. KNIGHT

AUSTIN F. S. LEE

INTRODUCTION

Few criminal offenses are more despised than the sexual abuse of children, and few are so little understood in terms of incidence (the number of offenses committed), prevalence (the proportion of the population who commit offenses), and reoffense risk. Despite long-standing public concern over the medical, emotional, and monetary costs associated with child sexual victimization, rigorous programs to enhance the accuracy of predictive decisions involving sexual offenders are of fairly recent origin. Because of inadequate methodologies, studies on the psychology,

behavior, treatment, and recidivism rates of child molesters have often yielded inconsistent findings. The uncertainty of information about sexual offenders raises questions about the effectiveness of special commitment statutes and ad hoc discretionary and dispositional decisions directed toward this group.

Before it can combat child molestation effectively, the criminal justice community must first understand it. Empirical knowledge of the factors that lead individuals to sexually abuse children can support and inform the sentencing, probationary, clinical, and supervisory decisions that must be made with regard to child molesters.

Editors' Note: This is a research report published by the U.S. Department of Justice, National Institute of Justice, June 1997, NCJ 163390. The Executive Summary has been omitted.

This report is divided into four main sections. Section 1 discusses the frequency of child sexual molestation and factors leading to sexual deviancy in individual offenders. Section 2 includes classification models for typing and diagnosing child molesters and describes treatment approaches and strategies for community-based maintenance and control. Section 3 talks about reoffense risk as it relates to criminal justice decisions and discusses predictors of sexual recidivism. To illustrate the variability of recidivism among child molesters, Section 4 presents the findings of a 25-year follow-up study of 115 released offenders. [Editors' note: Section 4 is omitted here.] Finally, some of the shortcomings of current approaches to reduce child molester reoffense risk are touched on in the report's conclusion, and an argument is made for post-release treatment and aftercare programs.

The information included in this research report has been distilled from several interrelated reports and studies sponsored by the National Institute of Justice (NIJ) to strengthen the efficacy of intervention and prevention strategies and ultimately reduce child sexual victimization rates.

SECTION 1. OCCURRENCE AND ETIOLOGY

Frequency of Child Sexual Abuse

The assumption that sexual crimes against children and teenagers are underreported is now commonly accepted. Sexual offenses apparently are more likely than other types of criminal conduct to elude the criminal justice system. This inference is supported by the reports of both sex offenders and sexually abused children. Offenders report vastly more victim-involved incidents than those for which they were convicted (Abel et al., 1987). It is impossible to determine how representative these anonymous self-reporting offenders are, compared to all of the nonincarcerated and unidentified sex offenders in the population.

A telephone survey of a national probability sample of 2,000 children between the ages of 10 and 16 revealed that 3.2% of girls and 0.6% of boys had suffered, at some point in their lives, sexual abuse involving physical contact. If one infers that those statistics can be generalized to the rest of the country, children have experienced (but not reported) levels of victimization that far exceed those reported for adults (Finkelhor & Dziuba-Leatherman, 1994). This finding is consistent with a recent report indicating that teenagers are at greater risk than adults for rape (Bureau of Justice Statistics, 1996).

In addition to underreporting, incidence estimates are also affected by a number of methodological problems. Although research on criminal conduct of any type may be hampered by these difficulties, sexual crimes seem to be especially susceptible. For instance, sexual offenses involve behavior that is not as clear-cut as that occurring in nonsexual crimes (such as robbery, burglary, or auto theft) because they often include nonsexual offenses (e.g., kidnapping, breaking and entering, or simple assault) as well as a variety of different sexual violations. The criminal charges springing from such a litany differ from one jurisdiction to another, and the resulting conviction may be for a "lesser," that is, nonsexual, offense (e.g., pleading out to simple assault). Given this unevenness in legal system dispositions, it is not surprising to find wide variations among—and wide ranges within—incidence/prevalence estimates.

Characteristics of the Offender

The sexual abusers of children are highly dissimilar in terms of personal characteristics, life experiences, and criminal histories. No single "molester profile" exists. Child molesters arrive at deviancy via multiple pathways and engage in many different sexual and nonsexual "acting-out" behaviors.

Sexual focus. Evidence shows that sexual focus in child molesters comprises two separate components. The first is intensity of pedophilic interest, i.e., the degree to which offenders are focused or "fixated" on children as sexual objects. The second component involves the exclusivity of their preference for children as sexual objects. The second component is inversely related to social competence, as measured by the extent and depth of adult social and sexual relationships, and it is independent of the intensity of pedophilic interest.

Physiological arousal. Logic suggests that a behavioral dimension of sexual interest in children would be accompanied by varying degrees of physiological arousal to them. Plethysmographic assessment (i.e., measurement of penile volume changes [phallometry] in response to sexual stimuli) has demonstrated an ability to discriminate between child molesters and comparison groups of nonmolesters (Barbaree & Marshall, 1988; Freund & Blanchard, 1989 . . .) as well as among subgroups of child molesters defined by victim gender preference (same sex vs. opposite sex) and by relationship to victim (incest vs. nonincest). For example, exclusive incest offenders demonstrate far less sexual arousal in response to children than do extrafamilial child molesters. Offenders with strong pedophilic interest show more sexual arousal to depictions of children than their low-fixated counterparts.

Victimization of offenders as children. Some support exists for the notion that child molestation may be related to an offender's restaging or recapitulation of his own sexual victimization. Tests of the recapitulation theory on a sample of 131 rapists and child molesters revealed that child molesters who committed their first assault when they were 14 or younger were sexually victimized at a younger age than were offenders who committed their first assault in adulthood. They also experienced more severe sexual abuse than offenders with adult onset of sexual aggression (Prentky & Knight, 1993). No evidence of recapitulation of sexual abuse among rapists was

found in this study. It should be pointed out, however, that regardless of whether or not they were sexually abused (and, if so, by whom and at what age), *all* offenders in the sample went on to commit sexual offenses.

By itself, sexual victimization is too narrow a factor to explain child molestation. No inexorable link exists between experiencing sexual abuse as a child and growing up to be a child molester; the "outcome" of child molestation is a much more complex phenomenon. Most victims of childhood sexual abuse do not go on to become perpetrators. As is true for other kinds of maltreatment, childhood sexual victimization becomes a critical element in the presence or absence of a variety of other factors (e.g., co-occurrence of other types of abuse, availability of supportive caregivers, ego strength of child-victim at the time of abuse, and treatment), all of which moderate the likelihood of becoming a child molester. In addition, the severity of the long-term effects of childhood sexual abuse is influenced by clear morbidity factors (e.g., age at onset of abuse, duration of abuse, the child's relationship to the perpetrator, and invasiveness and/or violence of the abuse). The weight and significance of having been sexually abused are specific to the individual child molester.

Social competence. A variety of studies have documented the inadequate social and interpersonal skills, underassertiveness, and poor self-esteem that, in varying degrees, characterize individual offenders (Araji & Finkelhor, 1985; Marshall, Barbaree, & Fernandez, 1995 . . .). Social competence deficits are pervasive among child molesters and must be considered clinically significant. As is true for sexual abuse suffered by offenders during childhood, however, social competence deficits constitute but one important factor in the complex etiology of child molestation.

Impulsive, antisocial personality. Research shows that child molesters who committed their first sexual offense in adolescence had histories of being disruptive in school (verbally or physically assaulting peers and teachers); showed high levels of juvenile antisocial behavior; and, as adults, manifested a greater degree of nonsexual aggression. For some types of child molesters, sexual offenses are part of a longer criminal history, reflecting an antisocial lifestyle and impulsive behavioral traits that probably had been present from childhood (Prentky & Knight, 1993; Prentky, Knight, & Lee, 1997; Quinsey, Rice, & Harris, 1995). A history of impulsive, antisocial behavior is a well-documented risk factor associated with some child molesters.

Developmental influences. Recognition of the multiple factors that determine child molestation has led clinicians and investigators to examine the antecedent and concurrent experiences that place sexual abuse in a developmental context. One variable, "caregiver inconstancy," measures the frequency of changes in primary caregivers and the longest time spent with any single caregiver; it reflects the permanence and consistency of the child's interpersonal relationships with significant adults. Caregiver inconstancy, a powerful predictor of the degree of sexual violence expressed in adulthood (Prentky et al., 1997) interferes with the development of long-term supportive relationships, increasing the likelihood of an attachment disorder. Attachment disorders may be characterized by intense anxiety, distrust of others, insecurity, dysfunctional anger, and failure to develop normal age-appropriate social skills. Thus, specifiable early childhood experiences may lead to interpersonal deficits and low self-esteem that severely undermine development of secure adult relationships. Individuals having these interpersonal and social shortcomings are more likely than others to turn to children to meet their psychosexual needs.

Section 2. Typology and Treatment

Classification of Child Molesters

Diagnosis and assessment. Just as the childhood and developmental experiences, adult competencies, and criminal histories of child molesters differ considerably, so do the motives that underlie the behavior patterns that characterize their sexual abuse of children. Thus, informed decisions about these offenders require some understanding of the dimensions believed to be important in discriminating among them. Diagnosis aims to reduce this diversity by assigning the offender to a class or group of individuals with similar relevant characteristics. Identifying and measuring these relevant characteristics is the task of assessment.

A reliable, valid classification system can improve the accuracy of decisions (1) in the criminal justice system (where dangerousness and reoffense risk are assessed and resources are allocated), (2) in the clinical setting (where a more informed understanding of particular classes of offenders can be used to optimize treatment plans), and (3) in the design of more effective primary prevention strategies. A classification model may also help in deciphering critical antecedent factors that contribute to different outcomes (i.e., different "types" of child molesters).

DSM-IV classification. The 1994 edition of the *Diagnostic and Statistics Manual of Mental Disorders (DSM-IV)* places pedophilia under the heading, "Sexuality and Gender Identity Disorders" (American Psychiatric Association, 1994). According to *DSM-IV,* the onset of pedophilia "usually begins in adolescence," and its course is "usually chronic." Specific behavioral criteria for diagnosing pedophilia are listed as follows:

- The subject has experienced, for at least 6 months, recurrent intense sexual urges or fantasies involving sexual activity with a prepubescent child (age 13 or younger).
- The subject has acted on these urges or is markedly distressed by them.
- The subject is at least 16 years old and at least 5 years older than the victim. (Late adolescent subjects who are involved in ongoing relationships with 12- or 13-year-old youngsters are excluded.)

Three other specifications figure in this classification system: (1) whether the client is sexually attracted to males, females, or both; (2) whether the offenses are limited to incest; and (3) whether the client is an "exclusive" (attracted only to children) or "nonexclusive" type.

Although the *DSM-IV* classification system may succeed in isolating the "pedophilic" child molester, it fails to capture those incest and extrafamilial offenders without known 6-month histories of sexualized interest in children. Requiring evidence that an individual has met the first (and critical) diagnostic criterion dealing with "recurrent intense sexual urges or fantasies" involving children will inevitably screen out a large number of child molesters.

Sex-of-victim model. Classification of child molesters on the basis of their victims' sex—same-sex, opposite-sex, or mixed-group offenders—has shown stability over time (Fitch, 1962; Langevin et al., 1985). In addition, it has demonstrated predictive validity as well as some concurrent validity (e.g., it corresponds as expected with penile plethysmographic responsiveness to stimuli depicting specific ages and sexes) (Freund, 1965, 1967; Frisbie, 1990; . . .). Many reports have suggested that, among extrafamilial offenders, same-sex child molesters are at highest risk to reoffend, and opposite-sex child molesters are at lowest risk. However, the sex-of-victim distinction has not received consistent support. In contrast to the typical finding, at least four recent studies found either no differences in recidivism rates among groups, or differences that were opposite of prediction (Abel, Becker, Murphy, & Flanagan, 1981; Prentky & Quinsey, 1988; . . .).

The reasons for discrepant findings based on the sex-of-victim distinction are unclear, although several possibilities come immediately to mind:

- The large number of unreported sexual assaults on children
- Possible biases against reporting homosexual encounters
- Situational factors that might lead to assaults on the less-preferred sex
- Incarceration after a single assault

Further, some studies do not distinguish between incest offenders, who are almost exclusively heterosexual in their choice of victims, and nonincest offenders. Assuming that "true" incest offenders (that is, those whose offenses are exclusively intrafamilial) constitute a clinically and theoretically meaningful group of child molesters, the proportion of such cases in any particular sample might affect the differences found between same- and opposite-sex offenders.

Clinically derived multidimensional systems. In the earliest taxonomic systems for child molesters, which were based exclusively on clinical experience, three subtypes consistently appeared:

- Offender with an exclusive and long standing sexual and social preference for children (Common Type 1)
- Offender whose offenses are seen as a shift or regression from a higher, adult level of psychosexual adaptation, typically in response to stress (Common Type 2)
- Offender who is a psychopath or sociopath with very poor social skills and who turns to children largely because they are easy to exploit—not because they are preferred or even desired partners (Common Type 3)

The most historically important of these hypothetical subtypes are the "fixated" and the "regressed" (Common Types 1 and 2, respectively). Implicit or explicit in the various systems that attempted to define fixated and regressed types was an assessment of achieved level of social competence. In addition to being described as having more intense pedophilic interest, fixated offenders were also typically differentiated from regressed offenders by marital status, number and quality of age-appropriate heterosexual relationships, and achieved educational and occupational levels. The fixated child molester was hypothesized to have a negligible history of dating or peer interaction in adolescence and adulthood, and, if married, the quality of his relationship was considered to be poor.

Regressed offenders, in contrast, were described as more likely to have been married and to have developed appropriate heterosexual relationships prior to their "regressive" sexual offenses. Thus, the construct of social competence was clearly involved in the distinction between fixated and regressed types, but, when empirically tested (Conte, 1985), this distinction was found to be flawed. Results showed that the two groups were not homogeneous. Indeed, social and interpersonal competence were found to be independent of fixation (Finkelhor & Araji, 1986).

The MTC:CM3 model. To meet the need for a clearly operationalized, reliable, valid taxonomic system for child molesters, researchers at the Massachusetts Treatment Center (MTC) for Sexually Dangerous Persons developed MTC:CM3, a two-axis typology (see Exhibit 1). On Axis 1, fixation and social competence are completely independent dimensions, and each has distinct developmental antecedents and adult adaptations (Knight, Carter, & Prentky, 1989). The concept of regression was dropped in developing MTC:CM3, and a newly defined fixation dimension (i.e., "intensity of pedophilic interest") was crossed with a dimension of social competence, yielding four independent types:

- High fixation, low social competence (Type 0)
- High fixation, high social competence (Type 1)
- Low fixation, low social competence (Type 2)
- Low fixation, high social competence (Type 3)

A new behavioral dimension ("amount of contact with children") was added on a separate coordinate (Axis II) and became a powerful discriminator with respect to reoffense risk. In addition, the degree of violence employed by an offender was differentiated into dimensions of physical injury (high/low) and sadism (present/absent), yielding six distinct Axis II subtypes whose hypothetical characteristics are shown in Exhibit 2. Exclusive incest offenders were omitted in the design of MTC:CM3; including such offenders in this system would require considerable reconceptualization and revision. Although

further revision of MTC:CM3, including integration of Axis I (fixation and social competence) and Axis II (amount of contact with children, degree of injury to victim, and sadism), is necessary, validity studies conducted thus far clearly support the primary structural changes in this model (Knight, 1989, 1992; Prentky et al., 1997).

Course and prognosis among child molesters. Among child molesters, both the course (progression of symptoms associated with the condition) and the prognosis (forecast of the probable course and likelihood of recovery) vary considerably. For example, onset ranges from early adolescence to middle adulthood (as in the case of some exclusive incest offenders). The prognosis ranges from cases of lifelong, intractable pedophilic interest that is resistant to treatment to isolated instances of incest in adults with a sexual preference for peers, ample remorse and victim empathy, and a high likelihood of "recovery."

Clinical Management of Offenders

Treatment. Over the past decade, the provision of therapeutic services for sex offenders has increased significantly. A 1994 survey reported 710 adult and 684 juvenile treatment programs (Longo, Bird, Stevenson, & Fiske, 1995), up from 1985 survey results that showed 297 adult and 346 juvenile treatment programs (Knopp, Rosenberg, & Stevenson, 1986). Broadly speaking, sex offender treatment programs employ four approaches:

- Evocative therapy, which focuses on (1) helping offenders to understand the causes and motivations leading to sexually deviant and coercive behavior and (2) increasing their empathy for the victims of sexual assault. This approach may include individual, group, couples/marital, and family therapy. Group therapy may be eclectic or issue focused (i.e., specialty groups may target substance abuse, adult children of alcoholics, victim empathy, victim survivors, social skills/assertiveness training, black awareness, gay identity, or Vietnam veterans).

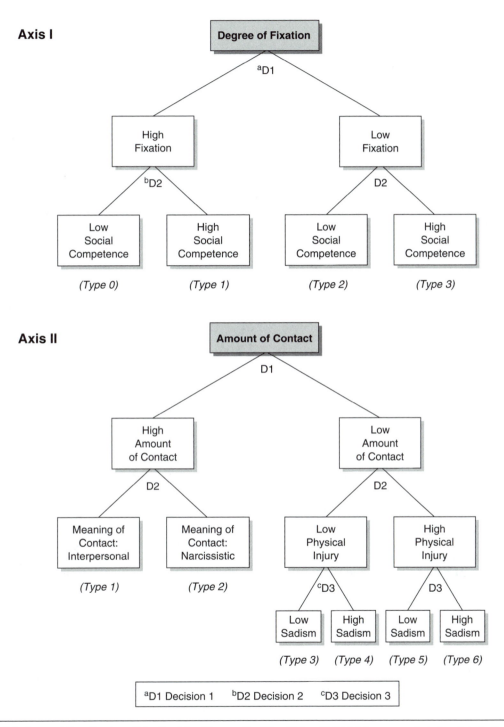

Axis I

Degree of Fixation

[a]D1

High Fixation

Low Fixation

[b]D2

D2

Low Social Competence *(Type 0)*

High Social Competence *(Type 1)*

Low Social Competence *(Type 2)*

High Social Competence *(Type 3)*

Axis II

Amount of Contact

D1

High Amount of Contact

Low Amount of Contact

D2

D2

Meaning of Contact: Interpersonal *(Type 1)*

Meaning of Contact: Narcissistic *(Type 2)*

Low Physical Injury

High Physical Injury

[c]D3

D3

Low Sadism *(Type 3)*

High Sadism *(Type 4)*

Low Sadism *(Type 5)*

High Sadism *(Type 6)*

[a]D1 Decision 1   [b]D2 Decision 2   [c]D3 Decision 3

Exhibit 1   Flow Design of the Decision Process for Classifying Child Molesters on Axis I and Axis II of MTC:CM3

	Interpersonal (Type 1)	Narcissistic (Type 2)	Exploitative (Type 3)	Muted Sadistic (Type 4)	Nonsadistic Aggressive (Type 5)	Sadistic (Type 6)
Amount of Contact With Children	High	High	Low	Low	Low	Low
Sexual Acts	Fondling, Caressing, Frottage Non-phallic sex	Phallic Non-sadistic sex	Phallic Non-sadistic sex	Sodomy "Sham" sadism[a]	Phallic Non-sadistic sex	Sadism
Relationship of Offender to Victim	Known	Known or Stranger	Stranger	Stranger	Stranger	Stranger
Amount of Physical Injury to Victim	Low	Low	Instrumental[b]	Instrumental[b]	High	High
Amount of Planning in Offenses	High[c]	Moderate	Low	Moderate	Low	High

Exhibit 2   Hypothetical Profiles of MTC:CM3 Axis II Types

a. "Sham" sadism implies behaviors or reported fantasies that reflect sadism without the high victim injury present in Type 6.

b. Instrumental aggression implies only enough force to gain victim compliance.

c. Interpersonal types know their victims and may spend a considerable amount of time "grooming" them (setting them up), but the offenses often appear to be unplanned or spontaneous.

- Cognitive behavior therapy, which focuses on sexual assault cycles and techniques that interrupt those cycles; altering the beliefs, fantasies, and rationalizations that justify and perpetuate sexually aggressive behavior; and controlling and managing anger. Studies of relapse prevention, the most commonly employed cognitive behavioral model, report that, for child molesters, the most frequently identified experiences prior to committing an offense were planning the offense (73% of sample) and low victim empathy (71% of sample) (Pithers, 1990; Pithers, Martin, & Cumming, 1989).
- Psychoeducation groups or classes, which use a more didactic approach to remedy deficits in social and interpersonal skills; they teach anger management techniques, principles of relapse prevention, and a range of topics that includes human sexuality, dating and communication skills, and myths about sexuality and relationships.

- Pharmacological treatment, which focuses on reducing sexual arousability and the frequency of deviant sexual fantasies through the use of antiandrogen and antidepressant medication.

These approaches are not mutually exclusive, and the ideal treatment program (yet to be identified) would employ combinations of them. State-of-the-art intervention at this point (cognitive behavior therapy and, when appropriate, medication) can effectively reduce reoffense rates. For example, recidivism rates for new sexual offenses by child molesters treated under the cognitive behavior therapy model, with a focus on relapse prevention, were 4.6% in a 3-year follow-up study (Marques et al., 1993) and 3% in a 6-year follow-up study (Pithers & Cumming, 1989). The nonvolunteer control group in the 3-year follow-up had a sexual recidivism rate of 8.2%, yielding an apparent treatment effect of 3.6%.

When these failure rates are compared to those for Years 3 and 5 in the MTC study . . . of sex offenders who did not receive cognitive behavior therapy, the presumptive effectiveness of treatment in reducing the probability of sexual reoffense is between 7 and 15%. A recent meta-analysis of 12 sex offender treatment studies ($N = 1,313$) found that the overall recidivism rate for untreated sex offenders was 27%, while for treated offenders it was 19%—an apparent treatment effect of 8% (Hall, 1995). These statistics suggest that treatment can reduce child molester recidivism. The wide variability in study findings on reoffense rates of both treated and untreated offenders, however, makes efforts to find optimal treatment interventions as problematic as efforts to assess and predict recidivism.

Community-based maintenance and control. The vast majority of sex offenders are released eventually. Thus, community-based clinical management and control of child molesters are indispensable parts of any rehabilitation program if public safety is to be ensured. An effective community-based maintenance program for child molesters should include the following components:

- Coordination by highly trained and well-supervised parole agents and probation officers who carry small caseloads (15 to 20 offenders) to ensure intensive surveillance/supervision
- Mandatory treatment by therapists trained and supervised in cognitive behavioral theory with sex offenders; this is especially critical for adjustment and maintenance.
- Evaluation for medication
- Proper monitoring and supervision of vocational, social, recreational, and leisure activities
- Confidential notification of local police departments and/or the district attorney's office

Registration with the criminal justice system is a widely practiced, reasonable procedure that should be considered a part of an offender's aftercare plan. Community notification, however, is an untested management technique—that has at least as many potential problems as benefits—and must be empirically evaluated.

Indeed, the general notification of laypersons outside the criminal justice system may increase, rather than decrease, the risk of recidivism by placing extreme pressure on the offender; examples of stressors include threats of bodily harm, termination of employment, on-the-job harassment, and forced instability of residence.

Continuity of treatment is considered a critical factor in managing sex offenders. Maintenance is forever, and relapse prevention never ends. Community-based clinical management must be supportive, vigilant, and informed by current wisdom about maximally effective maintenance strategies.

SECTION 3. REOFFENSE RISK

Dispositional Decisions

Recidivism rates are highly variable, making it impossible to draw any reliable conclusions about reoffense among child molesters as a group. Most recent studies have been conducted in order to evaluate treatment efficacy; consequently, little is known about recidivism independent of some treatment intervention. Moreover, variations in recidivism rates associated with different treatment programs are difficult to interpret. [Comparing] recidivism rates across studies is confounded by [a number of factors]. These include differences in the statutes and sentencing and parole guidelines among jurisdictions; duration of exposure (i.e., time in the community, where the child molester is at liberty to reoffend); offender characteristics; treatment-related variables (including differential attrition rates, program integrity, and amount of treatment); amount and quality of posttreatment supervision; and many other factors.

The criminal justice system is responsible for certain discretionary decisions concerning sex offenders, most of which rest on a presumption about an individual offender's dangerousness or reoffense risk. Examples of decisions driven by underlying assumptions about the probability of recidivism include

- Whether to leave an offender in the community on probation.
- Whether to parole an offender and, if so, the level/duration of supervision needed.
- Whether to recommend compulsory treatment.
- Whether to require registration with the police.
- Whether to notify the community.

From a forensic standpoint, potential danger-ousness is a question central to the disposition of sex offenders. Yet, there is no reliable body of empirically derived data that can inform and guide decision making about reoffense risk—primarily because of methodological differences in existing studies. . . .

Predictors of Sexual Recidivism

Although ample evidence exists to demon-strate the predictive superiority of statistical (actuarial) risk assessment methods over clinical judgment, few concerted efforts have been made to develop and empirically test actuarial predic-tion devices for sexual offenders. The one obvi-ous exception is the work of investigators in Canada, who have focused on psychopathy, measures of prior criminal history, and phallo-metric assessment to predict sexual recidivism (Quinsey et al., 1995). A recent study on risk assessment among extrafamilial child molesters included three of the dimensions used in MTC:CM3 (fixation, social competence, and amount of contact with children). Study research-ers argued that the MTC:CM3 assessment of fixation—a behavioral measure of the strength of an offender's pedophilic interest—may serve as a viable substitute for phallometry, which is intrusive and much more expensive (Prentky et al., 1997).

Risk assessment study of extrafamilial offenders. The predictive value of a rationally derived com-posite of variables for assessing reoffense risk, based on archival data (prison and criminal records), was tested in a follow-up study of extrafamilial child molesters who had been discharged from the Massachusetts Treatment Center over a period of 25 years. The sample of 111 represents 96.5% ($N = 115$) of all child molesters discharged between 1960 and 1984.

Data reveal differential predictive accuracy depending on the type of criminal behavior being examined. Three variables—degree of sexual preoccupation with children (fixation), paraphil-ias (fetishism, transvestism, and promiscuity), and number of prior sexual offenses predicted sexual recidivism, while those variables that reflect impulsive, antisocial behavior predicted recidivism for nonsexual crimes involving physical contact with a victim and violent (sex-ual and nonsexual) crimes.

Unlike other recent studies (e.g., R. K. Hanson, Steffy, & Gauthier, 1993), this study found no evidence for the utility of alcohol history, social competence, and sex of child-victim as predictors of reoffense. In the case of victim sex, one explanation for these inconsistencies may be due to sampling differences. The sample of child molesters examined in this study had an average of three known sexual offenses prior to release. This sample had a higher base rate probability of reoffense than would likely be observed in an unscreened sample of child molesters recruited from the general prison pop-ulation. Among child molesters who are at higher risk to reoffend, the victim's sex may be less important to accurate prediction than such factors as degree of sexual preoccupation with children and impulsivity.

Predictive accuracy. The variables associated with reoffense risk among child molesters that were examined for discriminant validity had reasonable predictive accuracy with regard to both sexual and nonsexual reoffending; overall predictive accuracy was approximately 75%. The results of this study are sample-specific and may not be generalizable. The potential unique-ness of this sample is suggested by the study's failure to find any predictive efficacy for the victim-sex variable.

Although risk assessment procedures that rely exclusively on archival data may never achieve the efficiency of much more time-intensive procedures—such as the penile plethysmo-graph or a comprehensive interview that assesses psychopathy (e.g., the Hare Psychopathy Checklist—Revised, PCL-R) (Hare, 1991)—the distinct advantages of an archival scale include its ease of use (i.e., it does not require the com-pliance or even the presence of the offender), cost efficiency, and relatively high reliability. Despite these presumptive advantages, the abil-ity of such an archivally based procedure to rea-sonably discriminate across samples remains to be demonstrated.

***

CONCLUSION

Sexual offenders constitute the one category of dangerous criminals most subject to either special commitment statutes or ad hoc discre-tionary and dispositional decisions. These laws and the decisions that they require are often based on assumptions about sex offenders that are, at best, misleading and, at worst, erroneous. Given the serious concerns about sex offenders within the criminal justice system and society at large, the need for valid diagnostic and assess-ment tools is urgent. Indeed, the most formidable task is to develop empirically corroborated esti-mates of sexual reoffense probabilities for differ-ent subgroups of sex offenders under standardized operational conditions.

Practitioners, researchers, and legislators should be guided by moderation, clear vision, and empirical evidence. Over the years, many laws governing sex offenders have been enacted and later repealed (Carter & Prentky, 1993; Grubin & Prentky, 1993). Two timely examples of presumably well-intentioned but problematic legislation are the much-discussed community notification laws and the new California law requiring repeat sex offenders to choose between "chemical castration" (i.e., treatment with antiandrogenic medication) or surgical cas-tration. The California statute poses difficulties on several counts:

- From an ethical standpoint, mandating either an intrusive, irreversible surgical procedure or treatment with a drug that the U.S. Food and Drug Administration has not approved for use with sex offenders is highly questionable.
- From a practical standpoint, sex offenders cannot be relied on to comply with a drug regimen to which they have not consented and from which they cannot withdraw. Moreover, the apparently compliant offender can easily circumvent the effects of the drugs or the surgery by buying testosterone (steroids) on the street.
- From an empirical standpoint, the law makes the invalid assumption that all sex offenders are motivated by uncontrollable sexual urges. Chemical reduction of testosterone is appropri-ate for some, but not all, child molesters; when medication is used, it must be included as one component of a treatment plan that includes therapy. It is critical to keep in mind, however, that surgical or chemical reduction of testos-terone will not, by itself, solve the problem of child molestation.

Reducing the risk of recidivism among sex offenders is a problem for which no easy answers or shortcuts exist. Treatment provided in prison must be continued after offenders are released into the community. Reintegration is especially problematic for child molesters. Detailed after-care plans, orchestrated by well-trained and supervised parole agents and probation officers, are essential to reducing reoffense risk and should include consideration of the vocational, psychotherapeutic, pharmacological, social, and recreational needs of the offender.

Clearly, the most compelling motive for treat-ing child molesters is the reduction in victimiza-tion rates that is presumed to result. Society resists treating sexual offenders, however, because to do so is perceived as a humane response to intolerable behavior. If treatment can be demonstrated to reduce the probability of reoffense, then working on the development and refinement of treatment methods and procedures is an essential secondary intervention.

The criminal justice community faces dif-ficult, but not insuperable, challenges as it moves to balance the right of the community to be protected with the rights of offenders. If those professionals who deal with the victims and perpetrators of child molestation are willing to harness their collective energy, pull in a common direction, and speak with a single firm voice, properly informed laws can be enacted that will better control child molesters and make communities safer for children.

UNIT IV

Victimology and Victim Services

Introduction and Commentary

Services to victims and research focusing on victims of crime have only recently been recognized as important components of forensic psychology. Yet, many psychologists are more likely to come into contact with victims than with offenders. As we noted in Chapter 1, forensic psychologists evaluate and treat crime victims, testify about the effects of their experience in both criminal and civil courts, and train law enforcement officers on effective approaches to interviewing them. Death notification—informing individuals of the sudden death of a loved one—is another example of their many tasks. The articles in this section help us better understand the prevalence as well as the psychological effects of victimization.

The first article, by **Sarah E. Ullman,** is a recent update of her 1987 article reviewing the empirical literature on rape avoidance. Ullman focuses on both effective and ineffective strategies that a potential victim may adopt when confronted by an attacker. She also discusses risky situations, the role of alcohol, and victim–offender relationships, and she offers crucial and sensible advice with regard to rapist typologies. In an interesting section on barriers to resistance, Ullman highlights social psychological factors that lead some women to *not* resist, including fear and the perception of stigmatization.

The reading by **Bonnie S. Fisher and her colleagues** reports on findings from a national random sample of female college students, the extent to which they have been sexually victimized, and information on whether they reported their victimization. Whereas the great majority did not report the crime to police or college officials, three-fourths of the respondents indicated they had told *someone,* usually a friend rather than a family member or mental health worker. While not a surprising finding, it leads the authors to discuss implications for college and university officials as well as treatment providers. The article also includes an interesting discussion on the differences between feminist and conservative interpretations of the results of this study.

A different form of self-reported victimization—anti-gay violence—is highlighted in the article written by **Kristen Kuehnle** and **Anne Sullivan**. Bias or hatred of an individual or group because of their sexual orientation is the second most frequent form of hate or bias crimes, following those motivated by racial hatred. In this descriptive study, the authors report on the characteristics of 241 incidents of violence against gays, lesbians, or transgendered individuals.

In contrast to past research on victimization, the typical victim of *anti-gay* violence is not a young African American male, but rather an older male or transgendered individual, Latino or white. The authors also report where the victimizations occurred, relationships between victims and offenders, and whether the victims reported the incidents to police and sought medical attention.

In recent years, some researchers have been paying more attention to "covictims" of homicide and other violent crimes. These are individuals who are deeply affected by the crime but have been largely ignored by researchers and the criminal justice system. Covictims are generally believed to be relatives or close friends of the primary victim, but workplace colleagues, the individual who discovers a brutal homicide, or even the officers who investigate it may be covictims as well. The last reading in this section reminds us that the family or close friends of the perpetrator also may experience this secondary victimization. **Sarah Eschholz and her fellow researchers** conducted interviews with family members of individuals tried for murder. Eschholz et al. found that these family members were extremely sympathetic to the crime victims and their families. However, relatives of the offenders also experienced significant psychological trauma. The article highlights the importance of restorative justice, an approach that addresses the need to make communities whole again after crimes have been committed.

As a group, these readings sensitize us to the psychological effects of victimization and possible relationships between and among various forms of victimization. Although the selections focus on violent victimization, readers should be aware that researchers are beginning to pay more attention to the psychological effects of nonviolent victimization, such as fraud or burglary. While the harm resulting from these offenses does not tend to be physical in nature, victims of these offenses often feel vulnerable, helpless, and cynical about persons and institutions in which they previously had had trust.

13

A 10-Year Update of "Review and Critique of Empirical Studies of Rape Avoidance"

Sarah E. Ullman

To understand women's resistance to rape in contemporary society, it is important to understand the historical and legal context of the phenomenon of women's resistance to rape. Resistance strategies refer to verbal and physical actions that women may engage in when confronted by potential rapists. Historically, women were held responsible for resisting rape to the utmost according to English common law, which is the basis of contemporary rape laws that have evolved in the United States. Rape has been defined as vaginal penetration of a female against her will by force or threat of force without her consent. The FBI continues to define rape in this way, although legal definitions in many states have been broadened in recent years. The traditional definition emerged from the fact that, historically, women were the legal property of their fathers and husbands, and rape was considered a crime against a man's property (i.e., his wife or daughter), which was damaged or spoiled by the offense. Resistance, especially physical resistance, was considered evidence of nonconsent. Injuries suffered in the struggle were expected to corroborate a woman's complaint that the sexual activity was indeed nonconsensual (i.e., rape). Although rape laws have been reformed and legal standards expecting victim resistance have been loosened in most states, victims are often still expected to resist so that others believe that sexual activity was indeed without their consent. Police and prosecutors still use evidence regarding victim's use of resistance as a way to support the credibility of rape claims (Abarbanel, 1986). The expectation that women resist serves to hold women responsible for controlling male sexual aggression and contributes to victim blaming in cases of rape.

Editors' Note: This article first appeared in *Criminal Justice and Behavior,* Vol. 34, No. 3, March 2007, pp. 411–429. Reprinted with permission of Sage Publications.

The early study of the causes of crime victimization by victimologist Menachem Amir (1971) is reflected in his theory of victim precipitation, which states that at least some rapes are the result of behaviors engaged in by victims that led to or precipitated their attacks.

In the 1970s, second-wave feminists attacked this theory for blaming victims (Russell, 1975) and decried the poor treatment of rape victims by criminal justice and medical systems (Bevacqua, 2000). Except for cases where women were raped by strangers in circumstances resulting in excessive injuries (seen as proof that the sexual activity was forced) with no morally questionable behavior on their part (e.g., being out in public at night, drinking), rape victims were considered less than innocent in their own attacks. Few women (typically less than 10%) reported attacks to police, and this remains true today (Bachman, 1998; B. S. Fisher, Daigle, Cullen, & Turner, 2003). Two thirds of rapes are committed by men known to their victims, according to large-scale epidemiological studies (Kilpatrick, Edmunds, & Seymour, 1992; Tjaden & Thoennes, 2000) that show most rapes do not fit the stranger stereotype.

Because rape was defined as a crime committed mostly by strangers until the mid-1980s, most rape prevention efforts were focused on telling women to restrict their behavior (e.g., refrain from going out at night, wearing revealing clothing, or drinking). Although this advice has been criticized for restricting women's freedom and full participation in society, it is still recommended in some self-help books and by some police officers. Advice to women to restrict their behavior is also supported by lifestyle and routine activities theories of victimization, which posit that one's risk of being victimized results from being out at night in places where situational opportunities, vulnerable targets, and motivated offenders come together without capable guardians to protect potential victims (see Meier & Miethe, 1993, for a review). These theories assume that most crime is committed by strangers or people who do not know each other

well, outside, at night, in public places. However, we now know that most violent crime is committed by people known to each other and very often in the home. This is especially true of rape and other violence against women (Bachman, 1994). Police traditionally warned women not to fight back if attacked by a rapist. They were instead told to play along or try to talk their way out of rapes (Storaska, 1975)—strategies that subsequent research shows to be ineffective (Ullman, 1997).

Despite contemporary awareness of the high prevalence of date rape and acquaintance rape, first revealed by Mary Koss's (1985) national survey of college students in the mid-1980s and followed by other community-wide prevalence surveys showing that most rapes occur between intimates and acquaintances (Fisher, Cullen, & Turner, 2000; Tjaden & Thoennes, 2000), victims are still disbelieved, stigmatized, and held responsible for their attacks (Ullman, 1999a). These negative reactions are harmful to women's psychological functioning and may lead to or reinforce their own self-blame for being raped (Ullman, Townsend, Filipas, & Starzynski, 2007).

In response to this problem, rape prevention programs have been developed, many of which are in college settings, but they focus mostly on increasing knowledge about rape and changing attitudes that are believed to contribute to rape, such as rape myths, which are false beliefs about rape (e.g., women who dress in provocative clothing are asking to be raped). Although rape-supportive attitudes are held by many in society, there is no evidence that prevention programs can effectively change these attitudes over long periods of time or that changing these attitudes will necessarily lead to less rape (Anderson & Whiston, 2005; Brecklin & Forde, 2001; Flores & Hartlaub, 1998; Sochting, Fairbrother, & Koch, 2004). On the other hand, research consistently shows that certain resistance strategies can be used by women to avoid rapes, implying that prevention programs should focus on teaching women effective resistance methods to protect themselves.

IMPACT OF RAPE: COSTS AND BENEFITS OF RESISTANCE

Resistance and rape avoidance are important because research shows that women who have experienced a completed rape have poorer mental health, such as more depression, anxiety, suicidal ideation, and suicide attempts, than women experiencing attempted rape (Kilpatrick, Saunders, Amick-McMullan, & Best, 1989; Ullman & Brecklin, 2002; Ullman & Siegel, 1993). Furthermore, sexual assaults of a more severe nature are related to poorer physical health outcomes, ranging from acute physical injuries, to immediate postassault acute health problems, to increased risk of developing chronic medical conditions (Golding, 1999; Koss & Heslet, 1992; Ullman & Brecklin, 2003; Ullman & Siegel, 1995). In addition, women's risks of contracting sexually transmitted diseases or becoming pregnant are higher if they suffer completed rapes. Therefore, reducing completed rapes may reduce victims' health problems and associated medical care costs. Some evidence suggests women feel better about themselves and less depressed if they resist rape, even if they are unable to avoid rape completion (Bart & O'Brien, 1985). Because costs to individual women and society are greater when more rapes are completed, any efforts to reduce completed rapes are important. Of course, concurrent prevention efforts must focus on men who are the primary perpetrators of rapes and on stopping rape from ever occurring. Unfortunately, effective prevention programs have yet to be identified that reduce male perpetration. Therefore, "risk reduction" programs that teach women facts about rape, risky situations, and effective resistance are needed. At the same time, rape prevention programs that target men can be developed and evaluated.

RAPE RESISTANCE STRATEGIES

Many women try to resist verbally and physically aggressive assailants in one or more ways.

Research shows that using more resistance strategies and resisting immediately are related to avoiding completed rape (Ullman, 1997). Different types of resistance are related to different odds of suffering completed rape and physical injuries. Furthermore, assailants' assault tactics occur in varying circumstances that differentially constrain women's options for resistance. Research shows that attacks at night, with weapons, and in indoor and/or isolated locations are related to rape completion (Ullman, 1997). However, victim resistance may lead to avoiding rape, even in such circumstances, and must be examined in detail, paying close attention to relationship contexts and alcohol/substance use, which can affect women's ability and willingness to resist as well as the perceived efficacy of resistance.

Effective strategies. A number of studies find that several active resistance strategies are effective for avoiding rape without increasing risk of physical injury. Forceful physical resistance or fighting refers to physical actions women use against their attackers, including biting, scratching, hitting, using a weapon, and martial arts or other physical self-defense techniques. These strategies are not commonly used by victims in rape situations, with studies showing only approximately 20% to 25% of women using these types of forceful physical resistance. Studies of police-reported rapes (Zoucha-Jensen & Coyne, 1993) and unreported rapes identified in the National Crime Victimization Survey (NCVS) (Clay-Warner, 2002) continue to show that women who fight back forcefully are more likely to avoid completed rape (see Ullman, 1997, for a review).

Despite this positive news, some researchers have expressed concern that women who physically fight back forcefully, in particular, in response to rape may sustain more physical injuries by increasing the offender's use of violence against them in the attack (Prentky, Burgess, & Carter, 1986). Unfortunately, most studies showing that women's physical fighting is related to more physical injury still fail to take into account whether the women were already being physically attacked when they resisted. This is important because of the possibility that the offender's initial physical attack was the determinant of victim injury. The sequencing of offender violence and victim resistance in relation to assault outcomes must be assessed to draw accurate conclusions about the effects of resistance on attack outcomes. Results are misleading when simple correlations of victim resistance with assault outcome are performed, without regard for when the resistance occurs during the attack.

Specifically, positive correlations of forceful fighting by victims with physical injury appear to be spurious, resulting from the fact that victims were being more violently attacked in these situations before they resisted. When the sequence of attack-resistance-injury has been taken into account, studies show that fighting leads to less completed rape and no increase or decrease in physical injury (Quinsey & Upfold, 1985; Ullman, 1998; Ullman & Knight, 1992). It is clear that these different results have important implications for rape avoidance advice given to women who must weigh the options and potential consequences of resistance in deciding how to respond to an attack. Most important, women should be encouraged (if they are able and so choose) to resist rape (especially by men who are physically attacking them) with forceful strategies, including fighting, known to increase their chances of avoiding completed rape.

Nonforceful physical resistance strategies used by women against attackers include fleeing, guarding one's body with one's arms, struggling, and so forth. Most research continues to find that women using these forms of physical resistance are more likely to avoid completed rape and no more or less likely to be physically injured. Recent evidence supports the efficacy of physical resistance. Clay-Warner's (2002) recent study of NCVS data show that a variable combining nonforceful and forceful forms of physical resistance (as contrasted with verbal resistance) was related to avoiding rape, controlling for situational factors and other resistance strategies in a logistic regression.

Forceful verbal resistance refers to strong verbal responses such as screaming, yelling, and swearing at the attacker. These are effective strategies for avoiding rape, particularly in response to offenders using verbal threats (Ullman, 1997, 1998). However, a study of NCVS data, without sequence information, shows that physical resistance was more effective than verbal resistance for avoiding rape (Clay-Warner, 2002). Clay-Warner concluded that forceful verbal resistance was ineffective in a logistic regression analysis controlling for assault characteristics and other resistance strategies. This study constitutes a more conservative test of the efficacy of resistance strategies.

Ineffective strategies. Nonforceful verbal resistance strategies include verbal responses of pleading, crying, and reasoning (e.g., trying to talk the offender out of rape). All are related to greater odds of rape completion. Not resisting, sometimes also called "immobility" or freezing, also is related to completed rape. Nevertheless, women are sometimes unable to resist rape if taken by surprise or if they freeze when confronted by an attacker. Recent studies using NCVS data (Clay-Warner, 2002) and police data (Scott & Beaman, 2004) continue to confirm this finding. Not resisting the offender is related to greater odds of experiencing completed rape, but it is unrelated to physical injury (Ullman, 1997).

Summary. In summary, fighting, fleeing, and screaming/yelling are all associated with decreased odds of completed rape. It is possible that verbal resistance is less effective than physical resistance, but without sequence information, this is unclear. Furthermore, these effective strategies do not appear to increase the odds of physical injury in studies that examine the sequence of offender attack, victim resistance, and injury/rape outcomes. Thus, research suggests that women should not be told to refrain from resisting as this increases their odds of experiencing completed rape. Research on resistance strategies continues to support the efficacy of forceful resistance, especially physical resistance, for avoiding rape.

Clay-Warner's (2002) research shows that the efficacy of resistance strategies changes when controls for use of multiple resistance strategies and situational factors are included in multivariate analyses. Specifically, resistance may not have different effects according to situational factors. This is an important advance compared to prior studies. However, more work is needed with different samples to replicate these findings and to consider the sequence of attack-resistance on assault outcomes.

More research is needed about what resistance works in which situations, but thus far, it still appears that resistance needs to be as forceful as the offender's attack and to match the type of strategy used by the attacker. In other words, if a woman is threatened, screaming may be enough to avoid rape, whereas if she is physically attacked, she may need to fight to be able to escape. Studies typically show that women do respond with verbal resistance to verbal threats and physical resistance to physical attacks (Siegel, Sorenson, Golding, Burnam, & Stein, 1987; Ullman, 1998; Ullman & Knight, 1992). Recent studies of acquaintance rape confirm this pattern of results (Macy, Nurius, & Norris, 2006) previously documented in stranger rapes. Research on resistance and self-defense training also supports more qualitative work showing that formal self-defense training enhances women's psychological well-being and belief they can avoid rape (McCaughey, 1997). Some data suggest that such training can help women avoid rapes, but rigorous evaluations have yet to be done (see Brecklin, in press, for a review of self-defense training studies).

Despite the fact that resistance can help women to avoid rape, this should not be taken to mean that they must resist rape or that it is their fault if they are unable to stop it. Although it should not be women's responsibility to avoid rape, society and the legal system still expect women to do so (Estrich, 1987). Because of this expectation, advising women to resist may reinforce society's expectation that women must resist and that they are to blame if they do not. On the other hand, women need to be told what works and then be free to choose how they want

to respond. Failing to inform them about how to avoid rape makes it less likely they will resist because of fear or belief they cannot avoid rape. The result can be less resistance and more completed rape with its negative consequences. Teaching women that resistance works and how to actually resist or use self-defense may not always be sufficient for helping them avoid completed rapes, however. There are other barriers to resistance, discussed later, especially with men whom women know well or with whom they are in a relationship. In addition, various situational and contextual factors affect rape resistance.

SITUATIONAL FACTORS AFFECTING RAPE RESISTANCE

Situational factors are characteristics of the attack itself and/or contextual factors surrounding the scene of an assault. Many situational factors are associated with whether women are likely to avoid completed rape and physical injuries. These factors include whether there is a social situation surrounding the assault, such as a party or bar environment. Another factor is the prerape behavior of victims and offenders. For instance, drinking by offenders and victims prior to attack may affect both women's likelihood of being attacked and the assault outcomes. The victim–offender relationship refers to whether the victim knew the offender prior to the attack and the nature of that relationship (e.g., stranger, nonromantic acquaintance, romantic acquaintance, husband/lover) and may also affect the outcome of rape.

Other characteristics of the attack, such as whether a weapon is involved, where the attack takes place, the time of day, and whether environmental intervention occurs (e.g., presence of other people or factors that might intervene or otherwise deter the assailant from continuing an attack), affect whether rape is likely to be completed as well as the physical injuries women experience. Finally, some have argued that the type of rapist committing the attack may affect women's ability to avoid rape.

Risky situations. Few studies examine the efficacy of resistance across situations, although Clay-Warner's (2002) recent study of NCVS data suggests that effectiveness of resistance strategies does not vary across most assault situations. More research is needed on the efficacy of specific resistance strategies in different assault situations because type of resistance may vary by assault characteristics (Clay-Warner, 2003).

Certain places and situations may put women at a greater risk of rape and affect their ability to effectively resist an attacker. Criminologists have tried to explain individuals' risk of violent crime with lifestyle and routine activities theories of victimization (Meier & Miethe, 1993). According to these theories, one's risk of being victimized can be explained by the convergence of several factors: risky situations, suitable targets, motivated offenders, and an absence of capable guardians. For example, a young woman drinking alone in a bar who meets a sexually aggressive man may face a higher risk of sexual victimization. These theories have traditionally been useful for explaining risk of violent stranger victimization, which is typically associated with engaging in activities outdoors, at night, with delinquent peers. Therefore, they may help to explain women's risk of stranger rape. However, because different contexts and relationship factors characterize attacks by acquaintances and intimate partners, different theories (or modifications of existing theories) may be needed to understand risk and avoidance of sexual assault by known men.

Rapes by acquaintances and intimates often occur indoors, in isolated locations, and sometimes are part of a series of attacks by the same perpetrator (e.g., in cases of intimate partner rape). Research also shows additional factors are related to risk of acquaintance rape, such as women initiating dates, men paying for dates, use of alcohol or drugs by one or both parties, and women going to men's homes (Muehlenhard & Linton, 1987). A recent study of college women shows that women who had been victimized in the past, drank more alcohol, had multiple sexual partners, had poor psychological adjustment, and experienced insecurity about relationships with men were more likely to report being sexually victimized at a follow-up assessment (Greene & Navarro, 1998).

Bars appear to be quite risky settings for women because they are more likely to be both physically and sexually attacked in and around these contexts (Parks & Miller, 1997). Just being in a bar, regardless of how much one has been drinking, appears to put one at greater risk of being targeted by sexually aggressive men, according to research on women who frequent bars (Parks & Zetes-Zanatta, 1999). This finding is consistent with experimental research, which shows that people view drinking victims as legitimate targets of sexual aggression and hold them more responsible for their own assaults (Abbey, Ross, McDuffie, & McAuslan, 1996).

Fraternity and sports participation may be associated with increased risk of sexual assault (Koss & Dinero, 1988; Koss & Gaines, 1993). Current research, however, is unable to answer whether fraternity members or college athletes are more likely than other men to commit sexual aggression either alone or in groups (Frintner & Rubinson, 1993; Humphrey & Kahn, 2000; Koss & Cleveland, 1996). It is possible that behaviors often associated with these groups are in fact what predict sexual aggression. A recent study of college men shows that greater problematic alcohol use and adherence to masculinity norms supportive of violence against women were associated with self-reported sexual aggression but not with athletic involvement (Locke & Mahalik, 2005).

Rapes committed by more than one man (e.g., gang rapes) appear to be more violent in nature, and women are less able to avoid completed rape and other sexual acts in these cases than in single-offender rapes (Ullman, 1999b; Ullman, 2007). More research is needed on potentially high-risk populations, such as fraternities and sports teams. Foubert's (2000) empirical study evaluating actual sexually aggressive behavior of fraternity men is the only such study to have been published. Fraternity men participating in a rape prevention program were less accepting of rape myths and said they were less likely to commit rape 7 months after program completion. However, there was no decline in how much sexually coercive behavior they admitted to committing after the prevention program compared with those not receiving the program.

Environmental/bystander intervention. Environmental interventions are persons, events, and noises that interrupt assaults in progress and appear to facilitate rape avoidance by allowing victims a chance to escape (Bart & O'Brien, 1985; Ullman & Knight, 1991). Few studies of rape avoidance have examined the impact of environmental interventions or presence of bystanders on rape avoidance. Clay-Warner (2002) found that the presence of bystanders was associated with avoiding rape in the NCVS, as it was in two studies in Ullman's (1997) review. Recently, Banyard, Plante, and Moynihan (2004) argued that prevention messages should be targeted to community members to increase their willingness to take an active role in prevention training and intervening in rape situations.

Drinking by offenders and victims. Men and women who drink heavily have an increased risk of perpetrating or being victimized by sexual assault . . . (see Ullman, 2003, for a review). This suggests that interventions to reduce drinking-related assaults may need to address abusive drinking in general. The role that alcohol plays in actual rape attacks is unclear, but drinking is involved in . . . one half to two thirds of all sexual assaults (including stranger and known offenders). Alcohol's presence does not necessarily mean that it is a causal factor in the occurrence of rapes or in the resulting injuries offenders inflict on their victims. For example, drinking before an assault is correlated with other factors also related to the rape outcome, such as social situations in which victim and offender are less acquainted with each other (e.g., parties, bars). It may be these risky social contexts, and not the drinking itself, that confer sexual assault risk. Recent research involving both college and community samples indicates

that both victim and offender drinking are associated with more completed rapes. Victims who have been drinking may be less able to effectively resist rapes on a behavioral level (Harrington & Leitenberg, 1994; Scott & Beaman, 2004; Ullman, Karabatsos, & Koss, 1999). However, other social-psychological barriers to resisting rape have been reported by women, including fear of rejection by the man and/or one's peer network, embarrassment, and perceiving that one is too intoxicated to escape even if one resists (Norris, Nurius, & Dimeff, 1996). Recent studies of college women also suggest that women who drink blame themselves more, both of which are associated with tonic immobility and less effective resistance (Macy et al., 2006; Nurius, Norris, Macy, & Huang, 2004), although these are cross-sectional retrospective data. It is possible that women who drink resist assault less, which leads to greater self-blame and possibly greater rape completion.

Current research on the relationship of drinking and outcomes of sexual assaults is inconsistent. Offender drinking has been thought to decrease men's inhibitions against using violence, which could translate into more severe assault outcomes (e.g., completed rape, physical injuries) to women. This disinhibition theory of alcohol-related violence is based on experimental evidence showing that men who drink engage in more aggression in laboratory settings (see Bushman & Cooper, 1990, for a review). Furthermore, representative sample studies show that offender drinking is related to more victim physical injury in sexual assault incidents (Martin & Bachman, 1998). Recent studies of college students and National Crime Survey data show that rapists' use of violence is related to more rape completion when offenders are not drinking (Cleveland, Koss, & Lyons, 1999; Ullman & Brecklin, 2000). Instead of drinking and physical aggression having a synergistic (combined) effect, they may be independent strategies used by offenders to complete rapes (Cleveland, Koss, & Lyons, 1999), because each one is more predictive of physical injury in the absence of the other (Ullman & Brecklin, 2000). If victims perceive their attackers to be drunk and fear they are out of control and may become more violent, they therefore may decide not to resist. Alternatively, offenders who get their victims drunk may impair their ability to resist, whereas offenders may need to use more violence to complete rape if drinking is not involved. Drinking is more common in assaults occurring with less well-known offenders and in unplanned social situations, but some research shows more severe sexual victimization of college women in unplanned social situations and in cases where offenders were not drinking (Abbey et al., 1996; Brecklin & Ullman, 2001; Ullman et al., 1999).

It is clear that drinking is associated with the outcomes of sexual assaults, but more research is needed to understand the role of drinking in the physical injury experienced by women, not just the rape outcome, which is examined in most studies. Alcohol abuse prevention efforts are clearly integral to prevention of alcohol-related sexual assaults, and more research is needed on the role of drinking in different assault contexts so that specific information about alcohol's role in sexual assaults can be integrated into prevention programs. Two conclusions may be drawn from current research in relation to drinking and rape. First, it should not be assumed that drinking prior to assault causes offenders to become more violent and complete more rapes. Sex offender researchers have argued that drinking is unlikely to cause someone not otherwise predisposed to sexual aggression to commit rape (Seto & Barbaree, 1995). Second, women's drinking in and of itself should not be assumed to increase their risk of sexual victimization. National studies show that rapes where only offenders were drinking (as opposed to both victim and offender) were related to greater rape completion (Brecklin & Ullman, 2002) and victim injury (Ullman & Brecklin, 2000), suggesting a greater role of offender, not victim, drinking in assault outcomes. Although drinking appears to put women at greater risk of completed rape, this may be because of other situational, behavioral, and social-psychological factors not yet completely understood.

Victim–offender relationship. At least two thirds of rapes are committed by men known to the victim (Kilpatrick et al., 1992; Tjaden & Thoennes, 2000). A woman's relationship to the attacker prior to the assault is related to the rape outcome. There is some inconsistency as to whether resistance is more or less effective in response to strangers or known men, but women appear to be more likely to avoid stranger rapes (Ullman, 1997; Ullman, Filipas, Townsend, & Starzynski, 2006), probably because they are more willing to resist these attackers (Martin & Bachman, 1998). Most research shows that women resist much less when attacked by known perpetrators, but their resistance is equally effective for avoiding rape completion in these cases. The fact that women are less predisposed to resist attacks by known men makes them much more vulnerable to completed sexual assaults, particularly by intimate partners (Ullman & Siegel, 1993). Although Koss (1985) found that all victims were equally likely to physically resist rapes in a college population, other studies show less physical resistance to intimates than to stranger and acquaintance assailants (Clay-Warner, 2002; Scott & Beaman, 2004; Ullman & Siegel, 1993).

Approximately 25% to 30% of rapes are perpetrated by intimate partners (Mahoney & Williams, 1998). A significant proportion of domestic violence situations also involve sexual assaults, which may be repeated within an intimate relationship and are obviously much more difficult for victims to avoid. Married women reported not resisting assaults by their husbands because they felt it was their duty to submit, feared resisting would make husbands more violent, wanted to protect their children, knew from past experience that resistance was useless, or did not feel psychologically and physically trained to fight (Finkelhor & Yllo, 1985). It is clear that preventing rape in intimate relationships may require dealing with chronically violent men who repeatedly assault their partners in marital, cohabiting, or dating relationships (Bergen, 1996). Resisting rapes by intimate partners is likely to be more difficult, and some women find that ending their relationships may be the only way to stop sexual assault by partners. More research is needed on how women avoid rape by men they know and whether specific resistance strategies differ in effectiveness for different types of known offenders. Research suggests that forceful resistance strategies can enhance women's ability to avoid completed rape by both known and stranger assailants.

Weapons. Another factor that may affect women's ability to resist and avoid rape is whether a weapon is involved. Fortunately, few rapes involve weapons (less than 11%) according to recent national data (Bachman, 1998). This is especially true of rapes by known attackers. Offenders who display weapons to their victims are more likely to complete rape, but evidence is mixed about whether offenders with weapons are more likely to injure their victims (see Ullman, 2002). Victims attacked with weapons are more likely to develop posttraumatic stress disorder because of fear they might have been killed during the attack (Kilpatrick et al., 1989). Even when offenders have weapons, the physical injury they inflict tends to be minor, and completion of the rape itself is usually the most serious outcome for victims. Only about one third of sexual assault victims sustain injuries, usually of a minor nature, such as cuts, bruises, and scratches (Ullman, 1997).

Fortunately, resistance appears to be just as effective for avoiding rape by armed assailants (Ullman, 1997). Rapists appear to use weapons to inhibit victim resistance, not to cause gratuitous injuries. Victims are more likely to be injured by rapists carrying nonlethal weapons of convenience (e.g., sticks, stones) than lethal weapons, possibly because victims resist less when confronted with lethal weapons. However, some data suggest that victims respond with more physical resistance to assailants bearing weapons in police-reported cases (Scott & Beaman, 2004). If victims have weapons, they are less likely to be raped (Kleck & Sayles, 1990; Quigley, 1989), but few women have weapons ready to use in situations involving men they

know and trust, who commit the majority of sexual assaults. More research is needed to understand the role of different types of weapons in rapes. Specifically, information is needed about how different types of resistance strategies used by women may vary in effectiveness in response to offenders with different types of weapons. Clay-Warner (2002) examined this issue in NCVS data and found no effect of physical resistance in assaults with weapons, whereas physical resistance was related to less completed rape in attacks without weapons. This may temper our prior conclusion (Ullman, 1997) that women can successfully avoid completed rape, even by offenders bearing weapons (by using forceful resistance). Although it does appear that women may be more likely to avoid rape if they have a weapon themselves, more research is needed on this issue. Unfortunately, no research using sequence data examines the role of weapons in relationship to subsequent victim resistance and injury outcomes of rapes, including Clay-Warner, so this issue is unresolved.

Rapist type. Researchers have identified different types of rapists that differ according to various psychological and behavioral characteristics (R. A. Knight, 1999). There is little research examining whether women's resistance may vary in effectiveness to attacks by different types of rapists. This issue may be of concern if certain types of rapists (e.g., sadists) are more likely to respond to victim resistance with increased physical violence, as some have warned. The only study of resistance using an empirically validated rapist typology (e.g., classification system for typing offenders) shows no differences in the effectiveness of women's different resistance strategies for avoiding rape and injury according to rapist type (Ullman & Knight, 1995). More research is needed, but concerns that sadistic rapists or other specific rapist types (e.g., pervasively angry, opportunistic, nonsadistic sexual, vindictive) will inflict more injury on victims who forcefully resist (Prentky et al., 1986) remain unfounded to date. The most important factor affecting the amount of injury to victims is how much violence offenders use during the attack. Fortunately, this is an observable behavior that does not require women to figure out the type of rapist attacking them before deciding how or whether to resist. Until research shows otherwise, women should not be discouraged from resisting rape based on fears that offenders will respond with increased violence.

BARRIERS TO RESISTANCE: SOCIAL-PSYCHOLOGICAL FACTORS AND VICTIMIZATION HISTORY

Teaching women what resistance strategies are effective and how to use these strategies may not be enough to help them avoid rape, especially by known men. Various social-psychological barriers exist for women in dating situations that may need to be addressed in high school and college women, including embarrassment and fear of peer group rejection for resisting men's sexual aggression (Norris et al., 1996). These barriers may also be rooted in gender role socialization that encourages women to put the needs of others, especially men, above their own needs. Because society holds women responsible for rape and often blames them for men's sexually aggressive behavior, many women deny they have been raped and will not label themselves as rape victims (Koss, 1985). Because of this, they may internalize self-blame for experiences that make them feel victimized but for which costs of acknowledgment are too high. Women report that they perceive they face low personal risk for sexual aggression from acquaintances and low preparedness to protect themselves against this threat (Nurius, 2000). Therefore, to develop effective resistance efforts, more research is needed on factors shaping risk perceptions and how these factors influence women's risk reduction and self-protection behaviors. Gidycz, McNamara, and Edwards (2006) reviewed the literature on women's risk perception and sexual assault and concluded that although women generally underestimate their risk, relative to peers, of being assaulted, it is not

clear from existing studies that they have deficits in their ability to perceive risk. Even women with prior victimization histories can detect risk, sometimes as well [as] or better than nonvictimized women, but they show different behavioral responses to sexual assault situations, namely, less assertive responding.

Concerns about rejection by men, embarrassment at how others might negatively judge their resistance (e.g., by blaming women for asking for it), and fears of being stigmatized by friends or peers affect women's decisions of how to respond to acquaintance sexual aggression. Women's fears of negative reactions from others are well founded, as they often receive negative social reactions (e.g., blame, stigma, controlling responses, egocentric responses, disbelief) when disclosing sexual assaults (Ullman, 1999a). These social concerns may override their ability to recognize danger and take action in acquaintance rape situations. In addition, drinking may lead women to focus on cues concerning positive aspects of social situations, such as having fun and meeting men, instead of potential danger cues.

In a study of acquaintance sexual assault, Nurius, Norris, Young, Graham, and Gaylord (2000) found that college women were more likely to respond assertively to a man's sexual aggression when he used physical force, when she was concerned about injury, when she was not concerned about preserving the relationship, and when she felt angry and confident. On the other hand, women used diplomatic responses when the man used verbal coercion, when she was self-conscious of her responses, and when she felt sadder and less angry. These findings suggest that risk reduction interventions need to address women's emotional responses to sexual assault situations and that increasing women's confidence may help them actively resist sexual aggression, as suggested by self-defense experts. Another study of 415 college women assaulted by acquaintances shows that women who were less concerned about the offender's judgment, engaged in less self-blame, and had greater resentment were more likely to use more resistance (Nurius et al., 2004). Using structural equation modeling, this study also shows that women's alcohol use was related to greater self-blame for rape, which was associated with more immobility and diplomatic responding. However, alcohol use was not related to complete immobility but instead, to attempts to verbally negotiate out of sexual assault. These results suggest a complex relationship of alcohol use, social cognitive responses, and resistance to acquaintance sexual assault.

Only one study evaluates whether addressing social-psychological barriers in a prevention program reduces risk of sexual victimization in college women. Breitenbecher and Scarce (2001) gave a treatment group a 90-minute educational program that included information about sexual assault prevalence, rape myths, sex role socialization, and rape as an act of power. A component was added to build skills in sexual communication to teach women effective verbal and behavioral responses to sexual assault after imagining the emotions and thoughts they would expect in such a situation. The treatment group showed no reduction in sexual assault risk compared to a control group of women at a 7-month follow-up. In addition, knowledge about sexual assault, dating behaviors, sexual communication, and perception of risk were unaffected by participating in the program. Possible reasons that victimization was not reduced include small sample size, the fact that one-shot interventions may be inadequate, and the program's lack of actual physical training in resistance/self-defense to sexual assault. In summary, social-psychological barriers may affect women's ability to resist sexual victimization and may need to be addressed in risk reduction efforts. More research is needed to determine whether efforts to reduce these barriers in women can lower their risk of being attacked and help them to avoid completed rapes once attacked. Educating women about these barriers may help them to become more aware of and less influenced by internal barriers to their own self-protection and resistance during attacks.

Although awareness of barriers is likely an important target for prevention, another study of 212 college women (Macy et al., 2006) finds that outcomes of acquaintance rapes are affected by not only assailant behavior and victim responses but also women's emotions and appraisals. Macy et al. concluded that reducing self-blame was needed. Self-blame was higher for victims who were drinking prior to assault and led to less victim resistance and poorer psychological aftermath. In addition, the authors suggested training women to detect threat and be aware of perpetrator tactics (e.g., isolating women, giving them drinks); to use effective resistance strategies; and to understand how their expectancies, behaviors, and prior victimization histories may affect their decisions about resistance. In particular, women with prior victimization histories appear to be more likely to use passive resistance strategies and less likely to use active resistance strategies than nonvictimized women (Norris et al., 1996). However, in the same study (Macy et al., 2006), victimization history was unrelated to resistance when assailant actions were in the model. Thus, multiple factors must be considered to understand women's ability and willingness to resist acquaintance rape.

SELF-DEFENSE TRAINING

Teaching women how to defend themselves has long been part of feminists' efforts to help empower women to avoid rape. Although no published empirical evaluations of the efficacy of self-defense training exist, anecdotal data suggest that this type of training helps women thwart future assaults. Self-defense training has beneficial psychological effects such as increased confidence, assertiveness, perceived control of one's life, self-efficacy, and increased mastery of actual physical skills. In a controlled experimental study, Ozer and Bandura (1990) found that women trained in physical self-defense skills had enhanced efficacy and coping, decreased perceived vulnerability to assault, increased freedom of action, and decreased avoidance behaviors. Gidycz, Rich, Orchowski, King, and Miller (2006) evaluated a sexual assault risk reduction program that included a physical self-defense component using random assignment to program or a wait-list control group. Although women receiving the program had increased protective behaviors during a 6-month follow-up, there were no differences between women receiving the program and the control group in rates of sexual victimization, assertive communication, or self-efficacy. The authors suggested that the lack of a significant effect of this program on sexual victimization rates may have been because of greater awareness and labeling of sexual assault by program participants, sharing of information between women in the two groups, and lack of a powerful enough program.

Feminists argue that self-defense training empowers women and girls to overcome passive female gender role socialization that encourages them both to be out of touch with their bodies and to perceive themselves as too weak to protect themselves from men's violence (McCaughey, 1997). This socialization may explain women's fear of sexual assault in contemporary American society that leads them to restrict their behavior to avoid rape. Self-defense educators first try to help women to overcome their fear of hurting the attacker, their aversion to using violence, and feelings that they do not deserve to protect themselves. These social-psychological factors impede women from seeing themselves as active agents capable of protecting themselves and thwarting attacks. Mastering physical self-defense techniques appears to help women overcome these barriers and feel efficacious (Hollander, 2004). According to self-defense instructors, child sexual abuse survivors may have an especially difficult time defending themselves and overcoming these barriers. This may be why they are more likely to be revictimized (e.g., raped again) as adults and also may explain the ineffectiveness of current rape prevention programs with previously victimized women (Hanson & Gidycz, 1993). Although more research is needed to evaluate self-defense training, rape intervention programs need to provide access to self-defense training for women, given consistent research showing that forceful verbal and physical resistance enhance rape avoidance.

RAPE PREVENTION PROGRAMS

Although many rape prevention programs exist, most focus on changing attitudes such as rape myths or increasing women's self-efficacy (Anderson & Whiston, 2005; Brecklin & Forde, 2001; Flores & Hartlaub, 1998), with the rationale that decreasing rape-supportive attitudes may reduce rape. Little evidence shows that programs are effective in altering rape-related attitudes over time, and it is unclear whether changing attitudes will reduce rape. A review of studies of rape intervention programs for college students finds little change in rape myth attitudes as the follow-up time of assessment increased, less effectiveness for mixed-sex than single-sex programs, and less effectiveness of unpublished program evaluations (e.g., doctoral dissertations) than published evaluations (Brecklin & Forde, 2001). Other meta-analytic reviews of prevention programs with a variety of outcome measures reach similar conclusions (Anderson & Whiston, 2005; Flores & Hartlaub, 1998), and none show evidence of reduction in risk of rape. In one of the few published studies to date assessing future victimization risk, Hanson and Gidycz (1993) found a decrease in rates of sexual assault victimization during the course of a 9-week period in college women without a prior history of sexual assault exposed to a risk reduction program that included discussion of self-defense strategies and risky dating behaviors. However, two subsequent evaluations of similar sexual assault education prevention programs found no reduction in sexual assault risk at follow-up, regardless of sexual assault history (Breitenbecher & Gidycz, 1998; Breitenbecher & Scarce, 1999).

Because women's vulnerability to rape is heavily determined by situational factors that increase their proximity to motivated offenders, focusing on women's personality characteristics or backgrounds is unlikely to effectively reduce rape. Most studies reveal that victims are indistinguishable from nonvictims on attitudinal variables such as sex role beliefs, rape myth acceptance, acceptance of interpersonal violence, and adversarial sexual beliefs. Furthermore, Lonsway's (1996) review of rape prevention education programs concludes that sexuality education is not adequate for changing rape-related attitudes if it does not explicitly address sexual violence and that programs may be more effective if they discuss women's roles and status in society. More recently, some have argued that risk reduction programs should focus more on teaching women self-defense or resistance strategy training because changing attitudes may not reduce rape (Rozee & Koss, 2001; Ullman, 2002).

Some feminists have expressed valid concerns that interventions targeting women that either teach self-defense or educate them about effective resistance strategies hold women responsible for rape prevention. However, as long as males commit rape, women and girls should be given information and training in effective methods of self-protection. Women also need access to knowledge about risky situations and behaviors, just as society helps people protect themselves from other public health threats such as HIV infection. This type of education can be done without holding women responsible or blaming them for being assaulted. In addition, education and training about resistance can empower women by presenting this information in the context of programs about gender role socialization and social-psychological barriers to self-protection. Most experts believe that a two-pronged approach is needed to prevent rape: risk reduction programs for women and prevention programs for men (Gidycz, Dowdall, & Marioni, 2002; Rozee & Koss, 2001). Because programs targeting men and women separately may be more effective, information targeted to men and women should be somewhat different, although possibly not completely different. For example, women need to know about risky situations, perpetrator characteristics, and effective resistance strategies, including actual self-defense training, such as Model Mugging or other self-defense training programs. Men need to be taught what rape is (e.g., definition, rape myths, impact of rape) and how to interact with women respectfully without ignoring their needs or refusals of sexual advances. Men also need to know that

drinking is not an excuse for rape and that getting a woman drunk and having sex with her actually constitutes rape. Both men and women may benefit from information about rape statistics, gender role attitudes and socialization, and rape myths.

Most rape prevention programs do not focus on teaching women about risky situations, effective resistance strategies, and actual self-defense training. Few rape prevention program evaluations examine whether participants actually have a reduced risk of future victimization or perpetration in the future. Without such evaluations, we do not know whether existing rape prevention programs actually work. Unfortunately, the few programs that have assessed this outcome have mostly failed to show reductions in victimization risk. The two programs that showed some efficacy during brief follow-up periods did not work for all women (e.g., women with a history of previous victimization; Hanson & Gidycz, 1993) or still showed high revictimization rates among program participants (Marx, Calhoun, Wilson, & Meyerson, 2001). Finally, other studies fail to replicate these results (Breitenbecher & Gidycz, 1998; Breitenbecher & Scarce, 1999). It is important to note that these programs typically include various components, including education about rape prevalence, rape myths and attitudes, characteristics of victims and offenders, how to label sexually coercive behavior, risky situations, safe dating behaviors, how to resist rape, effects of rape on women, and local resources for victims (see Gidycz et al., 2002, for a review). When evaluations do show positive effects, it is not clear which program components are producing changes in participants. Educating women about risky situations and behaviors, including effective resistance, is likely to be important and is included in some of these programs. The overall ineffectiveness of these programs in reducing future victimization suggests that actual rape resistance and/or self-defense training is needed, especially because women with self-defense training before rape are more likely to say their resistance helped thwart the attack (Brecklin & Ullman, 2005).

Risk reduction programs typically try to keep women from ever being attacked by advising them to restrict their behavior by avoiding risky situations. Unfortunately, many women are attacked by men they know in situations they thought were safe, but they can still be empowered to thwart these attacks. Although society and even feminists may feel uncomfortable teaching women resistance strategies and self-defense, such intervention is needed. Effective resistance strategies of screaming, fighting, and fleeing should be taught to women in educational programs that include practical self-defense training. Evaluation of self-defense classes is needed to see if they help women avoid future rapes and improve their overall psychological well-being. Self-defense classes should be available for women in college and high school, and community programs providing self-defense training should be funded for women in the general population. Such risk reduction efforts will of course not stop rapists from selecting weaker targets, but they may help to reduce completed rapes for women who are attacked. Such programs also can show that society supports women's efforts to defend themselves against this crime. Interventions with women should address social-psychological barriers such as embarrassment, fear of social rejection by peers, and beliefs they are unable to resist rape or unworthy of being free from sexual assault. Evaluations of rape intervention programs for women are needed to see if components like self-defense training and education about risk reduction and social-psychological barriers are effective. Studies should include long-term follow-up assessments to determine whether positive attitude changes persist and whether future risk of actual victimization is reduced.

Risk reduction programs should be tailored to women with different victimization histories, such as child and adolescent sexual assault. A risk reduction program focused on discussion of self-defense strategies and risky dating behaviors decreased subsequent sexual victimization, but not for previously victimized women (Hanson & Gidycz, 1993). A subsequent multisite evaluation of a risk reduction program (Gidycz et al., 1998) shows that women victimized during a 2-month follow-up interval had a reduced risk of sexual revictimization at a 6-month follow-up. These results suggest that among women who had previously experienced a sexual assault, those who had the program were better able to use it. Another study of 66 college women with a history of sexual victimization (Marx et al., 2001) expands on a risk reduction program of Hanson and Gidycz (1993); it finds no differences in rates of sexual assault revictimization between program participants and a control group after 2 months but less completed rape for program participants. Changes in women, such as decreased self-competence or increased self-blame after an assault in adolescence, both of which are related to later revictimization, could be targeted in intervention programs with previously victimized women and may be particularly affected by self-defense training. Future research must identify consequences of being victimized that lead to higher risk of future completed rape to develop intervention programs tailored to these women's needs.

Arguing for resistance and self-defense training based on extant empirical results does not mean that women are responsible for rape prevention, which is a pitfall of interventions aimed at women. However, there is a distinction between prevention that restricts women's freedom (e.g., telling them to not go out at night or to not drink alcohol) and prevention that enhances women's freedom (e.g., providing information about risk, teaching self-defense skills). Failing to provide empirical information about effective resistance strategies and training in self-defense techniques allows men to continue completing more rapes of women, which causes serious psychological and physical harm. Rapists admit planning their attacks and looking for easy targets. Thus, women who act assertively can thwart them by resisting attack. Assailants may be surprised when women actively resist, as they may expect women to submit. Educators should help women to identify barriers to their own self-protection, such as feelings of unworthiness, and help them to define men's sexual aggression as wrong and the responsibility of men, not women.

Other prevention strategies in addition to risk reduction efforts with women are needed. The recommendation by Banyard et al. (2004) that we integrate bystanders into community-based prevention of rape is one such idea. Efforts are needed to develop such programs and evaluate whether community members can be encouraged to intervene to prevent sexual assault. Engaging the community in broader efforts to collectively prevent rape can avoid putting the sole burden of avoiding rape on potential victims. Primary prevention programs targeting males are also needed to reduce sexual aggression and can be integrated with other antiviolence prevention programming by focusing on generalized aggression and sex role socialization. Until effective rape prevention with boys and men is identified and implemented, intervention efforts are needed with women. Fortunately, research shows that women can effectively resist and avoid rapes, which provides evidence that risk reduction programs should focus on teaching women about risky situations, effective resistance strategies, and formal self-defense training.

14

REPORTING SEXUAL VICTIMIZATION TO THE POLICE AND OTHERS

Results From a National-Level Study of College Women

BONNIE S. FISHER

LEAH E. DAIGLE

FRANCIS T. CULLEN

MICHAEL G. TURNER

Figures have revealed that the majority of female rape and sexual assault victims are between the ages of 16 and 24 (Rennison, 1999). It is not surprising, then, that considerable attention has been given to the sexual victimization of college women. Existing research has shown that college women are at an elevated risk for victimization. Studies have estimated that between 8% and 35% of female students are victims of sexual offenses during their college years (DeKeseredy & Schwartz, 1998; B. S. Fisher, Sloan, Cullen, & Lu, 1998; Koss, Gidycz, & Wisniewski, 1987).

Despite the prevalence of sexual offenses, a large proportion of victims did not report their

Editors' Note: This article was originally published in *Criminal Justice and Behavior,* Vol. 30, No. 1, February 2003, pp. 6–38. Reprinted with permission of Sage Publications. In addition to several tables, we have omitted sections of the literature review and detailed reporting of the results.

sexual victimization to the police or to other authorities (Tjaden & Thoennes, 2000). Results from the National Crime Victimization Survey (NCVS) have consistently shown that rape and sexual assault have been the most widely underreported violent crimes. In fact, the 1999 NCVS results revealed that only 28.3% of these crimes were reported to the police (Rennison, 1999). Notably, other research has provided even lower estimates of reporting (Bachman, 1998; . . . Tjaden & Thoennes, 2000). . . .

Because of the extent of nonreporting, research has attempted to uncover the factors that affect the likelihood that sexual victimization will be reported to officials. Studies have discovered that demographic characteristics of victims are correlated with the likelihood of reporting victimization incidents (Bachman, 1998; Gartner & Macmillan, 1995; Lizotte, 1985; Pino & Meier, 1999). For example, older women were more likely to report their sexual victimization to the police than were younger victims (Gartner & Macmillan, 1995). Research has also revealed that reporting to police or law enforcement is shaped by incident-related characteristics and contexts (see, e.g., Bachman, 1998; . . . Hanson, Resnick, Saunders, Kilpatrick, & Best, 1999; . . .). Analyses of these incident factors have suggested that crime seriousness, victim–offender relationship, location of the offense, and the consumption of alcohol account for some of the variation in reporting. That is, offenses that resulted in injury, that involved a weapon, that were perpetrated by unknown assailants, [or] that occurred in unfamiliar places were the most likely to be disclosed to the police.

***

REASONS FOR NOT REPORTING

An analysis of the literature on reporting revealed that crime victims most often reported when they felt reporting would result in a positive outcome (Dukes & Mattley, 1977; Laub, 1981). That is, victims' belief that reporting will enable the police to catch offenders was often cited as an important motivator for reporting crime (Laub, 1981). Victims of sexual victimization, on the other hand, most often failed to report based on both the circumstances of the crime and on the psychological beliefs and fears of the woman herself. Coupled with the fact that sexual victimization is especially likely to be unreported to police, particular attention has been paid to these factors in hopes of discovering why such serious crimes go undisclosed.

It is thought that most crime victims do not feel responsible for their victimization; however, research has shown that rape victims tend to blame themselves for being raped. This self-blame tended to occur when victims were under the influence of alcohol at the time of the incidents and when they perceived that their own actions led to them being sexually victimized. Furthermore, when victims thought that these actions would be judged negatively by others, they were likely to internalize blame (see Finkelson & Oswalt, 1995). This self-blame due to victims' own actions is particularly salient when it is considered that alcohol consumption is often involved in sexual victimization (Koss et al., 1987) and has been reported as a method by which assailants obtain nonconsensual intercourse (Pitts & Schwartz, 1993).

In addition to incident-specific reasons, other research has uncovered psychological factors that influence reporting of sexual victimization. Some victims may have feared retaliation by offenders if they reported the incident to the police. If the victims knew the offenders, then it would have been possible they feared additional victimization resulting from reporting (Bachman, 1998; Greenfeld et al., 1998; Tjaden & Thoennes, 2000). . . .

***

FACTORS RELATED TO VICTIM REPORTING

Seriousness of the incidents. Although all victims of sexual victimization suffer some form of harm, some crimes are more serious in nature and cause more physical and/or psychological harm. Research has shown that those incidents that involved the highest degree of injury were more likely to come to the attention of the police (Bachman, 1998; Felson, Messner, & Hoskin, 1999; . . .). Other aspects of criminal events that have influenced the seriousness of the incidents are presence of weapons, threats or use of force, completion of rape, and monetary losses (Gartner & Macmillan, 1995; Orcutt & Faison, 1988). In a study of 897 women who reported experiencing victimization, Gartner and Macmillan found that harm, economic loss, and use of a weapon together explained approximately 15% of the variation in reporting to police. In light of this finding, it has been suggested that victims are most likely to report when they perceive their victimization to be serious in nature (Greenberg & Ruback, 1992).

Victim–offender relationships. One of the most widely researched areas of influence concerning reporting of sexual victimization involves the effect of the victim–offender relationship. In general, victims have been less likely to report incidents to the police when offenders were relatives, intimates, or acquaintances than when crimes were perpetrated by strangers (Gartner & Macmillan, 1995; Pino & Meier, 1999; . . .). Consistent with the general victimization-reporting research, reporting sexual assaults was seen as more appropriate when offenders were strangers than victims' boyfriends (Ruback, Menard, Outlaw, & Shaffer, 1999).

***

Victim characteristics. Research has revealed that demographic characteristics of victims were related to reporting sexual victimization to the police. Similar to the reporting of other crimes, older victims of sexual offenses were more likely than were younger victims to report to the police (Gartner & Macmillan, 1995). Income level, education level, and race of victims also appeared to affect the reporting of sexual victimization.

Thus, an analysis of NCVS rape data from 1979 to 1987 has shown that income was negatively related to reporting (Pino & Meier, 1999). A similar relationship has been found for education level: The more educated a woman was, the less likely she was to report being raped to the police (Lizotte, 1985).

The effect of the interracial nature of incidents has also been found to predict reporting to the police. Lizotte (1985), for example, reported that when offenders were African American and victims were Caucasian, victims were less likely to report the assault or rape to the police. Contradictory evidence, however, exists regarding the relationship between race and reporting of sexual victimization. Although some research has found that Caucasian women are most likely to report (Feldman-Summers & Ashworth, 1981), other studies have concluded that reporting was more likely when victims were African American (Bachman, 1998). Other research, however, has suggested that minority women were less likely to report rape to the police, evidence that those groups that have been historically distrustful of the police were less likely to see reporting to them as a desirable alternative (Feldman-Summers & Ashworth, 1981).

***

REPORTING TO OTHERS

Although it is well documented that sexual victimization has been likely to go unreported to the police, these incidents of victimization may have been disclosed to persons outside of the criminal justice system. In fact, research suggests that both juveniles and adults [are] more likely to tell authorities other than the police following incidents of violent victimization when the incidents occurred at school (Finkelhor & Ormrod, 1999). This pattern of disclosure was similar for victims of sexual offenses (see Koss et al. 1987). Thus, Pitts and Schwartz (1993) found that more than three fourths of rape victims tell someone, typically a female friend, about their experience.

Similarly, other research has found that the majority of persons who were sexually victimized confided in a friend; however, few told family members or health or social work professionals (Dunn, Vail-Smith, & Knight, 1999; Golding, Siegel, Sorenson, Burnam, & Stein, 1989). A separate study on the factors that influence potential rape victims to report incidents found that women were more likely to tell their husbands, boyfriends, or other intimates than the police about their experience (Feldman-Summers & Ashworth, 1981).

***

RESEARCH STRATEGY

This study attempted to build on the existing literature in several ways. First, this study analyzed national-level data with detailed measures to uncover sexual victimization–reporting practices by college women. Although research exists on college victimization, few studies have examined data from national samples in the United States. Perhaps the most notable national study of sexual victimization of college women was conducted during the mid-1980s by Koss et al. (1987). Despite substantively extending the literature, numerous changes in postsecondary education have occurred since Koss et al.'s 20-year-old study was done. . . . For example, enrollment of women in college[s] and universities has significantly increased during the past decade (U.S. Department of Education, 1993). Moreover, the changing social context and legal requirements mandated at these institutions may have altered the likelihood of women reporting their victimization on self-report surveys and to campus authorities (see B. S. Fisher, Hartman, Cullen, & Turner, 2002). To address these issues, this study used current national-level data to investigate the reporting of sexual victimization incidents by female college students.

A second advance this study attempted to make was methodological. This study has built on the methodological work done by Koss et al. (1987) and advances made by Kilpatrick and his colleagues (1992) and Tjaden and Thoennes (2000). . . . [W]e have extended their work by employing a two-stage measurement strategy used by the NCVS.

Third, few studies have examined the likelihood of reporting across multiple forms of sexual victimization. Most research has focused on the reporting of attempted or completed rapes (Bachman, 1998; J. E. Williams, 1984). Research that has employed a wider conceptualization of sexual victimization is limited and has focused on all adult women rather than on college women (see Gartner & Macmillan, 1995; Kilpatrick et al., 1987). To effectively measure reporting of a broad range of sexual victimization, this study measured incidents ranging from rape to sexual harassment, including attempted, threatened, and completed acts.

Fourth, as noted, studies have identified how characteristics of offenders, victims, and incidents influence reporting of sexual victimization. Few studies, however, have focused simultaneously on more than one of these categories of predictors or have explored the impact of multiple factors within each category. For example, studies rarely have included, in a single analysis, detailed information concerning victimization incidents and individual measures of victim and offender characteristics. To fill this void, this study used specific incident–level information for each victimization and measured incident characteristics and individual factors to assess the determinants of reporting.

Fifth, the majority of previous research examined the extent of and the factors that affect reporting of sexual victimization to the police. This study investigated reporting to police as well as reporting to campus officials and to third parties. In doing so, we were able to investigate the extent to which sexual victimization incidents are reported to people other than the police. Furthermore, we explored how determinants of reporting vary according to whether incidents are disclosed to the police, campus authorities, or other people known to victims.

Finally, the results of this study have implications for the ongoing debate between feminist and conservative scholars over the extent to which sexual victimization is a problem that warrants intervention. Accordingly, the closing sections of this article discuss the salience of the findings for these competing perspectives.

METHOD

Sampling Design

The results reported in this study are part of a larger project, the National College Women Sexual Victimization Study. Using computer-aided telephone interviews, professionally trained female interviewers administered the survey to a national-level sample of 4,446 female college students enrolled at 233 selected postsecondary institutions during the spring of 1997. Institutions were selected using a probability proportionate to the size of the female enrollment to ensure there was an adequate number of female students from which to randomly select to meet the needed sample size. Of the total institutions selected, there were 194 four-year schools and 39 two-year schools. Female students were then randomly selected within each institution included in the project. The response rate was 85.6% (for a detailed description, see B. S. Fisher, Cullen, & Turner, 2000).

***

DEPENDENT VARIABLES

Three measures of reporting were used in the analysis to determine if respondents decided to disclose an incident. First, respondents were asked if they or someone else reported the incidents to any police agency. If the incident was reported to any police agency, they were then asked to which police agency they reported.

Police agencies included on-campus police or security departments, off-campus local or city police, county sheriff, or state police. This variable was labeled *reporting to any police agency.*

In addition, reporting to others was measured by asking if they told anyone else other than or in addition to the police about the incident. If they did report the incident to a third party, respondents were then asked whom they told. The second measure, *reporting to at least one campus authority,* was created using this information. Campus authorities included campus law enforcement; residence hall advisors; deans; professors; other college authorities; and on-campus bosses, employers, or supervisors. The third measure employed was *reporting to at least one person other than a police agency or a campus authority. . . .* These categories were not mutually exclusive because respondents could have indicated they told more than one type of person. For example, respondents could have told their parents and a friend about their experience.

INDEPENDENT VARIABLES

Incidents, offenders, victims, and contextual characteristics were operationalized to measure their possible influences on victims' decisions to report their sexual victimization.

Incident characteristics. For our analysis, the following four types of sexual victimization were employed: (a) rape, (b) sexual coercion, (c) sexual contact, and (d) threats. Each of these types, with the exception of threats, includes completed and attempted acts. We recognize that not all of the incidents defined as sexual victimization would qualify as criminal acts. . . . The seriousness of incidents was measured with the following three variables: (a) if respondents suffered any injury, (b) the presence of a weapon, and (c) if victims considered the incident to be rape.

Table 14.1   Descriptive Characteristics of the Incidents of Sexual Victimization

Descriptive Characteristics of the Incidents of Sexual Victimization	%	n
Incident characteristics		
Type of sexual victimization		
Rape	11.9	157
Sexual coercion	16.8	221
Sexual contact	54.9	723
Threats[a]	16.5	217
Seriousness injury		
Yes	5.5	73
No[a]	94.5	1243
Presence of a weapon		
Yes	1.7	22
No[a]	98.3	1292
Victims considered incident rape		
Yes	6.3	82
No[a]	93.7	1222
Offender characteristics		
Victim-offender relationships		
Known others[b]	7.5	99
Current or ex-intimates[c]	12.6	165
Strangers	20.9	274
Fellow students[d]	27.8	365
Friends[a,e]	31.3	411
Offender-victim race/ethnicity		
Different	20.8	272
Same[a]	79.2	1037
Victim characteristic		
Age		
Mean age	21.4	1318
Standard deviation	3.1	
Younger than legal drinking age and drinking alcohol at time of incident		
Yes	21.4	280
No[a]	78.6	1030
Races/ethnicities		
African American non-Hispanic	5.0	66
Latina or Hispanic	6.8	90
Other non-Hispanic[a]	3.6	47
White non-Hispanic[a]	84.6	1112
Family classes		
Upper class	9.2	121
Upper middle class	41.1	541
Middle class	36.6	482
Working class	12.1	159
Poor	1.0	13

Descriptive Characteristics of the Incidents of Sexual Victimization	*%*	*n*
Contextual characteristics		
Locations		
Fraternity	6.5	85
Campus property	7.8	103
Living quarters	38.9	511
All other locations[a]	46.8	616
Drinking alcohol and taking drug behavior		
Both offender and victim drank alcohol and/or took drugs prior to incidents[f]	41.7	522
Offender drank alcohol and/or took drugs and victim did not do either	26.9	337
Offender did not drink alcohol and/or take drugs and victim did either or both	1.5	19
Neither offender nor victim drank alcohol or took drugs[a]	29.8	373

a. [This is the] Reference group used in the multivariate models.
b. This category includes professors, teachers, graduate assistants, teaching assistants, employers, supervisors, bosses, coworkers, stepfathers, and other male relatives.
c. This category includes current and former husbands, boyfriends, or lovers.
d. This category includes classmates or fellow students.
e. This category includes friends, roommates, housemates, suitemates, or acquaintances.
f. The categorization is based on victims' responses to questions about their behavior prior to the incidents and their perceptions of the offenders' behavior.

Offender characteristics. Research has consistently reported that characteristics of offenders may affect decisions to report. To take these types of characteristics into account, we included the following two measures: (a) the victim–offender relationship and (b) whether victims' race/ethnicity was different [than] or the same as offenders' race/ethnicity. The victim–offender relationship was measured using the following five categories: (a) current or ex-intimates, (b) fellow students, (c) known others, (d) strangers, and (e) friends.

Victim characteristics. A set of four independent variables measured the individual characteristics of victims. Consistent with previous victimization research, the demographic characteristics included age of the respondents and their race/ethnicity. A third victim characteristic, family class— measured by asking respondents to identify their class of origin while growing up—was included. Recent work by Ruback et al. (1999) has suggested

that being under the legal drinking age and drinking alcohol (underage drinker) may influence victims' decisions to report to the police. Hence, our fourth measure, *victims drinking alcohol and being under the legal drinking age when incidents took place,* was also included in the analysis.

Contextual characteristics. Studies have reported that both offender use and victim use of alcohol and/or drugs prior to or at the time of the incidents may affect victims' decisions to report incidents (Pitts & Schwartz, 1993; Ruback et al., 1999). To measure the context of incidents, we employed two variables. First, because sexual victimization can transpire in various places, we included a contextual measure of the locations of the incidents. The following four locations were used in our analysis: (a) in living quarters, (b) at a fraternity, (c) on campus property but not in living quarters, and (d) all other locations. Second, we included a measure of alcohol and/or drug use on the part of victims and offenders. We included a measure that took into account if both offenders and victims drank alcohol and/or took drugs prior to the incidents, if one did and the other one did not, and if neither did.

***

DESCRIPTIVE CHARACTERISTICS OF THE INCIDENTS

As a prelude to exploring the reporting behavior of the victims in the sample, we present the characteristics of the sexual victimization incidents, offenders, victims, and context in Table 14.1 [above]. As seen in this table, some of the incident-level characteristics exhibited much variation, whereas other characteristics did not. . . .

***

RESULTS

Tables 14.2 and 14.3 present the descriptive information on victims' decisions to report the incidents. As Table 14.2 reveals, a very low percentage of victims (2.1%) reported their victimization to the police and 4.0% reported their victimization to campus authorities. Among on-campus incidents, just more than 5% were reported to campus authorities.

A cross-tabulation of the data showed that all the incidents that were reported to any police agencies were also disclosed to someone else. This is also the case for all the incidents reported to any campus authorities because all the incidents reported to any campus authorities were also disclosed to someone else (see the last two rows of Table 14.2).

Table 14.2   Victims' Decisions to Report Incidents to Officials and Disclose Incidents to Someone Other Than Police or Campus Authorities

Victims' Decision	%	n
Reported to officials		
Reported to any police agencies	2.1[a]	27
Reported to any campus authorities	4.0	37
On-campus incidents only	5.3	27
Victims disclosed incident to people	69.9	919
other than police or campus authorities[b]		
Victims disclosed incident to friends[c]	87.9	808
Family members[d]	10.0	92
Intimates[e]	8.3	76
Other persons[f]	3.3	30
Other authority figures[g]	1.7	16
Counseling services[h]	1.0	9
Reported to any police agencies and disclosed to someone else	2.1	27
Reported to any campus authorities and disclosed to someone else	4.0	37

a. The percentages refer to telling at least one person in the specific category.
b. Percentage may exceed 100 as respondents could give multiple responses as to whom they told. Each specific category includes telling at least one type of person who was included in that category.
c. Category includes friends, roommates, suitemates, or housemates.
d. Category includes parent, parents, or family members other than parents.
e. Category includes husbands, boyfriends, or partners.
f. Category refers to other nonspecified persons.
g. Category includes off-campus employers, bosses, or supervisors.
h. Category includes women's programs or services, victims' services hotline, clergy, rabbi, or other spiritual leaders.

Looking at Table 14.3, the results indicated that even among completed and attempted rapes, fewer than 5% were reported to the police and an even lower percentage were reported to campus authorities. Reports for most other forms of sexual victimization ranged from none to very few of the incidents being reported to the police or campus authorities. Reports to officials of threats of rape and of sexual contact with force did climb to about 10% of the incidents, but the small number of incidents involved made the percentages potentially prone to substantial fluctuation, with only a couple of incidents being reported.

In contrast, although victims were unlikely to report incidents to formal officials, they tell others about their victimization experiences. Thus, in about 70% of the incidents, victims disclosed their victimization to someone other than the police. Most often, this person was a friend (in 87.9% of these incidents). Family members and current intimates were the second and third most cited people to be told, but they were contacted in only 10% and 8.3% of the incidents, respectively. As seen in Table 14.3, the percentages of incidents reported to someone other than police and/or campus authorities differed by type of victimization. To illustrate, a larger percentage of sexual contact incidents were told to someone else compared with the other three types of sexual victimization (74.1% compared with 66.2%, 62.9%, and 65.9%).

It is relevant that for completed and attempted rapes, approximately two thirds of the incidents were reported to someone else. Again, this was a large proportion in comparison with the percentage of incidents disclosed to the police, which was fewer than 5% for both rape categories. This pattern was evident across all the types of victimization. Again, Tables 14.2 and 14.3 reveal that most college women who are sexually victimized do not report their victimization either to the police or to campus authorities. . . . [T]he reasons for not reporting to law enforcement officials [were] explored by types of victimization. By far the most frequently given responses for not reporting were incident-related reasons. Across all victimization categories, in 81.7% of the incidents, college women stated they failed to report incidents to the police because the events were not serious enough. In 42.1% of the incidents, respondents did not disclose the events to the police because they were not sure a crime or harm was intended. In approximately 30% of the incidents, respondents believed the police would not think the incidents were serious enough, whereas in about 20% of the incidents, women stated that the police would not want to be bothered and/or that they lacked proof the incidents happened. Beyond incident and criminal justice characteristics, in approximately 20% of the incidents, women expressed a reluctance to report incidents because they did not want their

Table 14.3   Whether Told to Someone Other Than Police and/or Campus Authorities

Type of Victimization	Reported to Any Police Agencies		Reported to Any Campus Authorities		Told to Someone Other Than Police and/or Campus Authorities	
	%	*(n)*	*%*	*(n)*	*%*	*(n)*
Rape	4.5	(7)	3.2	(5)	66.2	(104)
Sexual coercion	0.0	(0)	.9	(2)	62.9	(139)
Sexual contact	1.4	(10)	2.8	(20)	74.1	(533)
Threats	4.6	(10)	4.6	(10)	65.9	(143)
Totals	2.1	(27)	2.8	(37)	69.9	(919)

families (18.3%) or other people to know about their victimization (20.9%). And in 19% of the incidents, respondents said they did not report the incidents because they were afraid of reprisals by their assailants or other people.

Although some variation was present, the general pattern of reasons given for not reporting to the police was fairly consistent across types of victimization. Still, there were some tendencies in the reasons given for not reporting rape incidents that may warrant attention. Similar to other victimization categories, the reason most frequently given for not reporting was that the incidents were not serious enough. In contrast, victims of completed and/or attempted rape were more likely to link their failure to report to not wanting family members and others to know of the victimization (38.9% of the incidents), not having proof of the incidents (36.9%), and being fearful of reprisals (32.9%). For these three reasons, the totals across all victimization incidents were, respectively, about 20%, 23.2%, and 19%. . . .

Victimization characteristics significantly affected the probability that incidents were reported to any police. First, similar to past studies, reporting to the police was more likely when the incidents were more serious (i.e., weapons were present or the victims defined the events as rape). Second, sexual contacts but not rapes were less likely than were threats of sexual victimization to be reported to the police.

Offender and victim characteristics played significant roles in determining the likelihood that victimization was reported to the police. First, incidents involving strangers were more likely to be reported than were those involving friends. Second, incidents in which the race/ethnicity of offenders and victims was not the same were more likely to be reported to the police than were incidents in which race/ethnicity was the same. Third, supportive of Bachman's (1998) results, incidents in which victims were African American students were more likely to be reported to the police than were those incidents involving White non-Hispanics or students of other races/ethnicities.

A contextual characteristic of the incidents was also important. The analysis revealed that incidents on campus property were more likely to be reported to the police than were those that occurred off campus.

The more serious incidents were significantly more likely to be reported to campus authorities (e.g., incidents that involved injuries or in which weapons were present). Victim–offender relationships were also salient as to the probability of incidents having been reported to any campus authorities. Compared with when offenders were friends, victims were more likely to report incidents in which the assailants were either strangers or known others (i.e., someone they knew but who was not a fellow student or a current or ex-intimate).

Victim characteristics were significant [regarding] the likelihood that incidents were reported to any campus authorities. Incidents involving younger and lower family class victims were significantly less likely to be reported to any campus authorities.

Two contextual characteristics of the incidents had significant impacts on reporting to campus authorities. As could be expected, incidents that happened on campus property were more likely to be reported to campus authorities. If both offenders and victims were drinking or had taken drugs, the incident was less likely to be reported to campus authorities.

As for reporting to someone other than police or campus authorities, victims' decisions to disclose their incidents were more likely for sexual contacts, when they sustained injuries, and when the offenders were known others. Notably, in contrast with the finding for campus authorities, they were more likely to tell someone of their victimization if their assailants and/or they [themselves] had been drinking or taking drugs prior to the incidents.

Across all three types of victimization, it was difficult to discern any factors that clearly prompted victims' decisions to report. Reporting to the police seems structured more by the characteristics that may make the victimization seem more believable to law enforcement officials: that is, the sexual victimization involved demonstrable evidence that the incident had taken place (e.g., injury) and was committed by a stranger. As for the other forms of reporting to campus authorities and someone other than the police (mainly friends), key factors were (a) whether any injuries occurred, (b) victim–offender relationship, and (c) whether alcohol and/or drugs were present. The precise impact of these factors on the two types of reporting, however, was not always consistent.

DISCUSSION

Similar to previous research, only a low percentage of college women who were sexually victimized reported these incidents to the police. Even when the offense involved was a completed or attempted rape, supportive of Koss et al.'s (1987) findings, fewer than 1 in 20 incidents was brought to the attention of law enforcement officials . . . [and] not all of the incidents defined as sexual victimization would qualify as criminal acts. Even so, regardless of where one might draw the line in defining victimization as criminal, the findings of this study do not change: Incidents, including rapes, are not reported to the police or to campus authorities but are reported to others. Consistent with previous research, including the literature on classic rapes (Estrich, 1987; J. E. Williams, 1984), there was a tendency for sexual victimization to be reported to police when incidents involved the presence of weapons, were committed by strangers, and took place on campus but outside living quarters. Again, these features are likely to serve as prima facie evidence that women were sexually victimized and thus provide confidence that a report to enforcement officials would be seen as believable. In contrast, the presence of alcohol and/or drugs made the reporting of incidents less likely, perhaps because victims perceived that their use of these substances would diminish their credibility. Finally, victims' definition of incidents as rape also increased the probability of reporting incidents to officials.

Still, the central point is that respondents refrained from contacting the police about most of their incidents of victimization. Furthermore, women in our sample also were reluctant to involve campus authorities. These authorities were notified in only 2.8% of all incidents of victimization and in 3.2% of all rapes. Why is there such a low reporting of sexual victimization incidents to the police and to campus authorities?

A feminist perspective might suggest that the extremely low proportion of incidents reported cannot be attributed simply to the general low reporting by college students of criminal events. In fact, as noted previously, college women report victimization by other violent crimes at a much higher level (B. S. Fisher & Cullen, 1999). Instead, feminists would likely maintain that patriarchal influences in society, including on college campuses, provide barriers to reporting. In our data on rape incidents, for example, one third to 40% of the sample stated they did not report incidents to the police because they lacked proof that the incident happened, were afraid of reprisals, and did not want their families or other people to know about their victimization. Reasons such as these suggest that sexual assault victims believed that proof beyond their testimony was needed to secure police action, that they would not be protected if they disclosed their assailants' identities, and that a sexual victimization was something sufficiently embarrassing or shameful that it should even be kept from their families. Our study does not have data on whether victims experienced self-blame, but the finding that alcohol limits reporting is consistent with the possibility that this may have had some influence. As noted, there is some evidence that when victims consume alcohol, they may perceive that they have contributed to their own sexual victimization. In a feminist view, however, such cognitions are a reflection of sexist cultural beliefs that create a context conducive to the continued victimization of women by men. Notably, in 7 of 10 incidents, alcohol and/or drugs were present.

The findings of our study, however, also might be interpreted by conservative commentators as reinforcing their view that most events reported as sexual victimization on surveys such as Koss et al.'s (1987) and ours are not really victimization (see Gilbert, 1997; Roiphe, 1993). In this conservative perspective, feminists are portrayed as advocacy researchers who employ survey methods that count as rape and sexual assault events that supposed victims do not define as criminal. Either implicitly or explicitly, ideology is held to trump science, with conservatives accusing feminists of interpreting shaky survey findings as showing definitively that the sexual victimization of women by men is not rare but widespread. The feminist political agenda, according to critics, is to use such claims to reinforce the notion that patriarchy's influence is extensive and in need of radical change. The real effects, say the critics, are that advocacy research creates unwarranted fears among college women, encourages women to view themselves as oppressed, increases gender conflict, and creates sexual turmoil in intimate relationships (Gilbert, 1995, 1997).

In our data, conservatives would likely use one finding to support their position that the sexual victimization of college students is overstated: in 8 of 10 incidents, respondents stated they did not report their victimization to the police because it was not serious enough. Even for rape, this reason was given for 7 of 10 incidents. The implication of these data is obvious: If college women, arguably a bright and privileged group, did not define the incidents in question as serious, then perhaps their failure to report matters to the police reflected a rational decision that nothing of consequence really occurred. In this view, the study's methodology manufactured sexual victimization that, revealingly, the women themselves perceived as nonserious and at worst as men acting badly, not criminally.

Three considerations lead us to question the conservatives' interpretation. First, a salient research issue is what students mean when they define incidents as not serious enough to report. For conservatives, the phrase *not serious* is taken in a strictly literal sense as meaning that the incidents were unimportant. For feminists, however, such a response may merely indicate a false consciousness expressed by women acculturated to see their victimization as somehow acceptable. It may also reflect a rational assessment in which female victims decide that reporting coerced sexuality is not worth turning in fellow students when such an act may incur negative reactions from their peers and no real action from the criminal justice system. That is, the events may be appraised as lacking seriousness not according to an objective standard but relative to what reporting the incidents actually entails. In any case, before definitive interpretations can be ventured, detailed qualitative studies need to be undertaken of women's cognitive understandings of sexual victimization incidents.

Second, conservative critics often question the methodological rigor of sexual victimization studies, with the endpoint being that the estimates produced by this research are artifacts of faulty measurement strategies. We cannot claim that our study is beyond reproach, but its design was formulated to ensure that incidents would only count as victimization when respondents answered detailed questions in the incident report. That is, we did not merely rely on behaviorally specific questions to determine whether victimization transpired but confirmed or disconfirmed its occurrence through the incident report. Accordingly, it is unlikely that the events counted as victimization in our study did not really happen or that they are the inventions of distraught women. In short, we believe that we are on fairly firm ground in maintaining that most incidents, including those that legally satisfy the definition of rape, are not reported to police or campus authorities.

Third and perhaps most important, our data show that approximately 7 in 10 sexual victimization incidents apparently are not treated as trivial but are serious enough for college women to tell others about what happened to them. In the case of rape incidents, for example, there is about a 60 percentage point difference between the percentage of rapes reported to the police or to campus authorities and the percentage told to others.

Although not definitive, findings such as these suggest that women counted as victims by our methodology did in fact experience sexual victimization[s] that could have been but were not reported to law enforcement and school officials.

These findings also suggest that we need systematic research into why victims of sexual assault, including rape, do not tell the police but do tell those in their social circles about what happened to them. We suspect that one profitable line of research will be to investigate more fully how the context surrounding victimization affects how women interpret not only what happened to them but also what represents appropriate responses on their part. Most of the incidents reported by respondents in our study involved assailants that women knew, occurred when offenders and/or victims had been drinking or taking drugs, and were often located in living quarters. Sexual victimization that occur in such contexts may leave women burdened and in need of support from friends. But such contexts may, in a number of ways, make turning to authorities unappealing. Thus, when women are alone and drinking with men in private residences, typically late at night, it is difficult to prove not only that an assault was perpetrated but also that consent was not given. Furthermore, in those circumstances, women not only may engage in self-blame but also may be unsure as to whether their assailants had the criminal intent to rape or assault. In contrast, because the victimization was real and disturbing, victims sought out help from friends and fellow students. In short, they handle the incidents informally, not formally.

Finally, college officials wishing to address the larger problem of the sexual victimization of female students might gain one important lesson from this research: Although officials are informed about only a fraction of incidents, many students on their campuses might have victimization incidents disclosed to them. We know relatively little about how disclosure of victimization affects recipients of this information and about whether these students should lend informal support, urge victims to seek counseling, and/or encourage victims to seek legal solutions by reporting the incidents to the police and campus authorities. Regardless, future research that explores these matters in more detail is needed. In a more applied domain, it would also seem prudent for campus officials charged with administering sexual assault awareness programs to provide the general population of students with guidance as to what steps they should take when sexual victimization is reported to them.

15

PATTERNS OF ANTI-GAY VIOLENCE

An Analysis of Incident Characteristics and Victim Reporting

KRISTEN KUEHNLE

ANNE SULLIVAN

Although the past decade saw a burgeoning of research investigating various aspects of victimization, few studies examined the factors related to anti-gay victimization. This research brings together available information on anti-gay victimization to gain an understanding about the type and extent of anti-gay incidents and the reporting practices of the victims.

A rich body of research presently exists on the nature and extent of criminal victimization in the general population. Studies have shown that the risk of victimization varies across different demographic groups (Cohen & Felson, 1979; Garofalo & Martin, 1993; Laub, 1997; Maxfield, 1989). For example, the risk of victimization is greater for males. Men are more likely than women to be victims of personal crimes such as robbery and assault. Similarly, young people between the ages of 16 and 24 face a much higher risk of becoming victims than do older members of society (Garofalo & Martin, 1993; Laub, 1997). Likewise, significant racial differences exist in the risk of victimization. African Americans are much more likely to be victims of crime than members of other groups.

Editors' Note: This article was originally published in *Journal of Interpersonal Violence*, Vol. 16, No. 9, September 2001, pp. 928–943. Reprinted with permission of Sage Publications. Though most of the article remains intact, we have removed two tables as well as information on coding of variables and analysis of some data.

These findings suggest that what people do, where they go, and who they associate with affect their likelihood of victimization (Cohen & Felson, 1979; Garofalo & Martin, 1993; . . . Laub, 1997; . . .). In other words, rather than being a random event, victimization appears to be a function of the risks associated with a person's lifestyle and routine activities. Specifically, the risk of victimization is greater for males, African Americans, and young people because their activities take them into public places at night, which increases their exposure to criminals. . . .

Another frequently examined aspect of victimization is the reporting of crimes to the police. Although crime reporting is relatively independent of the demographic characteristics of victims (Block & Block, 1980; Green, 1981; Skogan, 1984), crimes committed by relatives, friends, and lovers are less likely to be reported to the police (Skogan, 1984). Whether an offense was completed or only attempted and whether there was injury or financial loss are also strong determinants of victim reporting. . . . Specifically, violent crimes involving injury or weapons are most likely to be reported to the police (Laub, 1997).

Historically, hate crimes have been underreported in the United States. Several studies have found that lesbians and gay [men] are reluctant to report hate crimes to the police (Berrill & Herek, 1992; Comstock, 1989; Finn & McNeil, 1987; Gross, Aurand, & Addessa, 1988; Morgen & Grossman, 1988). Specifically, many gay [men] and lesbians believe that the police will treat them with indifference and insensitivity if they report a hate crime. Hence, many gays and lesbians do not report hate crimes to the police for fear of an unsympathetic or even hostile response (Berrill, 1992; . . .).

Research has also found that gay males experience more extreme levels of physical violence than lesbians. Males are also more likely to be victimized in public, including gay-identified areas, whereas females are more often victimized in or near their homes (Aurand, Addessa, & Bush, 1985; Comstock, 1989; Gross et al., 1988). A few studies have analyzed racial and/or ethnic differences in anti-gay victimization. Comstock (1989) found that gay men and lesbians of color experience higher rates of anti-gay violence than Whites.

This descriptive study investigates anti-gay victimization and reporting practices. An analysis of victims and incidents and reporting practices was conducted to examine whether victimization patterns and reporting practices are similar to those evidenced in prior research.

METHOD

This nonexperimental study includes a descriptive analysis of victim reports and examines the following questions:

1. Is anti-gay victimization similar to previous research on victimization, with differences in gender identity, race, and age?

2. Does lifestyle activity, such as location and the type of victim–offender relationship, affect the type of incident?

3. Is there a difference between unreported and reported incidents?

4. Are victim or incident characteristics a factor in reporting practices?

Sample

Because underreporting often occurs in formal arrest records, self-reported incidents were used for this analysis. Self-reports of victimization also present methodological difficulties; however, they can provide insight into the hidden data regarding certain types of crime. This nonprobability convenience sample consisted of self-reported incidents to a victim program in a large northeastern city from January 1995 through September 1998.

Procedure

When a victim reports an incident, the agency obtains information about the victim, the offender, the incident, the criminal justice response, and the referral services. An intake worker records this data on a standardized form.

The selection criteria for inclusion in this analysis were as follows:

1. The self-reported incident met the legal criteria to be considered a criminal act in the state.

2. The victim's gender identity was male, female, or transgendered or the individual was perceived to be gay, lesbian, or transgendered.

3. The victim was 18 years of age or older.

4. The incident had a bias motive.

5. No other motives, such as domestic violence or race, were involved.

Research Hypotheses

The following were the hypotheses guiding the research:

Hypothesis 1: Differences will exist between gender identity, race, and age in types of offenses.

Hypothesis 2: Differences will exist between gender identity and incident characteristics.

Hypothesis 3: Victim characteristics will affect reporting practices.

Hypothesis 4: Incident characteristics will affect reporting practices.

***

Sample Characteristics

A total of 241 incidents were included in the analysis. Table 15.1 provides a description of the demographic characteristics. Gender identity was 74.2% male; 21.6% were female, and 4.1% were transgendered. About 94.1% of the females were lesbian, and 5.9% were bisexual; 94.9% of the males were gay, 4% were bisexual, and 1.2% were heterosexual. All of the transgendered people were male to female.

Almost 75% of the sample was 30 years of age or older. About 6.3% were in the 18-to-22 age group; 19.2% were between 23 and 29 years of age, 60.3% were between 30 and 44 years of age, and 14.3% were 45 years of age or older.

About 84% of the sample was White, 5% were Latino/a, and nearly 6% were African American. Almost 4% fell into the "other" category, which included Asian, Native American, Pacific Islander, and unidentified groups.

Almost 45% of the sample was victimized by a stranger. In relationships that could be considered more intimate, ex-lovers were offenders in 2.3% of incidents, families in 1%, roommates in less than 1%, and pickups in 2.6%. About 5.5% of the victims had a social relationship with the offender, such as acquaintance or friend, whereas 5% were involved in a workplace relationship with the offender. Another 20.2% of the offenders were residential, that is, landlord, tenant, or neighbor. About 12.4% were victimized by law enforcement/security personnel, with 5.9% being victimized by a service provider.

Nearly 50% of the incidents were serious personal offenses, whereas 39.4% were other personal offenses. About 1% of the incidents were serious property offenses. Vandalism made up about 7.3% of the offenses, and unjustified arrest made up almost 3% of the cases. Out of the total number of incidents, 77.2% were reported to the police, which is higher than the rate found in earlier research (Berrill & Herek, 1992; Comstock, 1989; . . .).

Medical attention was not received in nearly 78% of the incidents. About 18% required outpatient medical attention. About 3% required hospitalization, and slightly more than 1% resulted in death.

Most incidents occurred in street areas or private residences. More than a quarter took place in a private residence, and 30% occurred in the street. About 12% occurred in public accommodations such as restaurants. About 8% occurred on public transportation; 5.9% in the workplace; 8% in cruising areas; 4.6% in a GLBT area; 1.3% at school; and 1.3% in police precinct, jail, or car.

Table 15.1   Sample Characteristics

	n	*Percentage*		*n*	*Percentage*
Gender identity			Relative/family	2	1
Female	52	21.6	Roommate	1	< 1
Male	179	74.2	Law enforcement/	27	12.4
Transgendered	10	4.1	security personnel		
	n = 241		Service provider	11	5.9
			Stranger	97	44.5
Sexual orientation			Other	1	< 1
Female				*n* = 218	
Lesbian	48	94.1			
Bisexual	3	5.9	**Offenses**		
Male			Serious personal	119	49.4
Gay	167	94.9	Other personal	95	39.4
Bisexual	7	4	Serious property	3	1.2
Heterosexual	2	1.2	Unjustified arrest	7	2.9
			Vandalism	17	7.3
Age				*n* = 241	
18 to 22	14	6.3			
23 to 29	43	19.2	**Reporting practices**		
30 to 44	135	60.3	Reported	186	77.2
45+	32	14.3	Not reported	55	22.8
	n = 224			*n* = 241	
Race			**Medical attention**		
African American	13	5.6	Not received	186	77.8
Latino/a	12	5.2	Outpatient	43	18
White	199	83.6	Hospitalization	7	2.9
Other	14	6	Death	3	1.3
	n = 238			*n* = 239	
Income			**Site**		
Less than $18,000	120	59	Police area	3	1.3
$18,000 to $28,000	30	15	Private residence	66	27.8
$28,000 or more	53	26	Public transportation	19	8
	n = 203		Street area	71	30
			Workplace	14	5.9
Victim-offender relationship			Public accommodation	29	12.2
Acquaintance/friend	12	5.5	Cruising area	19	8
Employer/coworker	11	5	School	3	1.3
Landlord/neighbor/	44	20.2	GLBT area	11	4.6
tenant			Other	2	< 1
Ex-lover	5	2.3		*n* = 237	
Pickup	6	2.6			

FINDINGS

Victimization Patterns

The cross-tabulation analysis suggested some trends in these self-reported victimizations (see Table 15.2). Generally, the victimizations involved actions against people, either serious or other personal offenses, rather than property offenses. The incidents against males (55.3%) and against transgendered people (70%) were more serious in type of alleged offenses than the incidents against females (25%). More than one half of the incidents against females involved less serious personal offenses, such as attempted assault and harassment, in contrast to males (35.2%) and to transgendered people (30%). The comparison between age groups did not yield consistent trends. Older victims between the ages of 46 and 64 were slightly more likely to experience a serious personal offense (66%) in comparison to any other age group. Younger victims (21%) were more likely to experience vandalism than any other age group.

The comparison between race groups suggests some differences. Those individuals who identified themselves as Latino/a were more likely to be victims of an alleged serious personal offense than other race/ethnic groups. A total of 67% of Latino/a victims experienced serious personal offenses in comparison to African Americans (36%), Whites (50%), and other races (33%).

In contrast to past research on criminal victimization in general, these self-reported victims of anti-gay bias crimes were not young African American males. Instead, the victims were older, male or transgendered, and Latino or White. The ethnic/racial differences noted by Comstock (1989) in a similar population continue to be present for this sample.

Routine Activities and Incident Characteristics

Because the concept of lifestyle is difficult to measure, incident characteristics were used for this analysis. As shown in Table 15.3, some patterns were present in the analysis [of the connection] between gender identity and the site of the incident, the victim–offender relationship, and medical attention.

Findings regarding the site of the incidents were similar to previous research (Aurand et al., 1985; Comstock, 1989; Gross et al., 1988) in that males were the only gender identity to be victimized in cruising areas and GLBT areas. About 50% of transgendered people reported victimizations in a private residence, compared to 36.5% of females and 23.5% of males. Both females and males were similar in reporting more victimizations in the street than did transgendered people (10%).

The relationship between the victim and offender displayed variation between gender identities. Strangers were more likely to be reported as the alleged offenders in 41.5% of the incidents with females and 46.7% with males, compared to 20% with transgendered people. Transgendered victimizations (20%) were more likely to involve a pickup than victimizations of males (1.8%) or females (2.4%).

This analysis raises questions about the combined effects of location and the victim–offender relationship. Are transgendered people more likely to be victimized in a private residence by someone they met socially there? And are strangers more likely to victimize males and females in more public areas such as the street, public transportation, or GLBT areas, as well as cruising areas for males?

Gender identity may be a factor in the seriousness of the injury. Generally, medical attention was not received for reported injuries. Females were less likely to receive medical attention than males and transgendered people. However, transgendered people had a significantly higher percentage of deaths than males or females. In particular, 22% of the incidents involving transgendered victims resulted in death compared to 2% of incidents involving lesbians and none involving gay [males].

Table 15.2 Gender Identity, Age, and Race by Type of Offense

| | Gender Identity | | | | | |
| | Female | | Male | | Transgendered | |
Type of Offense	n	%	n	%	n	%
Serious personal	13	25	98	55.3	7	70
Other personal	28	53.8	62	35.2	3	30
Serious property	2	3.8	1	< 1	0	
Vandalism	9	5	9	5	0	
Unjustified arrest	0		7	3.9	0	
	n = 52		n = 177		n = 10	

| | Victim's Age | | | | | | | |
| | 18 to 22 | | 23 to 29 | | 30 to 44 | | 45 to 64 | |
Type of Offense	n	%	n	%	n	%	n	%
Serious personal	7	50	19	44.2	68	50.4	21	65.6
Other personal	4	28.6	20	46.5	53	39.8	8	25
Serious property	0		1	2.3	2	2	0	
Vandalism	3	21.4	2	4.6	8	6	2	6.3
Unjustified arrest	0		1	2.3	3	2.3	1	< 1
	n = 14		n = 43		n = 134		n = 32	

| | Race | | | | | | | |
| | African American | | Latino/a | | Other | | White | |
Type of Offense	n	%	n	%	n	%	n	%
Serious personal	4	33.3	8	66.7	3	36	100	51
Other personal	6	50	2	16.7	4	50	76	38.6
Serious property	1	8	0		0		2	1
Vandalism	0		0		0		17	8.6
Unjustified arrest	1	8.3	2	16.7	1	14	2	1
	n = 12		n = 12		n = 8		n = 197	

REPORTING PRACTICES TO POLICE

Reported and Nonreported Incidents

Initially, reported and nonreported incidents were compared to identify basic differences between the two. . . . Gender identity of the victim and the victim–offender relationship were similar for both reported and nonreported incidents. Some slight differences were present in medical attention and in type of offense. In nonreported incidents, medical attention was less likely to be received. Specifically, medical attention was not received in 91% of nonreported incidents, compared to 74% of the reported incidents.

Table 15.3   Gender Identity and Incident Characteristics

	Female		Male		Transgendered	
	n	%	n	%	n	%
Site						
Precinct/jail/car	0		3	2	0	
Private residence	19	36	42	23.5	5	50
Public transportation	4	8	13	7	2	20
Street/public area	17	32.7	53	29.6	1	10
Workplace	3	5.8	11	6	0	
Public accommodations	5	9.6	22	12	2	20
Cruising area	0		19	11	0	
School	3	5.8	2	1	0	
GLBT area	0		11	6	0	
Other	1	2	3	2	0	
	n = 52		n = 179		n = 10	
Relationship						
Acquaintance/friend	3	7.3	8	4.8	1	10
Employer/coworker	2	4.9	9	5.4	0	
Landlord/neighbor/tenant	10	24.4	31	18.6	3	30
Ex-lover	2	4.9	3	1.8	0	
Pickup	1	2.4	3	1.8	2	20
Relative/family	1	2.4	1	< 1	0	
Roommate	1	2.4	0		0	
Law enforcement/security personnel	2	4.9	24	14.4	1	10
Service provider	0		10	6	1	10
Stranger	17	41.5	78	46.7	2	20
Other	1	2.4	0		0	
	n = 40		n = 167		n = 10	
Medical attention						
Not received	47	90	134	75.3	6	66.7
Outpatient	5	10	37	21	1	11.1
Hospitalization	0		7	4	0	
Death	0		0		2	22.2
	n = 52		n = 178		n = 9	

Reporting Factors

Treating reporting practices as an outcome, several variables were used as predictors: namely, gender identity, race, medical attention, and type of offense. . . . The findings provide some support to prior research showing that crime severity and extent of injury are strong determinants of victim reporting (Block & Block, 1980; Green, 1981; Skogan, . . . 1984). In this sample, gender identity did not appear to affect reporting

practices, and this finding is similar to previous research on demographic characteristics (Block & Block, 1980; Green, 1981; Skogan, 1984). One difference in this study, however, was that race did appear to affect reporting practices. Latinos were less likely to report than other groups. About 33% of Latino/as did not report incidents, compared to 15% of African Americans, 23% of Whites, and 22% of other races.

Medical attention also appeared to be a factor in reporting. All of the incidents involving hospitalization and death were reported. Similarly, 88% of the incidents involving outpatient care were reported. This reporting, however, may reflect mandated reporting by other individuals, such as medical personnel or law enforcement.

The type of offense seems to affect reporting. About 81% of serious personal offenses were reported. Likewise, all incidents involving serious property damage were reported. Victims may be motivated to report serious property damage for insurance purposes. These findings are consistent with prior research showing a positive relationship between financial loss and reporting (Block & Block, 1980; Green, 1981; Skogan, 1976, 1984).

Summary

Several victimization patterns were present and warrant further investigation. Nearly half of these anti-gay incidents were serious personal offenses, including murder, robbery, sexual assault, and assault with and without a weapon. Gender identity may have an effect on both the seriousness of the offense and the extent of medical attention. In particular, transgendered individuals were more likely to sustain serious personal injuries, such as hospitalization and death. Race and ethnicity may also be factors in the likelihood of victimization. Specifically, Latino/as were more likely to suffer a serious personal crime than members of other racial/ethnic groups.

Differences were also found when gender identity and lifestyles were analyzed. Transgendered people were more often victimized in private residences, either by someone in their immediate residential area or by a pickup. Females also experienced victimization in private residences or in the street by someone in their neighborhood or a stranger. In contrast, males were victimized by a stranger in the street, in GLBT areas, or in cruising areas.

In this study, a larger percentage of victims reported incidents to the police, compared to previous research. Three characteristics appear to be linked to reporting practices: being Latino/a,

receiving medical attention, and the type of offender. Latino/as were less likely to report their victimization to the police. When they did have contact with the police, Latino/as were more likely to be arrested. Incidents involving medical attention were more likely to be reported, which may be a function of mandatory reporting requirements for medical personnel. In addition, insurance may play a role in reporting to the police, because 100% of serious property crimes were reported.

Discussion

This descriptive analysis, although preliminary, provides insight into bias crimes against lesbians, gay [men], and transgendered individuals and those perceived to be of same-sex orientation. There are, however, some methodological limitations associated with the use of victim reports. For example, these incident reports were collected through a hotline, and there is a high turnover rate for intake workers. This could affect accuracy and consistency in completion of intake forms. In addition, there was no way to confirm whether all of these events actually occurred by cross-referencing police reports. Moreover, some victims did not wish to reveal characteristics about themselves or their assailants.

Despite these limitations, this descriptive study provides a basis for understanding various dimensions of anti-gay hate crimes. Moreover, there were some notable similarities [to] previous research. Specifically, offenders were more likely to be strangers, acquaintances, friends, or pickups. Likewise, incident reporting was affected by the extent of injury and financial loss. Differences from past research were also found. In particular, victims were as likely to report an incident involving a landlord, friend, and acquaintance as an incident involving a stranger.

The present analysis also found additional characteristics that appear to affect victimization. Latinos and transgendered people were more likely to be victims of serious personal offenses.

Our within-group analysis found some support for routine activities theory. For example, females were more likely to be victimized in or around a private residence by a stranger, landlord, tenant, or friend. Males were more likely to be victimized in public by a stranger, followed by a landlord or tenant. Like females, transgendered people were most likely to be victimized in a private residence, but the incident was more likely to involve an acquaintance, friend, or pickup. In terms of offenses, males and transgendered people were more likely to be victims of serious personal offenses, whereas females were more likely to be victims of less serious personal offenses.

Gender differences in the amount of serious personal victimization may result from women in general being more cautious in their routine activities. Prior research has shown that lesbians report higher levels of fear of anti-gay violence (Gross et al., 1988). As a result, lesbians may modify their behavior to protect themselves from victimization. For instance, lesbians may avoid holding hands or hugging . . . openly in public, whereas gay [males] may be more demonstrative.

CONCLUSION

This nonexperimental descriptive study provides results that partly support prior research on victimization and reporting practices and also presents a broader perspective by examining hate crimes committed against gay [males], lesbians, and transgendered individuals. Gay [males] and transgendered people were more likely than lesbians to be victims of serious personal offenses. Reporting these incidents to police varied by race, the victim–offender relationship, the type of offense, and the injury.

Although these findings should be treated as preliminary, they have implications. For example, Latinos/as were the least likely to report a hate crime to the police. Latinos/as may be less inclined to report because of cultural barriers. Victim advocates need to become familiar with these cultural barriers to encourage more Latinos/as to report hate crimes to the police. In addition, future research should expand on the present study by examining the routine activities of lesbians, gay [men], and transgendered people to determine if the risk of victimization is related to lifestyle.

16

OFFENDERS' FAMILY MEMBERS' RESPONSES TO CAPITAL CRIMES

The Need for Restorative Justice Initiatives

SARAH ESCHHOLZ

MARK D. REED

ELIZABETH BECK

PAMELA BLUME LEONARD

Discussions about the death penalty usually focus on either retributive justice or deterrence, both of which have long theoretical histories in the areas of crime and punishment. Restorative justice is rarely mentioned in the context of death penalty discussions, because in many ways the death penalty is antithetical to restorative justice, defying many of its underlying assumptions (Radelet & Borg, 2000). In death penalty cases, the victim is deceased and the state is seeking to execute the offender, both of whom normally form the core of the restorative justice community. In addition, family members of offenders and victims (although often allowed to testify in court) are placed in a setting where they become opponents

Editors' Note: This article appeared in *Homicide Studies,* Vol. 7, No. 2, May 2003, pp. 154–181. Reprinted with permission of Sage Publications. We have deleted sections on retributive and deterrence models as well as many of the qualitative comments from the results section.

in an adversarial process. This discourages recognition of harm to all involved and healing among victims' family members, offenders' family members, and the community.

This study examines the much-neglected topic of offenders' families in capital cases, with the expectation that as Justice Thurgood Marshall stated, "Death is different." Family members of offenders in capital cases have to deal with the possibility that their loved one may be sentenced to death and die at the hands of the state. Impending death is arguably different from life in prison. This possibility adds salience to the trials and terms of prison visitations that are not faced in noncapital crimes. Throughout the article, we highlight many instances in which family members deal with this burden and mention the added stress and feeling of responsibility because of the possibility of the death penalty. The purpose of the article is to describe how families cope with a loved one convicted of capital murder and how communities respond to these families. This article begins with a brief overview of both retributive justice and deterrence as they apply to the death penalty, and then shifts toward the need for restorative justice. The theoretical premises of this argument are explored using interviews with 19 family members of individuals tried for capital crimes.

The restorative justice movement and the victims' rights movement focus attention on the extreme devastation that is common to victims' family members (covictims) because of homicide. Offenders' family members also experience trauma and hardship following a homicide but have not been the focus of these movements. Victims' and offenders' family members experience intense trauma in capital cases (Freeman, Shaffer, & Smith, 1996), and these families receive little social service outreach or resources from formal organizations (Moriarty, Jerin, & Pelfry, 1998; Spungen, 1998).

Interaction with criminal justice personnel and processes can be quite distressing to covictims. Negative treatment of victims and covictims has been coined secondary victimization (J. E. Williams, 1984) and is defined as "a prolonged and compounded consequence of certain crimes; it results from negative, judgmental attitudes (and behaviors) directed toward the victim, [which results] in a lack of support, perhaps even condemnation and/or alienation of the victim" (p. 67). Secondary victimization initially described the treatment of rape victims in court cases (Madigan & Gamble, 1991), but recently it has been expanded to include responses from the criminal justice system and media to families of homicide victims (Mawby & Walklate, 1995; Rock, 1998; Spungen, 1998). Police and court personnel commonly keep personal property of the victims as evidence, withhold information about case status, and suggest that the victim contributed to his or her own death (Pasternack, 1995; Tomz & McGillis, 1997). As Rock (1998) explained, a family's alienation during the criminal justice process "constitutes one of the most potent symbolic assaults suffered by families in the wake of murder" (p. 76). Homicide covictims describe their contact with the criminal justice system as frustrating and protracted (Redmond, 1996).

Offenders' families also lack social services and are rarely examined in research (King & Norgard, 1999; Smykla, 1987; Vandiver, 1989). The few studies that include offenders' family members suggest that trauma experienced by these individuals stems from three sources. First, [there is] the effect of the offense and trial: Families often are ostracized, experience psychiatric and physical symptomology, hold profound guilt, and lack social service supports (Beck, Blackwell, Leonard, & Mears, 2003; King & Norgard, 1999; Smykla, 1987). Second, most offenders in capital cases have a history of early childhood trauma, including physical and sexual abuse and maltreatment, or chronic neglect (A. Andrews, 1991; Haney, 1995), and therefore their family members may be similarly suffering from this environment. This often comes up during the sentencing phase of the trial, where family violence and abuse is discussed as a mitigating factor for a death sentence (Haney, 1995; Vandiver, 1998). Finally, families are traumatized by the knowledge of an impending execution and the execution itself. The offender's family is in a constant state of anxiety and suspense, and their frustration is intensified by their knowledge of the racial and economic bias evidenced in capital sentencing (Radelet & Vandiver, 1983; Vandiver, 1998).

Despite a dramatic increase in restorative justice research and practice in the past 20 years, few restorative justice programs exist that attempt to apply this model to capital cases (Radelet & Vandiver, 1983; Smykla, 1987; Umbreit & Vos, 2000; Vandiver, 1989, 1998). Only four studies have explored restorative justice in the context of extremely violent offenses (Flaten, 1996; Roberts, 1995; Umbreit, 1989), and only one focused on capital cases (Umbreit & Vos, 2000).

***

RESTORATIVE JUSTICE MODEL

Restorative justice is based on the premise that crime (whether it be property or violent) creates a rift in the community in which it occurs. The most directly affected individuals are victims, offenders, and their respective families, but the social fabric of a community also suffers when a crime occurs (Bazemore & Pranis, 1997; Bazemore & Umbreit, 1995; Kurki, 1999; Northey, 1994; Schiff, 1998; Zehr, 1985). Individuals who live in communities that suffer from a crime problem (or where a particularly heinous crime has occurred) often lose trust in each other and their public officials and suffer from heightened fear and anxiety (Liska & Baccaglini, 1990; Perkins & Taylor, 1996; P. Williams & Dickinson, 1993). Lack of trust and fear of crime may, in turn, lead to a relaxing of social ties and create social disorganization (Kelling & Coles, 1996).

Unlike the retributive or deterrence models, the restorative justice model seeks to "engage key stakeholders" in the criminal justice process through the process of "conflict transformation" (Zehr, 1985). This process (a) provides for the needs of victims and their families, (b) addresses

safety and quality-of-life issues in communities damaged by offenses, (c) offers punishment/ treatment for the offender while maintaining community safety, and (d) provides mediation and reconciliation for those involved (Bazemore & Pranis, 1997; Bazemore & Umbreit, 1995; Kurki, 1999; Northey, 1994; Schiff, 1998; Zehr, 1985).

The restorative justice approach acknowledges that involvement with the criminal justice system often creates additional disorder in the lives of victims' and offenders' families (as well as community members) and can exacerbate the crime problem by not addressing the roots of the crime problem (Clear & Rose, 1998). Restorative justice seeks to involve all stakeholders in conflict resolution (Umbreit, 1998) and build social capital that leads to crime prevention within families and communities.

Restorative justice encompasses a range of practices. Along this continuum, restorative justice can completely replace the traditional judicial procedure, allow a case to return to court if the process breaks down or the involved parties cannot reach an agreement, or be used to supplement the traditional justice system (Braithwaite, 2002; Umbreit & Vos, 2000). Although restorative justice is a developing academic theory of how to deal with the crime problem, it is also a social movement with roots in different traditions and practices of several different cultures (Hadley, 2001; Van Ness & Strong, 2002). Therefore, there is no one restorative justice model that encompasses all aspects of this movement, but rather several related practices that are based on basic restorative justice principles. As a result, our research (and much of the research in the field) is grounded theory work, where researchers attempt to grow the theory and expand its utility by developing the practice of restorative justice and applying the theory to new populations.

One of the goals of restorative justice is to bring harmed parties together in the presence of the offender. This encounter "is greatly restricted in conventional criminal justice proceedings by rules of evidence, practical considerations, and the dominance of professional attorneys who speak on behalf of their clients" (Van Ness & Strong, 2002, p. 56; Launay & Murray, 1989). Nils Christie (1977) argued that in our present criminal justice system, the state has stolen the role of victim from the wronged party. This theft denies the victim (and related covictims) the process of working through the harm. Telling one's story and expressing the pain caused by the crime and having victimization validated often serves to foster the healing process for crime victims. Tutu's (1999) description of the truth and reconciliation process in South Africa, which used the restorative justice model, exemplifies this point:

Many who came to the commission attested afterward to the fact that they had found relief, and experienced healing, just through the process of telling their story. The acceptance, the affirmation, the acknowledgement that they had indeed suffered was cathartic for them. (p. 165)

In most restorative justice models, regardless of the form they take, parties to the original criminal event verbally share their respective roles in the crime and are allowed to take back ownership of the original dispute. Victim–offender mediation models usually focus on the victim and offender. Family group counseling (FGC) opens up this process to include family members of victims, offenders, and community stakeholders. Healing circles are modeled after support groups and often bring together individuals harmed by similar crimes. Victim impact panels allow victims to tell their stories to groups of offenders and community members (Bazemore & Umbreit, 1997; Braithwaite, 2002; Umbreit, 1998; Van Ness & Strong, 2002).

Regardless of the form that different restorative justice models take, victims can express their pain, fear, and the extent to which the criminal incident has affected their lives. Offenders have the opportunity to tell their side of the story and express sorrow and contrition. Throughout these encounters, there is an emphasis on holding the offender accountable, reconciling affected parties, and closure (Braithwaite, 2002; Flaten, 1996; Umbreit & Vos, 2000). In addition, all parties are

given the opportunity to ask questions and to clarify specifics of the criminal event and the backgrounds of involved parties. These encounters also give victims, offenders, and other stakeholders a chance to ask for forgiveness or grant forgiveness if they feel this is appropriate.

Although several criminological theories (e.g., social disorganization theory, social control theory) stress the importance of community cohesiveness and organization in preventing crime, few studies consider the effect that criminal cases and their outcomes have on the communities in which they occur (a notable exception is Clear and Rose's [1998] study of the negative effect of incarceration on social capital). If strong communities with high levels of social capital are important ingredients in crime prevention (Bursik, 1988; Coleman, 1988; Hagan, 1994), then corrections policy should consider ways to empower community members by recognizing their critical role in community restoration in the wake of criminal events. Restorative justice—particularly through practices such as family group conferences, healing circles, and victim impact panels—attempts to build social capital among all members of the group including victims, offenders, families, and the larger community (Van Ness & Strong, 2002).

Past Research

Restorative justice is the focus of much current research and correctional policy making, but the majority of these programs do not focus on violent crime. Many researchers, politicians, and representatives of restorative justice programs argued that the utility of restorative justice and mediation is limited to property crimes and less serious violent crimes (Umbreit & Vos, 2000; Van Ness & Strong, 2002). Violent offenders, particularly those committing homicide, are considered beyond the reach of the healing process involved in restorative justice.

The Truth and Reconciliation Committee in South Africa demonstrated the value of applying restorative justice to violent crimes, even offenses that were heinous in nature, for victims, communities, and offenders (Tutu, 1999). Although it is not the point of this article to argue that amnesty should be granted to violent offenders who confess in the United States, we believe that important lessons can be learned from South Africa. Indeed, the few studies conducted in the United States concerning extreme violence and restorative justice have found results very similar to those noted in South Africa (Flaten, 1996; Roberts, 1995; Umbreit,1989, 1998; Umbreit & Vos, 2000).

Umbreit (1989) explored the applicability of the restorative justice model to crimes of violence in a series of five case studies involving extremely violent criminals and their victims. The Victim/ Offender Reconciliation Program (VORP) model was used to mediate the encounter between the offender and the victim. A professional mediator performed an extensive needs assessment and had private meetings with offenders and victims before the victim–offender encounter. Reactions of offenders and victims varied; however, none of the participants regretted participating in the process. Some of the positive outcomes mentioned by respondents included the opportunity to forgive, a lessening of the intensity of anger felt as a result of the crime, the ability to apologize, moving toward healing and peace, and a sense of involvement among community members.

Flaten's (1996) work describes traditional victim–offender mediation between seven sets of victim(s) and offender(s) of serious crimes. All seven cases involved juveniles and included the crimes of murder, attempted murder, and burglary. Like Umbreit's 1989 study, all participants went through extensive preparation before the mediation sessions. The overwhelming majority of victims and offenders reported satisfaction with the mediation. Specific benefits included aid in the rehabilitation process, a chance to tell one's story and express emotions, a chance to have questions about the crime answered, the personalization of the victim and offender, apology/ forgiveness, fear and anger reduction, and healing. All the participants agreed that mediation was appropriate for serious crimes. Roberts (1995), in a study of 22 violent offenders

involved in a Victim Offender Mediation Project in Canada, found similar results. Victims and offenders expressed a high level of satisfaction with the encounter, and many victims left feeling they had more control over their lives.

Umbreit and Vos (2000) conducted the only study to date to assess the use of restorative justice on capital cases. Using in-depth case study analysis, the authors looked at the experiences of five individuals (three covictims and two offenders) who participated in victim–offender mediation. Offenders and covictims spent extensive time with a professional mediator before the encounters took place. Despite the fact that all these cases involved a murder and a death sentence, offenders and covictims reported satisfaction with the process. The experience served to humanize the offenders and covictims and gave both sides a chance to tell their stories and offer accompanying apology/forgiveness if desired. Finally, the encounter was described as healing by all who were involved.

The four studies that have attempted to apply restorative justice practices to serious crimes— particularly violent crimes—have all used mediation models rather than conferencing, healing circles, or impact panels, all of which attempt to incorporate family members and the larger community into the restorative justice process. Given the preliminary success of these studies, we feel it is important to explore additional applications of restorative justice in response to violent crime. Our article uses data to assess the need for restorative justice practices among family members of homicide offenders. The remainder of the article focuses on interviews with these family members. We use this data to

1. Determine whether family members of offenders in capital cases often suffer because of the homicide and arrest (which is essential to establish that these individuals are appropriate members of the restorative justice community) and, if so, whether this suffering is aggravated by the judicial process.

2. Illuminate feelings of offenders' family members toward victims' family members, and toward the community in which they reside.

3. Identify any need for restorative justice in these cases.

4. Provide examples of families who have attempted to practice restorative justice on their own.

METHOD

Data were collected from 19 family members of men convicted of capital homicide. Individuals were recruited through contacts with 16 defense attorneys in three southeastern states. The two criteria for participation in the study were that the family member had maintained a relationship with the offender throughout the trial and its aftermath, and that the victim was not a member of the offender's immediate family. Of the original 21 individuals, 90% (19) contacted agreed to participate in this study. Each participant was paid $50.00 for his or her time. Fourteen participants were the mother or father of the offender, 1 was an aunt, 1 a grandfather, and 3 were siblings. Fourteen of the participants indicated that they were the primary source of support to the convicted, and of these, 13 were parents and 1 was a sibling. Twelve respondents were White, 6 African American, and 1 Latino.

At the time of the interview, the family members were involved in various stages of capital proceedings. The length of time from the arrest to the interview varied widely among the sample. The longest time between arrest and interview was 19 years and the shortest was 2 years. Seventeen of the individuals were represented at the trial by a public defender, and in one of those cases, a private attorney was also retained; private attorneys represented 2 individuals.

Thirteen of the offenders related to individuals in our sample received death sentences—3 pleaded guilty, thereby avoiding a possible death sentence, and 3 received life without parole because of their trial. Subsequently, 1 of the death sentences was reversed on appeal, and the offender is now serving life without the possibility of parole. Of the remaining 12 men who received a death sentence, 3 were executed. The remaining 9 on death row are in various stages of appeals.

The families in this study may be different from a general sample of families of individuals convicted of capital crimes, because of our reliance on attorney recommendations of family members involved in the offender's case. It is possible that families who do not participate in the offender's trial are significantly different from those who do. Specifically, family members who are not participating in the trial are less likely to be emotionally supportive of the [offender]. These family members also may not feel the same sense of responsibility for the murder and its aftermath and, therefore, may not be looking for many of the things offered by restorative justice. Furthermore, individuals who did not get along with the attorneys in their family member's case are not likely to show up in this sample. Therefore, we expect a pro–defense attorney bias in our results.

A semistructured interview protocol was used in conducting interviews with family members. These interviews were not drawn from restorative justice sessions; rather, these interviews were conducted solely for the purpose of data collection. Participants were queried on their interactions with the criminal justice system and their attorneys; their relationships with family, loved ones, and their community; and changes within their lives during the capital proceedings. The shortest interview was 70 minutes and the longest was 3½ hours. The average length of interview was approximately 2 hours. The interviews were taped and transcribed. The transcriptions were coded and categorized using a variant of Strauss and Corbin's (1990) grounded theory. The 19 interviews were analyzed using a qualitative coding scheme that emphasized themes related to restorative justice. We systematically indexed the interviews (Berg, 1989; Glassner & Berg, 1980) using the following themes: trauma or damage caused by the murder or by the subsequent criminal justice processing of the case, feelings toward and interactions with victims' family members, relationships with the community, and issues relating to restorative justice processes. Interrater reliability yielded a 94%

agreement on major themes. Responses were annotated and then reanalyzed to sort the responses based on subthemes within each thematic area that had been identified during the initial coding process.

FINDINGS

Offender Family Member Trauma

To establish that offenders' family members are appropriate individuals to include in the restorative justice process, it is necessary to show that they have suffered harm from the original crime and the ensuing criminal justice process. Throughout our interviews with respondents, we asked several questions about their health and psychological well-being since the murder. From these responses, we found numerous examples of stress, trauma, and symptoms consistent with posttraumatic stress disorder. Although we did not administer the Davidson Trauma Scale, we used it as a reference when coding our qualitative interviews for trauma symptomology. Generally, Davidson (1996) identified three categories of symptoms:

1. Intrusion (characterized by repeated thoughts or dreams about the event[s]);

2. Avoidance/numbing (characterized by loss of recall, inability to visit certain people or places associated with the event(s), and withdrawal); and

3. Hyperarousal (characterized by inability to sleep, irritability, anger outbursts, and difficulty concentrating).

Indications of trauma were frequent in our sample, with all 19 cases showing some of the symptoms and over half of the sample demonstrating evidence of at least two of the three subcategories of trauma.

All respondents described the experience as extremely painful to them and their families. Coping responses to the homicide, the trial, and the sentence varied widely, with some respondents showing tremendous resiliency and other respondents expressing an inability to cope and continuous suffering.

***

COMMUNITY RESPONSES

Restorative justice recognizes the community as an important stakeholder in criminal events. Communities, through their treatment of families of victims and offenders, can either help restore peace after an event or allow a vicious cycle of violence, feelings of revenge, and division to continue. It was evident from our sample that communities frequently played both of these roles. A supportive community environment often mitigated the trauma of offenders' family members. Many families specifically emphasized the importance of their religious community and their employers in helping them through this process.

***

Individuals confronted with hostility in their communities were more likely to suffer from extreme, prolonged trauma. This hostility often led to fear, anger, shame, and isolation.

> My sisters ended up having to leave their church. . . . They were always like pillars of the church. Always giving time and money and everything. In their moment of pain they didn't feel like the church reached out and comforted them. Every time a new trial come. Somebody got a message. Some unusual thing would happen.

In one case, the community response was so negative that two younger siblings had to drop out of high school because their lives were being threatened and school administrators said they could not ensure their safety. In another case, someone defecated on the doorstep of an offender's mother.

Media is another aspect of the community. Media coverage of the crime was frequently framed in terms of good against evil, where the offenders and their families were assumed guilty before the trial began. The media often described the offenders as animals or monsters, symbolically severing the shared human connection between the offender and his or her community. Many family members felt that the media was at the root of the poor treatment they received in the community.

***

Media coverage was a continuous reminder of the trauma that both families suffered, and it prevented movement toward closure. In addition, family members rarely felt that their side of the story was told. Instead, they saw the media as sensationalizing the event and twisting the truth to the detriment of victims' and offenders' families.

Restorative justice. Throughout our interviews with family members, we noted many instances in which families were trying to do restorative justice on their own—without the help of the legal system. These efforts were oftentimes successful at bringing family members closer to healing and to feeling that they were valued members of their community. As Tutu (1999) stated, "Dealing with the real situation helps to bring real healing" (p. 271). These efforts usually involved finding someone, or a group of people, who were willing to listen to their stories and work with them to progress through the victimization experience to become survivors:

> The other thing that helped, and I found this to be very surprising, is talking about it. Not to the point where it becomes an obsession. Another thing I found out too, that people like his friends, that it got worse because they were afraid to say anything to me because they didn't know what to say and what I wanted them to say is what they felt.

> Something else that has helped me an awful lot and that's the togetherness. That there is the understanding that you have whenever you attend these conferences [describing a conference for offenders' family members].

Unfortunately, many of these families found that the traditional system of justice impeded their efforts at restorative justice.

> Seek someone to understand what you're saying. That would only be someone that's been through it. . . . There is nothing that can make them feel better unless we had a more just system. That would be the only thing: if we had a fair system. They don't work with the family, the criminal justice system doesn't.

Other family members desired restoration but needed help in their journeys. For some, this meant silent coping; others sought out new communities that were willing to help them work through their pain. These new communities were forged through working with counselors; talking with individuals who corresponded with death row inmates; or, in one case, several mothers of death row inmates united to form their own support group.

> I would love to be able to talk to her [victim's mother]. That's kind of another thing that doesn't happen a lot, is the interaction between two families. And I think that there should be some way to allow that to happen.

> All I can say is that it would be great if there was some type of support system for families because you don't know what you're going through.

> I've learned that you can go all the way back down and start all over again. You survive, but you got to make up your mind to do it.

By reaching out, these families are starting to find peace and are better able to support their loved ones in prison and through the death penalty itself, should it come. More significant, most of the respondents agreed to the interview because of a desire to help other families, whether they are victims' or offenders' families.

CONCLUSION

This qualitative analysis of interviews with 19 family members of individuals convicted of a capital crime clearly evidenced many restorative justice themes and calls for the inclusion of offenders' family members in the restorative justice healing circle. First, family members of offenders experience intense suffering, which is in many ways exacerbated by the criminal justice system and by their treatment within their communities (particularly by the media). These families are in need of healing. To that end, many desired to reach out and connect with victims' family members, their own communities, and to form new communities based on the shared experience of a homicide and a trial. Many family members needed to share their story with others as a part of the healing process. One father described the unresolved feelings of his wife concerning her recently executed son:

> We don't have a marker on the grave yet. She just can't put a marker there. But I think if we had that closure.

Restorative justice offers many benefits over solely relying on traditional services, such as counseling or pastoral care. The respondents in our sample experience murder from both sides. First, they often feel connected to (and in many cases partly responsible for) the original murder, and later they become victims as the state takes the [life] of their loved one. The use of healing circles brings offenders' family members together to share their experiences, and family group counseling brings together victims' and offenders' family members, as well as members of the affected community. These opportunities to hear the stories of family and community members from their own perspectives in a safe environment hold tremendous potential for offenders as well as victims' family members. Our preliminary assessment of the findings from this study indicates that only family members who have accepted their family member as guilty are ready for this type of intervention.

The majority of the individuals in our sample believed that their family member had committed a serious crime and deserved to be punished, although all felt the death penalty was not an appropriate punishment. A key element of restorative justice is accountability (Braithwaite, 2002; Umbreit, 1998). These families recognized this without prompting (on the researchers' part)

and routinely expressed a desire to relate this, along with a deep sense of sympathy, to the victims' families. Reparation is often coupled with accountability in restorative justice solutions (Braithwaite, 2002; Umbreit, 1998). This issue poses a couple of problems that are unique to murder cases. First, the victim is deceased. Second, many family members of victims are offended by the mention of reparation for murder (Friedman-Barone, 2002). Their loved one is gone, and any repayment may be seen as "blood money." Finally, reparations from an offender facing the death penalty are difficult to obtain because of limited financial resources of most individuals on death row. These problems do not preclude the possibility of symbolic reparation in the form of words, memorials, or community building.

Offenders' family members often feel isolated from their communities because of the murder, the trial, and a sentence of death. Restorative justice is the only approach that focuses on healing offenders and their family members, victims and their family members, and the community. Family group counseling could potentially bring all these stakeholders together to build stronger communities. This is particularly salient in cases where communities are divided on racial or religious lines following a murder. Although the results indicate a need to continue to explore restorative justice as a means to heal offenders' families, it is important to proceed deliberately in a manner that keeps the needs of victims and community members central to the process. We recognize that these interviews only represent one group in the restorative justice process. To reach true restoration, we have to explore the needs of the victims' families, community members, and offenders. Future research should be directed toward assessing the needs of victims' family members in capital cases, and developing individual healing circles for offenders' and victims' family members separately that could possibly set the stage for family group counseling between offenders' and victims' families in the near future. In addition, during the course of this study we noticed a couple of patterns: namely, women and men often experience trauma somewhat differently, some families readily sought out the victims' families whereas others did not, and communities often responded differently to offenders' family members, which affected the family members' resiliency in dealing with the capital case. More work is needed to validate these findings and to begin to explain these differences.

Looking at capital crimes through a restorative justice lens allows us to see that the decision between the death sentence and a life sentence is larger than the offender. Much like the death of the original victim, choosing capital punishment means a death in a larger community, which can delay healing and inhibit prevention efforts designed to end violence. Restorative justice asks that all losses be recognized and dealt with in a responsible manner so that humanity is elevated rather than devalued in the process of doing justice.

UNIT V

PSYCHOLOGY AND THE COURTS

INTRODUCTION AND COMMENTARY

Mental health professionals can have interactions with criminal and civil courts at virtually every stage of court proceedings. We most often think of them as testifying as experts in criminal or civil trials, but they are even more likely to be involved in pretrial activities, such as evaluating defendants, other litigants, or witnesses for competency. In addition, their expertise is often sought at the sentencing phase of criminal trials. They participate in numerous other court-related contexts, such as aiding in the preparation of witnesses, helping attorneys select jurors, assessing an individual's capacity to make a will, or evaluating plaintiffs in an age- or sex-discrimination suit.

Several of the readings in this section reflect the tension that can exist between courts and the mental health experts and practitioners who consult or testify in these settings. It has been observed that testifying in court as an expert witness is not for the timid, but—as some of the selections here suggest—many of these witnesses may err in the opposite direction; that is, they may exaggerate their abilities or misapply diagnostic instruments.

The first article, an editorial by **George B. Palermo,** addresses the ambivalence experienced by many mental health professionals when asked to be experts in courts, particularly criminal courts. Palermo highlights the ethical tensions these professionals face as a result of the rules of procedure that limit their testimony to "facts." Unable for the most part to address motivations or possible hidden organic pathology, experts often feel they cannot present the person behind the facts. After commenting on a variety of such legal limitations, Palermo nevertheless concludes that experts can testify or participate in court proceedings and still remain true to their ethical principles.

The assessment of individuals with purported brain disorders—neuropsychological assessment—is the topic of the reading by **Tedd Judd** and **Breean Beggs.** In both criminal and civil courts, forensic neuropsychologists may testify about the results of their assessments of plaintiffs, defendants, victims, and in some cases other witnesses. While the professional literature is giving increasing attention to these specialized assessments, rarely does the literature mention cross-cultural issues. Yet, as Judd and Beggs indicate, one's culture and language may well affect the outcome of a neuropsychological test. The authors review the elements of a neuropsychological assessment, offer guidelines for making it culturally sensitive, and review pertinent legal standards. The reading includes an interesting case study that illustrates many of the principles discussed.

One of the most complex and controversial practice areas for forensic psychologists is the child custody evaluation. It is such a potential minefield that the American Psychological Association (1994) has developed guidelines specifically for this purpose. As a result, it is generally believed that the quality of child custody evaluations has improved over the last decade.

The reading by **James N. Bow** and **Paul Boxer** focuses on one aspect of child custody evaluations, the appraisal of possible domestic violence. Not infrequently, one or both of the parents seeking custody allege violence on the part of the opposing parent. On the basis of their survey of custody evaluators, the authors conclude that the 115 clinicians in their sample were informed about domestic violence and were conscientious about obtaining information from a variety of sources. However, they tended not to use specialized questionnaires or instruments specifically designed to assess the risk of domestic violence. Although the article ends on a positive note, the authors emphasize that problems do exist and offer suggestions for continuing improvement of these important evaluations.

In the next article, **Marc Sageman,** a forensic psychologist (who also holds an MD), comments on the skills needed for conducting psychological assessments and communicating their results effectively to the courts. Sageman offers a clearly written general overview, emphasizing the importance of focusing on the legal question that is at issue and addressing one's testimony to the right audience. The author also reminds us that forensic psychologists are not always independent experts. They are often retained by one side or the other in a dispute, and consequently are expected to conform their written reports and their testimony to the strategy of the retaining attorney.

In the final article in this section, **Connie M. Tang** reviews basic psychological research that informs forensic practice concerning young children. This article is similar to Kamala London's in the first section of this book. However, whereas London's paper was most relevant to interviewing by police officers during early stages of an investigation, Tang's extends to interviews conducted by attorneys, judges, social workers, and psychologists and psychiatrists, as well as police officers. In addition, Tang focuses on preschool children. As she notes, there exists a large body of psychological research on language and conceptual development in young children. For example, she discusses research on the value of open-ended *wh* questions (who, what, when, where, why) as opposed to yes/no questions and research on the ability of preschoolers to weave conceptual scripts and understand symbols. Interviewer-aided recall is also discussed. The article includes guidelines for determining whether and how to interview young children.

As a group, the readings in this section remind forensic psychologists and other mental health practitioners who interact with the courts to remain informed about developments in their profession and to exercise caution in their interpretations and their use of assessment methods. They also must be continually aware of and familiar with the psychological and criminal justice research that is relevant to the courtroom, such as the research on eyewitness testimony, domestic violence, and risk assessment. As increasingly more psychologists participate in courtroom proceedings, guidelines and standards of practice will likely become more necessary. Finally, as legal professionals like judges and lawyers become more sophisticated about psychological principles and research, they also may demand more accountability on the part of the mental health professions.

17

FORENSIC MENTAL HEALTH EXPERTS IN THE COURT

An Ethical Dilemma

GEORGE B. PALERMO

D uring the past decades, mental health and legal scholars have debated the ethical role of psychiatrists and psychologists in the forensic setting, especially in those cases in which a not guilty by reason of insanity plea (NGRI) has been entered or competency to stand trial is an issue. The proper role of mental health professionals in the legal process certainly calls for clarification. . . . [T]he following factors should be taken into consideration: the moral values held by society and the difference, if any, between the ethics involved in the diagnostic or treatment-oriented patient–doctor relationship and those related to a forensic mental health expert examination of a defendant who is allegedly mentally ill. Also, consideration should be given to the relationship between the court of law and the forensic mental health expert.

Society upholds moral values that are accepted by the majority of its members. Those in the mental health professions abide by codes of ethics laid down by their associations (e.g., American Psychiatric Association, American Psychological Association, American Medical Association, and their respective forensic sections). Their conduct, whatever the professional setting, should comply with specific guidelines, which basically are respect for the patients/clients and their autonomous decisions, informed consent, beneficence, and nonmaleficence. The aforementioned are basic to the ethical relationships of mental health professionals

---

Editors' Note: This article was originally published in the *International Journal of Offender Therapy and Comparative Criminology,* Vol. 47, No. 2, 2003, pp. 122–125. Reprinted with permission of Sage Publications.

with their clients/patients. Deviation from the aforementioned guidelines rarely occurs, and any person who does not uphold them may receive some type of censure and in serious cases have [his or her] license revoked and legal charges instituted for whatever omission or commission in which the [person has] been involved.

Although it is widely believed that a trial is aimed primarily at resolving a dispute, the ethical foundation of any court trial should primarily be the search for truth. After all, witnesses swear to "tell the truth, the whole truth, and nothing but the truth." It is assumed that mental health professionals who testify in a trial uphold the truth and that they abide by the ethical guidelines of their professions. However, looking at the role of mental health experts in a trial, one is often left with the impression that at times the aforementioned is not fully taken into consideration by the triers of fact. Indeed, a certain degree of ethical tension exists in the forensic setting regarding the court testimony of mental health experts in NGRI or related cases.

It is well-known that the law gives primary importance to the facts of a case. Forensic mental health experts appreciate the importance of the facts as well, but because of their training, they go beyond them. While attempting to determine whether there is any relationship between the mental condition of a defendant and his or her criminal conduct, they inquire about the motivations behind the defendant's antisocial behavior with the purpose of reaching a total understanding of him or her—the person behind the facts. The total discovery of the expert (facts, personality structure, and motivating factors) often clashes with the rigidity of the rules of law, and a state of incomplete communication between the expert and the triers of fact ensues. This brings about a limitation of the testimony that the expert can offer to the court, and his or her role appears to be truncated.

It can be argued that the nonscientific rules of a judicial proceeding may actually infringe on the defendant's rights. Because of the nature of the game, the mental health experts—pressured into playing an ambiguous role—are limited in

their professional testimony to just presenting a behavioral assessment of a defendant. [They are unable to add a] psychodynamic explanation that could support a defendant's inability to comply with the requirements of the law. Rarely are they allowed to search for hidden organic pathology that may be at the basis of a defendant's behavioral manifestations, and when allowed to do so, it may not be given due importance. For example, in a fit of jealous rage, a 27-year-old man shot and killed his rejecting girlfriend. He claimed that he wanted to kill and be killed at the time of the offense, and prior to his apprehension, he was wounded by the police. At trial, he was unsuccessful in an NGRI plea even though an MRI of his brain revealed extensive multiple sclerosis plaques of a vast region of his brain involving the midtemporal lobes and the amygdala. The court dismissed the aforementioned findings as irrelevant even though such lesions are well-known to trigger impulsive, unreflective, destructive rage.

Furthermore, there is a tendency by the triers of fact to look on psychodynamic explanations for allegedly "sick" antisocial behavior as intriguing fancies or "junk science," and this attitude is often shared by juries. In all fairness, it should be noted that some judges do request a total psychological appraisal at the time of sentencing.

Limiting the testimony of forensic mental health experts not only creates identity confusion for them and an ethical quagmire, but is a disservice to all: the defendant, the triers of fact, and the experts themselves. Actually, it is a negation of those ethical values that mental health experts otherwise hold in their professional practice. This may contribute to the reluctance of some mental health experts to testify in a court of law. One would expect that the ethical rules of law within a trial would reflect those of society at large. At times one wonders, however, whether the courtroom is just an arena that primarily tests the skillfulness of the triers of fact, where animosity and partisanship regulate the ups and downs of a trial, and where the search for the truth becomes a secondary issue.

Motivational factors are not so-called psychobabble but are dynamically important feelings and thoughts that may prompt the irrational behavior of alleged mentally ill people and should be part of the narrative of meaningful forensic testimony. Stressing the motivational factors in a defendant's behavior is not a proposal to return to the Durham rule in mental health cases. [Rather], it is intended to provide additional information to the triers of fact that could help them to find, if not the truth, the best assessment of a defendant and the optimal solution in a case. The presentation of these factors to the court is not binding because any judge has the discretion to reject unreasonable expert testimony. We are told that forensic mental health expert testimony tends to be somewhat subjective, but a certain degree of subjectivity is present in all the participants in a trial. It is part of their human nature. Thus, all parties should exercise caution to avoid any degree of sympathy for—or antipathy toward—the defendant.

Mental health experts, in defending their reluctance to participate as experts in a trial, have claimed that the relationship between the forensic mental health experts and an alleged mentally ill defendant differs from that encountered in their professional practice outside of the legal system. Furthermore, they claim that they cannot pursue the best interests of the defendant . . . in a forensic examination of alleged mentally ill offenders. [This is] because such examinations are basically concerned with the determination of legal culpability; legal competency to stand trial; and at times, even competency to be executed in death penalty cases. All of these outcomes are viewed as maleficent versus a defendant and thus unethical. On the contrary, such examinations and eventual testimony are highly ethical in view of the consequences that the assessment might generate for a defendant who, even though a miscreant, may be mentally ill. It is then that the search for the truth is of the utmost importance.

Furthermore, mental health experts who in their private practice frequently diagnose their patients as persons affected by a functional or an organic illness should also recognize that many defendants can be diagnosed with personality disorders and suffer from organic or functional illnesses (e.g., schizophrenia, bipolar illness, or organic dementias). However, in the case of such defendants, their mental disorders are not self-limited but have created sociolegal problems. This is one more reason why mental health experts as members of society should overcome any reluctance to become involved in the assessment of defendants who are allegedly mentally ill. Professional ethics certainly do not preclude social ethics. These defendants/patients deserve the same expertise that is given to patients in general mental health assessments or to those patients placed in isolation because they are affected by contagious diseases. A defendant seen for a forensic mental health assessment should be looked on as a possibly sick individual who because of his or her mental disorder may spread his or her sick behavior to society and its members. Bad behaviors may influence predisposed individuals to act out in an antisocial manner. If one follows the aforementioned reasoning, it is evident that potential forensic mental health experts should not consider themselves to be acting in an unethical manner when doing assessments of allegedly mentally ill defendants for the courts. Obviously, they are not there to condone an offender's behavior but only to diagnose and advise treatment. And that treatment may at times take place within confinement, confinement that is at times necessary to protect both society and the defendants themselves.

The judicial system needs more flexibility, and the testifying experts should realize that they are not infringing on their professional ethical tenets of beneficence or nonmaleficence with their testimony, but instead are exercising their healing social duty and enabling the law of the land to take its therapeutic course. As members of society, they should view themselves as participants in the moral community and the moral microcosmic setting of a court trial.

18

CROSS-CULTURAL FORENSIC NEUROPSYCHOLOGICAL ASSESSMENT

TEDD JUDD

BREEAN BEGGS

In this chapter, we offer an introduction to cross-cultural forensic neuropsychological evaluation for the nonneuropsychologist. We will review the types of forensic questions a neuropsychological evaluation can address, the cross-cultural considerations that need to enter into each type of evaluation, the knowledge and skills needed to carry out such evaluations, and the impact of culture and language on neuropsychological tests. We aim to provide the users of such evaluations with the means to understand what can and cannot be determined, and a means for judging the quality of the work on a case-by-case basis.

NEUROPSYCHOLOGICAL EVALUATION

Clinical neuropsychology is a specialization of clinical psychology concerned with people with brain disorders. In neuropsychological evaluation, the clinician assesses the changes or impairments in thinking abilities, executive functions, emotions, behavior, and functional abilities of people with brain disorders. The evaluation typically involves review of records, interviews, and behavioral observations, but the most distinctive feature is the use of neuropsychological tests (Lezak, 1995; Mitrushina, Boone, & D'Elia, 1999; Spreen & Strauss, 1998).

Editors' Note: Previously published as Chapter 10 in K. H. Barrett & W. H. George (Eds.), *Race, culture, psychology, and law* (2005). Thousand Oaks, CA: Sage. Reprinted with permission of Sage Publications. In addition to a table and one case study, portions of material describing specific tests as well as a section on standards of proof have been deleted.

Forensic Roles of Neuropsychological Evaluation

Clinical neuropsychology was born in a medical setting and its primary allegiance is still to psychology and medicine. The science and practice of neuropsychological evaluation is aimed at medical and mental health diagnostic and treatment questions. Nevertheless, neuropsychological evaluation has come to have a growing role in the forensic setting, and certain aspects of research and practice have become increasingly directed at those needs (McCaffrey, Williams, Fisher, & Laing, 1997; Murrey, 2000; Sweet, 1999; Valciukas, 1995).

The amount of damage caused by a personal injury is one of the chief forensic issues addressed by neuropsychologists. But neuropsychological evaluation is also used to help determine personal competence to manage one's own affairs, to stand trial, to give testimony, to parent, and to benefit from schooling and rehabilitation. It is used to determine level of disability with respect to disability accommodations, qualification for disability benefits, and specialized education. It is used to determine qualifications on an accused criminal's culpability and appropriate sentencing. These many different types of legal needs require the neuropsychologist to answer a variety of questions at several different standards of proof and require a variety of clinical and investigative skills.

Forensic neuropsychological evaluations are typically much more thorough than medical or mental health neuropsychological evaluations and involve distinct skills and standards of proof. They may also involve distinct tests or uses of tests.

The person with the purported brain disorder may be the defendant, the plaintiff, the victim, the client, or [someone in another role]. For this reason, in this chapter we will call the person with the purported brain disorder the focus person. . . . This chapter will be oriented primarily toward the forensic issues and legal system of the [United States], recognizing that applications in other jurisdictions may require modification.

Cross-Cultural Evaluation

We will define a cross-cultural evaluation as taking place whenever there are cultural differences among the examiner(s), the focus person, and the examination materials and/or concepts. This includes not only majority culture examiners working with immigrants or linguistic, cultural, or subcultural minorities, but also immigrant or minority examiners working with those of other cultures including the majority culture. It also includes minority examiners working with people of their own culture, but using tests and materials from another culture.

In the arena of forensic evaluation, we also need to recognize that there are circumstances when what is at issue is the focus person's ability to conform [his or her] behavior to the norms (laws, justice system, institutional expectations) of another culture. This means that an evaluation may cross cultures between the focus person and that person's adaptive behavior within the host culture, even if the neuropsychologist, the tests, and the norms are all from the focus person's culture/language. For example, suppose an immigrant has marginal cognitive abilities due to a traumatic brain injury, a stroke, or the early stages of dementia. A neuropsychologist from [that person's] culture, in [his or her] language, could examine that person with tests normed on an appropriate population. The focus person could be competent to parent, manage money, or stand trial, in [his or her] country of origin. In a new culture, the [person's] cognitive limitations could render [him or her] unable to work with an interpreter, or to learn, understand, or track procedures competently in [the] new setting. The focus person might, therefore, be incompetent in the context of the host culture. The neuropsychologist may need to evaluate these adaptive abilities within the context of the host culture. This, too, would be a cross-cultural evaluation.

Psychologists and neuropsychologists face an ethical dilemma with cross-cultural work. They are bound by statute and professional ethics not to discriminate in the provision of services on the basis of race, ethnicity, language, or country of origin (American Psychological Association, 1993, 2002). Yet they are also bound by those same professional ethics to provide services that are ethnically, linguistically, and culturally sensitive, and to act within the confines of their competence. They cannot possibly provide services of equal quality and cultural competence to all ethnic and linguistic groups because it is not humanly possible to become equally knowledgeable of and competent in all cultures and languages. Even if a psychologist were fully bilingual and bicultural and thereby tried to serve just two cultural groups, it is likely that the service could not be of equal quality because it would not be backed by an equal body of research concerning both groups.

How does a neuropsychologist address this dilemma? In some cases, it is clear that the ethical thing to do is to refer the focus person to a clinician more skilled with that linguistic or cultural group. But at times the choice is not clear. There may be no such clinician available. The available clinician who is culturally appropriate may not have the needed neuropsychological or forensic skills. Unfortunately, ethical guidelines offer little help beyond leaving such decisions to the psychologist's judgment. We cannot offer rules to cover all such situations. But we do hope that this chapter will offer the clinician or attorney struggling with such issues some further guidelines on how to make such choices on a case-by-case basis. We also aim to demystify the forensic neuropsychological evaluation for the nonexpert so that its cultural limitations can be examined.

FORENSIC EVALUATION ISSUES

The Forensic Question

The forensic question being asked has a profound influence on the way the assessment is carried out. It determines the degree to which history is relevant, whether the testing focuses on neuropsychological functions or everyday adaptive abilities, whether or not a diagnosis or a cause of handicap is relevant, the level of proof required, and the degree of cross-cultural competence required of the examiner.

Medical Versus Cultural Determinants

Neuropsychological evaluations typically describe weaknesses and impairments in cognitive abilities, peculiarities and pathologies of emotions and behavior, and limitations in adaptive skills and activities. The source(s) of these various impairments and pathologies may be the result of a brain disorder, they may represent limitations or differences in education or cultural norms of an immigrant population, or they may result from a combination of factors.

For some forensic questions, it is important to determine the source of the problem. For example, in order for a child to qualify for public special education services due to learning disability, [his or her] academic impairment must be due to a medical condition. [Children] do not qualify as learning disabled if their poor academic achievement is due to cultural factors or poor teaching in the past. . . .

For other forensic questions, the medical or cultural source of an impairment may not matter. For example, many issues of competency such as competency to stand trial, to testify, to parent, or to manage one's own funds depend only upon the person's ability to carry out the required activity correctly (Grisso, 2003). . . . It does not matter if limitations in these competencies are due to cultural and educational background, a medical condition, or a combination of factors. Such distinctions are important, however, in predicting whether or not the person may be capable of acquiring a competence that is lacking, which may then dictate the length or the extent of a guardianship, an attempt to educate a defendant into competence to stand trial, a plan to restore parental rights, and so on.

Diagnosis

In some cases, a clinician may be reasonably certain that the focus person has an impairment due to a medical condition, but [he or she] may not know what medical condition caused the impairment. There may be multiple medical conditions that could have caused the impairment, or no known medical cause, but a clear impairment, nevertheless. In many instances, statutes require a specific diagnosis, and the clinician may need to resort to a "generic" diagnosis such as 294.9 Cognitive Disorder Not Otherwise Specified (American Psychiatric Association, 1994). In other circumstances, the specific diagnosis may not be very relevant. For example, an immigrant applying for a waiver from the English test requirement for U.S. citizenship may have a history of an untreated childhood fever with seizures that could have been encephalitis and two traumatic brain injuries. The relevant medico-legal question is whether or not [the person has] an impairment that prevents the learning of English, not which one of these brain insults caused the impairment.

Causality

In personal injury litigation, injured worker claims, and in certain criminal assault cases, it is necessary to demonstrate not only that the focus person has an impairment due to a medical condition, but also that that impairment was caused by a specific event. Most usually this involves a trauma to the brain, a toxicity, anoxia, or medical malpractice event. Determining this cause often requires a reconstruction of the history of an impairment and evidence of pre-injury ability levels. In many other forensic settings, however, the specific cause of an impairment is much less important.

Prognosis and Prediction

Looking ahead. Neuropsychological evaluation is often used to predict future behavior regarding competency, rehabilitation, education, disability accommodation, dangerousness, and compensation. For example, it can be important to know if someone is likely to recover from an incompetency, so that a trial might be postponed, or a guardianship or disability pension revisited.

It is also important to know what the prognosis of a condition is in order to set realistic education and rehabilitation goals.

Looking backwards. Neuropsychological evaluation can also be used as part of a determination of past behavior. It may play a role in reconstructing someone's past state of mind at the time of a crime, [or] one's previous competence to give testimony, to make a confession, to stand trial, to sign a will or contract, or to let a deadline pass.

Culturally Relative Standards

The need (or lack thereof) for culturally relative standards. For some forensic questions, it is critically important that the neuropsychological evaluation uses a culturally relative standard (Ferraro, 2002; Fletcher-Janzen, Strickland, & Reynolds, 2000; Nell, 2000). The neuropsychologist must determine if the focus person's abilities and behavior are deviant within [the person's] cultural context in order to determine if a medical condition is present. Tests used must compare the person to an appropriate population in order to have validity as measures of brain disorder. This is especially true for personal injury liability, disability accommodation, and special education.

For many forensic questions, the standard is absolute and it concerns competence within a specific U.S. cultural and institutional framework rather than culturally relative standards. For example, the question of competence to stand trial is a question of the focus person's ability to understand what is going on in a U.S. court and to collaborate in [his or her] defense with a U.S. attorney. Although an interpreter is provided, the focus person is not given the option of standing trial under another legal system or of having the system simplified. . . .

Many other forensic questions stand somewhere in between. For example, competence to parent, to work, or to manage funds must take into account cultural values and typical behaviors for these activities, but there are also some expectations with regard to U.S. culture and laws that the focus person is expected or needs to manage, such as not abusing or neglecting children, or being able to manage U.S. currency.

Specific cultural competence in neuropsychological evaluation. The neuropsychologist and his or her psychometrist, intern, and other assistants need to have knowledge of the culture of the focus person in order to perform a competent and ethical evaluation. The degree of knowledge needed may depend upon the nature of the question asked, as noted above. Some degree of general cultural competence is a prerequisite for specific professional cultural competence. . . .

The aspects of specific cultures that are most relevant to neuropsychological evaluation are as follows:

- Worldview—This includes how a culture tends to view the locus of control of the individual (whether things happen to you primarily because of your own choice and initiative, because of chance, because of the actions of family or society or God, etc.), how the culture views causality (scientific, magical, religious, chance, balances, etc.), how the culture views the purpose of life, and so on.
- Values—This includes concepts of honor, shame, justice, family expectations, time sense, and the like.
- Religion and beliefs—This includes not only the formal theological belief system but also the rituals, social structures, and functions of the religion in everyday life.
- Family structures—This includes not only how the culture describes kinship, but also the expectations for participation in a family and expectations for behavior toward specific family members according to role.
- Social roles—This includes expectations for interactions based on age, gender, social class, position of authority, and so on. This also includes how members of the culture view and interact with members of other cultures and ethnic groups.
- Recent history—This includes wars, famines, epidemics, immigration trends, and so on that may give indications of likely causes of brain illnesses, emotional traumas, or other life-shaping events.

- Epidemiology—This includes local diseases, genetic disorders, toxicities, etc., that may be characteristic of a particular population.
- Responses to psychotropic medications—These have been found to vary by ethnicity (Strickland & Gray, 2000).
- Attitudes and beliefs regarding health, illness, and disability
- Communication and interpersonal style:
  ○ Language (including features such as tonal languages, nature of the writing system, and use of an alphabet)
  ○ Expectations between individuals of various social roles
  ○ Personal disclosure (what is considered appropriate in what contexts)
  ○ Rapport and how to establish it
  ○ Nonverbal conventions such as interpersonal distance or eye contact
- Educational system—This includes the quality and nature of the educational system and the role of testing within that system.

***

Culturally Relative Standards—Testing

The rationale of normative-based testing in neuropsychology. In order to use tests to determine the degree of cognitive loss resulting from a brain disorder, it would be ideal to have neuropsychological test results from the focus person prior to the development of the brain condition. This is rarely the case (although limited cognitive testing is sometimes available from various sources). Lacking such data, neuropsychologists attempt to estimate what the focus person's test scores would have been by comparing them to a similar population. What constitutes a "similar population" can vary from test to test, as can the quality of the norming project. It is most usual to norm by age, and tests are also sometimes normed by gender, education, ethnicity, and other variables.

***

Determining the presence of brain dysfunction is only one of the roles of neuropsychological testing. These tests are also used to assist in diagnosing different types of brain dysfunction, to assist in determining various forms of competence, to predict future behavior, to predict educational and vocational potential, and other functions. Each of these functions has forensic applications, distinctive types of validation, and distinctive considerations in how norms are used.

The myth of culture-fair testing. Some naïve psychologists still believe that psychological testing is a universal phenomenon, and that it can be made culturally fair. There are even tests that incorporate "culture-fair" in their names. This myth has had an unfortunate role in advancing xenophobic and racist agendas (Fraser, 1995; Gould, 1996; Herrnstein & Murray, 1994). Psychological testing is not a universal phenomenon, and there is a great deal of cultural and individual variability in the knowledge and attitudes that people bring to the evaluation (Nell, 2000; Lonner & Malpass, 1994).

***

Some traditional cultures without formal educational systems may have no tradition of formal testing whatsoever. Others have markedly different attitudes toward testing. For example, independent thinking and making mistakes have long been regarded as dangerous in a large part of Russian culture, to the point that there is a Russian saying, "Thinking is the privilege of the intelligent" (Michael Zawistowski, personal communication, 2002). For cultural reasons, Russians will often say, "I don't know," in response to test items rather than risk an error, and may appear to be giving inadequate or even invalid effort. Similarly, although "quick" is (in some contexts) a synonym for "intelligent" in English, in many sub-Saharan African cultures, intelligence is associated with wisdom, thoughtfulness, and even taking time to make decisions (Mpofu, 2002). A common testing experience with people from these and other immigrant populations is that it is difficult to "hurry" the focus person on the tests. This can likewise give an erroneous impression of inadequate effort and malingering.

Because of these considerations, adjusting for culture is not simply a matter of new norms for the relevant cultural group or adjusting the interpretation of test scores. It involves an entire set of testing skills to understand how the focus person views the experience, to assure that the focus person understands what is expected, and to interpret the results in light of that understanding.

***

Mental status examination. All physicians and mental health care providers are trained in administering a mental status examination (although some maintain these skills better than others). The mental status examination is very useful for screening, but it is unstandardized, not quantified, and not normed. Its interpretation is based upon clinical judgment. . . .

Psychiatrists and other mental health professionals are often quite good at detailing specific qualitative aspects of the focus person's thought processes, such as the nature of [the person's] delusions, hallucinations, paranoia, and anxieties. They may supplement their examinations with personality tests. Behavioral neurologists are particularly skilled at teasing out mental status changes resulting from focal lesions to specific parts of the brain.

Mental status examinations are heavily dependent upon the skills and interpretation of the individual clinician. This can be quite variable, and the research literature indicates that the mental status examination is, in general, not very reliable across clinicians (Rodenhauser & Fornal, 1991; Tancredi, 1987).

Cultural considerations are also up to the individual clinician. These can be quite astute, but horror stories also abound. To give one small example, a psychiatrist was conducting a competence-to-stand-trial evaluation of a Spanish speaker and asked him to interpret the proverb, "People who live in glass houses shouldn't throw stones." The medical interpreter, in an aside, explained to the examiner that this was not a known proverb in Spanish. The examiner insisted that the focus person ought to be able to interpret it anyhow. The interpreter afterwards made her point by asking the examiner to interpret the Spanish proverb,

"A horse with a sore back will always flinch" (Sara Koopman, personal communication, 2003). (It should be noted, however, that not all professional interpreters can be counted on to be cultural brokers in this manner, and are often professionally proscribed from doing so.) Similarly, many English speakers may be baffled by the Russian expression, "to discover America" and the Spanish expression, "to discover warm water," while having no problem with the corresponding English expression, "to reinvent the wheel."

The Mini Mental State Exam is a brief exam widely used by physicians primarily to screen for level of delirium or dementia. It consists of items regarding orientation, memory, attention, drawing, reading, writing, repetition, naming, and following directions. It is scored on a 30-point scale and is normed by age and education. Many translations and cross-cultural adaptations and norms are now available (cf. Ostrosky-Solis, Lopez-Arango, & Ardila, 2000; Tang et al., 1999), but are not always known or used. It plays a useful role in the evaluation of mental status, but can rarely stand alone as the basis of a medico-legal opinion.

Cultural differences in judgments of insanity are also well-known. One need only read the headlines to find world leaders hurling accusations of paranoia, delusions, and irrationality at one another. Other chapters in this book treat this theme in more detail.

Cognitive tests. Cognitive tests, such as IQ tests, are designed to measure thinking abilities in a general population. They are usually designed to measure various components of thinking abilities in a general way as these relate to theories of cognition or to academic or life skills. The tests are not designed to measure specific brain functions. The tests are usually designed to give a "normal" distribution of scores, with most people's scores clustering around the average score (e.g., IQ of 100), with fewer and fewer people scoring farther and farther away from average. Many of the most common cognitive tests used in the [United States], such as most intelligence tests and memory tests, are normed on a population representative of the

U.S. general population by census matching. Typically, only English speakers are used in the norming sample and sometimes people are excluded because of various disabilities or limited education. Norms are available for the Wechsler Adult Intelligence Scale—III and the Wechsler Memory Scale—III for subtests and indexes that have been adjusted for age, education, sex, and ethnicity (African American, Hispanic, and Caucasian only) for individuals educated primarily in the [United States] (Taylor & Heaton, 2001). These norms are used for specific inferences, but not for IQs.

The most widely used cognitive tests, the Wechsler Intelligence Scales and others, have been widely translated and adapted and often renormed in other countries. It is less common for these tests to be revalidated. The translated and renormed versions are often relatively difficult to obtain in the [United States] because they are most typically published in the country where they were adapted (or not published at all), and may not be distributed in the [United States]. Even their existence may be noted only in regional journals published in the relevant language.

Whether or not it is "fair" or appropriate to use a U.S. IQ test or other cognitive test with someone from another culture depends in large part on the use to be made of that test and even on the results obtained. Certainly, there is potential for an egregious error to label a child as mentally retarded based upon a test administered in [the child's] second language [he or she has] not yet mastered or based upon a culture that is still foreign to [the child]. Similarly, it can be unfair to the defense in a personal injury case to conclude that a plaintiff has brain damage on the basis of poor test results if those poor test results are actually due to cultural considerations. On the other hand, normal test results and strong performances in certain areas might be helpful in qualifying someone for educational and vocational opportunities, for establishing . . . competence, or for inferring good recovery from injury when other information is insufficient to allow for such conclusions. Such results may also add confidence to a conclusion to meet the standards of a certain legal level of proof. Furthermore, impaired test performances may be used to contribute to a conclusion of brain damage, particularly when those impaired performances are congruent in their specifics with converging evidence from other sources (nature and location of the injury, adaptive behavior before and after the injury, etc.).

***

Neuropsychological tests. Neuropsychological tests are most often designed to measure impairments in specific brain functions such as attention, memory, executive functions (abstraction, reasoning, problem solving, decision making, self control), language, visual-spatial abilities, perceptual abilities, motor skills, and so on.

Many of these tests have a "low ceiling." Most people with intact brains will have few or no errors on such tests, but the tests will not discriminate well among normal people with strong or weak abilities in that area. However, people with specific brain impairments will usually fail the test. Some neuropsychological tests compare the focus person to him/herself by comparing sensory or motor abilities on one side of the body with the other side. For this reason, norms may be less critical for some of these tests.

Some more cognitively oriented neuropsychological tests have high ceilings and are normed by age and education so as to be able to predict more closely the expected performance of the focus person (Heaton, Grant, & Matthews, 1992; Ivnick et al., 1996).

Most neuropsychological tests in common use in the [United States] are normed on populations with at least 8 years of education. Research on groups with little or no education has suggested that the first 2 years of education have the greatest impact on neuropsychological test performance (Ostrosky, Ardila, Rosselli, López-Arango, & Uriel-Mendoza, 1998). U.S. neuropsychologists must be especially careful in their interpretations when working with low-education populations.

***

Functional abilities tests. Some tests are designed to measure functional abilities in specific skill areas. These tests are typically used to determine if the focus person is competent to exercise those skills. Such tests attempt to look as directly as possible at the area of competency. For example, the Independent Living Scales (Loeb, 1996) are designed to measure competence for community living primarily in the elderly. The focus person is actually tested on his or her ability to look up a number in the phone book and dial it, read a bill and write a check to pay it, read a clock, and so on. Measures of the competency to stand trial (Everington & Luckasson, 1992; Grisso, 2003) ask a series of questions about the functions of a criminal court, and about the person's knowledge of the alleged crime. . . .

Adaptive behavior rating scales. Adaptive behavior rating scales are not tests of abilities. The focus person and/or an informant who knows that person well rate the person on the ability to carry out various everyday activities. These scales are particularly important in the diagnosis of mental retardation because the accepted definitions of mental retardation (American Association on Mental Retardation, 2002; American Psychiatric Association, 1994) require impairment not only on IQ testing but also in adaptive behavior.

***

Adaptive behavior is clearly culturally relative, and this is evident in the rating scales. For example, the referenced scales contain items referring to the use of telephones, microwaves, small electrical appliances, clothes washers and dryers, repair services, cars, seatbelts, air conditioners, thermometers, handkerchiefs, televisions, menus, dictionaries, alphabetizing, phone books, zip codes, bathroom cleaning supplies, electricity, scales, rulers, schedules, Christmas, Hanukah, forks, reading materials, ticket reservations, shoelaces, clocks, classified ads, and checkbooks. Access to these items is not universal and is related to culture, urbanization, and social class. There are no items referring to clotheslines, chopsticks, domestic animals, Ramadan, and so on.

Other items depend upon cultural norms of behavior or values that are not universal. [This includes such aspects as] looking at others' faces when talking, ending conversations, not interrupting, carrying identification, traveling independently in the community, . . . obeying street signs, needing time alone, . . . punctuality, hospitality, controlling temper, "pleasant breath," saying "thank you," conversational distance, dating, and so on. Although several of these scales have been translated into Spanish (and possibly other languages), there has been minimal cultural adaptation of the items, and there are minimal instructions in the manuals concerning cross-cultural applications.

***

Adaptive behavior scales can play an important role in cross-cultural neuropsychology. At times they may help document that an individual who does not "test well" on standardized cognitive tests, perhaps for cultural reasons, nevertheless is able to function adequately and competently in this society. Adaptive behavior scales in brain injury cases can document the changes in a way that cognitive tests cannot. However, interpretation of low scores is problematic because the scales are culture bound. . . .

Symptom validity tests. In the last 15 years, there has been a rapid increase in the number and sophistication of forensic neuropsychology testing instruments and techniques. This is particularly true in personal injury cases where the answers to forensic questions have significant consequences for injured people and the insurance companies that pay their claims. Measures of memory and attention have become increasingly sophisticated so as to detect more and more subtle impairments resulting from mild injuries in plaintiffs. At the same time, techniques to detect inadequate effort or malingering during neuropsychological testing have also become increasingly sophisticated, and have been used to undermine plaintiff's claims (Reynolds, 1998).

***

Personality tests. Most "personality tests" used by neuropsychologists are actually psychopathology inventories. They are designed to detect psychopathology according to psychiatric classifications, but they are less sensitive to variations in normal personality. The most common tests (Minnesota Multiphasic Personality Inventory—2 [MMPI], Butcher, Dahlstrom, Graham, Tellegen, & Kaemmer, 1989; Millon Clinical Multiaxial Inventory—III [MCMI-III], Millon, 1994; Personality Assessment Inventory [PAI], Morey, 1991) were not designed with brain disorders or the changes in personality resulting from those disorders in mind. . . .

A new generation of neuropsychological personality tests is emerging. These are specifically designed to measure the changes in personality resulting from brain disorders (for reviews, see Judd, 1999; Judd & Fordyce, 1996). These may be normed by gender, age, and education. Their cross-cultural application is not yet validated.

***

SPECIFIC FORENSIC QUESTIONS

Personal Injury

When personal injury liability work is cross-cultural, it generally requires one of the highest levels of cross-cultural competence of the neuropsychologist. Although the level of proof required is only more-probable-than-not, the neuropsychologist often has to determine whether or not there is brain injury present in cases of subtle injury. The neuropsychologist is also asked to determine if that injury is due to a specific event. This usually requires considerable investigation beyond the testing and interview. It may require interviews of family members or others from the same cultural group as the focus person. The neuropsychologist must be very well versed in cross-cultural knowledge and skills in general as well as in the specific culture of the focus person. The neuropsychologist also needs to be familiar with any available neuropsychological knowledge specific to that culture. The neuropsychologist should also be able to describe the impact of the injury on the focus person's life and family, and this will include cultural considerations. In the case of severe injuries where there is clear impairment, the neuropsychologist's job may be simply characterizing that impairment. In such situations, the need for cross-cultural competence is still present but is not as acute.

Competencies

Issues of the focus person's competence (to stand trial, to testify, to make a will, to consent to medical treatment, to manage funds, to drive, to sign a contract, to parent, and so on) require less cross-cultural skill on the part of the neuropsychologist than personal injury liability. This is because diagnosis and causality are less at issue, and also because competence is, in part, a question of functioning within the U.S. culture. Nevertheless, the neuropsychologist should be sensitive to culturally typical ways of functioning around the issue at hand. For example, U.S. mainstream culture places a much greater premium on personal independence than many other cultures. These other cultures use a more interdependent mode of functioning, especially within families. For example, the focus person may rely on family assistance with transportation, the mechanics of money management, dealing with institutions, and childrearing, much more so than is typical for mainstream U.S. culture, and yet that person may be competent in [his or her culture's] context. Many immigrants deal only in cash and do not use bank accounts, credit cards, or money orders, which some may interpret unfairly as suggesting marginal financial competence.

Many forensic competence issues require a judgment of prognosis, that is, whether the person can become competent. These questions may require more cultural sensitivity, especially when culture is a contributing component to incompetence. The neuropsychologist must be able to take into account the focus person's ability to learn in the context of brain dysfunction and usual patterns of acculturation.

Vocational, Educational, and Disability Issues

Disability accommodations in education, vocational rehabilitation, social services, and other domains require that it be established that the focus person more probably than not has a disability due to a medical condition. Unlike personal injury liability, the disability need not be attributed to one specific cause or medical condition (except in the case of worker's compensation). The disability might be the result of multiple or unknown medical conditions. Toward this end, the neuropsychologist must have cross-cultural skills to be able to determine the presence or absence of brain dysfunction as in personal injury liability.

When disability is already established, the neuropsychological evaluation may be confined to questions of reasonable accommodations. This type of evaluation has a component that concerns adaptation to the U.S. context for which cross-cultural considerations are less important. However, the neuropsychologist must be able to understand the goals and expectations of the focus person and family in their cultural context. For example, someone whose inability to learn English and cognitive impairments might render [him or her] unemployable in the open market might nevertheless play a significant helpful role in a business run by [the] family.

***

CRIMINAL DEFENSES

Neuropsychology can play a role in criminal defense with regard to competence to stand trial (discussed above), the insanity defense, the accused's state of mind at the time of the crime, and the mitigating and aggravating circumstances that might contribute to sentencing considerations. Neuropsychological testing may contribute to establishing a diagnosis and a pattern of cognitive abilities and disabilities that, in many instances, can be reasonably inferred to have been present at the time of the crime. This aspect of evaluation is subject to all of the cross-cultural cautions regarding testing that have already been mentioned.

Frequently, however, what is at issue is a neurobehavioral syndrome—a change in emotions, personality, and self-regulation resulting from a brain condition. Many of these syndromes—especially those associated with damage to the frontal lobes—have few manifestations on most cognitive tests. Those cognitive tests that are somewhat sensitive to these changes are tests of executive functions (Cripe, 1996). However, these tests are among the most problematic in cross-cultural application and are among the least cross-culturally researched (Sbordone, Strickland, & Purisch, 2000). For these reasons, the cross-cultural neuropsychologist who works on these criminal issues must be particularly skilled in understanding and evaluating behavior that is incongruent for the culture, subculture, and individual. This type of evaluation will typically involve extensive interviewing of multiple sources and review of records. It may involve little or no testing (Artiola i Fortuny & Mullaney, 1998), or the testing may turn out not to be very relevant to the case. Rather, the neuropsychologist will be attempting to construct a plausible explanation of the behavior in question based upon the accused's perception of the situation and behavioral tendencies. These tendencies must be seen as congruent with other behavior at other times and with what is known about any brain insults or dysfunctions that are present. For these reasons, this type of evaluation is particularly demanding of clinical neuropsychological and cross-cultural skills.

PUTTING IT ALL TOGETHER: COMPETENT FORENSIC CROSS-CULTURAL NEUROPSYCHOLOGICAL ASSESSMENT

To perform a competent forensic cross-cultural neuropsychological evaluation, the neuropsychologist should have

- Knowledge and skills concerning cross-cultural evaluation in general (how to work with an interpreter, principles of acculturation, dimensions of cultural impact on behavior, principles of test translation and adaptation, and so on);
- Knowledge concerning the specific culture/language of the focus person;
- Knowledge of neuropsychological literature regarding the culture/language of the focus person;
- Access to appropriate test materials and norms;
- Knowledge concerning the specific forensic question(s); and
- Knowledge concerning the professional ethical principles applicable to the situation.

When the neuropsychologist is not fully prepared in all of these areas, it may be possible to make up some deficiencies through research and consultation. The neuropsychological report should reflect this background through description of

- The focus person's cultural, linguistic, and acculturation status;
- Any use of interpreters;
- Tests and their appropriateness and any translations and adaptations made; and
- Norms used and their appropriateness.

The evaluation should include information from as wide a variety of sources as is practical and necessary to answer the questions at hand to the standard of proof needed. This diversity of data can include

- Review of medical, mental health, educational, employment, criminal, and other records;
- Interviews with multiple informants;
- Behavioral observations; and
- Tests and scales of cognition, neuropsychological functions, personality, functional abilities, adaptive behavior, symptom validity, and personality.

These data should be integrated into one coherent and consistent account. Doubts and limitations of knowledge should be clearly stated. Where competing explanations are plausible, a competent neuropsychological report will weigh the evidence for each. Under the U.S. legal system, the ultimate standard is the ability of the neuropsychologist to convince the jury and judge of the line of reasoning that led to the conclusions. The competent cross-cultural forensic neuropsychologist, in addition to having the above-mentioned knowledge, skills, and qualifications, must be able to communicate that information convincingly to a lay and legal audience.

The U.S. legal system itself and the science and art of neuropsychology are cultural artifacts. They produce neither universal justice nor universal truth. U.S. justice may not be the same as Somalian or Mayan or Thai justice. "Disability" as defined by U.S. law and neuropsychology may be quite different from disability as perceived by the Hmong or Inuit. Causality as defined by U.S. law and neuropsychology may be perceived quite differently by the Navajo or Samoan. In many instances, those from other cultures may be unaware of their rights or reluctant to pursue them. Even when cross-cultural law and neuropsychology are done "correctly" by their own standards, the result may not feel appropriate or just to those of other cultures.

The roles of professionals are many in these cases, and it is not always our job to reconcile these differences. But to the degree that we can at least recognize, understand, and respect the distinctive perspectives of those from other cultures, we can all do our jobs better. More than just that, we can work to build better systems of justice and knowledge to better serve a broader segment of human diversity.

CASE STUDY: MIGUEL

It was a clean catch. The prosecutor had a videotape of Miguel, a 27-year-old undocumented Mexican immigrant, handing the cocaine to the undercover agent through the car window and accepting the money. His companion, the driver of the car, had already plea bargained. The public defender was concerned, because Miguel did not really seem to understand what was going on in his case. He did not seem concerned, he did not ask questions, and each time she went to see him he acted almost as if they had never met. All he would say about the crime was that he had gone for a ride with his friend because he had a nice radio in his car. The psychologist she hired to determine his competence to stand trial reported that he had completed the third grade in Mexico, similar to his siblings. On a translated test, his Spanish word reading was at the twelfth-grade level, with an estimate of average intelligence. On a commercially available Spanish IQ test, he was in the low normal range. When interviewed through an interpreter, he was cooperative, and there were no signs of psychopathology. On a translated personality test, however, his profile was invalid because of inconsistent responses and a "fake bad" validity scale. The psychologist concluded he had normal intelligence, was malingering mental illness, and was competent to stand trial.

Although her colleagues thought she was wasting her time, the public defender hired a cross-cultural forensic neuropsychologist. He spoke with Miguel's younger sister, with whom he had lived at the time of his arrest. She reported that Miguel worked as a dishwasher at a nearby Mexican restaurant owned by friends. He knew his way to and from the restaurant, but she did not allow him to walk around the neighborhood or take a bus because he would get lost. He had never learned to drive or to ride a bike. He did not shop, and handed all of his earnings over to her. He spent much of his free time watching cartoons on TV or playing with her young children. She did not trust him to baby-sit, because he did not have enough sense to know how to manage the unexpected. As far as she knew, Miguel had always been this way. The neuropsychologist called Miguel's mother in Mexico. She cried on the phone, and begged to have her son sent back to her, promising she would never let him leave home again. She said that she had come home one day 5 years earlier and a neighbor told her that a friend had come by and asked Miguel to go to the [United States] with him and he had left. She did not hear from him for 2 months until someone dropped him at his sister's apartment. She said that when Miguel started the fourth grade, the teacher sent him home because he was not learning. After that, he stayed very childlike and never learned skills like the other children. He could do only the simplest of chores. The other children made fun of him, but he did not seem to notice. He played with children much younger than himself. He always stayed close to home and never developed any romantic interests or attachments. When asked about his health, she recalled that he had had fevers and chills the summer after the third grade. He later had to take a bitter medicine when the government workers came through to spray for mosquitoes.

On testing, Miguel had severely impaired memory and executive functions, even when compared to Mexicans with no education. The cross-cultural neuropsychologist concluded that Miguel probably had contracted childhood malarial encephalitis and was left effectively mentally retarded. He explained to the public defender that Spanish is a regularly spelled language and so word reading is not a valid estimate of intelligence as it can be in English. He also noted that the first intelligence test used was normed over 40 years ago on a questionable population and has since been found to produce IQ scores that are about 25 points too high. On a formal test of competence to stand trial, Miguel had minimal knowledge of any legal system. Attempts to educate him about specific points were unsuccessful. The public defender negotiated with the judge, Miguel, and his family to arrange Miguel's deportation to his mother's home in Mexico in lieu of a trial.

The case of Miguel is an amalgam from several cases of the first author's experience, and illustrates many of the challenges of cross-cultural forensic neuropsychological evaluation.

19

ASSESSING ALLEGATIONS OF DOMESTIC VIOLENCE IN CHILD CUSTODY EVALUATIONS

JAMES N. BOW

PAUL BOXER

Because of the complexity of custody disputes, the court is increasingly relying on expert testimony in child custody cases. Child custody evaluators are faced with a complicated task (Bow & Quinnell, 2001). This task can be made even more difficult when allegations of domestic violence by one or both parents are involved. Domestic violence in the context of child custody evaluation has been receiving increased attention in recent years, most likely because of certain legislative initiatives, judicial decision making, and enhanced public awareness. As a result, child custody evaluators are conducting an increased number of evaluations involving this issue. Custody evaluations involving allegations of domestic violence hold special challenges for evaluators because of the alleged secrecy of the parties and the frequent lack of adequate investigation and documentation to support or refute the allegations. Variations in the empirical research base of domestic violence coupled with varying legal statutes (Lemon, 2000) and definitions lend an additional level of complexity to these evaluations.

A child custody evaluator's opinion about alleged domestic violence can have a profound impact on the ultimate custody decision. Thus, it is important to quantify and clarify the

Editors' Note: This article was originally published in the *Journal of Interpersonal Violence*, Vol. 18, No. 12, December 2003, pp. 1394–1410. Reprinted with permission of Sage Publications.

procedures followed by custody evaluators in constructing such an opinion. As prior studies of custody evaluation practices have indicated, such evaluations are typically quite comprehensive in nature, even without any special attention called to allegations of domestic violence (Bow & Quinnell, 2001, 2002). The current study was designed to examine the ways in which custody evaluators handle the critical issue of domestic violence allegations.

DOMESTIC VIOLENCE: THE VEIL OF SECRECY

In custody disputes, the legal system often becomes a symbolic background for the continuation of the domestic violence. Child support, visitation, and custody all become major issues of control for the perpetrator. This is particularly true, as more than two thirds of states have passed laws authorizing joint custody (Pagelow, 1993) unless evidence indicates otherwise. Perpetrators often use intimidation and harassment, and children become pawns in the legal process. Allegations and counter-allegations are common. Perpetrators of domestic violence are masters at denying, minimizing, and blaming the victim. They are also good at projecting a nonabusive image (Bancroft & Silverman, 2002), meaning they can present to the court and evaluator as calm, loving, and sensitive. The absence of a single psychological profile of the perpetrator or victim of domestic violence (American Psychological Association [APA], 1996; Guyer, 2000), along with the lack of adequate documentation of domestic violence in most cases, makes it difficult for the evaluator to ascertain the veracity of the allegation.

It can thus be quite problematic for custody evaluators to confirm the status of perpetrators. Recent improvements in documentation by law enforcement agencies, along with arrests, should assist in substantiating incidents of domestic violence. Prior to the 1980s, police departments wrote policies discouraging arrests in these cases (Lemon, 1999) as well as requiring the official documentation of police contacts. Currently, at least 24 states have mandatory arrest statutes when police are called for domestic violence (Austin, 2001). These steps have assisted in verifying incidents of domestic violence reported to the police. Even so, only a very small percentage of domestic violence incidents are ever reported (Harway & Hansen, 1994). Therefore, in most cases, direct verification is lacking, which complicates the assessment process for the child custody evaluator.

CURRENT STATUS OF THE EMPIRICAL RESEARCH ON DOMESTIC VIOLENCE

The overall prevalence rate of marital violence between partners is about 12% (Austin, 2000). However, in high-conflict and/or entrenched custody cases, the rate is significantly higher with estimates in the 72% to 80% range (Johnston & Roseby, 1997; Newmark, Hartell, & Salem, 1995). There is also an increased risk around the time of the marital separation (APA, 1996; Pagelow, 1993).

Domestic violence in marital situations (i.e., marital or family violence) involves many dimensions including physical, sexual, property, and/or psychological violence, which range on a continuum in severity from mild to severe. It is important to note that no single definition of family violence is established or agreed upon by researchers (APA, 1996). Furthermore, much research has focused on samples drawn from clinical and domestic violence shelter samples. Generalizing from these samples is ill advised (Straus, 1990), although it is often done. In child custody cases, domestic violence research has been performed primarily by Hanks (1992), Johnston and her colleagues (Johnston & Campbell, 1993; Johnston & Roseby, 1997), and Newmark et al. (1995). In particular, Johnston and colleagues have provided the most comprehensive typology of interparental violence and its detrimental impact on children.

Domestic violence affects families in a variety of ways. First, it creates serious concerns about the safety and welfare of the victim and children. Second, children who witness domestic violence are at high risk for emotional and behavioral problems (Dalton, 1999; Holden, Geffner, & Jouriles, 1998; Johnston & Roseby, 1997). Third, children in such situations are at high risk for child abuse (Dalton, 1999; Lemon, 1999). Fourth, a history of domestic violence predicts a poor prognosis for parenting cooperation (Austin, 2000). Therefore, a thorough and accurate assessment of this area is critical, even if it is not alleged or identified as an initial concern.

Another critical issue for child custody evaluators is the possibility of interactive (e.g., bidirectional) or female-initiated violence. The vast majority of research in the past has focused on male-initiated violence. However, some research using community samples indicates the presence of wife-to-husband assaults at roughly the same rate as husband-to-wife assaults (Straus, 1990; Straus & Gelles, 1988). Then again, the injury rate for wives is about six times greater than that for husbands (Straus, 1993) because of the greater physical size and strength of men. As a result, there is a greater chance that injuries to wives will be documented. Johnston and Campbell's (1993) typology of interparental violence in contested custody cases included interactive and female-initiated categories. Furthermore, 16% of the arrests for domestic violence in California in 1998 were women (Clifford's report as cited by Austin, 2001). Consequently, interactive or female-initiated violence cannot be dismissed and must be considered in the assessment process.

DOMESTIC VIOLENCE IN THE LEGAL ARENA

Recent concerns about domestic violence and its detrimental impact on the family have resulted in legislative action. The overwhelming majority of states currently have statutes that require the court to consider domestic violence in all custody determinations, and 14 states have adopted statutes creating a presumption against awarding custody to a perpetrator of domestic violence (Lemon, 2000). Professional associations such as the American Bar Association and the APA have taken strong positions against granting custody to perpetrators (APA, 1996). Consequently, a finding of domestic violence has a substantial impact on custody determination.

Given the high stakes, some parents might use false allegations of domestic violence to a strategic advantage in custody disputes. Stahl (1994) noted a rapid rise in such allegations in the late 1980s and early 1990s. Domestic violence allegations can be a powerful weapon to limit or deny custody and/or visitation in a vindictive manner. Custody evaluators should thus be aware of this possibility. This is especially important because judges tend to award primary physical custody to the parent who made the allegation of spousal abuse, even if the other parent's actions were not substantiated (Sorensen et al., 1995).

Determining Practice Standards

Child custody evaluations involving allegations of domestic violence are clearly challenging and complex with many factors that need to be investigated. Bancroft and Silverman (2002), Dalton (1999), Jaffe and Geffner (1998), and L. E. Walker and Edwall (1987) have harshly criticized such evaluations. Criticism of child custody evaluators has focused on the following: (a) lack of basic knowledge about the domestic violence field, (b) failure to use collateral sources and record review, (c) overreliance on psychological testing, (d) failure to consider domestic violence as a major issue in custody determination by assuming that the allegations are exaggerated or fabricated, and (e) evaluators having a severe bias in favor of male perpetrators. Bancroft and Silverman claimed there is an urgent need to establish oversight and review of child custody evaluators. However, formal research on the practices and procedures for child custody evaluations involving domestic violence is lacking. Nevertheless, one state—California—requires custody evaluators to take training in domestic violence issues for court appointment.

The APA (1994) and the Association for Family and Conciliation Courts (AFCC) (1994) have developed child custody guidelines that outline preparatory and procedural steps to follow. Although not mandatory, the guidelines set parameters for professional practice in the custody evaluation field. Both [sets of] guidelines mention that evaluators should have expertise in the specific area assessed (e.g., domestic violence); otherwise, additional supervision, consultation, and/or specialized knowledge or training should be sought. Neither set of guidelines offers specific procedural steps for assessing domestic violence. Also, only a few authors have specifically addressed procedures to use in assessing domestic violence allegations in custody evaluations (Austin, 2000, 2001; Stahl, 1999; Walker & Edwall, 1987).

Austin (2000, 2001) discussed a risk assessment approach within a clinical-forensic-scientific paradigm. His approach shows great promise and is comprehensive in nature. He also outlined a 6-factor test of credibility, which includes objective verification, pattern of abuse complaints, corroboration by credible others, absence of disconfirming verbal reports by credible third parties, psychological profile and past history of abusive behavior by the alleged perpetrator of marital violence, and psychological status of the alleged victimized spouse. Still, there are currently no studies documenting the actual practices of evaluators involved in child custody evaluations with domestic violence allegations.

The purpose of the present study was to assess the status of child custody evaluations involving allegations of domestic violence. Four major areas were addressed: (a) training in the domestic violence area, (b) the nature and types of abuse referred for such evaluations, (c) practices and procedures utilized, and (d) types of custody/visitation arrangements and interventions recommended by evaluators. It is hoped that this information will inform practice and help mental health professionals better meet the needs of children, parents, and the judicial system.

METHOD

Identification of Participants

Names of doctoral-level psychologists were obtained through public access forensic referral lists, Internet searches of clinical and forensic psychologists who specialize in child custody work, and Friend of the Court (FOC) nominations. A list of master's-level child custody evaluators was obtained from the Association of Family, Court, and Community Professionals. Overall, 348 potential participants were identified.

Instrument

A comprehensive, six-page survey was developed after a thorough review of the child custody and domestic violence literature. The following areas were assessed: demographic information of the evaluator, specific training in the area of domestic violence, nature and types of domestic violence cases referred for child custody evaluations, practices and procedures used in such cases, victim characteristics that support domestic violence, importance of different risk factors in the assessment of the perpetrator, and types of interventions and recommendations typically used. A copy of the survey may be obtained by contacting the first author.

Procedure

Each potential participant was sent a packet of information including a letter outlining the purpose of the study, an informed-consent sheet, a blank survey form, a request form for results, and a stamped return envelope. The blank survey forms for doctoral- and master's-level child custody evaluators were almost identical except the doctoral-level form asked for additional credentialing information and the master's-level form inquired about tests requested or given. The latter was necessary because some of the master's-level evaluators were social workers that do not administer tests but might request testing. Potential participants were informed that all data would be coded, analyzed, and reported on a group basis to protect individual confidentiality.

Potential participants were requested to complete anonymously and return the survey. If they no longer performed child custody evaluations or evaluations involving domestic violence, they were asked to return the blank survey indicating so. Results of the study were promised to those who returned an enclosed request form or e-mailed the first author, requesting such information. Approximately 1 month later, reminder letters were mailed.

A total of 148 surveys were returned (43%). Of these, 115 were usable surveys, that is, completed by master's- or doctoral-level professionals currently performing child custody evaluations involving domestic violence allegations. Twenty-four blank surveys were returned indicating that recipients no longer performed custody work or declined custody evaluations involving domestic violence; 1 survey was incomplete and 8 were [returned as] undeliverable.

Demographics of Participants

The gender of respondents was almost equal, with 52% female and 48% male. Almost all were Caucasian (97%), with 3% Hispanic. Sixty-eight percent were doctoral-level psychologists, 16% were master's-level psychologists or counselors, and 16% were master's-level social workers. One person from each of the latter two groups was also an attorney. The overwhelming majority worked in private practice (80%) followed by court clinics (11%). The remaining worked in other settings such as universities or community mental health clinics. Forty-eight percent practiced in an urban area and 44% in a suburban setting, with only 8% working in rural areas. Respondents were represented from 33 states, including Washington, D.C., with the following regional distribution: 31% West, 19% South,

27% Midwest, and 23% East. Professional experience averaged 22.09 years in the clinical area ($SD = 7.74$) and 13.84 years in the child custody area ($SD = 7.48$). The median number of evaluations completed by respondents in their career was 150. It is important to note that this sample was a highly experienced group of child custody evaluators working mostly in private practice in an urban area. Therefore, the findings may not represent the full spectrum of custody evaluators.

RESULTS

Training in Domestic Violence

The majority of respondents (68.2%) reported taking no graduate courses addressing domestic violence. The primary method for learning about domestic violence was through seminars (median = 4 seminars) and reading books and articles (median = 18 articles/books), although there was much variability ($M = 7.38$ seminars, $SD = 10.25$; $M = 43.28$ articles/books, $SD = 78.20$). Only 4.5% of respondents did not attend any seminars, and only 2.7% read fewer than 3 articles/books on the topic. Some respondents also indicated that they taught courses/seminars and/or had written articles on domestic violence.

Type and Nature of Referrals

Respondents reported that almost all child custody referrals were court ordered (93.24%). On average, they reported that 37% of their child custody referrals involved allegations of domestic violence. Forty-six percent of the cases involved domestic violence related to the separation, whereas 29% were episodic (i.e., occurring intermittently during the marriage) and 24% were enduring and chronic in nature. In terms of the alleged perpetrator, the following pattern was reported: 51% male instigator; 17% bidirectional, mostly male; 14% bidirectional, mutual; 11% female instigator; and 7% bidirectional, mostly female. Table 19.1 shows the specific types and frequency of domestic violence allegations.

Table 19.1   Specific Types and Frequency of Domestic Violence Allegations

	Frequency Ratings						
Type	1	2	3	4	5	M	SD
Emotional/verbal abuse	0	3.5	9.6	19.3	67.5	4.51	0.82
Physical aggression	0	9.6	18.4	43.0	28.9	3.91	0.93
Coercion/threats	1.0	7.1	27.4	31.0	33.6	3.89	0.99
Controlling finances[a]	1.0	17.0	25.9	45.5	10.7	3.48	0.93
Destruction of property	2.6	21.1	33.3	35.1	7.9	3.25	0.96
Isolation	7.1	29.2	18.6	31.0	14.2	3.16	1.20
Stalking	6.3	62.5	17.9	10.7	2.7	2.41	0.87
Forced sex	9.6	57.0	21.1	10.5	1.8	2.38	0.87
Kidnapping children	23.5	66.1	4.3	4.3	1.7	1.95	0.78

NOTE: Value was rated on a Likert-type scale from 1 *(never)* to 5 *(almost always)*. Numbers in frequency rating categories indicate the percentage of respondents indicating that value.

a. Refers to the overcontrol of finances or economic abuse as described by Harway and Hansen (1994).

Emotional/verbal abuse, physical aggression, and coercion/threats were most common. In terms of physical aggression, respondents were asked to rate the severity. Fifty-one percent rated it as mild (e.g., threw something, pushed, or grabbed), 33% as moderate (e.g., slapped, bit, or kicked), and 16% as severe (e.g., hit with fist, choked, or threatened with a weapon).

Practices and Procedures Used

Table 19.2 displays the frequency of procedures typically used by respondents in these evaluations along with the average time allotted and value of each in the decision-making process. Multiple methods of data collection were indicated with almost all respondents using the following procedures: history gathering with each parent, interview with each child, parent–child observations, review of police and medical documents, and collateral contact with therapist(s). Psychological testing was used by three-quarters of the respondents. It is important to note that a portion of the sample involved social workers that did not administer or request testing. Conjoint sessions were infrequently used. As expected, the most time-intensive procedure was the interview with each parent.

Much time was also spent reviewing police and medical documents. In terms of decision making, the greatest value was placed on the interview with the father and interview with the child along with the father-child observation. Next was the interview with the mother and mother-child observation. Police and medical documents were also seen as having high value. Interestingly, psychological testing of the parents and child was in the lower tier for value in decision making.

Only 30% of respondents indicated that they administered specialized questionnaires, instruments, or tests pertaining to domestic violence. Twenty-nine percent of these respondents indicated they developed their own questionnaires, 20% used the Spousal Assault Risk Assessment Guide (SARA), 15% used the Psychopathy Checklist–Revised, 11% gave the HCR-20: Assessing Risk of Violence, 9% gave the Conflict Tactics Scale, and 9% used the Child Abuse Potential Inventory.

Respondents were asked to list the top three signs, symptoms, or characteristics that support the contention of domestic violence during the assessment of the victim. Sixty percent of the respondents listed classic battered traits/signs such as shame and guilt, fear of perpetrator, low self-esteem, financial vulnerability, or inability to

Table 19.2   Average Usage Rate, Time Allotted, and Decision-Making Value of Procedures Used in Child Custody Evaluations Involving Domestic Violence Allegations

Specific Procedure	*% Using Procedure*	*M Hours*	*SD*	*M Weight in Decision Making*	*SD*
Interview/history with mother	100	3.49	1.72	4.46	1.06
Interview with each child	100	1.95	1.08	4.60	1.02
Interview/history with father	99.0	3.49	1.72	4.61	1.08
Mother-child observation	98.2	1.54	1.06	4.43	1.11
Father-child observation	98.2	1.56	1.06	4.46	1.07
Review of police documents	97.3	1.26	0.80	4.40	1.07
Review of medical documents	95.5	1.54	0.95	4.25	1.13
Collateral contact with therapist	94.6	1.35	0.88	4.22	1.14
Collateral contact with physician	83.0	0.90	0.54	3.91	1.21
Collateral contact with neighbors and friends	77.5	1.68	1.41	3.35	1.10
Psychological testing of father	75.9	3.25	1.93	3.98	1.15
Psychological testing of mother	75.0	3.25	1.95	3.93	1.18
Psychological testing of children	49.1	1.95	1.25	3.65	1.25
Conjoint session with both parents	25.0	2.10	1.20	3.71	1.46

NOTE: Weight in decision making was rated on a Likert-type scale from 1 *(none)* to 6 *(great)* for those that used the procedure.

leave the relationship. Thirty-seven percent identified physical injuries or medical problems; 31% reported independent confirmation of domestic violence by eyewitness report, records, photos, or conviction; 28% identified the creditability and consistency of the report; and 21% listed Axis I symptoms such as depression, anxiety, or Posttraumatic Stress Disorder.

Respondents rated on a 6-point Likert-type scale (1 = *none* to 6 = *great*) the value of different risk factors in the evaluation of the alleged perpetrator and importance in the decision-making process. . . . All factors, except for IQ, received a mean rating above 4. Drug usage, past use of weapons, ability to accept responsibility, power and control issues/attitudes, access to weapons, and past history of criminal behavior received the highest ratings.

IMPACT OF DOMESTIC VIOLENCE AND INTERVENTIONS/RECOMMENDATIONS

Of those respondents that offered an opinion on the veracity of the allegation (90%), a contention of domestic violence was supported in an average of 57% of the cases. In these cases, 76% of respondents claimed it greatly or extremely affected their recommendations. For a single perpetrator, respondents recommended sole legal/physical custody with the victim in 50% of cases and joint legal custody with primary physical custody with the victim in 39% of cases.

In cases involving bidirectional (mutual) domestic violence, there was much greater variability in custody/visitation recommendations. On average, respondents recommended joint legal custody with primary custody with the mother in 29% of the cases, joint legal and physical custody (50/50) in 18% of the cases, sole legal/physical custody with the mother in 16% of the cases, joint legal custody with primary custody with the father in 14% of the cases, third-party custody in 10% of the cases, and sole legal/physical custody with the father in 8% of the cases.

When parenting time was recommended for the perpetrator, on average, respondents reported that 40% of the cases involved supervised visits, 24% involved limited visitation, and 5% involved no visitation. The remaining 31% of cases involved regular visitations with no restrictions. When supervised visitation was proposed, respondents recommended a visitation center 40% of the time. The next most common places were a neutral party's place (15%), relative of the perpetrator (13%), and relative of the victim (12%).

Respondents also rated the frequency of recommended interventions on a Likert-type scale from 1 *(never)* to 5 *(almost always)*. Individual therapy for parties and children, domestic violence groups for the perpetrator, and parenting classes were most recommended (means > 4.0). Therapy for the perpetrator received the highest frequency rating (M= 4.63, SD = 0.69). Family therapy and the involvement of special masters or guardians ad litem were less often recommended (means < 3.0), and mediation received the lowest rating (M = 2.28, SD = 1.19).

On average, respondents claimed that custody evaluations involving domestic violence took 23.9 hours to complete plus 11.5 hours for the report with a time frame of 9.9 weeks. Respondents also reported, on average, that 25% of these cases required testimony in court.

DISCUSSION

Even in the absence of a custody dispute, domestic violence can have a serious negative influence on the physical and psychological well-being of children and adolescents exposed to it. Thus, it is critical for custody evaluators to assess the presence and impact of domestic violence regardless of whether it was raised as a specific issue at referral. Child custody evaluators have been harshly criticized in the past for their assessment of domestic violence allegations (Bancroft & Silverman, 2002; Dalton, 1999; Jaffe & Geffner, 1998). This criticism raises a concern that needs to be further explored, because domestic violence is an increasingly common allegation in child custody disputes. This study was conducted to assess the status of practice in this area.

In terms of training in domestic violence, only a minority of respondents had taken graduate

courses addressing this topic. However, this is expected considering that the vast majority of respondents attended graduate school more than 20 years ago when there was less focus, awareness, and research on domestic violence. In the present study, seminars and reading articles and books were the most common training methods, but there was wide variability among the respondents in the number of seminars attended and articles and books read. Only a small number of respondents (< 5%) had done neither. The vast majority had attended numerous seminars and read many articles and/or books. Therefore, as a group, they had basic exposure to the topic and were far from uninformed, contrary to common criticism.

Respondents reported using multiple methods of data collection in evaluating domestic violence allegations in child custody cases such as interviews with each parent, interviews with each child, parent-child observations, documentation review, collateral contacts, and psychological testing as stressed in child custody guidelines (APA, 1994; AFCC, 1994). All procedures involved as much time or more time than in typical custody evaluations as found by Bow and Quinnell (2001). Furthermore, the [average] total time involved (procedures plus report = 35.4 hrs) was significantly more than the time spent on the typical child custody evaluation (24.5 to 28.5 hours; Bow & Quinnell, 2001). Therefore, child custody evaluations involving domestic violence appear to be more time intensive than the typical child custody evaluation.

Parent-child observations were almost universally used by all evaluators. It is important to note that there is no empirical support that an observation of a child and parent will help accurately differentiate a perpetrator from a nonperpetrator, although it may provide information about attachment, parenting style, and comfort level.

Bancroft and Silverman's (2002) criticism that child custody evaluators fail to use collateral sources and record review was not supported. Respondents almost universally reported utilizing these procedures. They also reported spending considerable time contacting collateral sources and reviewing police and medical reports. Further, they rated the latter two in the upper tier in the decision-making process.

Psychological tests were administered or requested by the majority of respondents. The types of tests utilized compared favorably with typical child custody evaluations as found by Quinnell and Bow (2001). However, the average weight of psychological testing in the decision-making process was rated relatively low. Consequently, there is no indication that respondents are overvaluing or overrelying on psychological tests. One pertinent criticism might be that they are underutilizing specialized instruments for assessing domestic violence. Less than one third acknowledged using specialized questionnaires, instruments, or tests. Of this group, 29% of respondents developed their own, which may not be legally defensible. The latter issue is also applicable for published instruments and tests that lack adequate validity and reliability. Useful, empirically derived instruments, such as the SARA (Kropp, Hart, Webster, & Eaves, 1999) and Conflict Tactics Scales (Straus, 1979; Straus, Hamby, Boney-McCoy, & Sugarman, 1996) need to be utilized more in these cases.

Although respondents indicated much value in assessing risk factors for alleged perpetrators, few of them actually used risk management inventories. However, this might reflect appropriate caution given that many of these inventories (e.g., Psychopathy Checklist) were normed on criminal or institutional populations that may not represent the perpetrator.

Only a few respondents reported using a comprehensive domestic violence model in the assessment process such as Austin's (2001) violence risk assessment. This model incorporates different components such as interview data, psychological testing, collateral information, special domestic violence instruments such as the SARA, and evaluation of static (resistant to change over time) and dynamic (situational and changeable over time) factors. This integrative model may have much applicability, but it requires empirical validation.

Respondents in this study reported that 37% of their child custody referrals involved

allegations of domestic violence, which is higher than the prevalence rate of marital violence (12%; Austin, 2000) but significantly lower than researchers have found in high-conflict and/or entrenched custody disputes (72% to 80%; Johnston & Roseby, 1997; Newmark et al., 1995). In regard to the alleged perpetrator, 51% were reported to be male, 38% were bidirectional, and 11% were female. The latter two figures affirm that bidirectional and female-instigated complaints are made and need to be appropriately investigated.

In 57% of the cases, respondents supported the contention of domestic violence. In those cases, 76% of respondents claimed it greatly or extremely affected their recommendation. This finding supports previous research that found child custody evaluators rated domestic violence as one of the top factors in custody decision making (Bow & Quinnell, 2001).

In cases involving a single perpetrator, 89% of respondents reported recommending physical custody to the victim, thereby supporting the trend that preference should be given to the nonviolent parent whenever possible. Further, it was recommended by the respondents that the perpetrator's visitation be supervised, limited, or terminated in 69% of cases. Last, the most commonly recommended intervention was therapy for the perpetrator. These findings are fervently contrary to the contention that child evaluators do not take this issue seriously in custody determination. Also, there is no evidence of an evaluator bias in favor of the perpetrator.

In terms of interventions, as expected, family therapy and mediation were seldom recommended. Both interventions are intimidating for victims of domestic violence along with being unsafe. Most professionals argue against mediation in these cases (Hart, 1990; Jaffe & Geffner, 1998; Pagelow, 1993). Regardless, many states mandate mediation in contested custody and visitation disputes. Guyer (2000) also noted that family therapy is not the treatment of choice because of safety concerns and lack of attribution of responsibility to the perpetrator. A recommendation that was seldom used, but may have great utility, is a special master and/or case manager. This person, appointed by the court, acts as a go-between and assists in coordinating the parenting plan to hopefully help parents to resolve conflictive issues.

CONCLUSION

Although child custody evaluators are often criticized for their work in the domestic violence area, the findings of this study fail to support such an assertion. In general, evaluators reported adequate training in the field. Their custody procedures closely adhered to child custody guidelines, and the amount of time delegated for many procedures exceeded the typical child custody evaluation. A review of documents (e.g., police and medical reports) and collateral contacts were seen as valuable components in the evaluation process. Psychological testing was used, but respondents did not overvalue it in the decision-making process. However, the vast majority of respondents underutilized valid and reliable domestic violence instruments and questionnaires. Such instruments and questionnaires might be an asset in the evaluation process. In those cases that respondents supported a contention of domestic violence, it significantly affected custody recommendations.

20

THREE TYPES OF SKILLS FOR EFFECTIVE FORENSIC PSYCHOLOGICAL ASSESSMENTS

MARC SAGEMAN

Forensic work is becoming very popular among psychologists. Interesting stories, challenging problems, high pay, and involvement in high-drama litigation are temptations too difficult to resist for most. On the surface, the professions of psychology and the law both deal with behavior. This similarity conceals real differences in their practice and respective incentives. Clinical work is a cooperative, nonjudgmental enterprise in which rapport and alliance with the client is the rule. The client has little incentive to be deceptive, for appropriate treatment depends on accurate information. The legal process, on the other hand, is an adversarial system of conflict resolution. One party claims one thing; another disputes it. Eventually, fact finders may dismiss, find little merit in, or award significant damages in a civil suit or mete

out punishment for or exonerate a criminal defendant. The dramatic nature of these resolutions provides strong incentives for clients to try consciously or unconsciously to influence these outcomes.

Some of these disputes involve subtle questions about psychological science that are "beyond the ken of the laity." Psychologists are then invited to assist the trier of fact to understand the evidence or to determine a fact at issue. Forensic psychology is the application of the science of psychology to legal questions. Psychologists venturing into the legal arena must understand that they are simply guests in someone else's house. The host makes up all the rules and uses their contributions as he or she sees fit. The forensic psychologist's role is but a small part of the process of litigation. One of the main

Editors' Note: This article was originally published in *Assessment,* Vol. 10, No. 4, December 2003, pp. 321–328. Reprinted with permission of Sage Publications.

rules to remember is that psychologists never win or lose cases; lawyers do. It is the attorney's case, which consists of gathering the evidence, filing multiple motions, presenting the theory of the case, and refuting the adversarial theory. Over the years, I have learned to be humble; juries are not much swayed one way or another by expert testimony. Although psychologists' contributions are small in each specific litigated case, in the aggregate, they have much more to offer, framing the arguments in any issue and influencing appellate opinions through their arguments.

What is specific about the subspecialty of forensic psychology? Nothing prevents regular psychologists from practicing in a forensic setting. Many such generalists do a fine job despite the lack of specific training in forensic psychology. They intuitively understand what is asked of them and their professional acumen and sagacity guides them appropriately. However, most may fall short of the ideals of a competent forensic psychologist because of a lack of skills specific to the forensic arena that must be mastered to become an effective practitioner. These skills fall into three general categories that make a forensic assessment different from a regular clinical evaluation. First, such assessment must be relevant to and specifically address the specific legal question raised rather than generate a diagnosis. Second, it requires the special attention to evidence and the ability to reconstruct the past or predict the future; this is not usually demanded in the course of a clinical evaluation. Finally, the opinions from the evaluation must be persuasive to the appropriate audience, often an appropriate trier of fact, to assist in the resolution of the case at hand.

KNOWLEDGE OF LEGAL ISSUES REQUIRING PSYCHOLOGICAL EXPERTISE

Criminal Responsibility

To effectively assist the trier of fact on some subtle issue of psychology and law, a psychologist must understand the exact nature of the legal issue at hand. This does not mean going to law school, but it does mean that the psychologist must be familiar with the specific wording of the issues addressed in the specific jurisdiction where the litigation takes place. The U.S. legal system is a maze of jurisdictions that intersect, each with its own laws and legal precedents. Unlike the universal nature of science, the law is parochial; rules and precedents in one jurisdiction are usually different from those in another. For instance, people in Philadelphia, Pennsylvania, are subject to Pennsylvania and federal laws. They can be and often are different. For example, an insanity defense in state court must abide by the 1843 McNaughtan Rule[s], whereas in federal court, it is ruled by the 1984 Federal Insanity Defense Reform Act. Both rules have little in common with clinical mental disorders.

The best approach is for the psychologist to work closely with the retaining attorney to learn the specific language to address in the report. It might be useful to ask for the latest legal opinions when interpreting this language to ensure that one is addressing the relevant legal issue. Otherwise, good forensic work will be totally useless if the judge throws out the report and does not allow the proffered testimony because the report is not relevant to the issues under litigation.

For instance, some psychologists equate criminal insanity or lack of criminal competency with a severe mental disorder. This is not the case. Insanity is a legal concept and not a medical or psychological term. Criminal responsibility is about the mental state of the defendant at the time of the crime, not at the time of the examination, which takes place much later than the crime. The fact that a defendant is suffering from a mental disorder at the time of the examination may or may not be relevant to the legal question about the state of mind at the time of the crime. Incarceration is depressing, and the mental state at the time of the evaluation may be much worse than it was during the crime. The opposite may also be true. The defendant might have been manic at the time of the crime but under good medical control at the time of the evaluation.

A defendant may have been legally and temporarily insane at the time of the alleged crime but still carry no current *Diagnostic and Statistical Manual of Mental Disorders (DSM)* Axis I diagnosis. The defendant may have been involuntarily intoxicated at the time of the crime, which would be an exculpatory factor, or the defendant may have been suffering from what used to be called paradoxical intoxication (no longer in the *DSM* but still present in the *International Statistical Classification of Diseases [ICD–10]* under the diagnosis of pathological intoxication [F10.07]). Jurisdictions vary in their treatment of voluntary intoxication as a contribution to the commission of a crime. In some states, it may be considered diminished capacity, converting first-degree to third-degree murder. In others, it may not be raised in the guilt phase of a trial, but it may come in later in the penalty phase as a mitigating factor.

Antisocial personality disorder is not deemed to be a mental illness in criminal cases. This is as it should be. Five of the seven criteria required for its diagnosis involve criminal behavior. To turn around and argue that this criminal behavior is the result of a condition defined by such behavior is to lapse into solipsism. Criminal law wisely sidesteps this vicious cycle by removing this diagnosis as a possible exculpatory or mitigating factor in a crime.

Competencies: Civil and Criminal

Legal competencies have their specific definitions, and a forensic psychologist must know and address their exact wording in the law to help the layperson decide a legal dispute. In the law, competency is defined as the capacity or potential for the mental functioning required in a decision-specific manner and to understand and carry out certain tasks of decision making. It is presumed to be present unless a court rules otherwise. A specific incompetence means that a mental illness is causing a defect in judgment in the specific area in question. Competence is not a general function; it is issue specific. There are many competencies, each with its own legal

definition. Starting with civil competencies, testamentary capacity (competency to write a will) requires that one understands the nature of a will, knows the extent of one's "bounty" and who the "natural heirs or natural objects of one's bounty" are and has some appreciation of one's relationship to family members and the effect of the will on others. "Insane delusions" invalidate a will as might "undue influences," that is, pressures applied unfairly by a person with the intent of benefiting from that pressure in terms of the will.

Contractual competence means that one understands the nature, terms, and effects of a particular transaction. Lack of such competence, which must be the result of illness and not simple ignorance, may invalidate the contract. This competence requires greater decision-making capacity than testamentary capacity because of the adversarial nature of contracts. Occasionally, challenges to competency to marry, which requires one to understand the nature of the marriage relationship and the duties and obligations involved, arise in cases where family members are opposed to the marriage of their kin with moderate mental retardation, who might not be able to live with another person with the same condition.

There are many types of competencies in criminal cases. The most common is the competency to stand trial. Unlike criminal responsibility, which deals with past state of mind, this is the defendant's present ability to understand the nature and consequences of the proceedings and to assist in the defense. Mental illness may negate this competency. Its lack may be temporary, as in the case of an unmedicated defendant with schizophrenia, or permanent, as in the case of a defendant with moderate or more severe mental retardation.

Various other criminal competencies stress different elements of the criminal process. For instance, the competency to confess is the knowing, intelligent, and voluntary waiver of one's *Miranda* rights (*Miranda v. Arizona*, 1966). Only police coercion, but not psychosis (e.g., confessing from a command from God), may result in the suppression of one's confession. As psychologists are rarely present to evaluate a defendant's competency to confess at the time of the confession, they must assess the defendant's competency to waive *Miranda* rights in retrospect, as a reconstruction of the defendant's state of mind at the time.

In terms of other criminal competencies, the competency to plead guilty involves the waiver of one's rights of appeal, for pleading guilty resolves the criminal dispute with finality, whereas a jury verdict can be appealed on various grounds of unfairness. Here, a psychologist often has the luxury to evaluate the defendant at the time of the plea, and this is, therefore, a current competency. The competency to wave counsel is no greater or different from *Dusky* (*Dusky v. U.S.,* 1960). Finally, the competency to be executed rests on understanding the reason for this punishment. This has generated many controversies. Insanity and mental retardation are bars to execution.

Linking Mental States With the Legal Issue in Question

The law often requires the linkage between a mental state and a specific legal issue. In criminal cases, diagnosing a severe mental disorder is only half of the work. The other half is linking this mental disorder to the defendant's behavior at the time of the alleged crime. This is done through an examination of this behavior based on a careful consideration of the evidence. This cannot be based solely on the defendant's self-report because of its self-serving quality. The psychologist must weigh the available objective evidence of the defendant's behavior around the time of the alleged crime. Was there any evidence of psychosis or of goal-directed behavior, such as escaping detection or apprehension, or bizarre acting out just prior to or after the acts? To justify linkage, the mental state at the time of the crime had to be a substantial contributing factor to the commission of the crime. Only careful reasoning, taking into account the totality of the evidence in a case combined with the clinical findings of psychopathology, will assist lay fact finders when much of the knowledge about abnormal behavior is beyond their ken.

Similarly, in civil cases, a mishap must have been a substantial contributing factor to the mental damages. This involves knowing the mental health of the plaintiff prior to the mishap and comparing it to the plaintiff's mental health after the mishap. The subtraction of the latter from the former is the extent of the damages incurred. This assessment of the plaintiff's prior state of health requires a careful search of the evidentiary documents predating the mishap. The tendency to blame all of one's troubles on a specific incident is ubiquitous. It may even be a universal heuristic error. It provides a concise and understandable narrative for one's problems and removes one's responsibility for them. Without having to impute any cynicism, this is naturally very common among plaintiffs. Defense attorneys try to deny or minimize the impact of a specific incident under litigation in terms of mental damages. Forensic experts must strive toward not only a fair assessment of the damage but also its causation.

To show liability, the expert must analyze the nature of the event and show that it may reasonably have led to the claimed damages. For instance, cursing an employee at work does not cause schizophrenia or substance dependence. It may create a hostile environment, but this should not be stretched too far to postulate the emergence of a severe mental disorder. Although some experts have submitted reports to this effect, the courts are rightly skeptical of these arguments. The few times that they have been accepted are more likely the result of a fact finders' desire to punish outrageous behavior than a true acceptance of such opinions, which are just hooks on which to hang despicable civil defendants.

SKILLS REQUIRED BY THE DEMANDS OF THE LEGAL SYSTEM

A second general type of skill required of forensic psychologists is that which is demanded by the nature of the legal questions at hand. As previously mentioned, incentives are very different in clinical and forensic evaluations and the competent forensic psychologist must always keep them in mind. It is crucial to corroborate the information provided and keep a modicum of neutrality in the proceedings. Many questions from the law involve reconstruction of past events and prediction of the future. The forensic psychologist must keep abreast of new techniques in both fields.

Gathering Complete Information

Forensic psychology opinions must be based on complete information. A forensic expert needs to have the soul of a detective to ferret out all the available information on which to render an opinion, within any reasonable degree of psychological certainty, on the legal questions before him or her. It is of the utmost importance to gather the most comprehensive information on the litigant, including past medical and mental health records, previous neuropsychological testing, occupational history, depositions, all legal testimonies, diaries (if available), and contemporary pictures and/or videos. The standard for a mental health expert is to review all the available evidence before seeing the subject of a forensic examination, especially if retained by the opposite side. Usually, in this case, the expert has only one opportunity to examine the subject. The expert should, therefore, have all the facts in mind to ask about discrepancies in the records or between the subject's narrative in the face-to-face evaluation and the records. This is more than simple courtesy, for there might be an explanation that does not have a sinister meaning and might have a significant impact on the opinion. It is important to consider and comment on potentially inconsistent evidence rather than ignore it. It could discredit an otherwise good report if some of the inconsistent facts are ignored without explanation. It is far more effective to defuse a potentially refuting piece of evidence in the report than face ridicule on the witness stand when the cross-examining attorney brings it up. The psychologist will appear to have something to hide, and the credibility of the report and testimony will suffer accordingly. The witness, effectively neutralized, will be unable to advance the case of the retaining attorney.

Credibility is the expert's most important asset in court. An expert assessment derived from all available evidence is far more accurate and credible than one derived solely from self-report. If the records imply the existence of other records, the expert needs to inform the retaining attorney and insist that they be obtained through subpoena, court orders, or other legal means if necessary. The more thorough the review of the evidence, the greater is the credibility of the expert. Lawyers, judges, and jurors are not mental health experts. They do not understand how diagnoses are made, records are written, or treatment is performed. They rely on the expert to educate them. But attorneys take formal courses on evidence, and laypeople have an intuitive understanding of how poor evidence produces poor opinions.

Failure to consider all the evidence may also be a cause of action to sue an expert witness for malpractice. In most jurisdictions, experts have immunity for their testimony. However, if the method to reach their opinion falls below the usual standards of practice, which include relying on all the available evidence, and this faulty method costs the retaining party a case that might have been won or reduces the compensation, then the psychologist is at strong risk of being successfully sued for malpractice. In these litigious times, this will become more common as more psychologists enter this field.

Striving for Neutrality

Clinical psychologists are accustomed to forming alliances and taking an advocacy role where their clients are concerned. The law, however, is interested in the truth and hopes that retained experts may help in reaching it. Ethics, professional integrity, and the demands of the law compel experts to tell the truth. This means that they must abandon the advocacy role, strive for neutrality, and let the evidence speak for itself as much as possible. It is ethically appropriate to refuse to testify as an expert witness for one's client. The allegiance built into the therapeutic relationship is not compatible with the neutrality demanded by the courts. This does not prevent the clinician from testifying as a fact witness on behalf of the client. But "wearing two hats" as a fact and expert witness is ethically incompatible and clinically imprudent. Words said in court could easily backfire in the therapeutic context. Similarly, the temptation to unconsciously please the retaining attorney is sometimes difficult to resist. Nevertheless, it must be resisted as much as possible. On a related issue, one must maintain a healthy dose of skepticism in a forensic setting and not simply accept transparently self-serving self-reports. When inconsistency arises among contemporaneous evidence in the forms of documents or multiple testimonies, fact finders generally trust evidence closer in time to the events in question than later accounts. So should the forensic psychologist.

Distortions of the past are common in self-reports. These do not have to be intentional, as human memory is fallible. Narrative truth as opposed to historical truth is useful in the therapeutic setting. But the law is interested only in the historical truth. Test results also need to be interpreted within their contexts. It is possible to "fake bad" on tests, and the temptation to do so is strong in both civil cases (to increase the monetary award) and criminal cases (to avoid punishment). The recent case of Vincent Gigante in New York should be a warning to us all. He was accused of being the head of one of the New York Mafia families and responsible for a multitude of crimes. At trial, he presented an insanity defense. Leading lights in forensic psychology and psychiatry testified that the defendant was suffering from dementia. In a later pleading, Mr. Gigante admitted to faking his mental illness.

It is important in forensic reports and testimony to separate interpretation from facts, which should be presented as clearly as possible. The psychologist can then present an argument supporting the interpretation based on the facts. The trend in the law is for judges and appellate courts to become more interested in the process of reaching an opinion than in the actual opinion itself. If the process is valid and passes the peer-review test, then the opinion on which it is based can be admissible in a court of law. If it is reached with a poor foundation, it can be challenged and the proffered testimony can be ruled inadmissible.

Reconstructing the Past

Many of the demands put to forensic psychologists have to do with reconstruction of the past. This is not as commonsensical as it seems. The law often asks psychologists to reconstruct the past and opine about a state of mind in the past or establish liability between a mishap and present damages. This is a difficult process in all circumstances.

When I review the medical records and depositions in preparation for the personal examination, I necessarily develop a mental portrait of the litigant in my mind. The documents often include the best documented evidence, such as detailed clinical evaluations and sometimes lengthy and complete mental health treatment notes.

The face-to-face examination always surprises me; the litigant is different in some significant way from the constructed image. I suspect that this is generally true for other examiners as well. These experiences are very sobering. Reconstruction of the past based on extrapolation of current evidence should be done with a great deal of caution and humility about our ability to do so. Psychohistorical studies of people that one did not even have the opportunity to evaluate personally must be viewed with skepticism. Yet this is what the forensic psychologist is asked to do in psychological autopsies, as when trying to answer whether someone committed suicide or was the victim of an accident. This is of great interest to the heirs and life insurance companies.

As with other aspects of an expert's opinion, reconstruction of a state of mind should be based on all the evidence available. Some evidence is more helpful than other. Most helpful is evidence providing a "direct window" into the mind, evidence such as diaries, contemporaneous records as opposed to retrospective accounts, job evaluations, depositions of other witnesses, witnessed overt behavior, and [any other evidence that would help in] understanding the context of the past.

Even with the best information, psychologists can fall prey to some common fallacies of interpretation. One known to all psychologists is the fundamental error of attribution, discounting contextual factors accounting for behavior and imputing it instead to a permanent characteristic of an individual. But there are many other errors of interpretations based on logical fallacies that psychologists are not aware of. Anyone considering a career in forensic psychology should read a good text warning professional historians about such traps. One of the classical texts is David Hackett Fischer's (1970) *Historians' Fallacies*.

Predicting the Future

Sometimes, forensic psychologists are asked the opposite, that is, to predict the future. The law often requires a mental health expert to predict the future, especially in regard to the prognosis of a condition (extent of damage) or the prediction of violence (civil commitment and discharge from mental health hospitals, death penalty sentencing phase in some states, and waiver to adult court in juvenile cases). Unlike the reconstruction of the past, there are more methodological guidelines for predicting the future. Such reports can be vulnerable to *Daubert* or *Frye* challenges (*Daubert v. Merrel Dow,* 1993; *Frye v. U.S.,* 1923) if they cannot represent a valid use of scientific methodology.

One valid method of prediction is Bayesian probability. This requires knowledge of base rates in an appropriate comparison group and prospective studies. Unfortunately, most of the psychological literature is based on retrospective studies [studies that examine past behavior], which are not useful in Bayesian probability. It behooves the forensic psychologist to become familiar with the few long-term prospective databases [in which researchers follow the behavior of a cohort into the future] that are still ongoing. One involves the Grant study, namely a [study of a] cohort of privileged boys who attended Harvard in the early 1940s (Vaillant, 1977,

1993). A second is the Boston Juvenile Study, which involved juvenile boys in Boston in the 1930s (Sampson & Laub, 1993). A third is the Terman study of California school prodigies, a group of privileged boys and girls (Terman & Oden, 1947). The last study is the Children of Kauai Study, involving the cohort born on that island in 1950 (Werner & Smith, 1982, 1992). These studies are very sobering in terms of damage claims [or claims that children necessarily suffer long-term damage as a result of adversity]. [The studies] show strong resilience to adversity and resistance to descent into criminality. The contrast between prospective and retrospective studies is striking. Perhaps it may be the result of the biases of memory.

Bayesian probability runs into the problem of low base rates in many psychological predictions, such as homicide or suicide. To counter this problem, some researchers have started to use case detection of low probability events based on signal detection theory and receiver operator characteristics analysis (Sweet, Dawes, & Monahan, 2000). This involves more sophisticated methodology and more data than Bayesian probability.

A third methodology is a sophisticated stochastic model used in the recent MacArthur Study of Mental Disorder and Violence (Monahan et al., 2001). This is far too complicated to carry out by one person and requires computer technology and software that the authors of the study have promised to release shortly.

If the courts are serious about enforcing the precedents set forth by *Frye* and *Daubert,* the forensic psychologist will need to become familiar with and use the above methods of prediction. However, at present, it seems that courts will be happy to simply accept an expert's opinion based on experience and training, for it is better than anything a layperson can provide. In most cases, the courts will rely on cross-examination and allow juries to decide rather than dismiss proffered testimony on the basis of inadequate methodology. Litigation about the above methods is generally confined to high-profile cases involving a famous person or a large amount of money.

Practice Skills

Forensic psychology is not only an academic subspecialty but also a practice. The task of the forensic psychologists is not over when they reach an opinion on a specific issue. In many ways, it could be the beginning of their role in the litigation process. The forensic psychologist does not work in a vacuum, but within a very delicate context of litigation that is full of pitfalls and loopholes. Litigation is a pragmatic process that tries to resolve complex issues within a reasonable time and with reasonable results. Although I previously warned that forensic psychologists' input in the whole process is not determinative, it can still have a significant impact on the process. Many issues are not decided on merit, but rather on certain games that lawyers play. This knowledge of the practice of forensic psychology comes under the large set of skills that I have labeled "practice skills." For those who are considering expanding their forensic practice, I would strongly recommend reading some of the good pragmatic introductions to the field, such as Brodsky's (1991) classic *Testifying in Court* and the Group for the Advancement of Psychiatry's (1991) *The Mental Health Professional and the Legal System.*

There are many possible roles for a forensic psychologist. Being a potential expert witness is only one of them. The litigation process usually starts when lawyers are confronted with an issue outside of their area of expertise. In civil cases, this includes a plaintiff claiming damages directly linked to an incident. Here, it is common for the plaintiff's lawyer to refer the plaintiff to a forensic psychologist for evaluation of the claims before he or she agrees to take on the case. The attorney is interested in finding out the merits of the case as well as the potential difficulties associated with the case. Like a psychologist, once an attorney accepts a case, the client cannot simply be abandoned, and the attorney will be responsible for unexpected costs. Attorneys working on a strict contingency fee do not get paid if they lose the case; they may also lose money if the awards do not cover the costs. So taking on a case is a risk, and plaintiff attorneys like to hedge their bets by asking for a preliminary opinion. This is not a full-fledged opinion because collateral documents are not yet available for scrutiny. In criminal cases, defense attorneys may want to know whether their clients are competent to proceed or whether there might be some type of mental health defense justifying, excusing, or mitigating the alleged crime. Attorneys may want a preliminary opinion before investing resources in pursuit of such a defense.

Another role for forensic psychologists is similar to the above. It consists of acting as a consultant to attorneys to help them develop a theory regarding the case. This is the overall narrative that will eventually be presented to the fact finder. This consulting role may or may not involve face-to-face evaluation of the litigant. This may involve a review of the raw neuropsychological data without actual testing. If acting as a consultant, it is important to clarify one's role and not act in a dual capacity. The role of the consultant is not to seek the truth, but to help attorneys further their case. Sometimes, these two goals conflict, and it must be clear from the start what the role of the consultant is in a specific case.

Supporting the Retaining Attorney's Overall Strategy

Attorneys will use a retained expert only if it furthers their theory of the case. Whereas the expert is supposed to tell the truth, an attorney is supposed to defend the client with the utmost zeal. Again, these two roles conflict and, in the end, it is the attorney's case. Attorneys will use the expert's opinion only if it significantly helps their case. A competent psychologist must have a good rapport with the retaining attorney. After the evaluation, psychologists should call the attorneys and inform them as to the general turn of their opinion. This is more than mere courtesy. Attorneys may not want a written report, which may become discoverable to the other side, if the proffered opinion does not advance their case. If the attorney gives the go-ahead for the report, the psychologist should ask what the attorney's overall strategy of the case is, as this is important in the drafting of the report.

In many cases, attorneys want to use the report to force a settlement. In this case, they want the report to be as detailed and compelling as possible. The downside of this strategy is that if a settlement is not reached, the report will provide the other side with the theory of the case and allow better preparation to counter it at trial. It will also provide the opposite attorney with a lot of material for cross-examination of the psychologist. Even in cases headed for trial, some attorneys prefer a long, comprehensive report, believing that because the report includes everything, there will be little to cross-examine the expert on.

Many attorneys proceeding to trial would prefer a minimalist report. They would rather keep the other side guessing as to the proffered testimony and not allow their opponent much time to prepare for cross-examination. The downside here is that if some aspects of the proffered testimony are not within the "four corners" of the report, they may not be admitted at trial. The crucial point is that the expert and the attorney must communicate effectively so that the expert understands the attorney's strategy for the case and the attorney understands the strengths and weaknesses of the report style.

This does not mean that the expert's opinion should be affected by the attorney's preferred presentation style. It is the attorney's case, not the psychologist's, and as long as there is no change in the evidentiary basis or in the resulting opinion, it is fine to allow the attorney to have an input in the presentation of the report. The psychologist must feel comfortable with the suggested style, or it will show in court.

Addressing One's Testimony to the Right Audience

Legal conflicts are decided by many different types of fact finders who constitute different audiences that must be addressed differently. These audiences vary: lay juries in state or federal district courts, drawing from different segments of the population; judges in bench hearings; appellate courts in appeals from lower courts; lawyers in arbitration hearings; masters in various courts; or insurance company adjudicators. Unlike clinical practice, where one can simply provide one's opinion to the client, a report or testimony is addressed to such a specific audience. Forensic psychology is not simply an academic subject. It is a practice leading to serious and immediate results. A carefully reached opinion will amount to little if it does not persuade the appropriate audience. This involves certain communicative skills. Actually, very little is known about how most of these audiences reach their decision. Legal mythology as propagated in law reviews is rife with examples of legal reasoning based on "logic" and legal precedents.

Appellate opinions and some important lower court decisions are disseminated and articulate the reasoning behind these opinions. I strongly suspect that they are just rationalizations of opinions reached on public policy grounds that are dressed in legal language. A prime example is the U.S. Supreme Court decision regarding the results of the 2000 presidential election that happened to fall perfectly along party lines. The odds of this happening simply by chance or by adherence to logic are very small. The research on how decisions are reached in the legal arena is based on jury verdicts, mostly through retrospective interviews or through mock trials. Juries are just as susceptible to presentation style (similar to good bedside manners) as to substantive argument. There is evidence that they view even civil cases as morality tales, providing an anchor to the determination of damage awards. Jury behavior is an exciting new field that merges the subspecialty of forensic psychology with social psychology (but it cannot be fully addressed in a journal focusing on assessment).

Despite our lack of formal knowledge of what type of information a given audience finds persuasive, it is still very important to address one's testimony to the right audience. Its presentation depends on the target audience. There are two types of expert testimony, namely, depositions and live testimony at a trial, arbitration, or similar setting. A deposition is an opportunity for the opposing attorney to find out the essence of the proffered testimony. One can be as sophisticated as one wants in a deposition. Remember that many attorneys will try to trip up an expert at trial by showing some inconsistency between a deposition testimony and live testimony. Often, the apparently contradictory quotation is taken out of context. While on the stand, take your time, read it in context, and explain away the apparent contradiction. This gives you added credibility.

In live testimony, the expert is speaking directly to the fact finder when responding to questions from attorneys from both sides. It is important for the expert to adjust the presentation to the level of sophistication of the target audience. If this is a bench trial, that is, a trial before a judge, assume that the judge is a sophisticated layperson, and you can be as sophisticated as you want on the stand. Indeed, talking down to a judge may be irritating and perhaps prejudice the judge against your testimony.

A jury is usually less sophisticated than a judge. When testifying before a jury, use simple words, translate complex concepts into simple ones, and try to use simple phrases to convey the essence of your testimony. Also, take the time to explain any term you use that the jury might not understand. Do not do that before a judge, however, because the judge can interrupt you and ask you to clarify your statements.

Communication skills are crucial on the witness stand. Many jurors respond better to definite statements than to those that are too nuanced, even if more accurate. Such statements may make the expert appear too wishy-washy and hesitant about the knowledge. It is a sad truth that juries, like television audiences, fall prey to positive sound bites. One must balance effective delivery with scientific accuracy. It is an art mastered by only a select few.

Deferring to the Prerogative of the Fact Finder

The conventional advice for experts is not to answer the ultimate legal question. This is wise counsel, but it is not always observed by lawyers and judges, who often specifically ask experts about the ultimate issue. I often do not provide an opinion on the ultimate issue but, instead, address the exact wording of the legal text guiding that issue. I often do not provide an opinion on the ultimate issue but, instead, address the exact wording of the legal text guiding that issue. It is for the fact

finder to make the extra step. If a judge asks me point blank about a specific issue, I will answer within the limitations of my evaluation. However, there are two issues that experts must be careful of in terms of addressing the ultimate issue.

The legal profession is very jealous of its turf, especially in regard to its function as fact finder. Experts may sometimes believe that they know the facts better than lay people; however, any intrusion into this legal prerogative will be contested, if not in lower courts, [then] definitely in appellate courts. One of these crucial prerogatives is the notion that the fact finder alone is allowed to determine the truth value of a witness. Any psychological testimony implying that a witness is or is not truthful will be challenged on such ground, despite the fact that there is a burgeoning scientific literature on the ability of witnesses to remember events or faces. A psychologist might be allowed to testify as to the state of scientific knowledge on this topic in general, but the testimony will not be allowed to veer into territory concerning the credibility of a specific witness. Any hint in that direction may result in a mistrial.

The ultimate issue on criminal responsibility in a homicide case is another fact-finder prerogative that the mental health expert must respect absolutely. The expert may opine as to the existence of a severe mental illness at the time of the commission of the crime and testify as to the contribution of this illness to the commission of the crime but then must stop there and go no further. The last step, to decide whether the defendant was sane or insane at the time, is strictly for the fact finder to determine. Any misstep here again may result in a mistrial.

Psychologists must master the three types of skills covered above before they become competent forensic psychologists. These skills range from academic knowledge about common questions that the law asks of psychologists to certain practical evaluative skills uncommon in the usual practice of psychology to pragmatic, strategic, and tactical skills involved in the actual practice of forensic psychology. A growing body of literature addressing these skills is becoming the basis of a new subspecialty of psychology.

21

DEVELOPMENTALLY SENSITIVE FORENSIC INTERVIEWING OF PRESCHOOL CHILDREN

Some Guidelines Drawn From Basic Psychological Research

CONNIE M. TANG

Historically, the U.S. court system has treated children's testimony with suspicion. Young children, in particular, are believed to be incompetent witnesses because of concerns over their memory limitations, linguistic immaturity, and conceptual underdevelopment. Thanks to empirical research in the past decades showing that children, even preschoolers, can be competent witnesses, children are now allowed to testify in court. To examine how basic psychological research, like more applied research, can also inform public policy in the forensic interviewing of preschool children, the present article will first selectively review some basic psychological research on preschool children's memory development, language development, and conceptual development. Then, based on this review, the article will generate some guidelines for forensic interviewers of preschool children, such as police officers, attorneys, judges, and social workers. Finally, this article will point out directions for future research.

There is an extremely large body of research on the forensic interviewing of children. These research studies were mostly applied in nature, simulating various circumstances that might occur in forensic settings. For example, during

Editors' Note: This article originally appeared in *Criminal Justice Review,* Vol. 31, No. 2, June 2006, pp. 132–145. Reprinted with permission of Sage Publications.

forensic interviewing, children can be repeatedly or suggestively interviewed, and they can be interviewed by more or less supportive interviewers. A large number of studies have thereby used the paradigm of exposing children to the target event and then interviewing them repeatedly, suggestively, and conducting the interviewing using interviewers of varied levels of support. These applied studies have been very informative, shedding light on interviewing techniques that should be used and techniques that should be avoided. A number of reviews (e.g., Goodman & Shaaf, 1997; Quas, Goodman, Ghetti, & Redlich, 2000; Saywitz, Goodman, & Lyon, 2002) have summarized many of these studies. Relying on this literature, London (2001) generated a series of guidelines for police officers when interviewing children. Using the same empirical base, Poole and Lamb (1998) have also written a guidebook for professionals who routinely conduct investigative interviews of children. Because young children were found to be particularly susceptible to interviewer suggestion relative to older children and adults (see a review by Bruck & Ceci, 1999), much research effort has also focused on the suggestibility of young children, emphasizing the importance of not asking leading or suggestive questions when conducting forensic interviews (see reviews by Ceci, Bruck, & Battin, 2000; S. L. Davis, 1998; Saywitz & Lyon, 2002).

Despite the number of reviews and guidelines that have already been compiled on the forensic interviewing of children, the present article fills a void in the literature by focusing on the forensic interviewing of preschool children (i.e., approximately between ages 3 and 5). Although guidelines for interviewing children in general can certainly apply to preschool children, preschoolers may be particularly challenging to interview because of their very young age and increased vulnerability to suggestion. Therefore, the topic of interviewing preschool children is worthy of special attention. Because of this review's special focus on preschool children, there is an absence of recent work with children of this particular age group on certain topics; in

these instances, older but relevant work will be reviewed. The present article also adds to the literature by emphasizing basic psychological research. Although extant reviews have mostly summarized empirical studies of an applied nature, in which the main purpose was to investigate various interviewing strategies, more basic psychological research, where the focus is broader, can also contribute to our understanding of young children's capabilities as witnesses. With the above considerations in mind, let us turn to some basic psychological research on young children's memory, language, and conceptual development.

MEMORY DEVELOPMENT

For a long time, the phenomenon of "childhood amnesia," where adults cannot usually recall events that occur prior to 3.5 to 4 years of age, has been attributed primarily to poor memory early in development (Eacott, 1999; Fivush & Nelson, 2004; Hayne, 2004). However, empirical research would find that although adults experience "childhood amnesia," young children are often able to recall events experienced in the first few years of life (Fivush, Haden, & Adam, 1995; MacDonald & Hayne, 1996). For example, Fivush et al. repeatedly interviewed preschoolers about several personally experienced events when the children were at 40, 46, 58, and 70 months of age. Even when interviewed at 40 months, children's narratives were quite coherent, although older children's narratives were even more coherent. Children's recall of past events was also remarkably stable over long delays, such that recall at 70 months for events that occurred prior to 40 months was as structured and coherent as recall for more recent events. When the children were re-interviewed at the age of 8 (Fivush & Schwarzmueller, 1998), they continued to recall these events accurately and with much detail.

There are several caveats to the Fivush et al. (1995) and Fivush and Schwarzmueller (1998) studies when applying their findings to the forensic interviewing of young children. First, the repeated interviews in the study might have served as rehearsal opportunities to improve children's recall. In forensic settings, these rehearsal opportunities may or may not be present. In cases where a child is interviewed multiple times by different interviewers such as parents, teachers, police, social workers, or attorneys, the child has several opportunities to rehearse. Although this is certainly possible, it is also likely that research findings (e.g., see a review by Bruck, Ceci, & Hembrooke, 2002) regarding the negative impact of repeated suggestive interviews on young children's memory will persuade professionals in the field to reduce the number of times each child witness is interviewed. Therefore, children may or may not experience as many interviews in forensic settings as those in the studies conducted by Fivush et al.

Second, despite using parents as judges, accuracy of these autobiographical recalls could not be ascertained as parents' memory also fades with time. Finally, when researching children's autobiographical recall in naturalistic settings, one cannot know if the children truly remember the past events. They could have constructed the memories based on continued discussions with their parents. As Peterson (2002) observed, although some studies (such as the above conducted by Fivush et al.) found children's long-term autobiographical memory to be robust, other studies found substantial deterioration in children's autobiographical memory as the delay increases. One such study was conducted by Boyer, Barron, and Farrar (1994), which revealed that 3-year-old children failed to show memory of a nine-action event sequence (i.e., "Making Play-Doh spaghetti") that they learned at 20 months of age. Major differences between Fivush et al. (1995; Fivush & Schwarzmueller, 1998) and Boyer et al. (1994) [were] that children in the Fivush studies were considerably older, that they were interviewed about personally experienced events that were rich in verbal context, and that children were interviewed about events that had occurred when they were

much older than 20 months of age. These differences may account for the inconsistencies in research findings.

In summary, keeping these caveats in mind, Fivush et al. (1995) and Fivush and Schwarzmueller (1998) showcased the possibility for structure and coherence in middle to older preschool children's recall of personally experienced events. In addition to exhibiting structure and coherence, preschoolers' recall possesses other interesting features as well. In a longitudinal study of children's autobiographical recall between 2.5 and 4 years, Fivush and Hamond (1990) interviewed children at two time points about personally experienced events that were shared with their mothers. The first interview occurred when the children were about 2.5 years old, and the children were interviewed by their mothers. Six weeks later, a stranger interviewed the children for the second interview. Results revealed that children reported more information in the second interview with the stranger than in the first interview with the mother. The authors argued that this could be due to children's understanding of the difference between reminiscing and recounting. When the mother was the interviewer, children might know that the interview was more of a social conversation about shared experiences (reminiscing). When a stranger was the interviewer, children might sense that they needed to provide information (recounting) to the naïve stranger.

Because the interviews were not counterbalanced and the children were older at the second interview, alternative explanations of the above findings were possible. For instance, the second interview might have generated more information because the first interview served as a rehearsal opportunity for the children. Also, 6 weeks could have been a long time in a young child's developmental trajectory. Children might have simply developed better verbal skills in the second interview. In a similar study (MacDonald & Hayne, 1996) involving twenty 3- to 4-year-old children during which the children experienced a unique event without the parents present, children still reported a lot more information in an interview with a stranger than in discussions with their parents. If children of this age range indeed understand the difference between reminiscing and recounting, they should have recounted both to their parents and to the stranger, providing their parents and the stranger an equal amount of information. The fact that this was not the case cast doubt on Fivush and Hamond's (1990) conclusions. Although MacDonald and Hayne did differ from Fivush and Hamond in that the interview was initiated by the stranger . . . discussions with parents were initiated by the child. Children in Fivush and Hamond did not initiate the conversations with either. Methodological issues aside, Fivush and Hamond raised the possibility that preschool children may know when to reminisce and when to recount. Alternatively, adult-initiated conversations might encourage more reports from children. Finally, there is the possibility that preschool children will report more information to a stranger than to their parents.

In addition to structure, coherence, and the possible ability to differentiate between reminiscing and recounting, another characteristic of young children's memory development is that their recall can improve a great deal with outside help. N. A. Myers and Perlmutter (1978) studied 3- and 4-year-olds' memory capability and found that when recalling toys, retrieval aids that provided [a] realistic setting (such as a doll house with garden and garage) for the target items facilitated children's recall. In forensic settings, although young children are interviewed about objects (or people) that they saw, they are also questioned about behaviors, conversations, and the environment. Myers and Perlmutter's research did not address the question of whether young children's memory for different components of an event calls for different retrieval aids.

Consistent with Myers and Perlmutter (1978), Macklin (1994) also found that visual retrieval aids are helpful to preschoolers. In Macklin's research, eighty 4- to 6-year-old children watched an advertisement for a fictitious cereal. Half of the children who could not recall the cereal's name were presented with a visual retrieval cue (i.e., a cereal box with graphics), and the other half of the children were not given the cue. Children who were exposed to the visual retrieval cue remembered the name of the cereal better than the children without the cue. Kail (1990) theorized that the development of memory in large part is the development of mnemonic strategies. Because preschool children are still in the process of developing mnemonic strategies, external retrieval aids are especially helpful in improving their recall.

Now that we have some basic idea about how young children remember, let us examine a topic in young children's memory development that is especially important: the recall of trauma. Although Terr (1991) argued that traumatic events tend to be fragmentary or nonexistent, research seems to show otherwise. Reviews of empirical research on children's trauma memory (e.g., Berliner, Hyman, Thomas, & Fitzgerald, 2003; Cordon, Pipe, Sayfan, Melinder, & Goodman, 2004; Fivush, 1998) concurred that despite tending to have less sensory detail and coherence, memories for trauma for the most part resemble those of nontraumatic events. Fivush concluded in her review that traumatic events that occurred before 18 months are not reportable by preschool children. Those that experienced the event between 18 months and 2.5 to 3 years are reported in bits and pieces. For traumatic events occurring after age 2.5 to 3 years, children are able to give coherent accounts of them.

Because children's memories for trauma resemble their memories for other more positive events, retrieval aids should be helpful in assisting children with trauma memory as well. Because of the emotion-laden nature of traumatic events, Liwag and Stein's (1995) study on emotion-related retrieval cues has relevance here. Children between the ages of 3 and 5 participated in this study. Parents were first asked to generate events that occurred in the week or two before the interview in which their children experienced happiness, sadness, anger, and fear. Children recalled these events in four conditions: control, emotional label, emotion face, and emotional reinstatement. In the control condition, children were simply asked to recall the target event. In the emotional label condition, children were asked to generate a verbal label corresponding to their emotional reaction. The emotion face condition additionally required the children to make a face appropriate to the emotion. In the emotional reinstatement condition, children labeled the emotion, made a face that matches the emotion, and were asked to reinstate their original emotion. Children in the emotional reinstatement condition outperformed children in all other groups in the quantity, quality, and organization of their recall. Emotional reinstatement thus appeared to improve young children's recall through providing them with more associations to the target events.

Although young children's memory development is most relevant for forensic interviewers, young children's language development is another important area for interviewers to become familiar with. Unlike assessing memories using the method of recognition, the method used most often in forensic interviews is verbal recalling. Therefore, children's ability to verbally recall events determines the outcome of a forensic interview. Whether young children will be able to verbally recall what they remember is related to their language development.

LANGUAGE DEVELOPMENT

The first sign of language is the appearance of babbling, a phenomenon that generally occurs around 6 months (Reich, 1986). It appears that words are understood before they are spoken. After learning about words (lexicon) and word meanings (semantics) in the first 2 years of life, children start to understand sentence structure (syntax) and the context of language use (pragmatics) during the preschool years. Reich reported that by age 3, children are talking at least as much as adults. In addition, when engaged in conversations with others, preschoolers can speak clearly, use well-formed grammar, and adapt to the listener's perspective. Specifically, Klecan-Aker and Swank (1988) interviewed

preschoolers aged 2 to 5 using materials such as toys and pictures. They talked to the children to elicit eight language functions: labeling, description, revision, affirmation/negation, personal, requesting, greetings, and turn taking. The researchers found that appropriate responses increased with age, although [they leveled] off after age 3. All eight language functions were in most preschoolers' repertoire by 3.5 years.

Although 3-year-olds seem to have developed basic conversational skills in Klecan-Aker and Swank's (1988) laboratory, where the primary focus was to elicit language functions, it is important for forensic interviewers to know if 3-year-olds report personally experienced events using the language skills that they possess. Simcock and Hayne's (2002, 2003) research brought light to bear on the issue. [Children aged 2 to 4] played a game using the Magic Shrinking Machine and were subsequently interviewed about this experience after delays ranging from 24 [hours] to 1 year. Children's general language skill was assessed at the time of the experience and at the interview. Simcock and Hayne found the following: First, older children recalled better than younger children. Second, children performed better with a shorter delay. The most interesting finding was that children did not once use a word that had not been a part of their productive vocabulary at the time of the game playing in their later verbal recall. In other words, preschool children's verbal recall of events lags behind their verbal abilities. Per Simock and Hayne (2002), it appears that for preschool children, even after they have obtained basic language skills, their verbal reports of the event might be "frozen in time" (p. 229), reflecting their language ability at the time of the encoding, not retrieval. Therefore, the age and language skills of a child when the target event occurred are important factors to consider when evaluating the child's potential for recalling the experience.

Although preschool children have developed some language skills to be interviewed, all questions do not work equally well with them. Some formats of questions are found to be more problematic for young children than others. M. Hughes and Grieve (1980) examined 5- and 7-year-olds' response to nonsense questions. They found that when asked bizarre questions in the yes/no format (e.g., "Is milk bigger than water?" and "Is red heavier than yellow?"), children usually responded with "yes" instead of the correct answer of "I don't know." It would thus appear that children understand the need for a "yes" or "no" answer when asked questions in yes/no format, even though this understanding led them astray in this case. It is possible that young children operate under the assumption that adults always ask meaningful questions, and thus they should provide answers even for bizarre questions. Although this study examined children mostly older than . . . preschool age, there are no theoretical reasons to believe that younger children will not behave similarly.

Peterson and Biggs (1997) included such a group of younger children in their study. They interviewed 2- to 13-year-olds about their emergency room visits. The accuracy of children's recall was assessed through comparing their responses with those provided by the caregivers and information on the hospital records. Mirroring the Hughes and Grieve (1980) study, 2-, 3-, and 4-year-old children had a particular difficulty with yes/no questions relative to 9- and 13-year-olds: Although they seemed fairly accurate when answering yes/no questions with "yes," they were only correct about half of the time when they answered yes/no questions with the response "no." Along the same line, J. Myers et al. (2003) conducted two experiments with 3-year-old children on their memory of a physical examination. Using a recognition-based interview consisting of all yes/no questions, Myers et al. found a high rate of false alarms (answering yes when the correct answer was no) among the children, leading the researchers to conclude that young children's answers to yes/no questions need to be interpreted with great caution.

Unlike yes/no questions, forced-choice questions clearly stating both options provide children the flexibility to choose. Siegal and Peterson (1998) conducted a series of three experiments

with children between the ages of 3 and 5. Participants learned different stories concerning a bear that lied about a piece of bread's contact with bugs or made an honest mistake about the bread's contamination or was negligent when making the mistake. Instead of using yes/no questions (e.g., "Did the bear lie?") or forced-choice questions with the alternative term "mistake" unstated (e.g., "Did the bear lie or not?"), Siegal and Peterson employed forced-choice questions clearly stating both options (i.e., "Did the bear lie or make a mistake?"). This question format enabled most children, including the 3-year-olds, to distinguish between a lie and a mistake. More remarkably, most 3-year-olds even distinguished between an honest mistake and a negligent mistake. A previous study (Siegel & Peterson, 1996) using the question, "Did the bear lie or not?" found most children between the ages of 3 and 5 unable to distinguish between a lie and a mistake: They tended to respond that the bear lied. It is possible that because the alternative of making a "mistake" was not stated in the question, children were drawn by the suggested answer of lying. In other words, the term "or not" in the question "Did the bear lie or not?" might not represent a true alternative to "lie." Although you can change all yes/no questions into forced-choice questions by adding the phrase "or not" (e.g., "Did the bear make a mistake or not?" "Was it Johnny or not?"), these type[s] of forced-choice questions in actuality resemble yes/no questions even as they assume the appearance of forced-choice questions. Therefore, it is best for forced-choice questions to stress all possible options. Siegal and Peterson's studies demonstrated the importance of providing true options to young children when using forced-choice questions.

To compare yes/no questions with *wh* questions (questions that often start with "who," "what," "when," "where," and "why" and are a form of open-ended questions), Peterson, Dowden, and Tobin (1999) recruited 3- to 5-year-olds to individually participate in an artwork-making activity with experimenters. Children were then interviewed a week later with 18 questions. The questions covered the content areas of action, person, and environment. The error rate was 30% for yes/no questions and 15% for wh questions. When the 50% chance for correct answers in the yes/no questions was taken into consideration, the above difference became even bigger. Not only were *wh* questions superior to yes/no questions in reducing errors, *wh* questions also enabled preschool children to acknowledge their ignorance by responding with "I don't know" when answering some inquiries. "I don't know" was seldom elicited by yes/no questions even if it was the correct response, mirroring Hughes and Grieve's (1980) study on nonsense questions.

In addition to *wh* questions, other open-ended questions include invitations (e.g., "Tell me more about that."). The strengths of *wh* questions and invitations were highlighted in Sternberg et al.'s (1996) applied research interviewing 4- to 12-year-old children who reported sexual abuse. Invitations were found to produce more detailed reports than other forms of questions. Invitations or *wh* questions also elicited more relevant details from children who experienced multiple incidents of abuse. To summarize, research suggests that invitations and *wh* questions are superior to yes/no questions when interviewing preschool children, whereas forced-choice questions fall somewhere in between. Although memory development and language development build a foundation for the forensic interviewing of young children, conceptual development is the underlying component to both developments. Now we will turn our attention to young children's conceptual development.

CONCEPTUAL DEVELOPMENT

Thanks to the work of giants such as Swiss psychologist Jean Piaget, we now know that children are not miniature adults. Instead, young children think in very different ways from adults. Young children's understanding of scripts, symbols, and knowledge acquisition has direct relevance to the practices of forensic interview. According to Flavell, Miller, and Miller (1993), scripts are

generalized and abstract event representations. Scripts have also been defined as cognitive frameworks for events, which are memories about what usually or typically occurs in a particular situation (Santrock, 2005). For example, a script about going to the supermarket will likely include taking a shopping cart, selecting merchandise, putting the purchases in the shopping cart, and paying at the checkout counter.

To examine children's script development, Adam and Worden (1986) interviewed 3- to 4-year-olds and 7- to 8-year-olds to test the hypothesis that memory for script-related information would be poorer than memory for unique information. After hearing stories that contained many scripted items (e.g., brushing teeth, taking a shopping cart, or ordering food from [a] server) and atypical items (e.g., drinking a glass of water, dropping a can of tomatoes on the floor, or chewing on ice cubes) in the scripts of "getting up in the morning," "going to a grocery store," and "going to a restaurant," children were tested [on] their recognition memory about scripted and atypical items. As predicted, older children performed better, and atypical items were remembered better. There was also an interaction between age and typicality: Although younger and older children did not perform differently for scripted items, older children performed better recognizing atypical items. Therefore, Adam and Worden revealed that preschool children's memory on scripted items could be as good as those of older children. A word of caution about the application of this study to the forensic interviewing of young children is that because children's memory was tested through the method of recognition, it is unknown if changing the assessment method to verbal recall will generate similar results.

We have reasons to believe, however, that changing the memory assessment method from recognition to recall may also find young children remembering scripted items better than atypical items. Low and Durkin (2000) presented 5-, 7-, 9-, and 11-year-old children a TV story either in a scripted version or a jumbled (i.e., out of the usual order of events) version. Before the age of 9, young children recalled the scripted version better than the jumbled version. After 9, children recalled the jumbled version as well as the scripted version. In addition, the younger 5- and 7-year-old children tended to reorder the story units in the jumbled version in their recall, indicating their automatic use of script information in remembering.

Consequently, it seems that children understand scripts before they understand the atypical aspects of events. They understand the atypical in the context of the typical. Because older children have a firmer understanding about scripts than younger children, they are better able to detect things that are different from the usual. Paradoxically, this more tenuous understanding about scripts sometimes serves the younger children well. Ornstein et al. (1998) arranged for 4- and 6-year-olds to receive a special medical check-up that included or excluded some procedures that are expected (e.g., listening to chest) and some that are unexpected (e.g., asking the child to walk backward). The children were interviewed immediately and after a 12-week delay. Many children mistakenly remembered typical but omitted procedures (i.e., false alarm) at the 12-week interview. Specifically, 42% of the 4-year-olds and 72% of the 6-year-olds made at least one such intrusion. Four-year-olds' less solid script understanding seemed to have enabled them to have less spontaneous intrusions than 6-year-olds.

In addition to scripts, symbols are another important concept relevant to the forensic interviewing of preschool children. Symbols are objects that are used to represent other things.

Preschool children's understanding of symbols has a huge impact on the effectiveness of props and cues as memory retrieval aids. The foregoing section on memory development discussed the importance of using retrieval aids to assist young children's recall. Becoming knowledgeable about young children's understanding of symbols will in turn help forensic interviewers in the selection of the type of retrieval aids that will be most useful.

In a series of four experiments, DeLoache (1991) used scale models and pictures to assess symbolic understanding in 2.5-year-olds. Study 1 found that although only a minority of the 2.5-year-olds [were] able to find toys in a room based [on] a three-dimensional scale model of the room, a majority of them were able to find the toys using a photograph of the room. DeLoache theorized that the ability to dual represent (i.e., representing the scale model/ photograph as both an object and a symbol) is necessary for these retrieval aids to be used successfully. Because children younger than 3 have yet to develop dual representation, they are unable to benefit from the three-dimensional scale model: The three-dimensional scale model is very salient as an object to young children, and its symbolic function is masked. Photographs, in contrast, are familiar to children as symbols: Even young children have much experience using photos as symbols. Photographs are, therefore, not salient as objects. Because young children only perceive photographs as symbols, there is no need to dual represent to use photographs successfully. The next three experiments [conducted by DeLoache (1991)] found additional support for the dual representation hypothesis, in that as long as there is no need to dual represent, young children can benefit from the use of props and retrieval aids. It should be noted that there is rapid development in children's ability to dual represent, so that by age 3, most children can successfully complete the toy-seeking task using the scale model (DeLoache, 1987).

Overall, however, preschool children do not seem to benefit from three-dimensional scale models such as anatomically detailed dolls even after they have developed dual representation abilities. For instance, DeLoache and Marzolf (1995) interviewed 2.5-, 3-, and 4-year-old children and found that children of this age range were able to report more correct information without, than with, the assistance of an anatomically detailed doll. The authors posited that even after the understanding of dual presentation is developed, children still need to understand the doll-self mapping for the anatomically detailed dolls to be useful. In other words, after knowing that the doll represents their body, children need to know how body parts on the doll map onto their own body parts. The ability to understand the mapping process takes additional time to develop. It can be argued further that when the understanding of dual representation is tenuous, the anatomically detailed doll might continue to draw attention away from the interview process by presenting as a novel object. The above studies taught us the lesson that retrieval aids do not always improve young children's recall. Sometimes, they have the opposite effect. In summary, the weight of the evidence (also see Hungerford, 2005, who reviewed many applied research [studies] directly evaluating anatomically detailed dolls) does not support the use of anatomically detailed dolls in the forensic interviewing of preschool children.

Besides scripts and symbols, preschool children's understanding of knowledge acquisition is another area that is relevant to the forensic interviewing process. Preschool children seem to realize that informational access is essential to knowing (e.g., Wimmer, Hogrefe, & Perner, 1988). This might be why children reported more information in recounting than in reminiscing (Fivush & Hamond, 1990): Children might have realized that the naïve interviewer did not have access to the target event and thus did not know [its details]. Yet young children still have difficulty sorting out the sources of their knowledge. For example, Gopnik and Graf (1988) found that 3-year-olds were not able to discern whether they saw some objects, were told about the objects, or merely inferred about the objects. Five-year-olds, on the other hand, did not have such difficulty. Taylor, Esbensen, and Bennett (1994) additionally found that children as old as 5 experienced difficulty recognizing that they had just learned something new; instead they claimed to have always known what they had just learned a few minutes ago. In short, preschool children are developing metacognitive awareness, and their difficulty with recognizing the sources of their knowledge might have contributed to their susceptibility to suggestions during forensic interviews (e.g., Quas,

Schaaf, Alexander, & Goodman, 2000; Thierry & Spence, 2002; Welch-Ross, 2000). Young children's understanding of knowledge acquisition can be summarized as being fragile during the early preschool years and becoming more solid later in the preschool age.

The above selective review of basic psychological research relevant to the forensic interviewing of preschool children has revealed strengths as well as weaknesses in the ability of preschool children as witnesses. Next, we will use this knowledge on child development to generate some guidelines for the forensic interviewing of preschool children.

GUIDELINES FOR INTERVIEWING PRESCHOOL CHILDREN

When young children are suspected to be victims or eyewitnesses of crimes, forensic interviewers need to make a decision about whether to interview a particular child. Because there are no established guidelines about making this decision, many interviewers make the decision intuitively, often based solely on language abilities: If the child is not verbal, interviewing obviously will not work; if the child is verbal, interviewers often choose to proceed with the interview. From what we know about preschoolers' memory, language, and conceptual development, a few more guidelines can be generated.

We learn from the preceding review that on average, preschoolers give coherent accounts of personally experienced events, especially . . . those older than 3 years of age. In addition, around 3, children's mastery of major language functions plateau[s]. Overall, children are able to participate in basic conversations by age 3. Therefore, children 3 years of age and older can and should be interviewed. Yet preschoolers might experience something we would term *language-determined memory,* which limits their ability to verbally recall events experienced before age 2. Language-determined memory is the phenomenon that young children cannot translate their preverbal memory into later verbal recall during the preschool years (Simcock & Hayne, 2002, 2003). It seems critical that for children to verbally report a past event, the event needs to be encoded verbally. Because children younger than 2 are still in the word-learning stage of language development, they do not encode memory in coherent verbal format such as in sentences. Therefore, although preschoolers can give fairly good autobiographical recall, they might not be able to coherently report events that occurred before age 2 because of very limited language abilities at that age.

The guidelines for determining whether to interview a preschooler thus follow: First, the child needs to be able to engage in verbal conversations. Second, the child probably needs to be older than 3, although individual differences are to be accommodated. This means that the interviewer may choose to interview a very verbal 2.5-year-old or choose not to interview a 3.5-year-old who is slower in language development. Finally, if the crime occurred after the child [was] 2 years [old] . . ., the child may be able to report the event in coherent sentences. This "older than 3 after 2" principle can be used as a rule of thumb when making decisions about whether to interview a preschooler: Children older than 3 who fell victim to or witnessed a crime after the age of 2 are potentially good information providers. Of course, forensic interviewers should always expect exceptions to the rule because of individual developmental differences among young children.

After deciding to interview a preschooler, the first order of business for forensic interviewers is to elicit accurate information from the child. Because preschool children are particularly susceptible to interviewer suggestion, forensic interviewers need to reduce suggestion in their questions. An effective means of doing so is asking questions in the right format. The earlier review points out that preschool children have a particular difficulty with yes/no questions. As a result, transforming the questions into forced-choice format is recommended. Keep in mind, however, that merely adding "or not" at the end of a yes/no question (i.e., "Did he wear a white shirt or not?") does not necessarily make the question any better, even though the question now takes the form of a forced-choice question. A forced-choice question that helps children with the accuracy of their reports needs to clearly present both options (i.e., "Did he wear a white shirt or blue shirt?). To maximize children's reporting of accurate information, forensic interviewers should go into the interview with a game plan to include a hierarchy of questions, proceeding in a bottom-to-top fashion from invitations (e.g., "Tell me about yesterday.") to *wh* questions (e.g., "What happened in the supermarket yesterday?") to forced-choice questions stating all options (e.g., "Did he wear a white shirt, a blue shirt, or a red shirt?) and to yes/no questions (e.g., "Did he wear a white shirt?"). Because question formats near the top of the hierarchy tend to be more suggestive, forensic interviewers should use invitations and *wh* questions liberally. Forced-choice questions with choices clearly stated can be used sparingly. Yes/no questions should be avoided if possible.

Despite the best of efforts, interviewers sometimes have to fall back on forced-choice and yes/no questions to extract necessary details. In preparation for these instances, interviewers should let preschool children know that it is okay to say "I don't know" when appropriate. In addition to permitting children to say "I don't know," interviewers should also explain the reasons why saying "I don't know" is okay. Although most preschool children have made the connection between access to information and knowledge at this age, the understanding is still tenuous. Let young children know that because the interviewer was not present when the event occurred, the interviewer does not know what happened. Only the children have the correct information. In addition, even the children themselves might not have answers to all questions or remember everything. Therefore, it is perfectly acceptable to say "I don't know."

After ascertaining the accuracy of children's reports as much as possible, the next important task for forensic interviewers is to help young children give as complete a recall as possible.

Interviewers can increase the amount of information children provide by admitting or even emphasizing ignorance. Preschool children may be able to recount instead of reminisce when speaking with a naïve interviewer. Also, keep in mind that interviewer-initiated conversations and stranger interviewers are associated with a greater amount of recall. By initiating conversations through questioning and by reminding children that the interviewer is ignorant, a forensic interviewer increases the chance of extracting the greatest amount of information from children.

Although young children are weaker than older children and adults in all aspects of memory, their weakness in retrieval strategies stands out the most. Therefore, it is important that some kind of interviewer-aided recall takes place for preschool children to provide the most amount of information. One such aid is emotional reinstatement, considering that experiencing or witnessing a crime is often emotion laden. Emotional reinstatement is done first by asking children to label the feelings they had while experiencing the emotional event. Then ask children to make a face that matches the emotion label. Finally, ask children to act like they are feeling just like they were when the event occurred. Despite the beneficial effects of emotional reinstatement on preschoolers' recall, forensic interviewers should be cautious about employing this technique. Because negative emotions such as anxiety and fear are often associated with witnessing or being a victim of crime, emotional reinstatement runs the risk of reintroducing those negative emotions to children. As a result, the need for complete information must be balanced against the need to protect children's emotional welfare.

Another effective retrieval aid interviewers can use to maximize the amount of recall by preschoolers is scripts. Preschool children have started to understand scripts. However, they do not always use scripts spontaneously or effectively. Interviewers can provide scripts as a structure to probe children's memory. For example, interviewers can first talk to children about what usually happens when they go to the supermarket. Then, interviewers can probe for memory on the day in question when [the] children went to the supermarket. Having the script as a background, preschool children are better able to recall what happened that was different from the usual chain of events.

What kinds of retrieval aids are useful and how to use these retrieval aids without the accompanying drawbacks present continual challenge for future research. In addition, researchers need to conduct basic as well as applied research exploring individual differences in children's memory, language, and conceptual development. It is quite conceivable that one day, research will enable forensic interviewers to use different retrieval aids with different children to optimize each child's recall on a case-by-case basis.

UNIT VI

CORRECTIONAL PSYCHOLOGY

INTRODUCTION AND COMMENTARY

Correctional psychology represents a broad landscape of opportunities for researchers and practitioners, who operate in both institutional and community settings. Prisons and jails are in need of direct services to inmates, evaluation of programs, assessment for making classification decisions, and training of staff, among many things. In the community, psychologists and other mental health professionals provide a very wide range of services to persons on probation and parole. In addition, there is a multitude of opportunities in the juvenile equivalents of these adult settings.

In the first reading in this section, **Jennifer L. Boothby** and **Carl B. Clements** report on a nationwide survey of correctional psychologists working in U.S. state and federal prisons, where the estimated psychologist-to-inmate ratio is 1:750. The article provides us with a glimpse into their work, such as the types of assessments they conduct and the instruments and treatments they favor. The authors also asked their respondents to tell how their workload was divided and how they would like their time to be allotted. Respondents reported that nearly 30% of their time was spent on administrative tasks, and most wanted less time there and more time for direct treatment of prisoners.

In their article on rehabilitation and reintegration, **J. Stephen Wormith and his colleagues** review the empirical evidence on effective treatment programs, focusing on programs for substance abusers and sex offenders. The effectiveness of the former is somewhat better established; particularly promising are prison-based therapeutic communities with follow-up in the community once offenders are released. Cognitive behavioral programs for sex offenders also have promise, as Wormith et al. indicate. The authors also mention the current interest in positive psychology. They note, however, that even if a treatment program has been shown to be effective, problems surrounding program delivery may occur. For example, client motivation and client dropout are crucial issues to be considered. Recognizing that clinicians in corrections often do not have sufficient time to do research and researchers are not necessarily clinicians, the authors call for more collaboration between these two groups. The Wormith et al. article provides an excellent overview of the current landscape of rehabilitation and reintegration as well as recommendations for moving the field of correctional psychology ahead.

Next, **Philip R. Magaletta and colleagues** contribute an article relating to the academic preparation and training of correctional psychologists. Based on a survey of 309 correctional psychologists working in the Federal Bureau of Prisons, Magaletta et al. identify nine core bodies of knowledge that form the heart of their work. The psychologists they surveyed said knowledge about psychopathology was of greatest importance on a daily basis. Furthermore, they said graduate school prepared them for clinical knowledge, but that prison-based knowledge (e.g., safety issues, confrontation avoidance, managing the mentally ill in segregation) was learned on the job. Interestingly, and in keeping with a narrow definition of forensic psychology, these psychologists did not consider themselves forensic psychologists, but rather psychologists engaged in clinical practice in corrections. Magaletta et al. end by noting that psychologists involved in correctional work must become directly involved in developing and disseminating knowledge specifically relevant to this work.

The great majority of individuals under correctional supervision are not in jails, prisons, or juvenile treatment centers, but rather are under community supervision. The last article in this section focuses on community corrections, specifically as it relates to juveniles. Juvenile corrections on the whole is a rapidly developing area for theory, research, and treatment.

One of the most attention-getting community treatment programs for serious juvenile offenders is multisystemic therapy (MST). This approach provides intensive treatment services to juveniles and their family, with one goal being to preserve the family unit. **Willem H. J. Martens,** however, suggests a number of modifications to MST in the case of some juveniles. For example, he suggests that additional professionals (such as a pediatrician and a neurologist) should be added to the MST team. He also advocates treatment of some youths away from the influence of their families. If all of Martens's recommendations were to be implemented, MST as it was originally conceived would hardly be recognizable. However, integration of some of his suggestions may indeed be warranted. Although multisystemic treatment has received very favorable research reports, there are chinks in its armor, as Wormith and his colleagues remark in their chapter.

The articles in this section support the work of correctional psychologists, but they should also prompt questions about the policies of the criminal justice system in which they operate. Psychologists working in correctional settings are often frustrated by such practices as placement of inmates in solitary confinement for long periods or restrictions on visitation with families—considered necessary for safety reasons by prison officials. However, many psychologists find great satisfaction working in correctional facilities or consulting with a variety of correctional agencies. Although the challenges in these settings are often immense, there are numerous opportunities to contribute to significant positive change in practices and in the lives of individuals.

22

A NATIONAL SURVEY OF CORRECTIONAL PSYCHOLOGISTS

JENNIFER L. BOOTHBY

CARL B. CLEMENTS

Psychologists have long had distinct roles in the nation's correctional institutions. Their functions have been described as a blend of clinical and community psychology (Milan & Long, 1980). Assessment, treatment, training, and consultation functions take place in an environmental context that, itself, often calls for conflict resolution, program design and evaluation, and attention to stressful conditions. The number of persons incarcerated in the United States grows daily. . . . Also observed has been a substantial increase in the number and percentage of mentally disordered offenders in prison (Bureau of Justice Statistics, 1999c). Both traditional and emerging roles for psychologists are evident in this "growth industry." Though a number of articles have suggested functional models and specific areas of expertise in the application of psychology skills to prisons and offenders (Clements, 1987, 2000; Milan, Chin, & Nguyen, 1999), a comprehensive survey of actual contemporary practice has been notably absent.

Information with regard to the roles and duties of correctional psychologists has not been examined fully in nearly two decades (Otero, McNally, & Powitzky, 1981). As noted, a number of changes have occurred at the state and federal levels in corrections during the past 20 years. The prison population is booming, sentencing policies have become more severe, and public attitude seems to favor punishment over treatment. How the roles and responsibilities of correctional psychologists may have changed in the context of these trends is not known. In addition to the Otero et al. report, two other studies are in limited circulation (Bartol, Griffin, &

Editors' Note: This article was first published in *Criminal Justice and Behavior*, Vol. 27, No. 6, December 2000, pp. 716–732. Reprinted with permission of Sage Publications.

Clark, 1993, cited in Bartol, 1999; Gallagher, Somwaru, & Ben-Porath, 1999). These surveys involved, respectively, the distribution of duties of 120 correctional psychologists and the use of psychological tests in 41 state jurisdictions. In the current study, we sought both a larger sample size and greater breadth of inquiry.

METHOD

Procedure

Potential survey participants (doctoral psychologists and master's-trained psychology staff) were identified through contacting state corrections commissioners or directors of prison mental health services and comparable administrative officials for the Federal Bureau of Prisons. These individuals were asked to [either] provide . . . a list of all psychologists working within their system or . . . designate a contact person who would be responsible for distributing the surveys. Ten state systems (21%) supplied lists of their doctoral- and master's-level psychology staff, whereas the remaining systems chose to distribute the surveys internally. The different methods of survey distribution did not appear to influence response rates. Based on address lists and numbers of surveys requested by each system, we estimated a potential pool of some 2,000 professionals. Of note, we did not survey psychologists who work in local jails or in state juvenile justice institutions, nor other mental health professionals (e.g., social workers) employed by prison systems.

Materials

A four-page questionnaire was developed specifically for this study. Survey questions addressed multiple facets of the correctional psychologist's experience. Major topics included (a) demographics, (b) job duties and responsibilities, (c) the provision of mental health services, (d) assessment practices, and (e) training recommendations. Psychologists were encouraged to include their name and address on a detachable sheet to indicate their interest in receiving a brief summary of the survey results. If not already detached, these sheets were separated from the survey on receipt to ensure anonymity of the respondents.

RESULTS

Participant Characteristics

Survey respondents included 830 psychologists (estimated response rate = 42%) working in 48 state prison systems (78% of respondents) and the U.S. Federal Bureau of Prisons (22%). Generally, the response rate was higher within the federal system and among doctoral-level personnel. Variation in response rate across the 48 state systems was not remarkable. Most respondents (59%) held either a PhD or PsyD, whereas 37% were master's-level graduates. The mean age of respondents was 45 years, and an overwhelming majority (92%) identified themselves as Caucasian. Approximately 62% of respondents were male, and 38% were female.

Although most psychologists working in corrections report having degrees in clinical psychology, this specialization is not uniformly distributed across settings. Approximately 67% of psychologists employed by the Federal Bureau of Prisons have degrees in clinical psychology, and all have doctorates. State correctional systems employ psychologists with master's and doctoral degrees at approximately the same rate, and 49% of these professionals report training in clinical psychology. Table 22.1 provides additional information about training emphasis.

In recent years, an increasing number of psychologists are employed on a contractual basis by correctional facilities. Many professionals apparently prefer this type of employment as it often enables them to work fewer hours in the prison system and to continue other work activities, such as private practice. Of the survey respondents, 12% indicated that their work was contractual.

Some psychologists responding to this survey were relative novices in corrections; others were long-time career professionals. The average length of employment in corrections was 8 years, but experience ranged from a few months to 38 years. Salary was obviously related to the number of years employed, but psychologists employed for similar lengths of time by federal and state systems earned significantly different salaries. Doctoral-level psychologists employed by the federal system earned an annual income of $61,800 on average, whereas doctoral-level psychologists employed by state systems averaged approximately $53,400. In comparison, master's-level staff averaged about $40,100 in annual income.

Table 22.1 Percentage of Correctional Psychologists Reporting Training Emphasis

Training Emphasis	Federal (n = 172)	State (n = 614)
Clinical psychology	67	49
Counseling psychology	22	27
Educational/school psychology	3	5
General psychology	3	6
Other	5	11

Reflecting the gender ratio of America's prisons (93% male), most respondents (82%) reported working only with male offenders. Some (10%) work with both male and female inmates, and only 8% work solely with female offenders. Correctional psychologists appear to work with inmates representing a full range (and usually a combination) of custody levels. These include maximum custody (44%), close custody (23%), medium custody (51%), and minimum custody (30%). It is also of interest that correctional psychologists do not appear to specialize in the treatment of any one type of offender. Few respondents indicated that they provided services aimed at only a single type of inmate or a single problem area (e.g., substance abuse,

developmentally disabled, inpatient mental health). Rather, these professionals work with a variety of offenders.

JOB FUNCTIONS

Correctional psychologists have a wide range of responsibilities within their respective institutions. They describe a broad distribution of time across many tasks. On average, administrative tasks consume the largest percentage (30%) of work time, whereas direct treatment (26%) and assessment (18%) also occupy a substantial portion of the correctional psychologist's time. Survey respondents, on average, reported relatively little time devoted to research. We also asked how these professionals would prefer to spend their time within these same job categories. . . . [P]sychologists expressed interest in spending much less time on administrative duties. Conversely, they reported a desire to increase the amount of time spent in providing therapy to offenders and in staff training. Similarly, many expressed interest in increasing the amount of time available for research. When asked to list activities they wished they were involved in, 47% included research on their wish list. Even so, the desired amount of time for research remained low (6%), perhaps reflecting the reality of other demands and lack of institutional support.

Treatment Approaches and Problem Focus

Correctional psychologists spend, on average, one quarter of their time providing therapy to inmates. Respondents were asked to further describe the format of interventions offered to inmates and the theoretical underpinnings of the services provided. Despite the ever increasing number of prisoners needing mental health services, 60% of treatment continues to be provided in an individual format. This allocation of resources exists in the face of an average psychologist to inmate ratio of 1:750. In contrast, respondents indicated spending approximately 18% of therapy time on psycho-educational groups and 15% on process groups. With respect to the theoretical orientations that correctional psychologists use to guide their provision of services, most reported a combination of frameworks. An overwhelming majority (88%) use a cognitive model. A behavioral orientation was endorsed by 69%, and another 40% employed a rational-emotive approach. Though we did not specifically pose an "eclectic" option, most endorsed one or more secondary theoretical orientations, suggesting an eclectic approach to psychotherapy. Table 22.2 contains additional data on respondents' orientation.

Given the substantial proportion of time correctional psychologists spend evaluating (18%) and treating (26%) prisoners, it becomes important to understand the types of inmate problems typically being addressed. Respondents were asked to list the four inmate problems they most commonly treated. Depression was overwhelmingly cited as the most frequent problem presented by inmates. Eighty percent of psychologists cited depression within the "top four problems." Anger problems were also mentioned by many psychologists (40%). Psychotic symptoms, anxiety, and adjustment issues were frequently mentioned as well. Table 22.3 summarizes these responses.

ASSESSMENT PRACTICES

Approximately 65% of respondents indicated that they were involved, to varying degrees, in the psychological assessment of offenders. The types of evaluations described range from intellectual assessment to the assessment of risk (see Table 22.4). Most typically, however, psychological testing in the prison system is done to assess personality characteristics (42%). A smaller percentage of testing time is spent on intellectual assessment (19%), the evaluation of risk (13%), and symptom assessment (12%). Very little time is devoted to neuropsychological assessment (5%) or behavioral analysis (3%).

Table 22.2 Percentage of Respondents Reporting Theoretical Orientations

Orientation	Percentage of Respondents
Cognitive	88
Behavioral	69
Rational-emotive	40
Psychodynamic/psychoanalytic	23
Humanistic	19
Existential	15
Systems	14
Other	13

Table 22.3 Percentage of Correctional Psychologists Indicating Various Mental Health Problems as One of Four Most Frequent Problems Treated

Orientation	Percentage of Respondents
Depression	80
Anger	40
Psychoses	25
Anxiety	24
Adjustment issues	20
Personality disorders	18
Substance abuse	17
Sexual behavior	14
Acting out/impulse control	12

NOTE: Not all respondents listed four problem areas.

Although psychologists reported using a variety of assessment instruments, most continue to rely on very few tests. As might be expected, the Minnesota Multiphasic Personality Inventory (MMPI, MMPI-2) continues to be the most widely used psychological instrument in corrections. Approximately 87% of respondents reported using the MMPI in their clinical work with prisoners. It is probable that many psychologists in corrections do not administer instruments themselves, but rather, use psychological data gathered during the reception and classification process. The MMPI has long been a mainstay of the intake process. Other personality instruments cited by psychologists include the Millon Clinical Multiaxial Inventory (MCMI) (30%), Rorschach (20%), projective drawings (14%), and the Personality Assessment Inventory (10%).

Table 22.4   Percentage of Correctional Psychologists Reporting Usage of Specific Psychological Tests

Instrument	Percentage
MMPI	87
WAIS	69
MCMI	30
Bender-Gestalt	23
Rorschach	20
Projective Drawings	14
BDI/BAI	13
PCL-R	11
PAI	10
WMS	8
SIRS	7
TONI	6
Trails A & B	6
MSI	6
Halstead-Reitan	5
Luria Nebraska	4
Slosson	3
LSI	<1
V-RAG	<1

NOTE: MMPI = Minnesota Multiphasic Personality Inventory; WAIS = Wechsler Adult Intelligence Scale; MCMI= Millon Clinical Multiaxial Inventory; BDI/BAI = Beck Depression Inventory/Behavior Assessment Inventory; PCL-R = Psychopathy Checklist—Revised; PAI = Personality Assessment Inventory; WMS = Wechsler Memory Scale; SIRS = Structured Interview of Reported Symptoms; TONI = Test of Nonverbal Intelligence; MSI = Multiphasic Sex Inventory: LSI = Level of Service Inventory: V-RAG = Violent Risk Assessment Guide.

With respect to intellectual assessment, most correctional psychologists use the Wechsler Adult Intelligence Scale (WAIS) (69%). Of those performing neuropsychological evaluations, 23% reported using the Bender-Gestalt. Tests used less frequently by these psychologists included the Wechsler Memory Scale (8%), Trails A&B (6%),

the Halstead-Reitan (5%), and the Luria Nebraska (4%). Although 13% of respondents described involvement in the assessment of risk, few professionals reported the risk instruments they were using. Of the instruments reported, the Psychopathy Checklist—Revised (PCL-R) was most commonly indicated (11%). The Multiphasic Sex Inventory (MSI) was reported by 6% of respondents engaged in risk assessment, whereas the Level of Supervision Inventory (LSI) was cited by fewer than 1%. It seems that many correctional psychologists rely on instruments such as the MMPI regardless of the referral question.

PROFESSIONAL MEMBERSHIPS

To gauge their affiliation patterns, respondents were asked to report any national or state membership in psychological organizations. Approximately 43% were members of the American Psychological Association (APA). Membership in divisions of APA was also investigated, with specific attention directed to those divisions that involve some aspect of corrections (Division 18) or forensic issues (Division 41). Only 8% reported membership in an APA division, with 1% belonging to Division 18 and 3% belonging to Division 41. Similarly, few respondents (7%) belong to the American Association for Correctional Psychology, a group specifically devoted to the issues facing psychologists in corrections.

PRIOR EXPERIENCE AND TRAINING RECOMMENDATIONS

Approximately 37% of respondents reported some type of previous forensic or correctional experience prior to employment in corrections. This background differed significantly for those with master's degrees (27%) versus those with doctorate degrees (44%). Doctoral-level psychologists in federal versus state prisons also differed in prior experience. Approximately 63% of those working in federal prisons described some type of previous correctional or forensic experience compared to only 33% of those in state prisons. The majority of those reporting previous training had completed an internship (or rotation) (62%) or practicum (43%) in a correctional setting. Others described corrections-related experience in research (23%), coursework (36%), or independent study (16%).

We solicited opinions about training for those psychologists or graduate students interested in correctional work. Table 22.5 summarizes recommendations made by correctional psychologists currently working in this field. The most frequent preparation recommended for a career in correctional psychology was to undertake an internship or practicum in a prison facility. Many respondents indicated that such experience would not only give students a better idea of the job responsibilities and opportunities but would also clarify what it was like to work with inmates in a security-oriented facility. Other training recommendations frequently cited by respondents include gaining experience in psychological testing, training in the diagnosis and treatment of personality disorders, experience with issues specific to forensic psychology such as the evaluation of competency, and criminal justice or law-related coursework. Clinical skills such as interviewing and diagnosis were mentioned by practically all respondents; therefore, these items were not included in Table 22.5.

PREDICTIONS FOR THE FUTURE

Respondents were given the opportunity to make predictions about the future of correctional psychology as a career. Although it was clearly evident from reading survey responses to prior questions that these professionals viewed their jobs as important, interesting, and challenging, their predictions about the future were not nearly so optimistic. For example, many expressed concern that the number of available jobs will gradually decrease, despite the growing need for psychological services in corrections. Those with doctorate degrees feared their positions would be lost to master's-level professionals, whereas those with master's degrees expressed concern about losing their jobs to social workers. Many (15%) also reported a continuing trend toward administrative duties replacing treatment. It may be that correctional psychologists see their positions turning into managerial or administrative positions, leaving the less well-trained or paraprofessionals to deliver the majority of treatment. Some respondents (10%) predicted an increasing presence of managed care in corrections, and others (9%) indicated concerns about privatization.

DISCUSSION AND RECOMMENDATIONS

The authors were gratified by the impressive return rate (42%) for this project. This level of

Table 22.5   Percentage of Correctional Psychologists Making Specific Training Recommendations

Training Recommendation	Percentage
Practicum or internship in a correctional setting	30
Training in personality disorders	21
Training in issues related to forensic psychology	13
Criminal justice or law-related coursework	12
Training in assessment	11
Training in the detection of malingering	10
Training in crisis intervention	8
Training in substance abuse evaluation and treatment	7

response can be attributed, in part, to the encouragement of chief psychologists and other administrators in prison systems across the United States. We speculate, too, that eagerness for professional interchange and information [was a motive] for many respondents. Nearly 65% requested a summary of preliminary results. By contrast, correctional psychologists are not heavily involved in national psychology organizations. Beyond membership in the APA (46% of respondents), very few had joined either of the potentially most relevant APA divisions, Psychologists in Public Service (Division 18) or the American Psychology-Law Society (AP-LS) (Division 41). Membership in the American Association for Correctional Psychology (AACP), an affiliate of the American Correctional Association, also was sparse, even though AACP is directly targeted at these professionals. Some respondents requested more information about these organizations, and AACP and AP-LS have recently announced a joint membership initiative to attract correctional psychologists.

A number of differences emerged between our results and those of previous surveys. Several similarities were also noted. In terms of sample size and characteristics, we reached more than 800 respondents, including 172 federal psychologists. Clearly, the number of psychologists employed in corrections has risen dramatically since the survey by Otero et al. (1981). At that time, an estimated 600 master's- and doctorate-level psychologists worked in corrections in the United States and Canada. In contrast, our estimates show that number to have jumped to approximately 2,000 in the United States alone. Even so, this growth rate has not kept pace with the more than quadrupling of the number of offenders confined in correctional institutions. Interestingly, the demographics of psychologists working in corrections are largely comparable to those of psychologists working in other areas (Kohout & Wicherski, 1999). An exception is the smaller number of women employed by corrections as compared to other settings.

Despite the growth in absolute numbers of psychologists in corrections, the estimated psychologist-to-inmate ratio (1:750) appears to be approximately half that observed in the early 1980s. The still lower ratio of doctoral-level providers (1:2,000) is even more disturbing. Although the proportion of professional time devoted to treatment has remained steady over the past two decades, the actual amount of service delivered per inmate has obviously shrunk. Commentary supplied by many respondents indicated a growing concern, and potential ethical quandary, with the imbalance of limited resources and escalating demand/need for services. Most wanted to devote more time to intervention. It would not surprise us if some providers felt the frustration reflected in Rice and Harris'[s] (1997) observation that, "the huge problems in changing institutional and bureaucratic routines make implementing [treatment] programs with high integrity extremely difficult" (p. 432).

At the same time, management roles, sometimes called the unseen career path (Kilburg, 1984), have increased since 1981. Today, correctional psychologists spend almost one third of their time in administrative tasks. Interestingly, more involvement in core management was one of the stated wishes of Otero's sample some 20 years ago (Otero et al., 1981). In addition, staff training activities also occupy more time than previously reported. One could argue that these management and training roles serve to extend the impact of psychological perspectives, but a certain irreducible need for assessment and treatment services cannot be finessed by delegating to others or through administering programs. Reflecting this attitude, respondents with administrative duties would, on average, like to see such time cut almost in half. In addition, some psychologists in corrections would like more time to devote to research, an activity urged by a number of writers (e.g., Andrews & Bonta, 1998; Bartol, 1999). Our observation is that such aspirations are best realized through academic partnerships and systemwide mandates (and support) to conduct evaluation studies. Such conditions are enjoyed more noticeably by our colleagues in Canada (Motiuk, 1999).

Correctional psychologists appear more likely than psychologists in general to endorse cognitive and behavioral orientations as guides to treatment (Milan, Montgomery, & Rogers, 1994). Given the adaptability and relative success of these approaches with offenders (Clements, 1987; Gendreau, 1996; Milan et al., 1999), this finding is encouraging. Among the psychological problems of inmates most commonly dealt with by survey respondents, depression was widely seen and treated, as were anger, anxiety, and adjustment issues. All are amenable to cognitive-behavioral strategies.

Pressed for time and spread so thinly, correctional psychologists nevertheless remain dedicated to one-on-one treatment. Given the daunting number of offenders in need of treatment, the failure to shift toward a framework of group treatment seems like a potentially poor use of important resources. One recent survey of group therapy providers in corrections reports an estimated effectiveness rating of greater than 5 on a 7-point scale in such areas as anger and stress management, adjustment, and cognitive restructuring (Morgan, Winterowd, & Ferrel, 1999). These writers urge the development of treatment manuals and heightened attention to "what works" outcome studies. Though group-based treatments have not been directly tested against individual therapy, those methods finding the most empirical support, cognitive-behavioral interventions (Gendreau & Goggin, 1997), are quite adaptable to group delivery. Ready examples include the aggression replacement training (ART) model developed by Goldstein and colleagues (Goldstein & Glick, 1997; Rokach, 1987), as well as programs that focus on antisocial attitudes and other "criminogenic needs" (Andrews & Bonta, 1998). Based on shrinking staff resources, creative attempts to expand service capacity through group methods seem fully warranted.

Somewhat puzzling is the relative underemphasis on treating both serious mental illness and substance abuse. Given the growing proportion of mentally disordered offenders in prison—recently estimated at 16% (Bureau of Justice Statistics, 1999a)—it appears either that few resources are being directed toward these individuals or that psychologists are playing a relatively minor role. We know that in some jurisdictions, services for the severely mentally ill are provided under contract and/or within special settings. Perhaps those providers are underrepresented in this survey. By contrast, substance abuse treatment—itself a major thrust in many prisons (see Inciardi, 1993; Milan et al., 1999)—has historically been the purview of counselors and case workers. Nevertheless, in both of these areas, psychologists clearly have a stake in treatment planning, service delivery, supervision, and program evaluation. There is also a clear need to provide services to incarcerated women whose mental health and health problems are likely to be widespread and diverse (Acoca, 1998; Bureau of Justice Statistics, 1999b). Physical and sexual victimization, parental responsibilities, depression, and patterns of drug use often distinguish women offenders (Conley, 1998). The substantial increase in the number of aging prison inmates also presents a challenge and opportunity for psychologists and other health professionals.

We are also concerned about reported assessment practices. Popularity and tradition aside, one cannot argue that any test, even the revered MMPI—used by 87% of those involved in assessment—is generically applicable to all correctional issues. Increasingly though, for instruments like the MMPI-2 and MCMI, offender norms are available. We did not assess whether these norms were being regularly employed. By contrast, some newer instruments that reportedly aid in the assessment of risk and supervision needs were minimally used. For example, the PCL-R (Hare, 1991) was used by 11% of respondents who assessed offenders. The Level of Service Inventory—Revised (LSI-R) (Andrews & Bonta, 1995), widely used in Canada, is virtually absent in the United States. These observations are consistent with Gallagher et al. (1999), who report MMPI use at high rates during intake (65% of states) and even higher (96%) for pre-parole evaluations, a logical place for instruments such as the LSI-R. More surprisingly, projective tests (drawings, inkblots) were frequently used in both samples and enjoy an even heightened popularity in pre-release evaluations (Gallagher et al., 1999).

Attracting, recruiting, and retaining qualified professional staff remain a challenge. Recruitment of minority psychologists is especially needed, given the disproportionate representation of African Americans in the U.S. prison population. Although pay scales are now reasonably competitive, training avenues remain limited. However, evidence of growth in the field of psychology and law, including interests and research in corrections, suggests an expanding pipeline of professionals (Bersoff et al., 1997). The doctoral programs that are available are being buttressed by an increasing number of accredited internships with a strong correctional or forensic focus. Several of these are located at correctional institutions and medical centers within the Federal Bureau of Prisons. These and similar state correctional and forensic settings partially address respondents' clear call for practicum and internship training. Assessment skills, personality disorder treatment competencies, and other forensic knowledge are also seen as contributing to the correctional psychologist's role.

To these recommendations, we would add familiarity with newer instruments specifically relevant to offenders, knowledge of cognitive-behavioral (and social learning) treatment paradigms, an orientation to applying skills to the institutional milieu, and a commitment to outcomes assessment. These recommendations apply to master's level psychology staff as well. Corrections employs more master's than doctoral staff (though the Federal Bureau of Prisons and

selected states more exclusively employ doctoral-level, licensed psychologists), and their preparation to carry out important assessment and treatment functions should not be left to chance.

In some state institutions, psychologists function as sole practitioners. We suspect that professional isolation and burnout are possible consequences. In addition, the opportunity for supervision and consultation with regard to ethics, case management, or myriad other issues would seem to be sacrificed at these outposts. We recommend that regional systems of professional consultation be established, including, where necessary, employing part-time consultants to enrich the working environment. Indeed, part-time employment in corrections may be a viable model for some who wish to remain connected to community, academia, or mental health agenc[ies].

Although this study examines a cross-section of the current roles of correctional psychologists working in state and federal prisons, it does not address similar roles that are being filled by other professionals nor psychologists' presence and functions within the nation's jails, juvenile institutions, and youth detention centers. Our guess is that mental health professionals in these settings are even less well-connected to fellow professionals, especially if they work full-time in remote locations. The task of identifying psychologists who practice in the hundreds of local jails and juvenile facilities in the United States will present a challenge to understanding how their roles might diverge from their prison-based colleagues. As the field of correctional psychology continues to expand, such surveys might enlighten both the profession and future practitioners.

23

THE REHABILITATION AND REINTEGRATION OF OFFENDERS

The Current Landscape and Some Future Directions for Correctional Psychology

J. STEPHEN WORMITH

RICHARD ALTHOUSE

MARK SIMPSON

LORRAINE R. REITZEL

THOMAS J. FAGAN

ROBERT D. MORGAN

How far have we advanced in the decade since a special issue of *Criminal Justice and Behavior* commemorated its 20th anniversary (Glenwick, 1996)? At that time, sages of correctional psychology suggested that the place for rehabilitation was well established in corrections, although they also called for continued efforts in areas such as correctional

Editors' Note: This article was originally published in a special issue of *Criminal Justice and Behavior*, Vol. 34, No. 7, pp. 879–892. Reprinted with permission of Sage Publications. The guest editor of the special issue was Robert D. Morgan.

training and technology transfer (Brodsky, 1996; Gendreau, 1996). The purpose of this article is to assist researchers, clinicians, program developers, and correctional administrators chart a course for continued improvement in the rehabilitation movement by highlighting recent key developments and empirical findings in the adult-offender rehabilitation literature. In this context, *rehabilitation* refers to a broad array of psychosocial programs and services that are designed to assist offenders in addressing a range of needs related to their offending behavior and in achieving a more productive and satisfying lifestyle.

Rather than attempt an exhaustive description of 40 years of offender treatment research, our approach has been to conduct a selective review, focusing on the meta-analyses of empirically supported offender treatment programs in general and more specifically on the treatment of substance abuse offenders and sexual offenders. Yet we believe that this review is sufficiently representative that inferences may be made, knowledge may be transferred to practice, and directions may be derived for future research. Furthermore, we are conscious of the "correctional quackery" that is often promoted in the name of a safer society (Gendreau, Goggin, French, & Smith, 2006) and limited our review to empirically supported research.

Correctional treatment planners and service providers must be clear about the objectives of their many and varied interventions. Since 1990, much of the offender treatment literature has focused on the reduction of offenders' criminal behavior, most commonly measured as recidivism. However, other kinds of services, such as health care, mental health treatment, faith-based programs, and cultural activities, may have different goals and should be evaluated accordingly. Services that engender a greater sense of well-being are a trend in the emerging field of positive psychology (Seligman, Linley, & Joseph, 2004), and services designed to build on client strengths are suggested as an approach worthy of development within corrections. As community reintegration has emerged as a critical adjunct to the treatment of prisoners, special attention is given to prisoner reentry into the community (e.g., Petersilia, 2004).

Although successful reintegration means no return to crime, recidivism is a unified concept without a unifying definition. Definitions have ranged from reincarceration for any reason, to an arrest regardless of conviction, to arrest with conviction, to conviction of a new offense (as opposed to a technical violation of parole or probation). Treatment studies have defined recidivism as a return to jail or prison for committing an offense for which the offender had prior treatment (e.g., drug abuse, sexual offense; Beck, 2001) but have seldom considered severity of recidivism as a substitute for the dichotomous approach. Recidivism rates are also time sensitive. Finally, the mode of data collection—self-report versus various official databases—represents another dimension of recidivism. Given these vagaries, further insight about "what works" may have to await the acceptance of a more refined and sensitive outcome measure.

An examination of America's national average recidivism rate showed that two thirds of offenders released from 15 states in 1994 were rearrested within 3 years of their release, with the majority being reconvicted and incarcerated for new crimes (U.S. Department of Justice, 2006). Yet an analysis of specific programs paints a different picture about the capacity for success in American corrections. In a review of almost 300 evaluations of correctional programs during 35 years, general cognitive-based programs were estimated to reduce recidivism by 8%, therapeutic communities by 6%, and cognitive-behavioral treatment programs for sex offenders in prison by 15% (Aos, Miller, & Drake, 2006). Clearly, the answer to the question, "What works to reduce recidivism?" depends on where and how one looks. To that end, we turn to the general and specific evidence for correctional treatment.

WHAT DO WE KNOW ABOUT EFFECTIVE CORRECTIONAL INTERVENTION?

The accumulation of knowledge about "what works" in correctional rehabilitation owes a great deal to the approximately 2,000 studies that have addressed this question during the past half century (McGuire, 2002) and to the application of meta-analytic practices that generate empirically based summaries of this large and diverse research. The extent to which correctional researchers have increasingly chosen meta-analysis as opposed to narrative reviews to summarize their findings is encouraging. Between 1985 and 2005, at least 52 meta-analyses have been conducted on offender treatment (McGuire, 2005), although the majority have been on youth programs. Meta-analysis is replete with methodological complications that can compromise interpretation, including variations in program content, control conditions, offender characteristics, outcome variables, and the wider social context of the intervention (Lösel, 2001). Nonetheless, important inferences can be drawn from this research, and the study of effective correctional treatment has progressed steadily during the past 15 years. At least five important findings have emerged.

First, the overall impact of treatment and program services for offenders has led to an average effect size of about .10 (McGuire, 2002). Second, comparisons between all types of treatment programs and increased sanctions, with a mean effect size of −.07 for the latter (Andrews, Zinger, et al., 1990; Gendreau, Goggin, Cullen, & Andrews, 2001), have consistently favored the former. Third, more detailed analyses of specific treatment characteristics have generated a wide range of effect sizes, ranging from −.09, indicating a possible negative effect, to .38, when services adhere to the principles of risk, need, responsivity, and other contextual conditions (D. A. Andrews & Bonta, 2003). Collectively, the individual and meta-analytic studies have identified "what works" and offered insights about where (e.g., community-based intervention) and how it is likely to do so (e.g., D. A. Andrews, 2001). Fourth, meta-analyses of specific kinds of treatment, such as cognitive-behavioral therapy (Landenberger & Lipsey, 2005; D. B. Wilson, Bouffard, & MacKenzie, 2005), and treatments with specific types of offenders, such as substance abuse offenders (Lipton, 1995;

Wells-Parker, Bangert-Drowns, McMillen, & Williams, 1995) and sex offenders (Alexander, 1999), have provided direction in terms of "what works for whom." Finally, an emerging cost-benefit methodology offers another dimension to traditional meta-analysis and provides insight about the economic benefits of treatment (Aos, Phipps, Barnoski, & Leib, 2001).

These findings offer specific direction for technology transfer to the field. In particular, the principles of risk, need, and responsivity (D. A. Andrews, Bonta, & Hoge, 1990; D. A. Andrews, Bonta, & Wormith, 2006) now guide both administrators and clinicians in the selection of clients (i.e., targeting moderate- and high-risk offenders), the kinds of services to provide (i.e., addressing criminogenic needs), and the manner by which services are delivered (i.e., behavioral and cognitive-behavioral programs). The extent to which these principles are followed and treatment integrity is practiced correlates highly with client outcome as measured by recidivism (D. A. Andrews & Dowden, 2005; Latessa, 2004). Their importance is profound, as adherence to them determines whether or not the prescribed intervention affects recidivism, regardless of client demographics such as age, gender, and ethnicity (D. A. Andrews & Bonta, 2003). These principles also shed light on the pre-Martinson (1974) perspective about the effectiveness of offender treatment, as such services would have known nothing about them.

The proliferation of offender treatment program evaluations and the common inclusion of their results in meta-analysis have taken the corrections community far beyond Martinson's (1974) article that prompted the statement that "nothing works." Therefore, clinicians in corrections may feel that the struggle to establish offender treatment among the scientifically accepted list of empirically supported interventions is over. However, this is not the case. Although great advances have been made in our understanding of offender treatment and evidence for its effectiveness abounds (e.g., McGuire, 2002), critics remain suspicious about efforts to intervene in the lives of offenders (e.g., Israel & Chui, 2006; Merrington & Stanley, 2004; Wilkinson, 2005). Furthermore, some chinks have developed in the armor of what have been the "poster children" of offender treatment, notably cognitive skill training (Cairn, 2006) and multisystemic therapy (Leschied & Cunningham, 2001; Littell, Popa, & Forsythe, 2006) and raise research questions about the client group, the mode of delivery, and the precision of the outcome measure.

Much of the future understanding about correctional intervention is likely to come from moving beyond the simple, but important, treatment-recidivism study to the examination of in-program issues. For example, there is a great deal of latitude for offender services to vary within the parameters of these principles. The concept of program integrity—the extent to which the service being offered conforms to the manner of service intended by the developers of the service—focuses on these variations (D. A. Andrews & Dowden, 2005; Lowenkamp, 2004). Second, client resistance and dropout are chronic, nonrandom problems in correctional treatment (Wormith & Olver, 2002). Clinicians must incorporate strategies, such as pretreatment preparation and motivational interviewing, to minimize client attrition (Miller & Rollnick, 2002), whereas researchers must consider dropouts and treatment failures in their evaluation of correctional treatment to truly understand treatment effects. With this foundation in the general principles of offender intervention, we turn to a sample of specialized offender services to illustrate both achievements and unanswered questions about offender treatment.

Substance Abuse Treatment

Because of the high prevalence of drug abuse among offenders (Mumola, 1999), drug abuse treatment programs may be the most common form of rehabilitation offered to this population. The most commonly used and thoroughly researched prison-based, psychosocial treatment is the therapeutic community (TC). Originally designed by Maxwell Jones (1962) in response to the traditional medical approach to the treatment of mental health problems, these "open" communities that stress consensus building and two-way communication between staff and patients and are founded on social learning theory have been applied in numerous correctional environments (Toch, 1980). The philosophy and structure of TC make it a viable form of treatment for drug-abusing offenders, particularly for those whose criminality has resulted in their incarceration (De Leon, 2000; Tims, De Leon, & Jainchill, 1994). Meta-analytic reviews of corrections-based drug treatment found that TC was effective in reducing recidivism for incarcerated substance abuse offenders with a mean effect size of .14 (Lipton, Pearson, Cleland, & Yee, 2002) and reductions of recidivism ranging between 5.3% and 6.9% (Aos et al., 2006). Five-year outcome studies conducted for prison-based TC programs in Delaware (Martin, Butzin, Saum, & Inciardi, 1999), California (Wexler, Melnick, Lowe, & Peters, 1999), and Texas (K. Knight, Simpson, & Hiller, 1999) found that offenders who completed both prison TC treatment and aftercare treatment in the community showed significant reductions in recidivism and relapse when compared with untreated controls. In all three studies, aftercare treatment in the community proved critical in helping offenders make the transition from prison to the community and maintain TC gains. Reductions in recidivism and drug use relapse were found to disappear 3 years after release for offenders who completed only the prison-based TC. Five-year outcome data for the programs in Delaware (Inciardi, Martin, & Butzin, 2004) and California (Prendergast, Hall, Wexler, Melnick, & Cao, 2004) found similar results. Although a lack of random assignment makes conclusions questionable (Burdon, Farabee, Prendergast, Messina, & Cartier, 2002), an evaluation of drug abuse treatment programs within the Federal Bureau of Prisons found that inmates who had completed prison-based treatment and community-based aftercare were significantly less likely to relapse in drug use or recidivate than inmates in a comparison group, even after controlling for individual- and system-level selection factors (Pelissier et al., 2000).

These findings indicate that prison-based TC coupled with aftercare treatment in the community can reduce both recidivism and relapse into drug use. Prison-based programs can serve to motivate offenders to participate in drug abuse treatment following release from prison (Wexler, Prendergast, & Melnick, 2004). Findings from the Delaware study indicated that graduates of the institutional TC were more likely to remain in community treatment (Inciardi et al., 2004). Prison treatment may serve more as a preparation for community treatment than as a primary treatment, although it has been shown to reduce prison misconduct (French & Gendreau, 2006; N. P. Langan & Pelissier, 2001). On the other hand, Marlowe (2003) noted that intensive supervision and intermediate sanction programs, by themselves, have not demonstrated a reduction in criminal recidivism or relapse. Educational or drug-awareness sessions have no impact on later drug use or criminal behavior. Boot camps and drug-focused group counseling have also been ineffective (Pearson & Lipton, 1999), and insight- and group process–oriented programs for high-risk offenders are associated with higher rates of drug use and recidivism. Pragmatic, skills-based programs that assist patients to deal with their post-release environments enhance treatment generalization from the institution to the community.

Although most substance abuse treatment research has focused on outcome variables related to drug use and recidivism, Simpson (2004) examined treatment process variables that underlie the responsivity principle. These studies include patient variables (e.g., readiness and motivation for treatment, severity of substance disorder), treatment variables (e.g., engagement in treatment, therapeutic relationship), and variables related to treatment program philosophies and attributes. Early engagement in a program is critical in overcoming offenders' lack of commitment to treatment, and techniques such as early use of motivational interviewing improve

program affiliation and treatment retention (Hiller, Knight, & Simpson, 1999).

In sum, treatment-process research is needed to address numerous important questions about service delivery. For example, how do different versions of a commonly identified program vary in their effectiveness? Taxman and Bouffard (2002) suggested that researchers include a measure of treatment integrity to assess program adherence to its purported model. How do offenders' perceptions of their counselors affect treatment success (e.g., Broome, Knight, Hiller, & Simpson, 1996)? Variables related to treatment counselors are almost nonexistent in the literature. Do offenders' perceptions of their similarity (or dissimilarity) to treatment staff impact treatment engagement? Proponents of the TC model advocate the use of recovering addicts as staff (De Leon, 2000), yet many institutional policies prohibit the hiring of ex-offenders. How do perceptions of their relationships with their clients impact treatment engagement and success? Although therapist–client relationships are important to treatment success, the institutional culture in which programs are embedded often regard relationships with inmates with suspicion (Simpson, 2004). These process-oriented questions are offered so that future research may guide drug treatment providers to achieve maximum treatment effect.

SEX OFFENDER TREATMENT

Unlike the growing consensus about what works in the general correctional literature, there is substantial variability in the outcome of individual studies examining treatment effectiveness for sex offenders (e.g., Hanson, Broom, & Stephenson, 2004; Nicholaichuk, Gordon, Gu, & Wong, 2000). Meta-analyses and summative reviews of treatment effectiveness have also demonstrated a range of effect sizes for sex offender treatment (e.g., Furby, Weinrott, & Blackshaw, 1989; C. A. Gallagher, Wilson, Hirschfield, Coggeshall, & MacKenzie, 1999; Hall, 1995; Lösel & Schmucker, 2005). Apparent disparities in treatment effectiveness may reflect improvements in the state of practice, as more recent studies with predominantly cognitive-behavioral treatments show significant effects, whereas older studies, with obsolete or indiscernible treatments, do not (cf. Furby et al., 1989; R. K. Hanson et al., 2002). However, problems inherent in the current literature, such as inadequate documentation and inappropriate handling of treatment dropouts and refusers, make inference about effectiveness difficult (McConaghy, 1999; Rice & Harris, 2003). Consequently, these mixed results of the psychosocial treatment-effectiveness literature have left the field divided about whether, for whom, and how sex offender treatment works (Marques, 1999).

One of the better-designed studies in the adult sex offender literature is the Marques, Wiederanders, Day, Nelson, and van Ommeren (2005) randomized clinical trial of an inpatient, cognitive-behavioral, relapse-prevention program for incarcerated offenders. This well-designed study failed to support a treatment effect during an 8-year follow-up (Marques et al., 2005). These results have led to speculation about their 1985 version of treatment: the impact of offenders not "getting" relapse prevention; failure to adhere to principles of risk, need, and responsivity; and failure of aftercare to use an interdisciplinary, individualized case-management process. Although such tightly controlled studies are difficult and expensive to conduct (Marshall & Serran, 2000), integrity in research design is necessary to advance the field's understanding of "what works" in sex offender treatment (Craig, Browne, & Stringer, 2003). Methodological suggestions include random assignment, matching on risk, using an incidental design (Marshall & Serran, 2000), determining the type of offender for which treatment works (Craig et al., 2003; Rice & Harris, 2003), using intent-to-treat procedures for dropouts (Lösel & Schmucker, 2005), and investigating mechanisms underlying effectiveness and individual treatment components (Marshall & Serran, 2000; Rice & Harris, 2003).

Despite largely inconclusive results overall, most researchers and clinicians agree that widely used cognitive-behavioral treatments (McGrath, Cumming, & Burchard, 2003) represent the most promising approach to affect sexual recidivism (Craig et al., 2003). Sex offender treatment providers have also heeded elements of best practice found in general correctional treatment: the risk, need, and responsivity principles. The use of these principles makes sense given the diversity of sex offenders in treatment (McGrath et al., 2003), varying recidivism risk based on instant offense (R. K. Hanson & Bussiere, 1998), limited resources for treatment provision, potential danger of treating low-risk offenders too intensely (Hanson, 2000, as cited in Marques et al., 2005), relevance of criminogenic needs in sexual recidivism (e.g., R. K. Hanson & Morton-Bourgon, 2005), and special needs of some offender populations (e.g., those with intellectual limitations; Lambrick & Glaser, 2004). In this regard, R. K. Hanson and Morton-Bourgon's meta-analysis identified a number of dynamic risk factors for sexual recidivism, such as self-regulation problems and employment instability, as well as factors unrelated to sexual recidivism, such as offense denial and a lack of victim empathy. As the latter are common targets of sex offender treatment (McGrath et al., 2003), future research should examine whether improved "incremental" effectiveness is found for treatments targeting the criminogenic need factors linked to recidivism risk (R. K. Hanson & Morton-Bourgon, 2005).

The principles of effective practice have also rejected the "one treatment fits all" approach. For example, the self-regulation model (Ward & Hudson, 1998) describes multiple pathways to offending behaviors, each differentially affecting recidivism risk and approach to treatment (Fisher & Beech, 2005). This model allows for individualized offense cycles and treatment plans. It is congruent with the needs and responsivity principles and is consistent with recent evidence that flexibility in treatment enhances outcome (Marshall, 2005). It also complements findings about the importance of self-regulation to risk of recidivism (R. K. Hanson & Morton-Bourgon, 2005). Additional research on the effectiveness of a self-regulation approach to treatment is needed for general and specific offender populations (Keeling & Rose, 2005).

As found with other types of offenders, evidence has begun to mount about the importance of community-based support for sexual offenders following their release from custody (R. J. Wilson, Picheca, & Prinzo, 2005). Programs such as Circles of Support may prove to be particularly important for sexual offenders (R. J. Wilson & Prinzo, 2001), but they require more research.

Recent literature has also advocated a more client-responsive, "gentle" approach in the delivery of treatment to sex offenders (Marshall & Serran, 2000). A "good lives" model of treatment focuses on building hope and working cooperatively with offenders to build on their strengths to maximize the effectiveness of treatment (Marshall et al., 2005). Other methods of "positive" treatment delivery such as a motivational enhancement (cf. Miller & Rollnick, 2002) may impact treatment acceptance in resistant offenders and merit further exploration. Self-deterministic approaches to treatment (cf. Sheldon, Williams, & Joiner, 2003) suggest more attention to positive outcomes, such as getting and keeping offenders in treatment. Yet they require close empirical scrutiny to substantiate the current optimism (Carich & Smith, 2006).

We now turn to other approaches of correctional intervention that do not necessarily target criminogenic need or recidivism, at least [not] directly. In particular, "positive psychology" is a paradigm that appears to turn our traditional criminogenic focus on its head.

POSITIVE PSYCHOLOGY AND OFFENDER TREATMENT

The belief that criminal behavior is a product of cognitive, emotional, and mental deficits (e.g., J. Q. Wilson & Herrnstein, 1985; Yochelson & Samenow, 1976, 1977) has generated numerous models of offender treatment in the past four decades. However, research has indicated that treatment programs based on this belief have had

varied success in reducing recidivism. The overlooked question in deficit-based inquiries into offender behavior is, What militates against individuals offending in the first place? Exploring offender behavior and interventions from this perspective invites a paradigm shift from a deficit-based model to a strength-based model. The foundation for this shift can be found in positive psychology.

Positive psychology, as developed by Abraham Maslow and later adopted by Martin Seligman, promotes ideas and principles that facilitate optimal mental and physical health and militate against mental illness and dysfunctional thoughts, feelings, and behaviors (Seligman et al., 2004; C. R. Snyder & Lopez, 2001). By studying the cognitive, emotional, and character strengths of happy people and examining concepts such as purpose, productivity, future-mindedness, parenting, empathy, wisdom, and courage, positive psychology has identified variables that may facilitate a more satisfying life. They include satisfying work, helping others, being a good citizen, developing spirituality and integrity, realizing potential, and self-regulating impulses (Seligman, 2004). Thus, the overarching goal of positive psychology is to enable people to live flourishing lives with greater health, well-being, and meaning.

Researchers and clinicians have begun to consider the use of positive psychology in offender treatment. Whereas research has shown that a punitive, fear-based treatment approach focusing on avoiding "bad" behaviors has not been very successful in reducing relapse among sex offenders (e.g., Reitzel, 2006; Yates, 2005), a "good lives" approach has garnered increasing theoretical interest among sex offender treatment staff (e.g., Ward & Stewart, 2003). In this treatment model, sex offenders are regarded as actively seeking those things that most people desire (e.g., intimacy) but employing inappropriate strategies. Therefore, treatment begins by identifying the life goals the individual desires and helps [him or her] work toward achieving such goals. Preliminary research supports this approach (e.g., Webster, 2005). Likewise, the No

Free Lunch program promotes a cognitive shift among general offenders, from avoiding failure to achieving success, by presenting fundamental life principles and problem-solving strategies that offenders can use to become optimally successful and applying those strategies and skills to build character, accumulate financial security, ensure healthy living, and encourage life-plan development. Although much more research is necessary, results for those completing the program in a Wisconsin minimum-security facility are encouraging, with recidivism rates of 3% after 3 years of release.

Concepts such as "flourishing," "a meaningful life," and "offender happiness" are not consistent with the current social and political antipathy toward offenders or with the punitive-retributive model of criminal justice. However, data that reflect the lack of efficacy of our current crime-management system clearly invite a reexamination of that model. Positive psychology may provide a meaningful alternative to traditional modes of offender treatment. However, whether it is more effective than current approaches and whether it represents fundamental or semantic differences from current approaches remains unanswered.

OFFENDER REINTEGRATION

The Office of Justice Programs (2004) estimated that more than 630,000 offenders were released from federal and state custody in 2004. Because many of these offenders eventually relapse (P. A. Langan & Levin, 2002), public attention has focused on the issue of offender reentry (Rakis, 2005), and researchers have suggested factors that must be addressed to enhance community reentry and reduce recidivism. These include using more careful, empirically based risk-assessment procedures on entry into prison (Birmingham, Gray, Mason, & Grubin, 2000), careful screening of offenders with mental health problems prior to their release from prisons or jails (Gagliardi, Lovell, Peterson, & Jemelka, 2004; Petersilia, 2004), more corrections-based

educational and vocational training programs to teach marketable job skills (Rakis, 2005), more vocational and work programs to develop good work habits (Saylor & Gaes, 1997), and better discharge planning activities and meaningful community linkages to make services immediately available on release (Hammett, Roberts, & Kennedy, 2001).

Past practices of managing prisoner reentry by single agencies working in isolation have not been successful because they have resulted in needy offenders "falling through the cracks," vital services being interrupted, therapeutic alliances being disrupted, and agencies engaging in inefficient, duplicative data-gathering and treatment activities (Lurigio, Rollins, & Fallon, 2004). Consequently, a more collaborative, efficient, systems-oriented approach has been proposed and supported by such federal government efforts as the Reentry Partnership Initiative, which actively promotes collaboration in planning and implementation (Rakis, 2005), and the Criminal Justice/Mental Health Consensus Project, which seeks bipartisan agreement among the various stakeholders in the criminal justice and mental health systems (Thompson, Reuland, & Souweine, 2003). Under this collaborative model, a multitude of agencies are encouraged to work together to address the myriad issues associated with moving all types of offenders back into the community. Furthermore, collaborative roles have been proposed for police (Byrne & Hummer, 2004); probation and parole officers (Lurigio et al., 2004; Rakis, 2005); academic institutions (Kendig, 2004); community mental health agencies and clinicians (N. Wolff, 2005); correctional educational, vocational, and treatment practitioners (Rakis, 2005); community-based substance abuse treatment agencies (Butzin, Martin, & Inciardi, 2005); and community-based hospital and medical practitioners (Hammett et al., 2001). However, what happens when agencies such as these, with their diversity of ideologies and practices, are brought together in a collaborative model remains largely unknown and is, in itself, a topic for further research.

Innovative electronic technologies (e.g., electronic monitoring, telehealth, and video-conferencing) have been suggested to connect correctional and community-based services and to enhance community supervision (Pattavina, 2004). However, little empirical research has been conducted to determine which combinations of services offered by which agencies targeting which offender needs will prove most successful in reducing offender recidivism. Other innovative suggestions include a restructuring of data-collection systems so that various agencies can share information and avoid duplication (Rakis, 2005), more cross-training and cultural awareness among agencies and organizations involved in the reentry process (Lurigio et al., 2004), and better public education.

Although our focus has been on reintegration, "front end" entry also deserves attention. There are now many criminal justice entry pathways, particularly for mentally disordered and substance-abusing offenders. Anecdotal evidence and some program-evaluation research suggest that these programs are effective (e.g., Broner, Mayrl, & Landsberg, 2005). For example, Steadman (2001) demonstrated the value of diversion programs that include well-integrated community services for mentally disordered offenders who would otherwise be in jail. Marlowe (2003) reported that drug courts that use structured behavioral and cognitive-behavioral programs are associated with the greatest reductions in drug use and recidivism, and meta-analyses suggest a 7.5% to 10.7% reduction in recidivism rates (Aos et al., 2006). However, others have noted that scientifically rigorous empirical research is still lacking (N. Wolff & Pogorzelski, 2005). The evaluation of specialized courts is complicated by the nonstandardized nature of these programs and the various definitions used to measure success. Drug court research has been criticized for its inadequate comparison groups, relatively brief follow-up periods, and limited range of outcome measures (Belenko, 2002). Future evaluation of specialized courts should address these issues.

CONCLUSION

First, we call for more collaborative efforts between correctional practitioners and researchers. Although correctional professionals who provide treatment may be in a position to evaluate the effectiveness of their services and contribute to the current correctional knowledge base, they may be impeded by constant clinical demands. Researchers, on the other hand, may have the luxury to design ideal studies but may lack access to and insight about the dynamics of prison life. Jointly, they can plan and conduct treatment-outcome studies that need not be overly intensive or cumbersome. The evaluation of outcomes, including clinical trials, should use reliable and valid measures, administered over time, to afford insight into the long-term benefits of the provided services. In developing an evaluation plan, researchers should not focus solely on recidivism but conduct a multiple source assessment, including behavioral assessment, functional domain assessment, collateral assessments, and quality of care.

Second, we ask, What are the kinds of advances that should be sought by the time *Criminal Justice and Behavior* celebrates its 40th anniversary in the next decade? Although we probably will still be asking about "what works," answers to the more specific questions about for whom does it work, when does it work, and how does it work should become clearer, particularly in the treatment of sexual offenders for which further direction is very much required. We should also know more about offender motivation and preparation for treatment to minimize client attrition and maximize treatment impact. Emerging approaches to offender intervention, such as those based on "good lives" and positive psychology, require the same kind of detailed process and outcome evaluation from which cognitive-behavioral interventions have learned and benefited during the past three decades. Finally, we should know more about combinations of treatment and treatment in its various criminal justice contexts, including diversion from prison, transition from prison, and reintegration after prison.

24

What Is Correctional About Clinical Practice in Corrections?

Philip R. Magaletta

Marc W. Patry

Erik F. Dietz

Robert K. Ax

The ever-growing need for mental health services in corrections is resulting from an escalation in incarceration rates, the high prevalence of mental illness and substance abuse among offenders, and several decades of social changes that expanded opportunities for mental health professionals in the field of corrections (Bartol & Bartol, 2004a; Diamond, Wang, Holzer, Thomas, & Cruser, 2001; Harrison &

Beck, 2004; Magaletta & Boothby, 2003; Otto & Heilbrun, 2002). Beyond the application of mental health principles to individuals who "just happen" to be in prison, clinical practice in corrections is a complex enterprise. It requires a keen understanding and broad mastery of the profession's unique body of knowledge as it is applied in the prison. Considering the salient outcomes in effective clinical practice in corrections

Editors' Note: This article was first published in *Criminal Justice and Behavior,* Vol. 34, No. 1, January 2007, pp. 7–21. Reprinted with permission of Sage Publications. We have deleted three tables, some results on training, and parts of the discussion section.

(i.e., preventing suicide, self-harm, [and] physical and sexual assault; increasing the likelihood of drug and alcohol recovery and successful community reentry), it is clear that adequate academic and continuing education/training for correctional mental health professionals is imperative (Carter, 1991; Magaletta & Verdeyen, 2005).

Unfortunately, little objective knowledge exists to indicate which core bodies of knowledge should underlie such training. Although academics have a mission partially focusing on generating new and objective knowledge, clinical practice in corrections has rarely been the focus of such knowledge. Equally problematic is the fact that correctional employees typically function under an "action imperative." In resolving one crisis after another, they rarely have the time, mission, budget, or human capital needed to generate knowledge regarding effective clinical practices (Kendig, 2004; Magaletta & Boothby, 2003). Adding to this reality are the considerable complexities involved in actually providing, coordinating, or evaluating clinical services in corrections. Offenders display numerous combinations of mental health problems rarely encountered in other settings, and service providers rarely assume just one role. Furthermore, the correctional system itself comprises nested systems, each of which exerts its own unique influence on clinical practice.

Psychologists remain the most frequently employed mental health professional practicing in today's correctional environment (Camp & Camp, 2000). Studies that have examined such psychologists have mainly focused on their most frequently performed job duties. Since the 1940s, this literature has consistently suggested that psychologists are likely to spend their time providing assessment and treatment to offenders (Boothby & Clements, 2000; Burton, 1948; Corsini, 1945; Corsini & Miller, 1954; Levinson, 1985; Sell, 1955; Silber, 1974; R. R. Smith & Sabatino, 1990). More recent research (Boothby & Clements, 2000) has also indicated that administrative tasks consume the largest amount of work time, 30%. Although this literature provides a starting point for understanding the nature of psychologists' work from a temporal perspective (i.e., what do they spend most of their time doing), the meaning of frequently performed tasks may simply reflect the mandates of policy and the volume of offenders, not the contextual and more nuanced dimensions of the work. Aspects of the work that are important despite their infrequent use remain unexplored, as do those areas that prison administrators expect from their mental health staff, such as the management of risk.

To grow the science in this area beyond analyses of frequently performed job duties, a training survey was developed to obtain a range of relevant, objective information about the knowledge used and training needed by contemporary psychology service providers in the Federal Bureau of Prisons (BOP). The BOP, with more than 187,000 offenders in custody, is now the United States' largest prison system (Harrison & Beck, 2004). With a doctoral-level hiring standard, the system employs more than 350 psychologists, who provide direct mental health care and consultative services in more than 110 facilities. Facilities range in mission (e.g., detention centers that function like jails and in-house medical centers that provide inpatient medical services) and security level (minimum, low, medium, and high security).

To inform the training, clinical practices, and evaluation techniques used by these BOP psychologists, we empirically examined the core bodies of knowledge that psychologists use in their various roles and duties. In addition, the developmental sequence of training in and for those areas was explored. As such, this work represents an important first step in delineating empirically supported training domains germane to the needs of psychologists practicing in this highly complex environment with one of the neediest mental health populations in the United States.

METHOD

Participants

Eligible participants for this study were psychology service providers in all BOP institutions during the summer of 2002 who returned a copy of the training survey. Of the distributed surveys, 309 were returned, resulting in a 52% return rate. Of the returned surveys, 177 were from doctoral-level psychologists, and 132 were from treatment program specialists. The educational backgrounds and direct services provided by these two groups remain distinct. The present analysis will focus on the frontline mental health/psychology service providers—the doctoral-level psychologists.

A summary profile of all psychologist respondents is provided in Table 24.1 and reveals adequate representation within each of the professional demographics measured. The modal psychologist who responded to the survey was a licensed, doctoral-level psychologist working at a medium-security facility with about 7.5 years of service. For those psychologists sampled, 38% held a PhD in clinical psychology, another 38% possessed the PsyD in clinical psychology, and 20% had a PhD in counseling psychology. Thirty-six percent had completed a predoctoral internship with the BOP and 64% had not. In terms of participants' current positions, there was approximately one third of the sample in each of three core positions: staff psychologist, treatment program coordinator, and chief psychologist.

Instrumentation

To conduct this study, the "Federal Bureau of Prisons Training Analysis of Psychology Services and Staff Positions Survey" (July 2002) was created. An expert consensus method was used to generate survey items. Seven senior psychology services staff from the BOP, representing a mix of clinicians and administrators with an average of 16 years with the agency, were recruited for this group. They were asked to construct a comprehensive list of clinical and administrative bodies of knowledge that would characterize the operation of maximally effective psychology service departments. For the purpose of consistency in survey design, these bodies of knowledge were referred to as job functions.

Through consensus, similar initial job functions were combined to form a final list of 41 functions. Next, individual items to define each job function were created. These too were refined and combined through consensus until 96 individual items tapping the 41 job functions were agreed on.

Next, two measurement structures, training and descriptive, were created and applied to each job function. Respondents were asked to provide information regarding these structures as they related to their current positions. In the training structure, respondents were asked to indicate the points during their education at which they had received (if at all) training in a job function. Response options included graduate school, internship, postgraduate BOP-sponsored new psychologist training, continuing education, on-the-job, and no training.

In the descriptive structure, information was gathered on three questions for each individual item in the survey. These questions, called importance, frequency, and risk (IFR), allowed for each knowledge domain to be simultaneously assessed from multiple vantage points. In this way, IFR served as a three-dimensional model from which training goals and priorities could be identified. Each of the IFR questions was scaled along a 5-point, Likert-type index (from 0 to 4). The importance question read, "How important is this [job function] in your current position? How central is this knowledge, skill, or ability in fulfilling your role or completing the tasks assigned to you?" and was scored $0 =$ no importance, $1 =$ blank, $2 =$ average importance, $3 =$ blank, and $4 =$ greatest importance. The frequency question read, "How frequently do you use this [job function] in your current position?" and was scored $0 =$ never, $1 =$ quarterly, $2 =$ monthly, $3 =$ weekly, and $4 =$ daily. The risk question read, "How risky/critical is this [job function]? In your current position, to what degree would it compromise the safe and orderly running of an institution if the knowledge were lacking or ability/skill were deficient/negligent?" and was scored $0 =$ low risk, $1 =$ blank, $2 =$ moderate risk, $3 =$ blank, and $4 =$ high risk.

Table 24.1   Profile of Psychologist Respondents (N = 177)

Position Title	Percentage	Frequency
Chief psychologist	31.1	55
Treatment program coordinator	32.2	57
Staff psychologist	31.1	55
Direct clinical training	4.0	7
Forensic examiner	1.7	3
Degree held		
Clinical (PhD)	38.4	68
Clinical (PsyD)	37.9	67
Counseling (PhD)	19.2	34
Clinical/counseling (EdD)	2.8	5
Predoctoral BOP internship?		
Yes	36.0	59
No	64.0	105
Licensed?		
Yes	73.4	130
No	26.6	47
Less than 1 year	4.5	8
1 to 5 years	34.5	61
6 to 10 years	33.9	60
11 to 15 years	18.6	33
16 or more years	7.9	14
Facility type		
Maximum	2.8	5
High	8.5	15
Medium	33.9	60
Low	22.6	40
Minimum	11.9	21
Admin/medical referral	11.3	20
Admin/detention	8.5	15

NOTE. BOP = Federal Bureau of Prisons

Procedure

A research team located in the Psychology Services Branch of the Correctional Programs Division designed, distributed, and collected the survey by mail in the summer of 2002. Approximately 595 surveys were distributed in packets to 99 institutions. Each packet was addressed to the chief psychologist of the institution's psychology services department. A cover letter was enclosed that invited the chief to participate voluntarily in the anonymous survey and to invite all treatment staff . . . to complete the enclosed surveys as well. Treatment staff included doctoral-level psychologists and nonpsychologist correctional treatment program staff. The latter staff are non-doctoral providers, usually substance abuse treatment specialists.

Several data-analytic strategies were used to create manageable, parsimonious, and meaningful units of analysis and thus meet the primary objective of identifying job functions most salient in terms of IFR. In the interest of parsimony, once the internal consistency of the individual-level items was obtained, item-level measurements were aggregated within each job function by using participants' mean ratings for each of the IFR measurement dimensions. These job function–level mean scores for each category were then rank ordered, and the top 10 most important, most frequently used, and highest risk (conceptualized as the most critical) bodies of knowledge were retained for the next level of analysis. [The researchers then employed additional methods to refine their selection of core bodies of knowledge.]

****

Once each core body of knowledge was selected, the types of training received for each was explored.

RESULTS

Core Bodies of Knowledge

Overall, 9 of the original 41 job functions emerged as core bodies of knowledge. The titles of the core bodies of knowledge are listed in Table 24.2, and the individual items that made up each core body are delineated in Table 24.3. The two core bodies of knowledge rated as most important were psychopathology and suicide prevention (for means higher than the grand mean of the top 10 job functions in the importance category, see Table 24.2). Psychopathology and interdepartmental communications/relationships were tapped almost daily and were the most frequently used core bodies of knowledge (for means higher than the grand mean of the top 10 job functions in the frequency category, see Table 24.2). Environmental factors (special housing unit; SHU), suicide prevention, psychopathology, safety, and confrontation avoidance were the top job functions in the risk category (for means higher than the grand mean of the top 10 job functions in the risk category, see Table 24.2). Participants indicated that these were the areas most likely to compromise the safe and orderly running of an institution if in

their current position the knowledge were lacking or ability/skill were deficient/[negligible].

Among this aforementioned list of statistically significant job functions, six remained unique (psychopathology, suicide prevention, interdepartmental communications/relationships, environmental factors [SHU], safety, and confrontation avoidance). Psychopathology actually appeared in each IFR category, and suicide prevention appeared in the importance and risk categories. Thus, there were only six statistically significant job functions that were retained among the core bodies of knowledge and examined in subsequent analyses.

To further determine if nonstatistically significant but operationally meaningful trends existed in the data, job functions that were simultaneously endorsed across each of the top 10 IFR categories were captured. Overall, three knowledge bases met these criteria and were added to core bodies of knowledge: ethical issues, medical/psychopharmacology, and clinical psychopathy.

DISCUSSION

Findings from this study provide a basic empirical answer to the question, "Just what is correctional about clinical practice in corrections?" At least in part, the answer is the prison environment itself. The core bodies reflect the reciprocal influence of individual-level psychopathology and the correctional environment in the day-to-day clinical practice of correctional psychology. These discrete bodies of knowledge can serve to shape the training of those who wish to enter clinical practice in corrections or have already begun their public service careers in corrections.

At the center of the psychologist's work, only one core body of knowledge was statistically significant [with respect to . . . each of the three IFR [questions (i.e., importance, frequency, and risk)]. Psychopathology was statistically distinguished from other core bodies of knowledge by being of greatest importance, being used daily, and being of high risk when knowledge in that area was absent. It is clearly the body of knowledge around which much of the BOP psychologists' work is organized. Indeed, many of the other knowledge bases selected (e.g., suicide prevention, environmental factors/SHU, psychopharmacology) are conceptually linked to a deep understanding of psychopathology.

Overall, the finding that the knowledge of psychopathology is important and frequently used in the correctional environment is of little surprise. Once thought of as an indicator of "special need," the presence of psychopathology in correctional populations has actually become one of their defining features. A recent summative review on the topic suggested that the prevalence of mental illness in prisons is higher than in the community and that comorbidities are common (Diamond et al., 2001). With psychologists increasingly involved in the biological aspects of mental health treatment, psychopharmacology was also found in each of the top 10 IFR rankings. Given that psychologists continue to serve as liaisons in prison psychiatry clinics through [T]elehealth (Magaletta, Fagan, & Ax, 1998) or with psychiatrists consulting directly in BOP institutions (R. D. Morgan, 2003), the need for and interest in this knowledge is only expected to increase. Furthermore, Fagan et al. (2004) recently found that interns and training directors (combined) in correctional settings were more interested in pursuing prescription privileges than their counterparts in other surveyed internship programs (e.g., at Veterans Affairs Medical Centers). Not coincidently, Ax and Morgan (2002) found that most BOP internship programs were already offering training in psychopharmacology, highlighting an increasing ability to meet training with need and interest.

An interesting pattern emerged when considering the IFR pattern for interdepartmental communications/relations. Although it is not even ranked in the top 10 for importance or risk, it makes a statistically significant entry with its weekly use. Knowledge of the prison environment and its interrelated systems (Magaletta et al., 1998) is used daily and remains an essential resource for carrying out

or supporting the content of other important and/or risky work (e.g., suicide prevention and working in segregation).

Ranked among the most important and riskiest bodies of knowledge, suicide prevention remains a major focus of BOP psychologists' work. Every year, psychologists train all new and existing staff in the identification and referral of suicidal inmates. During the 5-year period from [January] 1999 to [December] 2003, the number of completed suicide risk assessments rose 32%. In 2005, BOP psychologists completed more than 4,100 suicide risk assessments and 1,700 suicide watches.

The core body of knowledge ranked highest in the risk category was environmental factors, or knowledge of managing the mentally ill in SHU. This finding again highlights the degree to which an understanding of both psychopathology and the correctional environment itself undergird clinical practice in corrections. Given the historical trend of completed suicides and other acting-out behaviors often witnessed in segregation units (Rhodes, 2004), it is not surprising that this knowledge base entered through the risk category. The risk management work that psychologists perform in segregation remains most crucial to prisons' dual mission of custody and care. More than any other, it is their work in SHU that distinguishes psychologists as specialists and requires the use of their unique training and knowledge (Magaletta, Ax, Patry, & Dietz, 2005).

Confrontation avoidance was measured along two risk-related dimensions in this study. One definition was the first step in the progressive use of force model: active listening/verbal communication/crisis intervention. Because most use of force occurs in segregation units (Collins, 2004), this core body is thought to link very closely to segregation knowledge. The second item tapping confrontation avoidance dealt more globally with knowing how to intervene with an inmate to avoid further confrontation. At this more general level, confrontation avoidance suggests a quality, process, or aspect of effective management and treatment conducted with offenders.

Conceptually linked to this second definition of confrontation avoidance and again through the risk category was safety. When confrontation avoidance is effective, it prevents harm to staff and inmates and assists in maintaining the orderly running of the institution. An examination of the item-level comparisons and the high alpha coefficients suggests that psychologists conceptualize safety along both clinical and custodial lines, just as they do confrontation avoidance. Consistent with previous and more recent literature, safety is conceptualized as an important risk area even among psychology graduate students who are considering working at a secure facility (Morgan, Beer, Fitzgerald, & Mandracchia, [2007]; Norton, 1990). It is interesting that safety is one of the most salient factors leading to job satisfaction among correctional psychologists (Boothby & Clements, 2002).

Consistent with their status as mental health care professionals and their assumption of a public trust, BOP psychologists clearly identified ethics as a core body of knowledge. Clinical practice in corrections presents several unique professional features (Dignam, 2003), including multiple roles, and psychologists continue to endorse an understanding of ethical issues and how to resolve them for its importance, frequency of use, and risk if absent.

TRAINING AND BUILDING KNOWLEDGE FOR CLINICAL PRACTICE IN CORRECTIONS

The data clearly show that those entering clinical practice in corrections can be expected to arrive with solid academic exposure to core clinical areas such as psychopathology, suicide prevention, psychopharmacology, psychopathy, and ethics. For these clinicians, the "already received" academic training/exposure areas should be reinforced with specialized training. This may be conceptualized as moving from the mastery of knowledge to the application of skills for effective correctional practice. For example, clinicians could build on knowledge of standard suicide risk markers. They could be taught to query correctional staff as part of the suicide risk assessment process and to investigate if the offender has been giving away [his or her] possessions, a behavior recognized as a suicide risk factor in correctional work.

It does appear that aspects of graduate school curriculums are tapping and exposing students to areas of knowledge relevant to correctional work. For faculty and students interested in correctional work, these aspects can be highlighted and condensed to form a specialized course of study. In addition, for those students already involved in a correctional practicum or predoctoral internship, didactics might be revised to align with, emphasize, and build on the core domains outlined in this study.

A second trend seen in the training data was observed for areas more central to working in the prison environment, such as managing the mentally ill in segregation, confrontation avoidance, and staying safe on the job. For these areas, low reported rates for the more formal training (i.e., academic or continuing education training) and very high rates of OJT (on-job training) were observed. In fact, less than 25% of the sample received exposure during graduate school for any of these areas. This finding warrants further consideration and suggests that at least some of the knowledge needed for clinical practice in corrections is generated and transmitted by the prison itself. That is, although psychologists may understand the importance of this work and the risk related to it, they actually gain the knowledge by doing the work. For better or for worse, this knowledge is transmitted experientially as they use first-hand experience as the vehicle for learning.

Beyond the uniqueness of the prison environment itself, another possible reason for the heavy emphasis on experiential learning is that very little formal textbook knowledge or research concerning best clinical practices in this environment exists. For example, no published studies have been found in the literature of psychology, criminology, or sociology that dictate the use of particular assessment tools or intervention techniques within a segregation unit. In essence, those providing services in this highly specialized environment must rely largely on experience and clinical impression that are neither supported nor refuted on scientific grounds.

To meet the challenges that this poses, it is imperative that psychologists involved in correctional work become increasingly involved in the development of such knowledge and flowing from that, its dissemination through continuing education workshops, preemployment training, and written media.

25

MULTISYSTEMIC THERAPY FOR ANTISOCIAL JUVENILES

Suggestions for Improvement

WILLEM H. J. MARTENS

Multisystemic therapy (MST) is an intensive family- and community-based treatment that was developed in the late 1970s to address the mental health needs of youth who were seriously antisocial . . . and their families (Letourneau, Cunningham, & Henggeler, 2002). . . . It is based on a theory of human behavior (i.e., social ecological theory) that is strongly supported by the extant literature. Social ecological theory views individuals as nested within increasingly complex systems. Thus, problem behavior is maintained by problematic interactions within and across the multiple systems in which the child is embedded (Letourneau et al., 2002). MST treats factors that might pertain to individual characteristics of the youth (e.g., poor problem-solving skills), family relations (e.g., inept discipline), peer relations (e.g., association with deviant peers), and school performance (e.g., academic difficulties). On a highly individualized basis, treatment goals are developed in collaboration with the family, and family strengths are used as levers for therapeutic change (Henggeler, Schoenwald, Borduin, Rowlan, & Cunningham, 1998; Henggeler et al., 1999). Intervention strategies include strategic family therapy, structural family therapy, behavioral parental training, and cognitive behavior therapies. The use of a home-based model of service delivery (i.e., low caseloads, time-limited duration of treatment) removes barriers of access

Editors' Note: This article was originally published in the *International Journal of Offender Therapy and Comparative Criminology,* Vol. 48, No. 3, 2004, pp. 389–394. Reprinted with permission of Sage Publications.

to care and provides the high level of intensity needed to successfully treat youth presenting serious clinical problems and their multineed families (Henggeler et al., 1998, 1999). Multisystemic therapy is conducted by two or four therapists and an onsite supervisor, who work together for purposes of group and peer supervision and to support the 24–7 on-call needs of the team's client families. MST staff must be highly accessible to their clients (Henggeler et al., 1998, 1999).

Rowland et al. (2000) and Borduin, Heilbrun, Jones, and Grabe (2000) believed that MST appears to be a clinically effective and cost-effective alternative to out-of-home placements (e.g., incarceration, psychiatric hospitalization) for youth presenting serious clinical problems, such as antisocial behavior. Kazdin (2002), however, asserted that none of the existing intervention/ treatment approaches would ameliorate antisocial disorder and overcome the poor long-term prognosis. Kazdin (2002) and Martens (1997) suggested that there is only mixed evidence for (long-term) success of current MST. The author speculates that a lack of long-lasting [effectiveness] of MST in juveniles who are antisocial might be the consequence of lack of attention to [the following]: (a) neurological treatment of neurobiological dysfunctions that correlate with core features of antisocial behavior (Martens, 2000a, 2001a); (b) specific needs, condition, and coexistent mental disorders of the patient (Martens, 1997, 2000a; van Marle, 1995); (c) specific therapeutic models that are proven effective, such as psychoanalytic or psychodynamic treatment (Kernberg, 1984; van Marle, 1995); and (d) crucial environmental (Minuchin, Montalvo, Guerney, Rosman, & Schumer, 1967) and cultural factors (Martens, 1997) that interfere with treatment affectivity. I suggest that the following important topics, which are hardly considered in current MST approaches, should be included to make this treatment approach more adequate:

• The antisocial patient's old social environment will simply not accept when the patient's

behavior is transformed into harmless, social behavior (Martens, 1997; Minuchin et al., 1967). Thus, most of these juveniles who are antisocial are afraid to demonstrate a prosocial attitude because of rejection by their old environment. Moreover, many juveniles who are antisocial believe that a normal prosocial life and career is boring and only acceptable for stupid/dull people and losers. Without a solution to these problems, any intervention or prevention will have only limited success. Possible solutions could be (a) transfer of the juvenile with antisocial personality disorder (ASPD) and his or her family to a better neighborhood or structural improvement of neighborhood (Martens, 2000a); (b) creation of a more prosocial network; improvement of academic skills, success, and social competence that will lead to increased possibilities for successful prosocial jobs/careers (Martens, 1997, 2000a), higher socioeconomic status, increased self-esteem, social awareness, and as a consequence, a possible decrease of impulsivity/ hostility (Martens, 1997); and (d) stimulation of patient's awareness that a normal, social career and life is not necessarily boring.

• Specific treatment of coexisting mental disorders—most frequently substance abuse disorders, schizophrenia, and other personality disorders (Martens, 2000a) In addition, treatment of trauma or post-traumatic stress disorder (PTSD) (see DSM-IV, 1994) is needed, because many juveniles who are antisocial suffer from (recent) traumatic experiences as a consequence of physical/sexual abuse, neglect and rejection, homelessness, chaotic and violent family life, threatening neighborhood, and so on (Martens, 2000a, 2001/2002). Solomon and Johnson (2002) concluded in their review of outcome research that the strongest support is found for treatments that combine cognitive and behavioral techniques, and that hypnosis, psychodynamic anxiety management, and group therapies also may produce short-term symptom reduction. Because of the neurobiological correlates of PTSD, neurological treatment of these patients might be necessary (Yehuda, 2002).

• Combination of specific psychotherapeutic, neurologic, and neurofeedback treatment of ASPD traits Antisocial features that are frequently neurobiologically determined and thus need neurobiological attention are impulsivity, aggression (Martens, 2000a), sensation seeking (Martens, 2000a; Zuckerman, 1994), poor socialization and lack of guilt or remorse (Fowles & Kochanska, 2000), poor fear conditioning and associated incapacity to learn from experiences (Lykken, 1995; Martens, 2000a), criminality (Raine, Venables, & Williams, 1996), and a lack of moral capacity (Martens, 2000b). Juvenile ADHD, CD, and ODD behavior could be treated effectively with the help of neurofeedback (Horacek, 1998).

• By means of structured fantasy therapy (Garrison & Stolberg, 1983; Giannini, 2001), children and adolescents who are antisocial might be able to transform their hostile and paranoid fantasy world into a social and trustful one.

• Possibilities to learn from aggressive behavior in a controlled setting by means of agitation therapy (Martens, 2001a): This would increase the patient's awareness of his or her core problem and the roots and consequences of his or her aggression as a result of adequate guidance and confrontation with and feedback from others and psychotherapeutic aftercare, which may lead to self-insight and increased social, emotional, and moral capacities. Impressive confrontations with fellow patients and staff members may contribute to the process of remission in ASPD (Martens, 1997, 2000a). However, this treatment approach can only be realized in in-ward settings.

• Possibility for ethical and/or spiritual development, possibly by means of ethics therapy (Martens, 2001d) and/or spiritual psychotherapy (Martens, 2003b) because remission in ASPD may be linked to ethical and spiritual activities and development (Black, Baumgart, & Bell, 1995; Martens, 1997; Robins, 1966).

• Increased responsibilities (as a consequence of parenthood, marriage, joining the armed services, getting a stable job, etc.) might be linked to remission in ASPD (Black et al., 1995; Martens, 2000a; Robins, 1996). Ideal treatment conditions will include a structural enhancement of the patient's responsibilities by means of stimulation of forming of bonds, attachments, or commitments, which are characterized by [the] important dimension of loyalty, sympathy, and/or care.

• Because many children and adolescents who are antisocial are homeless or frequently gadabouts, these juveniles should be offered adequate housing and guidance (hygiene, medical treatment of physical illness; Martens, 2001c, 2001/2002). Current MST programs are hardly tailored for and directed toward homeless juveniles (or those who often run away, are left alone, or are gadabouts).

• Facilities for privacy and relaxation, which might be necessary for adequate reflection, contemplation, and preparation for change, [are needed]. The life of many juveniles who are antisocial is characterized by restlessness, lack of safety, chaos, and a lack of privacy and relaxation, which interferes with healthy development and opportunities for recovery (Martens, 1997, 2000a). Moreover, the patient may experience the facility for privacy as an expression of respect, deep understanding, and constructive attention on the part of the treatment staff.

• Therapeutic circumstances/approaches that are also targeted toward enjoying life, which may include vacations, excursions, and trips, may relate to remission in ASPD (Martens, 2000a): Important learning moments (positive experiences, contacts, refreshing changes) occur frequently and could be stimulated easily during these pleasant events.

• Cultural influences may play an important role in the development of antisocial behavior. For instance, some refugees have different moral ideation and some behavioral manifestations that are regarded in the West as socially undesirable that are in the refugees' eyes acceptable (Martens, 1997). Only therapists with an understanding of these cultural dimensions of antisocial behavior may be able to change the patient's attitude.

• To meet the psychosocial, neurobiological, and psychiatric therapeutic needs of antisocial youth and to enhance the effectiveness and positive long-term outcome of MST, I suggest that a neurologist, a forensic psychiatrist, a neurofeedback specialist, a pediatrician, a trauma therapist, and a social worker involved with the homeless worker should be added to the standard MST team.

I conclude, in contrast to others (Borduin et al., 2000; Henggeler et al., 1998, 1999; Letourneau et al., 2002), that MST is mainly appropriate for those individuals who are antisocial and their families who are motivated for it, and who are not severely (a) emotionally, socially, and morally disturbed and/or traumatized; (b) abused, rejected, and neglected by their relatives; (c) angry, hostile, and rancorous; and (d) at risk of reoffending, and who are capable of cooperating with relatives and MST staff and understanding instructions. Otherwise, a forensic psychiatric treatment community would be more suitable because it is evident that only therapeutic community treatment is effective in juveniles who are severely impaired, abused, and neglected (Martens, 1997; 2003a; Ministry of Justice, 2002; van Marle, 1995). Treatment of such juveniles should take place explicitly (at least in the initial phase) away from the influence of abusive, chaotic family and friends, even when these people are willing to change their attitudes. Only when the patient becomes strong enough and able to cope with his or her negative memories, traumas, and the impact of peers and relatives is it useful that he or she be gradually involved in the MST process.

REFERENCES

Abarbanel, G. (1986). Rape and resistance. *Journal of Interpersonal Violence, 1,* 100–111.

Abbey, A., Ross, L. T., McDuffie, D., & McAuslan, P. (1996). Alcohol and dating risk factors for sexual assault among college women. *Psychology of Women Quarterly, 20,* 147–169.

Abel, G. G., Becker, J. V., Mittelman, M. S., Cunningham-Rathner, J., Rouleau, J. L., & Murphy, W. D. (1987). Self-reported sex crimes of nonincarcerated paraphilics. *Journal of Interpersonal Violence, 2,* 3–25.

Abel, G. G., Becker, J. V., Murphy, W. D., & Flanagan, B. (1981). Identifying dangerous child molesters. In R. B. Steward (Ed.), *Violent behavior: Social learning approaches to prediction, management and treatment.* New York: Brunner-Mazel.

Abramovitch, R., Higgins-Biss, K., & Biss, S. (1993). Young persons' comprehension of waivers in criminal proceedings. *Canadian Journal of Criminology, 35,* 309–322.

Abramovitch, R., Peterson-Badali, M., & Rohan, M. (1995). Young people's understanding and assertion of their rights to silence and legal counsel. *Canadian Journal of Criminology, 37,* 1–18.

Acoca, L. (1998). Defusing the time bomb: Understanding and meeting the growing health care needs of incarcerated women in America. *Crime & Delinquency, 44,* 46–69.

Adam, L. T., & Worden, P. E. (1986). Script development and memory organization in preschool and elementary school children. *Discourse Process, 9,* 149–166.

Ainsworth, P. B. (1995). *Psychology and policing in a changing world.* New York: Wiley.

Ajaelo, I., Koenig, K., & Snoey, E. (1998). Severe hyponatremia and inappropriate antidiuretic hormone secretion following ecstasy use. *Academy of Emergency Medicine, 5,* 839–840.

Aldridge, J., & Cameron, S. (1999). Interviewing child witnesses: Questioning techniques and the role of training. *Applied Developmental Science, 3,* 136–147.

Aldridge, M., & Wood, J. (1997). Talking about feelings: Young children's ability to express emotions. *Child Abuse & Neglect, 21,* 1221–1233.

Aldwin, C. M. (1994). *Stress, coping, and development: An integrative perspective.* New York: Guilford Press.

Alexander, M. A. (1999). Sexual offender treatment efficacy revisited. *Sexual Abuse: Journal of Research and Treatment, 11,* 101–116.

Alison, L. J., Bennell, C., Mokros, A., & Ormerod, D. (2002). The personality paradox in offender profiling: A theoretical review of the processes involved in deriving background characteristics from crime scene actions. *Psychology, Public Policy, and Law, 8,* 115–135.

Allison, K. W., Crawford, I., Echemendia, R., Robinson, L., & Kemp, D. (1994). Human diversity and professional competence: Training in clinical and counseling psychology revisited. *American Psychologist, 49,* 792–796.

American Association on Mental Retardation. (2002). *The AAMR definition of mental retardation.* Retrieved June 1, 2003, from http://www.aaidd.org/Policies/faq_mental_retardation.shtml

American Educational Research Association, American Psychological Association, & National Council on Measurement in Education. (1999). *Standards for educational and psychological testing* (3rd ed.). Washington, DC: Author.

American Psychiatric Association. (1968). *Diagnostic and statistical manual of mental disorders* (2nd ed.). Washington, DC: Author.

American Psychiatric Association. (1980). *Diagnostic and statistical manual of mental disorders* (3rd ed.). Washington, DC: Author.

American Psychiatric Association. (1994). *Diagnostic and statistical manual of mental disorders* (4th ed.). Washington, DC: Author.

American Psychological Association. (1985). *Standards for educational and psychological testing.* Washington, DC: Author.

American Psychological Association. (1993). Guidelines for providers of psychological services to ethnic, linguistic, and culturally diverse populations. *American Psychologist, 48,* 45–48.

American Psychological Association. (1994). Guidelines for child custody evaluations in divorce proceedings. *American Psychologist, 49,* 677–680.

American Psychological Association. (1996). *Violence and the family: Report of the American Psychological Association Presidential Task Force on Violence and the Family.* Washington, DC: Author.

American Psychological Association. (2002). *Ethical principles of psychologists and code of conduct.* Washington, DC: Author.

American Psychological Association. (2003). Ethical principles of psychologists and code of conduct. *American Psychologist, 57,* 1060–1073.

Americans with Disabilities Act of 1990, 42 U.S.C.A. § 12101 et seq. (West 1993).

Amir, M. (1971). *Patterns in forcible rape.* Chicago: University of Chicago Press.

Anderson, L. A., & Whiston, S. C. (2005). Sexual assault education programs: A meta-analytic examination of their effectiveness. *Psychology of Women Quarterly, 29,* 374–388.

Andrews, A. (1991). Social work expert testimony regarding mitigation in capital sentencing proceedings. *Social Work, 36,* 440–444.

Andrews, D. A. (2001). Principles of effective correctional programs. In L. L. Motiuk & R. C. Serin (Eds.), *Compendium 2000 on effective correctional programming* (pp. 9–17). Ottawa: Correctional Service of Canada.

Andrews, D. A., & Bonta, J. (1995). *The Level of Service Inventory—Revised.* Toronto, Ont., Canada: Multi-Health Systems.

Andrews, D. A., & Bonta, J. (1998). *The psychology of criminal conduct* (2nd ed.). Cincinnati, OH: Anderson.

Andrews, D. A., & Bonta, J. (2003). *The psychology of criminal conduct* (3rd ed.). Cincinnati, OH: Anderson.

Andrews, D. A., Bonta, J., & Hoge, R. D. (1990). Classification for effective rehabilitation: Rediscovering psychology. *Criminal Justice and Behavior, 17,* 19–52.

Andrews, D. A., Bonta, J., & Wormith, J. S. (2006). The recent past and near future of risk and/or need assessment. *Crime & Delinquency, 52,* 7–27.

Andrews, D. A., & Dowden, C. (2005). Managing correctional treatment for reduced recidivism: A meta-analytic review of program integrity. *Legal and Criminological Psychology, 10,* 173–187.

Andrews, D. A., Zinger, I., Hoge, R., Bonta, J., Gendreau, P., & Cullen, F. (1990). Does correctional treatment work? A clinically relevant and psychologically informed meta-analysis. *Criminology, 28,* 369–404.

Annon, J. S. (1995). Investigative profiling: A behavioral analysis of the crime scene. *American Journal of Forensic Psychology, 13,* 67–75.

Aos, S., Miller, M., & Drake, E. (2006). *Evidence-based adult corrections programs: What works and what does not.* Olympia: Washington State Institute for Public Policy.

Aos, S., Phipps, P., Barnoski, E., & Leib, R. (2001). *The comparative costs and benefits of programs to reduce crime.* Olympia: Washington State Institute for Public Policy.

Araji, S., & Finkelhor, D. (1985). Explanations of pedophilia: Review of empirical research. *Bulletin of the American Academy of Psychiatry and the Law, 13,* 17–37.

Artiola i Fortuny, L., & Mullaney, H. A. (1998). Assessing patients whose language you do not know: Can the absurd be ethical? *The Clinical Neuropsychologist, 12,* 113–126.

Åsgard, U. (1998). Swedish experiences in offender profiling and evaluation of some aspects of a case of murder and abduction in Germany. In *Case Analysis Unit (BKA), Method of Case Analysis: An International Symposium* (pp. 125–129). Wiesbaden, Germany: Bundeskriminalamt Kriminalistisches Institut.

Ash, P., Slora, K. B., & Britton, C. F. (1990). Police agency officer selection practices. *Journal of Police Science and Administration, 17,* 258–269.

Association for Family and Conciliation Courts. (1994). Courts model standards of practice for child custody evaluations. *Family and Conciliation Courts Review, 32,* 504–513.

Ault, R. L., & Reese, J. T. (1980). A psychological assessment of crime profiling. *FBI Law Enforcement Bulletin, 49,* 22–25.

Aurand, S. K., Addessa, R., & Bush, C. (1985). *Violence and discrimination against Philadelphia lesbian and gay people.* Philadelphia: Philadelphia Lesbian and Gay Task Force Report.

Austin, W. G. (2000). Assessing credibility in allegations of marital violence in the high-conflict child custody case. *Family and Conciliation Courts Review, 38,* 462–477.

Austin, W. G. (2001). Partner violence and risk assessment in child custody evaluations. *Family Court Review, 39,* 483–496.

Ax, R. K., & Morgan, R. D. (2002). Internship training opportunities in correctional psychology: A comparison of settings. *Criminal Justice and Behavior, 29,* 332–347.

Aylward, J. (1985). Psychological testing and police selection. *Journal of Police Science and Administration, 13,* 201–210.

Babiak, P. (1995). When psychopaths go to work. *International Journal of Applied Psychology, 44,* 171–188.

Bachman, R. (1994). *Violence against women: A National Crime Victimization Survey Report.* Washington, DC: U.S. Department of Justice, Bureau of Justice Statistics.

Bachman, R. (1998). The factors related to rape reporting behavior and arrest: New evidence from the National Crime Victimization Survey. *Criminal Justice and Behavior, 25,* 8–29.

Bancroft, L., & Silverman, J. G. (2002). *The batterer as parent: Addressing the impact of domestic violence on family dynamics.* Thousand Oaks, CA: Sage.

Bandura, A. (1989). Human agency in social cognitive theory. *American Psychologist, 44,* 1175–1184.

Bandura, A. (1997). *Self-efficacy: The exercise of control.* New York: Freeman.

Banyard, V. L., Plante, E. G., & Moynihan, M. (2004). Bystander education: Bringing broader community perspective to sexual violence prevention. *Journal of Community Psychology, 32,* 61–79.

Barbaree, H. E., & Marshall, W. L. (1988). Deviant sexual arousal, offense history, and demographic variables as predictors of reoffense among child molesters and incest offenders. *Behavioral Sciences & the Law, 6,* 267–280.

Barbarin, O. A. (1993). Coping and resilience: Exploring the inner lives of African American children. *Journal of Black Psychology, 19,* 478–492.

Bard, M. (1969). Family intervention police teams as a community mental health resource. *Journal of Criminal Law, Criminology, and Police Science, 60,* 247–250.

Bard, M., & Berkowitz, B. (1969). A community psychology consultation program in police family crisis intervention: Preliminary impressions. *International Journal of Social Psychiatry, 15,* 209–215.

Barrick, M. R., & Mount, M. D. (1991). The big five personality dimensions and job performance: A meta-analysis. *Personnel Psychology, 44,* 1–26.

Bart, P. B., & O'Brien, P. (1985). *Stopping rape.* New York: Pergamon.

Bartol, C. R. (1991). Predictive validation of the MMPI for small-town police officers who fail. *Professional Psychology: Research and Practice, 22,* 127–132.

Bartol, C. R. (1996). Police psychology: Then, now, and beyond. *Criminal Justice and Behavior, 23,* 70–89.

Bartol, C. R. (1999). *Criminal behavior: A psychosocial approach* (5th ed.). Englewood Cliffs, NJ: Prentice Hall.

Bartol, C. R, & Bartol, A. M. (2008). *Criminal behavior: A psychosocial approach* (8th ed.). Upper Saddle River, NJ: Prentice Hall.

Bartol, C. R., & Bartol, A. M. (1987). History of forensic psychology. In I. B Weiner & A. K. Hess (Eds.), *Handbook of forensic psychology.* New York: Wiley.

Bartol, C. R., & Bartol, A. M. (1994). *Psychology and law: Research and application* (2nd ed.). Pacific Grove, CA: Brooks/Cole.

Bartol, C. R., & Bartol, A. M. (2004a). *Introduction to forensic psychology.* Thousand Oaks, CA: Sage.

Bartol, C. R., & Bartol, A. M. (2004b). *Psychology and law: Theory, research, and application* (3rd ed.). Pacific Grove, CA: Brooks/Cole.

Bartol, C. R., & Bartol, A. M. (2009). Forensic psychology: Introduction and overview. In C. R. Bartol & A. M. Bartol, *Introduction to forensic psychology* (2nd ed.) (Chapter 1). Thousand Oaks, CA: Sage.

Bartol, C. R., & Bartol, A. M. (in press). *Juvenile delinquency and antisocial behavior: A developmental perspective* (3rd ed.). Upper Saddle River, NJ: Prentice Hall.

Bartol, C. R., Bergen, G. T., Volckens, J. S., & Knoras, K. M. (1992). Women in small-town policing: Job performance and stress. *Criminal Justice and Behavior, 19,* 240–259.

Bartol, C. R., Griffin, R., & Clark, M. (1993, July). *Nationwide survey of American correctional psychologists.* Unpublished manuscript.

Bates, J. E., Pettit, G. S., Dodge, K. A., & Ridge, B. (1998). Interaction of temperamental resistance to control and restrictive parenting in the development of externalizing behavior. *Developmental Psychology, 34,* 982–995.

Bazemore, G., & Pranis, K. (1997). Hazards along the way: Practitioners should stay true to the principles behind restorative justice. *Corrections Today, 59*(7), 25–38.

Bazemore, G., & Umbreit, M. (1995). Rethinking the sanctioning function in juvenile court: Retribution or restorative responses to youth crime. *Crime & Delinquency, 41,* 296–316.

Bazemore, G., & Umbreit, M. (1997). *A comparison of four restorative conferencing models.* Washington, DC: U.S. Department of Justice, Office of Juvenile Justice and Delinquency Prevention.

Beck, A. R. (2001). *Recidivism: A fruit salad concept in the criminal justice world.* Kansas City, MO: Justice Concepts.

Beck, E., Blackwell, B. S., Leonard, P., & Mears, M. (2003). Seeking sanctuary: Interviews with family members of capital defendants. *Cornell Law Review, 88,* 382–418.

Beeghly, M., & Cicchetti, D. (1994). Child maltreatment, attachment, and the self-system: Emergence of an internal state lexicon in toddlers at high social risk. *Development and Psychopathology, 6,* 30.

Behrens, G. (1985). *Current psychological screening trends in the selection of law enforcement and corrections personnel in the United States.* Champaign, IL: Institute for Personality and Ability Testing.

Belenko, S. (2002). Drug courts. In C. G. Leukefeld, F. Tims, & D. Farabee (Eds.), *Treatment of drug offenders: Policies and issues* (pp. 301–318). New York: Springer.

Bennell, C., Jones, N. J., Taylor, P. J., & Snook, B. (2006). Validities and abilities in criminal profiling: A critique of the studies conducted by Richard Kocsis and his colleagues. *International Journal of Offender Therapy and Comparative Criminology, 50,* 344–360.

Ben-Shakhar, G., & Furedy, J. J. (1990). *Theories and applications in the detection of deception.* New York: Springer-Verlag.

Berg, B. (1989). *Qualitative research methods for the social sciences.* Needham Heights, MA: Allyn & Bacon.

Bergen, R. K. (1996). *Wife rape: Understanding the responses of survivors and service providers.* Thousand Oaks, CA: Sage.

Berliner, L., Hyman, I., Thomas, A., & Fitzgerald, M. (2003). Children's memory for trauma and positive experiences. *Journal of Traumatic Stress, 16,* 229–236.

Berrill, K. (1992). Anti-gay violence: Causes, consequences, and responses. In R. Kelly (Ed.), *Bias crime: American law enforcement and legal responses.* Chicago: University of Chicago Press.

Berrill, K., & Herek, G. (1992). Primary and secondary victimization in anti-gay hate crimes: Official response and public policy. In G. Herek & K. Berrill (Eds.), *Hate crimes: Confronting violence against lesbians and gay men.* Thousand Oaks, CA: Sage.

Bersoff, D. N., Goodman-Delahunty, J., Grisso, J. T., Hans,V. P., Poythress, N. G., & Roesch, R.G. (1997). Training in law and psychology: Models from the Villanova Conference. *American Psychologist, 52,* 1301–1310.

Beutler, L. E., Storm, A., Kirksih, P., Scogini, F., & Gaines, J. A. (1985). Parameters in the prediction of police officer performance. *Professional Psychology: Research and Practice, 16,* 324–335.

Bevacqua, M. (2000). *Rape on the public agenda: Feminism and the politics of sexual assault.* Boston: Northeastern University Press.

Birmingham, L., Gray, J., Mason, D., & Grubin, D. (2000). Mental illness at reception into prison. *Criminal Behaviour and Mental Health, 10,* 77–87.

Bjerregaard, B. (2000). An empirical study of stalking victimization. *Violence and Victims, 15,* 389–405.

Black, D. W., Baumgart, C. H., & Bell, S. E. (1995). A 16- to 45-year follow-up of 71 men with antisocial personality disorder. *Comprehensive Psychiatry, 36,* 130–140.

Black, H. C. (1990). *Black's law dictionary* (6th ed.). St. Paul, MN: West.

Blackburn, R. (1993). *The psychology of criminal conduct.* Chichester, UK: Wiley.

Blau, T. H. (1994). *Psychological services for law enforcement.* New York: Wiley.

Block, R., & Block, C. (1980). Decisions and data: The transformation of robbery incidents into official robbery statistics. *Journal of Criminal Law and Criminology, 71,* 622–636.

Blumstein, A., Cohen, J., Roth, J. A., & Visher, C. A. (Eds.). (1986). *Criminal careers and career criminals* (Vol. 1). Washington, DC: National Academy Press.

Bonanno, G. A. (2004). Loss, trauma, and human resilience: Have we underestimated the human capacity to thrive after extremely aversive events? *American Psychologist, 59,* 20–28.

Boney-McCoy, S., & Finkelhor, D. (1995). Psychosocial sequelae of violent victimization in a national youth sample. *Journal of Consulting and Clinical Psychology, 63,* 726–736.

Bonsignore v. City of New York, 521 F. Supp. 394 (1981).

Boothby, J. L., & Clements, C. B. (2000). A national survey of correctional psychologists. *Journal of Criminal Justice and Behavior, 27,* 716–732.

Boothby, J. L., & Clements, C. B. (2002). Job satisfaction and correctional psychologists: Implications for recruitment and retention. *Professional Psychology: Research and Practice, 33,* 310–315.

Borduin, C. M., Heilbrun, N., Jones, M. R., & Grabe, S. A. (2000). Community-based treatments of serious antisocial behavior in adolescents. In W. E. Martin & J. L. Swartz-Kulstad (Eds.), *Person environment psychology and mental health: Assessment and intervention.* Hillsdale, NJ: Erlbaum.

Born, M., Chevalier, V., & Humblet, I. (1997). Resilience, desistance and delinquent career of adolescent offenders. *Journal of Adolescence, 20,* 679–694.

Borum, R., & Stock, H. (1993). Detection of deception in law enforcement applicants: A preliminary investigation. *Law and Human Behavior, 17,* 157–166.

Bove, A. W., Goldstein, N. E., Appleton, C., & Thomson, M. R. (2003, March). *Gender differences in IQ among juvenile offenders.* Paper presented at the annual conference of the International Association of Forensic Mental Health Services, Miami, FL.

Bow, J. N., & Quinnell, F. A. (2001). Psychologists' current practices and procedures in child custody evaluations: Five years post American Psychological Association guidelines. *Professional Psychology: Research and Practice, 32,* 261–268.

Bow, J. N., & Quinnell, F. A. (2002). A critical review of child custody evaluation reports. *Family Court Review, 40,* 164–176.

Boyer, M., Barron, K. L., & Farrar, M. J. (1994). Three-year-olds remember a novel event from 20 months: Evidence for long-term memory in children? *Memory, 2,* 417–445.

Bradley, A. R., & Wood, J. M. (1996). How do children tell? The disclosure process in child sexual abuse. *Child Abuse & Neglect, 9,* 881–891.

Braithwaite, J. (2002). *Restorative justice and responsive regulation.* Oxford, UK: Oxford University Press.

Brecklin, L. R. (2008). Evaluation outcomes of self-defense training for women: A review. *Aggression and Violent Behavior, 13,* 60–76.

Brecklin, L. R., & Forde, D. R. (2001). A meta-analysis of rape education programs. *Violence and Victims, 16,* 303–321.

Brecklin, L. R., & Ullman, S. E. (2001). The role of offender alcohol use in rape attacks: An analysis of National Crime Victimization Survey data. *Journal of Interpersonal Violence, 16,* 3–21.

Brecklin, L. R., & Ullman, S. E. (2002). The roles of victim and offender alcohol use in sexual assaults: Results from the National Violence Against Women Survey. *Journal of Studies on Alcohol, 63,* 57–63.

Brecklin, L. R., & Ullman, S. E. (2005). Self-defense or assertiveness training and women's responses to sexual attacks. *Journal of Interpersonal Violence, 20,* 738–762.

Breitenbecher, K. H., & Gidycz, C. A. (1998). An empirical evaluation of a program designed to reduce the risk of multiple sexual victimization. *Journal of Interpersonal Violence, 13,* 472–488.

Breitenbecher, K. H., & Scarce, M. (1999). A longitudinal evaluation of the effectiveness of a sexual assault education program. *Journal of Interpersonal Violence, 14,* 459–478.

Breitenbecher, K. H., & Scarce, M. (2001). An evaluation of the effectiveness of a sexual assault education program focusing on psychological barriers to resistance. *Journal of Interpersonal Violence, 16,* 387–407.

Brennan, M., & Brennan, R. E. (1988). *Strange language: Child victims under cross examination* (3rd ed.). Wagga Wagga, New South Wales, Australia: Riverina Literacy Centre.

Brigham, J. C. (1999). What is forensic psychology, anyway? *Law and Human Behavior, 23,* 273–298.

Brodsky, S. L. (1991). *Testifying in court: Guidelines and maxims for the expert witness.* Washington, DC: American Psychological Association.

Brodsky, S. L. (1996). Twenty years of criminal justice and behavior: Observations from the beginning. *Criminal Justice and Behavior, 23,* 5–11.

Broner, N., Mayrl, D. W., & Landsberg, G. (2005). Outcomes of mandated and nonmandated New York City jail diversion offenders with alcohol, drug, and mental disorders. *The Prison Journal, 85,* 18–49.

Broome, K. M., Knight, K., Hiller, M. L., & Simpson, D. D. (1996). Drug treatment process indicators for probationers and prediction of recidivism. *Journal of Substance Abuse Treatment, 13,* 487–491.

Bruck, M., & Ceci, S. J. (1996). Issues in the scientific validation of interviews with young children. Comment on "Interviewing young children about body touch and handling." *Monograph of the Society for Research in Child Development, 61* (4–5, Serial No. 248).

Bruck, M., & Ceci, S. J. (1999). The suggestibility of children's memory. *Annual Review of Psychology, 50,* 419–439.

Bruck, M., Ceci, S. J., & Francoeur, E. (2000). Children's use of anatomically detailed dolls to report genital touching in a medical examination: Developmental and gender comparisons. *Journal of Experimental Psychology–Applied, 6,* 74–83.

Bruck, M., Ceci, S., & Hembrooke, H. (2002). The nature of children's true and false narratives. *Developmental Review, 22,* 520–554.

Bruck, M., Hembrooke, H., & Ceci, S. J. (1997). Children's reports of pleasant and unpleasant events. In J. D. Read & D. S. Lindsay (Eds.), *Recollections of trauma: Scientific evidence and clinical practice.* New York: Plenum.

Budd, T., & Mattinson, J. (2000). *Stalking: Findings from the 1998 British Crime Survey* (Research Findings No. 129). London: Home Office Research.

Burdon, W. M., Farabee, D., Prendergast, M. L., Messina, N. P., & Cartier, J. (2002). Prison-based therapeutic community substance abuse programs—implementation and operational issues. *Federal Probation, 66,* 3–8.

Bureau of Justice Statistics. (1996). *Criminal victimization in the United States, 1993.* Washington, DC: U. S. Department of Justice.

Bureau of Justice Statistics. (1999a). *Substance abuse and treatment, state and federal prisoners, 1997.* Washington, DC: Department of Justice.

Bureau of Justice Statistics. (1999b, July). *Mental health and treatment of inmates and probationers* (NJC 174463). Washington, DC: Department of Justice.

Bureau of Justice Statistics. (1999c, August). *Prisoners in 1998* (NJC 175687). Washington, DC: Department of Justice.

Buros, O. K. (1989). *The tenth mental measurements yearbook.* Lincoln: University of Nebraska Press.

Bursik, R. (1988). Social disorganization and theories of crime and delinquency: Problems and prospects. *Criminology, 26,* 519–551.

Burton, A. (1948). The status of correctional psychology. *Journal of Psychology, 28,* 217–222.

Bushman, B. J., & Cooper, H. M. (1990). Effects of alcohol on human aggression: An integrative research review. *Psychological Bulletin, 107,* 341–354.

Butcher, J. N., Dahlstrom, W. G., Graham, J. R., Tellegen, A., & Kaemmer, B. (1989). *Minnesota Multiphasic Personality Inventory—2: Manual for administration and scoring.* Minneapolis: University of Minnesota Press.

Butzin, C. A., Martin, S. S., & Inciardi, J. A. (2005). Treatment during transition to community and subsequent drug use. *Journal of Substance Abuse Treatment, 28,* 351–358.

Byrne, K. M., & Hummer, D. (2004). Examining the role of the police in reentry partnership initiatives. *Federal Probation, 68,* 62–70.

Cairn, J. (2006). Cognitive skills programmes: Impact on reducing reconviction among a sample of female prisoners. In *Findings 276.* London: Home Office. Retrieved June 16, 2006, from http://www.homeoffice.gov.uk/rds/pdfs06/r276.pdf.

Calhoun, S. R., Wesson, D. R., Galloway, G. P., & Smith, D. E. (1996). Abuse of flunitrazepam (Rohypnol) and other benzodiazepines in Austin and South Texas. *Journal of Psychoactive Drugs, 28,* 1–7.

California Penal Code, Section § 646.9 (1990).

Camp, C. G., & Camp, G. M. (2000). *The corrections yearbook 2000, adult corrections.* Middletown, CT: Criminal Justice Institute.

Canter, D. V. (1989, January). Offender profiles. *Psychologist, 2,* 12–16.

Canter, D. V. (1994). *Criminal shadows: Inside the mind of the serial killer.* London: HarperCollins.

Canter, D. V. (2004). Offender profiling and investigative psychology. *Journal of Investigative Psychology and Offender Profiling, 1,* 1–15.

Canter, D. V., & Kirby, S. (1995). Prior convictions of child molesters. *Science and Justice, 35,* 73–78.

Carich, M., & Smith, S. (2006, Spring). Fads in the field of sex offense treatment. *The Forum, 18,* 11–17.

Carter, D. (1991). The status of education and training in corrections. *Federal Probation, 55,* 17–23.

Carter, D. L., & Prentky, R. A. (1993). Forensic treatment in the United States: A survey of selected forensic hospitals, Massachusetts Treatment Center. *International Journal of Law and Psychiatry, 16,* 117–132.

Case Analysis Unit. (1998). *Methods of Case Analysis: An International Symposium.* Bundeskriminalamt, Wiesbaden, Germany: Kriminalistisches Institut.

Casey, C. (1993). Mapping evil minds. *Police Review, 101,* 16–17.

Castro, F. G. (2005). A cultural approach for promoting resilience among adjudicated Mexican American youth. In K. H. Barrett & W. H. George (Eds.), *Race, culture, psychology, & law.* Thousand Oaks, CA: Sage.

Ceci, S. J., & Bruck, M. (1993). Suggestibility of the child witness: A historical review and synthesis. *Psychological Bulletin, 113,* 403–439.

Ceci, S. J., & Bruck, M. (1995). *Jeopardy in the courtroom: A scientific analysis of children's testimony.* Washington, DC: American Psychological Association.

Ceci, S. J., Bruck, M., & Battin, D. B. (2000). The suggestibility of children's testimony. In D. F. Bjorklund (Ed.), *False-memory creation in children and adults: Theory, research, and implications* (pp. 169–201). Mahwah, NJ: Erlbaum.

Ceci, S. J., Huffman, M. L. C., Smith, E., & Loftus, E. F. (1994). Repeatedly thinking about a nonevent: Source misattributions among preschoolers. *Consciousness and Cognition, 3,* 388–407.

Ceci, S. J., Loftus, E. F., Leichtman, M. D., & Bruck, M. (1994). The possible role of source misattributions in the creation of false beliefs among preschoolers. *International Journal of Clinical and Experimental Hypnosis, 42,* 304–320.

Ceci, S. J., Ross, D. F., & Toglia, M. P. (1987). Suggestibility of children's testimony: Psycholegal implications. *Journal of Experimental Psychology, 116,* 38–49.

Chandler, J. T. (1990). *Modern police psychology: For law enforcement and human behavior professionals.* Springfield, IL: CC Thomas.

Chappell, D. (1995). How violent is Australian society? In D. Chappell & S. Egger (Eds.), *Australian violence: Contemporary perspectives II.* Canberra: Australian Institute of Criminology.

Chess, S., & Hassibi, M. (1986). *Principles and practice of child psychiatry* (2nd rev. ed.). NY: Plenum.

Christie, N. (1977). Conflicts as property. *British Journal of Criminology, 7,* 1–15.

Civil Rights Act of 1991, 42 U.S.C. 1981, et seq.

Clark, D. (2002). *Dark paths, cold trails: How a Mountie led the quest to link serial killers to their victims.* Toronto, Ontario, Canada: HarperCollins.

Clay-Warner, J. (2002). Avoiding rape: The effects of protective actions and situational factors on rape outcome. *Violence and Victims, 17,* 691–705.

Clay-Warner, J. (2003). The context of sexual violence: Situational predictors of self-protective actions. *Violence and Victims, 18,* 543–556.

Clear, T., & Rose, D. (1998). Incarceration, social capital and crime: Implications for social disorganization theory. Criminology, 36: 471–479.

Cleckley, H. M. (1964). *The mask of sanity* (3rd ed.). St. Louis, MO: C. V. Mosby.

Cleckley, H. M. (1976). *The mask of sanity* (5th ed.). St. Louis, MO: C. V. Mosby.

Clements, C. B. (1987). Psychologists in adult correctional institutions: Getting off the treadmill. In E. K. Morris & C. J. Braukmann (Eds.), *Behavioral approaches to crime and delinquency.* New York: Plenum.

Clements, C. B. (2000). Prisons and correctional institutions. In A. E. Kazdin (Ed.), *Encyclopedia of psychology.* Washington, DC, and New York: American Psychological Association and Oxford University Press.

Cleveland, H., Koss, M., & Lyons, J. (1999). Rape tactics from the survivor's perspective. *Journal of Interpersonal Violence, 14,* 532–547.

Cohen, L., & Felson, M. (1979). Social change and crime rate trends: A routine activity approach. *American Sociological Review, 44,* 588–608.

Coie, J. D. (2004). The impact of negative social experience on the development of antisocial behavior. In J. B. Kupersmidt & K. A. Dodge (Eds.), *Children's peer relations: From development to intervention.* Washington, DC: American Psychological Association.

Coie, J. D., & Miller-Johnson, S. (2001). Peer factors and interventions. In R. Loeber & D. P. Farrington (Eds.), *Child delinquents: Development, intervention, and service needs.* Thousand Oaks, CA: Sage.

Coleman, J. (1988). Social capital and the creation of human capital. *American Journal of Sociology, 94,* S95–S120.

Collins, W. C. (2004). *Supermax prisons and the constitution: Liability concerns in the extended control unit.* Washington, DC: National Institute of Corrections.

Committee on Ethical Guidelines for Forensic Psychologists. (1991). Specialty guidelines for forensic psychologists. *Law and Human Behavior, 15,* 655–665.

Comstock, G. (1989). Victims of anti-gay/lesbian violence. *Journal of Interpersonal Violence, 4,* 101–106.

Condie, L., Goldstein, N. E., & Grisso, T. (2003). *The Miranda Rights Comprehension Instruments—II.* Manuscript in preparation.

Conduct Problems Prevention Research Group. (2004). The fast track experiment: Translating the developmental model into a prevention design. In J. B. Kupersmidt & K. A. Dodge (Eds.), *Children's peer relations: From development to intervention.* Washington, DC: American Psychological Association.

Conley, C. (1998). *The women's prison association: Supporting women offenders and their families.* National Institute of Justice: Program focus (NJC 172858). Washington, DC: Department of Justice.

Conte, J. R. (1985). Clinical dimensions of adult sexual abuse of children. *Behavioral Sciences & the Law, 3,* 341–354.

Conte, J. R., Sorenson, E., Fogarty, L., & Rosa, J. D. (1991). Evaluating children's reports of sexual abuse: Results from a survey of professionals. *American Journal of Orthopsychiatry, 61,* 428–437.

Cooke, D. J., Michie, C., Hart, S. D., & Hare, R. D. (1999). Evaluating the screening version of the Hare Psychopathy Checklist—Revised (PCL:SV): An item response theory analysis. *Psychological Assessment, 11,* 3–13.

Copson, G. (1995). *Coals to Newcastle? Part 1: A study of offender profiling.* London: Home Office, Police Research Group.

Copson, G., Badcock, R., Boon, J., & Britton, P. (1997). Editorial: Articulating a systematic approach to clinical crime profiling. *Criminal Behaviour and Mental Health, 7,* 13–17.

Cordon, I. M., Pipe, M-E., Sayfan, L., Melinder, A., & Goodman, G. S. (2004). Memory for traumatic experiences in early childhood. *Developmental Review, 24,* 101–132.

Cornell, D., Warren, J., Hawk, G., Stafford, E., Oram, G., Pine, D., et al. (1993, August). *Psychopathy and anger among instrumental and reactive violent offenders.* Paper presented at the Annual Meeting of the American Psychological Association, Toronto, Ontario, Canada.

Corsini, R. J. (1945). Functions of a prison psychologist. *Journal of Consulting Psychology, 9,* 101–104.

Corsini, R. J., & Miller, G. A. (1954). Psychology in prisons, 1952. *American Psychologist, 9,* 184–185.

Cortina, J. M., Doherty, M. L., Schmitt, N., Kaufman, G., & Smith, R. G. (1992). The big five personality factors in the IPI and the MMPI: Predictors of police performance. *Personnel Psychology, 45,* 119–140.

Coulton, G. F., & Field, H. S. (1995). Using assessment centers in selecting entry-level police officers: Extravagance or justified expense. *Public Personnel Management, 24,* 223–254.

Coyote v. U.S., 380 F.2d 305 (1967).

Craig, L. A., Browne, K. D., & Stringer, I. (2003). Treatment and sexual offense recidivism. *Trauma, Violence, & Abuse, 4,* 70–89.

Crawford, N. (2002, November). Science-based program curbs violence in kids. *Monitor on Psychology, 33,* 38–39.

Cripe, L. I. (1996). The ecological validity of executive function testing. In R. J. Shordone & C. J. Long (Eds.), *Ecological validity of neuropsychological testing.* Delray Beach, FL: GR Press/ St. Lucie Press.

Dahlstrom, W. M., & Welsh, G. S. (1960). *An MMPI handbook: A guide to use in clinical practice and research.* Minneapolis: University of Minnesota Press.

Dalton, C. (1999). When paradigms collide: Protecting battered parents and their children in the family court system. *Family and Conciliation Court Review, 37,* 273–296.

Damasio, A. (1994, October). Descartes' error and the future of human life. *Scientific American,* p. 144.

Damasio, A., Tranel, D., & Damasio, H. (1987). Individuals with sociopathic behavior caused by frontal damage fail to respond autonomically to social stimuli. *Behavioral Brain Research, 41,* 81–94.

Damasio, H., Grabowski, T., Frank, R., Galaburda, A. M., & Damasio, A. R. (1994). The return of Phineas Gage: Clues about the brain from the skull of a famous patient. *Science, 264,* 1102–1105.

Damon, W. (2004). What is positive youth development? *Annals, AAPSS, 591,* 13–24.

Daubert v. Merrel Dow, 509 U.S. 579 (1993).

Davidson, J. (1996). *Davidson Trauma scale.* Toronto, Ont., Canada: Multi-Health Systems.

Davies, A. (1994). Editorial: Offender profiling. *Medicine, Science and the Law, 34,* 185–186.

Davies, W., & Feldman, P. (1981). The diagnosis of psychopathy by forensic specialists. *British Journal of Psychiatry, 138,* 329–331.

Davis, G. M., Tarrant, A., & Flin, R. (1989). Close encounters of a witness kind: Children's memory for a simulated health inspection. *British Journal of Psychology, 80,* 415–429.

Davis, S. L. (1998). Social and scientific influences on the study of children's suggestibility: A historical perspective. *Child Maltreatment, 3,* 186–194.

Davison, G. C., & Neale, J. M. (1994). *Abnormal psychology* (6th ed.). New York: Wiley.

DeKeseredy, W., & Schwartz, M. D. (1998). *Woman abuse on campus: Results from the Canadian National Survey.* Thousand Oaks, CA: Sage.

De Leon, G. (2000). *The therapeutic community: Theory, model, and method.* New York: Springer.

DeLoache, J. S. (1987). Rapid change in the symbolic functioning of very young children. *Science, 238,* 1556–1557.

DeLoache, J. S. (1991). Symbolic functioning in very young children: Understanding of pictures and models. *Child Development, 62,* 736–752.

DeLoache, J. S. (1995). Early understanding and use of symbols: The model model. *Current Directions in Psychological Science, 4,* 109–113.

DeLoache, J. S., & Marzolf, D. P. (1995). The use of dolls to interview young children: Issues of symbolic representation. *Journal of Experimental Child Psychology, 60,* 155–173.

Delprino, R. P., & Bahn, C. (1988). National survey of the extent and nature of psychological services in police departments. *Professional Psychology: Research and Practice, 19,* 421–425.

Dennison, S., & Thomson, D. M. (2000). Community perceptions of stalking: What are the fundamental concerns? *Psychiatry, Psychology and Law, 7,* 159–169.

Dennison, S., & Thomson, D. M. (2002). Identifying stalking: The relevance of intent in commonsense reasoning. *Law and Human Behavior, 26,* 543–561.

Dent, H. R., & Stephenson, G. M. (1979). An experimental study of the effectiveness of different techniques of questioning child witnesses. *British Journal of Social and Clinical Psychology, 18,* 41–51.

Diamond, P. M., Wang, E. W., Holzer, C. E., Thomas, C. R., & Cruser, D. A. (2001). The prevalence of mental illness in prison: Review and policy implications. *Administration and Policy in Mental Health, 29,* 21–40.

Dickerson v. U.S., 530 U.S. 428 (2000).

Dignam, J. (2003). Correctional mental health ethics revisited. In T. J. Fagan & R. K. Ax (Eds.), *Correctional mental health handbook* (pp. 39–58). Thousand Oaks, CA: Sage.

Dionne, G., Tremblay, R., Boivin, M., Laplante, D., & Pérusse, D. (2003). Physical aggression and expressive vocabulary in 19-month-old twins. *Developmental Psychology, 39,* 261–273.

Dodge, K. A. (2002). Mediation, moderation, and mechanisms of how parenting affects children's aggressive behavior. In J. G. Borkowski, S. L. Ramey, & M. Bristol-Power (Eds.), *Parenting and the child's world: Influences on academic, intellectual and social development.* Mahwah, NJ: Erlbaum.

Dodge, K. A. (2003). Do social information-processing patterns mediate aggressive behavior? In B. B. Lahey, T. E. Moffitt, & A. Caspi (Eds.). *Causes of conduct disorder and juvenile delinquency.* New York: Guilford Press.

Dodge, K. A., & Pettit, G. S. (2003). A biopsychosocial model of the development of chronic conduct problems in adolescence. *Developmental Psychology, 39,* 349–371.

Doll, B., & Lyon, M. A. (1998). Risk and resilience: Implications for the delivery of educational and mental health services in schools. *School Psychology Review, 27,* 348–363.

Douglas, J. E., & Burgess, A. E. (1986, December). Criminal profiling: A viable investigative tool against violent crime. *FBI Law Enforcement Bulletin, 55,* 9–13.

Douglas, J. E., Burgess, A. W., Burgess, A. G., & Ressler, R. (1992). *Crime classification manual.* New York: Lexington Books.

Douglas, J. E., & Olshaker, M. (1995). *Mind hunter: Inside the FBI's elite serial crime unit.* New York: Simon & Schuster.

Douglas, J. E., & Olshaker, M. (1997). *Journey into darkness: The FBI's premier investigator penetrates the minds and motives of the most terrifying serial criminals.* New York: Simon & Schuster.

Douglas, J. E., Ressler, R. K., Burgess, A. W., & Hartman, C. R. (1986). Criminal profiling from crime scene analysis. *Behavioral Sciences & the Law, 4,* 401–421.

Dubow, E. F., Edwards, S., & Ippolito, M. F. (1997). Life stressors, neighborhood disadvantage, and resources: A focus on inner-city children's adjustment. *Journal of Clinical Child Psychology*, 26, 130–144.

Dukes, R. L., & Mattley, C. L. (1977). Predicting rape victim reportage. *Sociology and Social Research, 62,* 63–84.

Dunn, P. C., Vail-Smith, K., & Knight, S. M. (1999). What date/acquaintance rape victims tell others: A study of college recipients of disclosure. *Journal of American College Health, 47,* 213–222.

Dunnette, M. D., & Motowidlo, S. J. (1976). *Police selection and career assessment.* Washington, DC: Government Printing Office.

Dusky v. U.S., 362 U.S. 388 (1960).

Eacott, M. J. (1999). Memory for the events of early childhood. *Current Directions in Psychological Science, 8,* 46–49.

Easteal, P. W., & Wilson, P. (1991). *Preventing crime on transport: Rail, buses, taxis, planes.* Canberra: Australian Institute of Criminology.

Edens, J. F., Skeem, J. L., Cruise, K. R., & Cauffman, E. (2001). Assessment of "juvenile psychopathy" and its association with violence: A critical review. *Behavioral Sciences & the Law, 19,* 53–80.

Egger, S. A. (1990). Serial murder: A synthesis of literature and research. In S. A. Egger (Ed.), *Serial murder: An elusive phenomenon.* Westport, CT: Praeger.

Egger, S. A. (1997). *The killers among us: An examination of serial murder and its investigation.* Upper Saddle River, NJ: Prentice Hall.

Egger, S. A. (1999). Psychological profiling: Past, present, and future. *Journal of Contemporary Criminal Justice, 15,* 242–261.

Eisenberg, N. (1998). *Social, emotional, and personality development* (5th ed., Vol. 3). New York: Wiley.

Equal Employment Opportunity Commission, ADA Division, Office of Legal Counsel. (1995). *Enforcement guidance: Preemployment disability–related inquiries and medical examinations under the Americans with Disabilities Act of 1990.* Washington, DC: Equal Employment Opportunity Commission.

Eschholz, S., Reed, M. D., Beck, E., & Blume Leonard, P. (2003, May). *Homicide Studies, 7,* 154–181.

Estrich, S. (1987). *Real rape.* Cambridge, MA: Harvard University Press.

Everington, C., & Luckasson, R. (1992). *Competence Assessment for Standing Trial For Defendants with Mental Retardation test manual.* Worthington, OH: IDS.

Everson, M., & Boat, B. (1990). Sexualize doll play among young children: Implications for the use of anatomical dolls in sexual abuse evaluations. *Journal of the American Academy of Child and Adolescent Psychiatry, 29,* 736–742.

Fagan, T. J., Ax, R. K., Resnick, R. J., Liss, M., Johnson, R. T., & Forbes, M. R. (2004). Attitudes among interns and directors of training: Who wants to prescribe, who doesn't, and why. *Professional Psychology: Research and Practice, 35,* 345–356.

Farberman, R. (2007). Council extends its stances on torture. *Monitor on Psychology, 38*(9), 14.

Fare v. Michael C., 442 U.S. 707 (1979).

Farrington, D. P., & Lambert, S. (1997). Predicting offender profiles from victim and witness descriptions. In J. L. Jackson & D. A. Bekerian (Eds.), *Offender profiling: Theory, research, and practice* (pp. 133–158). Chichester, UK: Wiley.

Federal Bureau of Investigation. (1992). *Killed in the line of duty.* Washington, DC: U.S. Department of Justice.

Feldman-Summers, S., & Ashworth, C. D. (1981). Factors related to intentions to report a rape. *Journal of Social Issues, 37,* 53–70.

Felson, R. B., Messner, S. F., & Hoskin, A. (1999). The victim–offender relationship and calling the police in assaults. *Criminology, 37,* 931–947.

Ferguson, A. B., & Douglas, A. C. (1970). A study of juvenile waiver. *San Diego Law Review, 7,* 39–54.

Ferraro, R. (Ed.). (2002). *Minority and cross-cultural aspects of neuropsychological assessment.* Royersford, PA: Sets & Zeilinger.

Finkelhor, D. (1984). *Child sexual abuse: New theory and research.* New York: Free Press.

Finkelhor, D., & Araji, S. (1986). Explanations of pedophilia: A four-factor model. *Journal of Sex Research, 22,* 145–161.

Finkelhor, D., & Dziuba-Leatherman, J. (1994). Children as victims of violence: A national survey. *Pediatrics, 94,* 413–420.

Finkelhor, D., & Ormrod, R. (1999, November). Reporting crime against juveniles. *OJJDP Juvenile Justice Bulletin,* pp. 1–7.

Finkelhor, D., & Yllo, K. (1985). *License to rape: Sexual abuse of wives.* New York: Free Press.

Finkelson, L., & Oswalt, R. (1995). College date rape: Incidence and reporting. *Psychological Reports, 77*, 526.

Finn, P., & McNeil, T. (1987). *Bias crime and the criminal justice response: A summary report (prepared for the National Criminal Justice Association)*. Cambridge, MA: Abt Associates.

Fischer, D. H. (1970). *Historians' fallacies: Toward a logic of historical thought*. New York: Harper Perennial.

Fisher, B. S., & Cullen, F. T. (1999). *Violence against college women: Results from a national level study: Final report submitted to the Bureau of Justice Statistics, March 1999*. Washington, DC: U.S. Department of Justice, Bureau of Justice Statistics.

Fisher, B. S., Cullen, F. T., & Turner, M. G. (2000). *The sexual victimization of college women*. Washington, DC: U.S. Department of Justice, National Institute of Justice and Bureau of Justice Statistics.

Fisher, B. S., Daigle, L. E., Cullen, F. T., & Turner, M. G. (2003). Reporting sexual victimization to the police and others: Results from a national-level study of college women. *Criminal Justice and Behavior, 30*, 6–38.

Fisher, B. S., Hartman, J., Cullen, F. T., & Turner, M. G. (2002). Making campuses safer for students: The Clery Act as a symbolic legal reform. *Stetson Law Review, 32*, 61–90.

Fisher, B. S., Sloan, J. J., Cullen, F. T., & Lu, C. (1998). Crime in the ivory tower: The level and sources of student victimization. *Criminology, 36*, 671–710.

Fisher, D., & Beech, A. (2005, November). *Identification and treatment implications of the Ward & Hudson pathways: A manualized approach*. Paper presented at the 14th Annual Association for the Treatment of Sexual Offenders Research and Treatment Conference, Salt Lake City, UT.

Fisher, R. P., Geiselman, R. E., Raymond, D. S., Jurkevich, L. M., & Warhaftig, M. L. (1987). Enhancing enhanced eyewitness memory: Refining the Cognitive Interview. *Journal of Police Science and Administration, 15*, 291–297.

Fitch, J. H. (1962). Men convicted of sexual offenses against children. *British Journal of Criminology, 3*, 18–37.

Fivush, R. (1998). Children's recollections of traumatic and nontraumatic events. *Development and Psychopathology, 10*, 699–716.

Fivush, R., Haden, C., & Adam, S. (1995). Structure and coherence of preschoolers' personal narratives over time: Implications for childhood amnesia. *Journal of Experimental Child Psychology, 60*, 32–56.

Fivush, R., & Hamond, N. R. (1990). Autobiographical memory across the preschool years: Toward reconceptualizing childhood amnesia. In R. Fivush & J. A. Hudson (Eds.), *Knowing and remembering in young children, Emory Symposia in Cognition, 3* (pp. 223–248). New York: Cambridge University Press.

Fivush, R., & Nelson, K. (2004). Culture and language in the emergence of autobiographical memory. *Psychological Science, 15*, 573–577.

Fivush, R., & Schwarzmueller, A. (1998). Children remember childhood: Implications for childhood amnesia. *Applied Cognitive Psychology, 12*, 455–473.

Fivush, R., & Shukat, J. (1995). What young children recall: Issues of content, consistency, and coherence of early autobiographical recall. In M. S. Zaragoza, J. R. Graham, G. C. N. Hall, R. Hirschman, & Y. S. Ben-Porath (Eds.), *Memory and testimony in the child witness*. Thousand Oaks, CA: Sage.

Flaten, C. (1996). Victim–offender mediation: Application with serious offenses committed by juveniles. In B. Galaway & J. Hudson (Eds.), *Restorative justice: An international perspective* (pp. 387–402). Monsey, NY: Criminal Justice Press.

Flavell, J. H., Miller, P. H., & Miller, S. A. (1993). *Cognitive development* (3rd ed.). Englewood Cliffs, NJ: Prentice Hall.

Fletcher-Janzen, E., Strickland, T. L., & Reynolds, C. R. (Eds.). (2000). *Handbook of cross-cultural neuropsychology*. New York: Kluwer Academic/ Plenum.

Flores, S. A., & Hartlaub, M. G. (1998). Reducing rape myth acceptance in male college students: A meta-analysis of intervention studies. *Journal of College Student Development, 39*, 438–448.

Folkman, S., & Moskowitz, J. T. (2000). Positive affect and the other side of coping. *American Psychologist, 55*, 647–654.

Forth, A. E., Hart, S. D., & Hare, R. D. (1990). Assessment of psychopathy in male young offenders. *Psychological Assessment, 2*, 342–344.

Forth, A. E., & Kroner, D. (1994). *The factor structure of the Revised Psychopathy Checklist with incarcerated rapist and incest offenders.* Unpublished manuscript.

Foubert, J. D. (2000). The longitudinal effects of a rape-prevention program on fraternity men's attitudes, behavioral intent, and behavior. *Journal of American College Health, 48,* 158–163.

Fowles, D. C., & Kochanska, G. (2000). Temperament as a moderator of pathways in conscience in children: The contribution of electrodermal activity. *Psychophysiology, 37,* 788–795.

Fraser, S. (Ed.). (1995). *The bell curve wars: Race, intelligence, and the future of America.* New York: Basic Books.

Fredrickson, B. L. (2001). The role of positive emotions in positive psychology: The broaden-and-build theory of positive emotions. *American Psychologist, 56,* 218–226.

Freeman, L. N., Shaffer, D., & Smith, H. (1996). Neglected victims of homicide: The needs of young siblings of murder victims. *American Journal of Orthopsychiatry, 66,* 337–345.

Fremouw, W. J., Westrup, D., & Pennypacker, J. (1997). Stalking on campus: The prevalence and strategies for coping with stalking. *Journal of Forensic Science, 42,* 666–669.

French, S. A., & Gendreau, P. (2006). Reducing prison misconducts: What works! *Criminal Justice and Behavior, 33,* 185–218.

Freund, K. (1965). Diagnosing heterosexual pedophilia by means of a test for sexual interest. *Behavior Research and Therapy, 3,* 229–234.

Freund, K. (1967). Diagnosing homo- and heterosexuality and erotic age preference by means of a psychophysiological test. *Behavioral Research and Therapy, 5,* 209–228.

Freund, K., & Blanchard, R. (1989). Phallometric diagnosis of pedophilia. *Journal of Consulting and Clinical Psychology, 57,* 100–105.

Frick, P. J., O'Brien, B. S., Wooton, J. M., & McBurnett, K. (1994). Psychopathy and conduct problems in children. *Journal of Abnormal Psychology, 103,* 700–707.

Friedman, W. J. (1991). The development of children's memory for the time of past events. *Child Development, 62,* 139–155.

Friedman-Barone, R. (2002, March 1–2). *Responses of murder victims' families to restitution and implications for policy reform.* Paper presented at the Law & Politics of the Death Penalty: Abolition, Moratorium or Reform? Conference, Eugene, OR.

Frintner, M. P., & Rubinson, L. (1993). Acquaintance rape: The influence of alcohol, fraternity membership, and sports team membership. *Journal of Sex Education and Therapy, 19,* 272–284.

Frisbie, L. V. (1990). *Another look at sex offenders in California. California Mental Health Research Monograph* (No. 12). Sacramento: California Department of Mental Hygiene.

Frye v. U.S., 293 F. 1013 (D.C. Circ 1923).

Fulero, S. M. (1995). Review of the Hare Psychopathy Checklist—Revised. In J. C. Conoley & J. C. Impara (Eds.), *Twelfth mental measurements yearbook.* Lincoln, NE: Buros Institute.

Furby, L., Weinrott, M. R., & Blackshaw, L. (1989). Sex offender recidivism: A review. *Psychological Bulletin, 105,* 3–30.

Gacono, C. B., Meloy, J. R., Sheppard, K., Speth, E., & Roske, A. (1995). A clinical investigation of malingering and psychopathy in hospitalized insanity acquitees. *Bulletin of the American Academy of Psychiatry and Law, 23,* 387–397.

Gagliardi, G. J., Lovell, D., Peterson, P. D., & Jemelka, R. (2004). Forecasting recidivism in mentally ill offenders released from prison. *Law and Human Behavior, 28,* 133–155.

Gallagher, C. A., Wilson, D. B., Hirschfield, P., Coggeshall, M. B., & MacKenzie, D. L. (1999). A quantitative review of the effects of sex offender treatment on sexual reoffending. *Corrections Management Quarterly, 3,* 19–29.

Gallagher, R. W., Somwaru, D. P., & Ben-Porath, Y. S. (1999). Current usage of psychological tests in state correctional settings. *Corrections Compendium, 24,* 1–3, 20.

Gallegos v. Colorado, 370 U.S. 49 (1962).

Gamma-hydroxy butyrate use—New York and Texas, 1995–1996. (1997). *Morbidity and Mortality Weekly Reports, 46,* 281–283.

Ganger, J., & Brent, M. R. (2004). Reexamining the vocabulary spurt. *Developmental Psychology, 40,* 621–632.

Garbarino, J., & Kostelny, K. (1992). Child maltreatment as a community problem. *Child Abuse and Neglect, 16,* 455–462.

Garbarino, J., Kostelny, K. E., & Dubrow, N. (1991). What children can tell us about living in danger. *American Psychologist, 46,* 376–383.

Gardner, H. (1983). *Frames of mind: The theory of multiple intelligences.* New York: Basic Books.

Gardner, H. (1986). The waning of intelligence tests. In R. J. Sternberg & D. K. Detterman (Eds.), *What is intelligence?* Norwood, NJ: Ablex.

Gardner, H. (1993). *Multiple intelligences.* New York: Basic Books.

Gardner, H. (1998). Are there additional intelligences: The case for naturalist, spiritual, and existential intelligences. In K. Kane (Ed.), *Education, information, and transformation.* Englewood Cliffs, NJ: Prentice Hall.

Gardner, H. (2000). *Intelligence reframed: Multiple intelligences for the 21st century.* New York: Basic Books.

Garmezy, N. (1991). Resiliency and vulnerability to adverse developmental outcomes associated with poverty. *American Behavioral Scientist, 34,* 416–430.

Garofalo, J., & Martin, S. (1993). *Bias-motivated crimes: Their characteristics and the law enforcement response. Final report to the National Institute of Justice.* Carbondale: Southern Illinois University, Center for the Study of Crime, Delinquency, and Corrections.

Garrison, S. R., & Stolberg, A. L. (1983). Modification of anger in children by affective imagery training. *Journal of Abnormal Child Psychology, 11,* 115–129.

Gartner, R., & Macmillan, R. (1995). The effect of victim–offender relationship on reporting crimes of violence against women. *Canadian Journal of Criminology, 37,* 393–429.

Geiselman, R. E., & Padilla, J. (1988). Cognitive interviewing with child witnesses. *Journal of Police Science and Administration, 16,* 236–242.

Gendreau, P. (1996). Offender rehabilitation: What we know and what needs to be done. *Criminal Justice and Behavior, 23,* 144–161.

Gendreau, P., & Goggin, C. (1997). Correctional treatment: Accomplishments and realities. In P. Van Voorhis, M. Braswell, & D. Lester (Eds.), *Correctional counseling and rehabilitation* (3rd ed.). Cincinnati, OH: Anderson.

Gendreau, P., Goggin, C., Cullen, F. T., & Andrews, D. A. (2001). The effects of community sanctions and incarceration on recidivism. In L. L. Motiuk & R. C. Serin (Eds.), *Compendium 2000 on effective correctional programming* (pp. 18–21). Ottawa, Ont.: Correctional Service of Canada.

Gendreau, P., Goggin, C., Cullen, F. T., & Paparozzi, M. (2002). The common-sense revolution and correctional policy. In J. Maguire (Ed.), *Offender rehabilitation and treatment: Effective programmes and policies to reduce re-offending* (pp. 359–386). Chichester, UK: Wiley.

Gendreau, P., Goggin, C., French, S., & Smith, P. (2006). Practicing psychology in correctional settings. In I. B. Weiner & A. K. Hess (Eds.), *The handbook of forensic psychology* (3rd ed., pp. 722–750). Hoboken, NJ: Wiley.

Gettys, V. S. (1990, August). *Police and public safety psychologists: Survey of fields of study, activities, and training opportunities.* Paper presented at the annual convention of the American Psychological Association, Boston.

Giannini, A. J. (2001). The use of fiction in therapy. *Psychiatric Times, 8*(7), 1–7.

Gidycz, C. A., Dowdall, C. L., & Marioni, N. L. (2002). Interventions to prevent rape and sexual assault. In J. Petrak & B. Hedge (Eds.), *The trauma of adult sexual assault: Treatment, prevention, and policy* (pp. 235–259). New York: Wiley.

Gidycz, C. A., Dowdall, C. L., Marioni, N. L., Loh, C., Lynn, S. J., Marmelstein, L., et al. (1998, August). *The evaluation of a risk reduction program: A multi-site investigation.* Paper presented at the annual meeting of the American Psychological Association, San Francisco.

Gidycz, C. A., McNamara, J. R., & Edwards, K. M. (2006). Women's risk perception and sexual victimization: A review of the literature. *Aggression and Violent Behavior, 11,* 441–456.

Gidycz, C. A., Rich, C. L., Orchowski, L., King, C., & Miller, A. K. (2006). The evaluation of a sexual assault self-defense and risk reduction program for college women: A prospective study. *Psychology of Women Quarterly, 30,* 173–186.

Gilbert, N. (1995). Violence against women: Social research and sexual politics. In R. J. Simon (Ed.), *Neither victim nor enemy: Women's Freedom Network looks at gender in America.* Lanham, MD. Women's Freedom Network and University Press of America.

Gilbert, N. (1997). Advocacy research and social policy. In M. Tonry (Ed.), *Crime and justice: An annual review of research.* Chicago: University of Chicago Press.

Gillstrom, B. (1994). *Abstract reasoning in psychopaths.* Unpublished doctoral dissertation, University of British Columbia, Vancouver, Canada.

Gillstrom, B., & Hare, R. D. (1988). Language-related hand gestures in psychopaths. *Journal of Personality Disorders, 2,* 21–27.

Glassner, B., & Berg, B. L. (1980). How Jews avoid alcohol problems. *American Sociological Review, 45,* 647–664.

Gleason, J. B. (1977). Code switching in children's language. In E. M. Hetherington & R. D. Parke (Eds.), *Contemporary readings in child psychology.* New York: McGraw-Hill.

Glenwick, D. S. (1996). Introduction to the special issue: The state of science and art of criminal justice and behavior. *Criminal Justice and Behavior, 23,* 3–4.

Godwin, M., & Canter, D. (1997). Encounter and death: The spatial behavior of U.S. serial killers. *Policing: An International Journal of Police Strategy and Management, 20,* 24–38.

Golding, J. M. (1999). Sexual assault history and long-term physical health problems: Evidence from clinical and population epidemiology. *Current Directions in Psychological Science, 8,* 191–194.

Golding, J. M., Siegel, J., Sorenson, S. B., Burnam, M. A., & Stein, J. A. (1989). Social support sources following sexual assault. *Journal of Community Psychology, 17,* 92–107.

Goldstein, A., & Glick, B. (1997). *Aggression replacement training.* Champaign, IL: Research Press.

Goodman, G. S., Aman, C., & Hirschman, J. (1987). Child sexual and physical abuse: Children's testimony. In S. J. Ceci, M. P. Toglia, & D. F. Ross (Eds.), *Children's eyewitness memory.* New York: Springer-Verlag.

Goodman, G. S., Hirschman, J. E., Hepps, D., & Rudy, L. (1991). Children's memory for stressful events. *Merrill-Palmer Quarterly, 37,* 109–158.

Goodman, G. S., & Reed, R. S. (1986). Age differences in eyewitness testimonies. *Law and Human Behavior, 10,* 317–332.

Goodman, G. S., Rudy, L., Bottoms, B. L., & Aman, C. (1990). Children's memory and children's concerns: Issues of ecological validity in the study of children's eyewitness testimony. In R. Fivush & J. Hudson (Eds.), *What young children remember and know.* New York: Cambridge University Press.

Goodman, G. S., & Shaaf, J. M. (1997). Over a decade of research on children's eyewitness testimony: What have we learned? Where do we go from here? [Special issue]. *Applied Cognitive Psychology, 11,* S5–S20.

Gopnik, A., & Graf, P. (1988). Knowing how you know: Young children's ability to identify and remember the sources of their beliefs. *Child Development, 59,* 1366–1371.

Gorenstein, E. E., & Newman, J. P. (1980). Disinhibitory psychopathology: A new perspective and a model for research. *Psychological Review, 87,* 301–315.

Gorman-Smith, D., Tolan, P. H., Zelli, A., & Huesmann, L. R. (1996). The relation of family functioning to violence among inner-city minority youths. *Journal of Family Psychology, 10,* 115–129.

Gough, H. (1969). *Manual for the California Psychological Inventory.* Palo Alto, CA: Consulting Psychologists Press.

Gould, S. J. (1996). *The mismeasure of man* (Rev. and expanded ed.). New York: Norton.

Green, G. (1981). *Citizen reporting of crime to the police: An analysis of common theft and assault.* Doctoral dissertation, University of Pennsylvania.

Greenberg, M. S., & Ruback, R. B. (1992). *After the crime: Victim decision making.* New York: Plenum.

Greene, D. M., & Navarro, R. L. (1998). Situation-specific assertiveness in the epidemiology of sexual victimization among university women: A prospective path analysis. *Psychology of Women Quarterly, 22,* 589–604.

Greenfeld, L. A., Rand, M. R., Craven, D., Flaus, P. A., Perkins, C. A., Ringel, C., et al. (1998). *Violence by intimates: Analysis of data on crimes by current or former spouses, boyfriends, and girlfriends.* Washington, DC: U.S. Department of Justice, Bureau of Justice Statistics.

Grisso, T. (1981). *Juveniles' waiver of rights: Legal and psychological competence.* New York: Plenum.

Grisso, T. (1996). Pretrial clinical evaluations and criminal cases: Past trends and future directions. *Criminal Justice and Behavior, 23,* 90–106.

Grisso, T. (1998). *Instruments for assessing understanding and appreciation of Miranda rights.* Sarasota, FL: Professional Resources.

Grisso, T. (2003). *Evaluating competencies: Forensic assessments and instruments* (2nd ed.). New York: Kluwer/Plenum.

Grisso, T., Miller, M. O., & Sales, B. (1997). Competency to stand trial in juvenile court. *International Journal of Law and Psychiatry, 10,* 1–20.

Gross, L., Aurand, S., & Addessa, R. (1988). *Violence and discrimination against lesbian and gay people in Philadelphia and the Commonwealth of Pennsylvania.* Philadelphia: Gay and Lesbian Task Force.

Grossman, L. S., Haywood, T.W., Ostrov, E., Wasyliw, O., & Cavanaugh, J. L. (1990). Sensitivity of MMPI validity scales to motivational factors in psychological evaluations of police officers. *Journal of Personality Assessment, 55,* 549–561.

Group for the Advancement of Psychiatry. (1991). *The mental health professional and the legal system* (Report No. 131). New York: Brunner/Mazel.

Grubin, D. (1995). Offender profiling. *The Journal of Forensic Psychiatry, 6,* 259–263.

Grubin, D., & Prentky, R. A. (1993). Sexual psychopathy laws. *Criminal Behavior and Mental Health, 3,* 381–392.

Gudjonsson, G. H., & Singh, K. K. (1984). Interrogative suggestibility and delinquent boys: An empirical validation study. *Personality & Individual Differences, 5,* 425–430.

Guerra, N. G., Huesmann, L. R., Tolan, P. H., Van Acker, R., & Eron, L. R. (1995). Stressful events and individual beliefs as correlates of economic disadvantage and aggression among urban children. *Journal of Consulting and Clinical Psychology, 63,* 518–528.

Guion, R. M., & Gibson, W. M. (1988). Personnel selection and placement. *Annual Review of Psychology, 39,* 349–374.

Gutek, B. A., O'Connor, M. A., Melancon, R., Stockdale, M. S., Geer, T. M., & Done, R. S. (1999). The utility of the reasonable woman legal standard in hostile environment sexual harassment cases. *Psychology, Public Policy, and Law, 5,* 596–629.

Guyer, C. G. (2000). Spouse abuse. In F. Kaslow (Ed.), *Handbook of couple and family forensics.* New York: Wiley.

Guze, S. B. (1976). *Criminality and psychiatric disorder.* New York: Oxford University Press.

Hadley, M. L. (2001). *The spiritual roots of restorative justice.* Albany: State University of New York Press.

Hagan, J. (1994). *Crime and disrepute.* Thousand Oaks, CA: Pine Forge Press.

Hagan, M. (1992). Special issues in serial murder. In H. Strang & S. Gerull (Eds.), *Homicides: Patterns, prevention and control: Proceedings of a conference held 12–14 May 1992.* Canberra: Australian Institute of Criminology.

Hall, G. C. N. (1995). Sexual offender recidivism revisited: A meta-analysis of recent treatment studies. *Journal of Consulting and Clinical Psychology, 63,* 802–809.

Hammett, T. M., Roberts, C., & Kennedy, S. (2001). Health-related issues in prisoner reentry. *Crime & Delinquency, 47,* 390–410.

Hampson, J. E., Rahman, M. A., Brown, B., Taylor, M. E., & Donaldson, C. J. (1998). Project SELF: Beyond resilience. *Urban Education, 33,* 6–33.

Hancock, B. W., & McClung, C. (1984). Abstract-cognitive abilities in police selection and organization. *Journal of Police Science and Administration, 12,* 99–104.

Haney, C. (1995). The social context of capital murder: Social histories and the logic of mitigation. *Santa Clara Law Review, 35,* 547–609.

Hanks, S. E. (1992). Translating theory into practice: A conceptual framework for clinical assessment, differential diagnosis, and multi-modal treatment of maritally violent individuals, couples, and families. In E. C. Viano (Ed.), *Intimate violence: Interdisciplinary perspectives.* Philadelphia: Hemisphere.

Hanson, K. A., & Gidycz, C. A. (1993). Evaluation of a sexual assault prevention program. *Journal of Consulting and Clinical Psychology, 61,* 1046–1052.

Hanson, R. K., Broom, I., & Stephenson, M. (2004). Evaluating community sex offender treatment programs: A 12-year follow-up of 724 offenders. *Canadian Journal of Behavioural Science, 36,* 87–96.

Hanson, R. K., & Bussiere, M. T. (1998). Predicting relapse: A meta-analysis of sexual offender recidivism studies. *Journal of Consulting and Clinical Psychology, 66,* 348–362.

Hanson, R. K., Gordon, A., Harris, A. J., Marques, J. K., Murphy, W., Quinsey, V. L., et al. (2002). First report of the collaborative outcome data project on the effectiveness of psychological treatment for sexual offenders. *Sexual Abuse: A Journal of Research and Treatment, 14,* 169–194.

Hanson, R. K., & Morton-Bourgon, K. E. (2005). The characteristics of persistent sexual offenders: A meta-analysis of recidivism studies. *Journal of Consulting and Clinical Psychology, 73,* 1154–1163.

Hanson, R. F., Resnick, H. S., Saunders, B. E., Kilpatrick, D. G., & Best, C. (1999). Factors related to the reporting of childhood rape. *Child Abuse and Neglect, 23,* 559–569.

Hanson, R. K., Steffy, R. A., & Gauthier, R. (1993). Long-term recidivism of child molesters. *Journal of Consulting and Clinical Psychology, 61,* 646–652.

Hare, R. D. (1978). Electrodermal and cardiovascular correlates of psychopathy. In R. D. Hare & Schalling (Eds.), *Psychopathic behavior: Approaches to research.* Chichester, UK: Wiley.

Hare, R. D. (1980). A research scale for the assessment of psychopathy in criminal populations. *Personality and Individual Differences, 1,* 111–119.

Hare, R. D. (1991). *Manual for the Hare Psychopathy Checklist-Revised.* Toronto, Ont., Canada: Multi-Health Systems.

Hare, R. D. (1993). *Without conscience: The disturbing world of the psychopaths among us.* New York: Pocket Books.

Hare, R. D. (1995). Psychopaths: New trends in research. *Harvard Mental Health Letter, 12,* 4–5.

Hare, R. D. (1998). The Hare PCL-R: Some issues concerning its use and misuse. *Legal and Criminological Psychology, 3,* 99–119.

Hare, R. D., & Cox, D. N. (1978). Clinical and empirical conceptions of psychopathy, and the selection of subjects for research. In R. D. Hare & D. Schalling (Eds.), *Psychopathic behavior: Approaches to research.* Chichester, UK: Wiley.

Hare, R. D., Harpur, T. J., Hakstian, A. R., Forth, A. E., Hart, S. D., & Newman, J. P. (1990). The Revised Psychopathy Checklist: Descriptive statistics, reliability, and factor structure. *Psychological Assessment, 2,* 338–341.

Hare, R. D., & Hart, S. D. (1995). A commentary on the Antisocial Personality Disorder Field Trial. In W. J. Livesley (Ed.), *The DSM-IV personality disorders.* New York: Guilford Press.

Hare, R. D., Hart, S. D., & Harpur, T. J. (1991). Psychopathy and the DSM-IV criteria for antisocial personality disorder. *Journal of Abnormal Psychology, 100,* 391–398.

Hare, R. D., & McPherson, L. M. (1984). Violent and aggressive behavior by criminal psychopaths. *International Journal of Law and Psychiatry, 7,* 35–50.

Hare, R. D., McPherson, L. M., & Forth, A. E. (1988). Male psychopaths and their criminal careers. *Journal of Consulting and Clinical Psychology, 56,* 710–714.

Hare, R. D., & Schalling, D. (Eds.) (1978). *Psychopathic behavior: Approaches to research.* Chichester, UK: Wiley.

Harpur, T. J., Hakstian, R., & Hare, R. D. (1988). Factor structure of the Psychopathy Checklist. *Journal of Consulting and Clinical Psychology, 56,* 741–747.

Harpur, J. T., & Hare, R. D. (1994). The assessment of psychopathy as a function of age. *Journal of Abnormal Psychology, 103,* 604–609.

Harpur, T. J., Hare, R. D., & Hakstian, A. R. (1989). Two-factor conceptualization of psychopathy: Construct validity and assessment implications. *Psychological Assessment, 1,* 6–17.

Harrington, N., & Leitenberg, H. (1994). Relationship between alcohol consumption and victim behaviors immediately preceding sexual aggression by an acquaintance. *Violence and Victims, 9,* 315–324.

Harris, G. T., Rice, M. E., & Cormier, C. A. (1991). Psychopathy and violent recidivism. *Law and Human Behavior, 15,* 625–637.

Harris, G. T., Rice, M. E., & Quinsey, V. L. (1994). Psychopathy as a taxon: Evidence that psychopaths are a discrete class. *Journal of Consulting and Clinical Psychology, 62,* 387–397.

Harrison, P. M., & Beck, A. J. (2004). Prisoners in 2003. *Bureau of Justice Statistics Bulletin.* Washington, DC: U.S. Department of Justice.

Hart, B. J. (1990). Gentle jeopardy: The further endangerment of battered women and children in custody mediation. *Mediation Quarterly, 7,* 317–330.

Hart, S. D., Cox, D. N., & Hare, R. D. (1995). *The Hare Psychopathy Checklist: Screening Version.* Toronto, Ont., Canada: Multi-Health Systems.

Hart, S. D., Forth, A. E., & Hare, R. D. (1990). Neuropsychological assessment of criminal psychopaths. *Journal of Abnormal Psychology, 99,* 374–379.

Hart, S. D., & Hare, R. D. (1989). Discriminant validity of the Psychopathy Checklist in a forensic psychiatric population. *Psychological Assessment, 1,* 211–218.

Hart, S. D., Hare, R. D., & Forth, A. E. (1993). Psychopathy as a risk marker for violence: Development and validation of a screening version of the Revised Psychopathy Checklist. In J. Monahan & H. Steadman (Eds.), *Violence and mental disorder: Development in risk assessment.* Chicago: University of Chicago Press.

Hart, S. D., Hare, R. D., & Harpur, T. J. (1992). The Psychopathy Checklist: Overview for researchers and clinicians. In J. Rosen & P. McReynolds (Eds.), *Advances in psychological assessment* (Vol. 8). New York: Plenum.

Hartman, B. J. (1987). Psychological screening of law enforcement candidates. *American Journal of Forensic Psychology, 1,* 5–9.

Harway, M., & Hansen, M. (1994). *Spouse abuse: Assessing and treating battered women, batterers, and their children.* Sarasota, FL: Professional Resource Press.

Haugaard, J. J., & Seri, L. G. (2000). Stalking and other forms of intrusive contact in adolescent and young-adult relationships. *UMKC Law Review, 69,* 227–238.

Hayne, H. (2004). Infant memory development: Implications for childhood amnesia. *Developmental Review, 24,* 33–73.

Heaton, R. K., Grant, I., & Matthews, C. G. (1992). *Comprehensive norms for an expanded Halstead-Reitan battery: Demographic corrections, research findings, and clinical application with a supplement for the WAIS-R.* Odessa, FL: Psychological Assessment Resources.

Hempel, C. (2003, February 9). TV's whodunit effect. *Boston Sunday Globe Magazine,* 13–17.

Hemphill, J. (1991). *Psychopathy and recidivism following release from a therapeutic community treatment program.* Unpublished master's thesis, University of Saskatchewan, Saskatoon, Canada.

Henderlong, J., & Lepper, M. R. (2002). The effects of praise on children's intrinsic motivation: A review and synthesis. *Psychological Bulletin, 128,* 774–795.

Henderson, N. D. (1979). Criterion-related validity of personality and aptitude scales. In C. D. Spielberger (Ed.), *Police selection and evaluation: Issues and techniques.* Washington, DC: Hemisphere.

Henggeler, S.W., Rowland, M. D., Randall, J., Ward, D. M., Pickrel, S. G., Cunningham, P. B., et al. (1999). Home-based multisystemic therapy as an alternative to the hospitalization of youths in psychiatric crisis: Clinical outcomes. *Journal of the American Academy of Child and Adolescent Psychiatry, 38,* 1331–1339.

Henggeler, S. W., Schoenwald, S. K., Borduin, C. M., Rowlan, M. D., & Cunningham, P. B. (1998). *Multisystemic treatment of antisocial behavior in children and adolescents.* New York: Guilford Press.

Henry, M. S., & Rafilson, F. M. (1997). The temporal stability of the National Police Officer Selection Test. *Psychological Reports, 81,* 1259–1265.

Herman, J. L. (1992). *Trauma and recovery.* New York: Basic Books.

Herrnstein, R. J., & Murray, C. A. (1994). *The bell curve: Intelligence and class structure in American life.* New York: Free Press.

Hiatt, D., & Hargrave, G. E. (1988). Predicting job performance problems with psychological screening. *Journal of Police Science and Administration, 16,* 122–125.

Hibler, N. S., & Kurke, M. I. (1995). Ensuring personal reliability through selection and training. In M. I. Kurke & E. M. Scrivner (Eds.), *Police psychology into the 21st century.* Hillsdale, NJ: Erlbaum.

Hicks, S. J., & Sales, B. D. (2006). *Criminal profiling: Developing an effective science and practice.* Washington, DC: American Psychological Association.

Hiller, M. L., Knight, K., & Simpson, D. D. (1999). Risk factors that predict dropout from corrections-based treatment for drug abuse. *The Prison Journal, 79,* 411–430.

Hills, A. M., & Taplin, J. L. (1998). Anticipated responses to stalking: Effect of threat and target stalker relationship. *Psychiatry, Psychology and Law, 5,* 139–146.

Ho, T. (1999). Assessment of police officer recruiting and testing instruments. *Journal of Offender Rehabilitation, 29*(3–4), 1–23.

Holden, G. W., Geffner, R., & Jouriles, E. N. (Eds.). (1998). *Children exposed to marital violence: Theory, research, and applied issues.* Washington, DC: American Psychological Association.

Hollander, J. (2004). "I can take care of myself": The impact of self-defense training on women's lives. *Violence Against Women, 10,* 205–235.

Holmes, R. M., & Holmes, S. T. (1996). *Profiling violent crimes: An investigative tool* (2nd ed.).Thousand Oaks, CA: Sage.

Homant, R. J., & Kennedy, D. B. (1998). Psychological aspects of crime scene profiling: Validity research. *Criminal Justice and Behavior, 25,* 319–343.

Horacek, H. J. (1998). *Brainstorm: Understanding and treating the emotional storms of ADHD and related disorders.* Northvale, NJ: Jason Aronson.

Howe, M. L., Kelland, A., Bryant-Brown, L., & Clark, S. L. (1992). Measuring the development of children's amnesia and hyperamnesia. In M. L. Howe, C. J. Brainerd, & V. F. Reyna (Eds.), *Development of long-term retention* (pp. 56–102). New York: Springer-Verlag.

Huffman, M. L., Warren, A. R., & Larson, S. M. (1999). Discussing truth and lies in interviews with children: Whether, when, and how? *Applied Developmental Science, 3,* 6–15.

Hughes, C., Dunn, J., & White, A. (1998). Trick or treat? Uneven understanding of mind and emotion and executive dysfunction in "hard-to-manage" preschoolers. *Journal of Child Psychology and Psychiatry, 39,* 981–994.

Hughes, C., White, A., Sharpen, J., & Dunn, J. (2000). Antisocial, angry, and unsympathetic: "Hard to manage" preschoolers' peer problems, and possible cognitive influences. *Journal of Child Psychology and Psychiatry, 41,* 169–179.

Hughes, M., & Grieve, R. (1980). On asking children bizarre questions. *First Language, 1,* 149–160.

Humphrey, S. E., & Kahn, A. (2000). Fraternities, athletic teams, and rape: Implications of identification with a risky group. *Journal of Interpersonal Violence, 15,* 1313–1322.

Hungerford, A. (2005). The use of anatomically detailed dolls in forensic investigations: Developmental considerations. *Journal of Forensic Psychology Practice, 5,* 75–87.

Hunter, J. E., & Hunter, R. F. (1984). Validity and utility of alternative predictors of job performance. *Psychological Bulletin, 96,* 72–98.

Inbau, F. E., Reid, J. E., & Buckley, J. P. (1986). *Criminal interrogation and confessions* (3rd ed.). Baltimore: Williams & Wilkins.

Inciardi, J. A. (1993). *Drug treatment and criminal justice.* Thousand Oaks, CA: Sage.

Inciardi, J. A., Martin, S. S., & Butzin, C. A. (2004). Five-year outcomes of therapeutic community treatment of drug-involved offenders after release from prison. *Crime & Delinquency, 50,* 88–107.

In re Gault, 387 U.S. 1 (1967).

International Association of Chiefs of Police. (1998). *Pre-employment psychological evaluation guidelines.* Alexandria, VA: Author.

Intrator, J., Hare, R., Stritzke, P., Brichtswein, K., et al. (1997). A brain-imaging (Single Photon Emission Computerized Tomography) study of semantic and affective processing in psychopaths. *Biological Psychiatry, 42,* 96–103.

Inwald, R. E. (1988). Five-year follow-up study of departmental terminations as predicted by 16 pre-employment psychological indicators. *Journal of Applied Psychology, 73,* 703–710.

Inwald, R. E., & Knatz, H. (1988, August). *Seven-year follow-up of officer terminations predicted by psychological testing.* Paper presented at the Annual Meeting of the American Psychological Association, Atlanta, GA.

Israel, M., & Chui, W. H. (2006). If "something works" is the answer, what is the question? *European Journal of Criminology, 3,* 181–200.

Ivnik, R. J., Malec, J. F., Smith, G. E., Tangalos, E. G., & Peterson, R. C. (1996). Neuropsychological tests' norms above age 55: COWAT, BNT, MAE Token, WRAT-R Reading, AMNART, STROOP, TMT, and JLO. *Clinical Neuropsychologist, 10,* 262–278.

Jackson, J. L., Herbrink, J. C. M., & van Koppen, P. J. (1997). An empirical approach to offender profiling. In V. G. S. Redondon, J. Perez, & R. Barbaret (Eds.), *Advances in psychology and law: International contributions* (pp. 333–345). Berlin: de Gruyter.

Jeffers, H. P. (1991). *Who killed precious?* Chicago: Congdon & Weed.

Jenkins, P. (1994). *Using murder: The social construction of serial homicide.* New York: Aldine de Gruyter.

Jenkins, P. (1996). The social construction of serial homicide. In J. E. Conklin (Ed.), *New perspectives in criminology.* Boston: Allyn & Bacon.

Johnson v. Zerbst, 304 U.S. 458 (1938).

Johnston, J. R., & Campbell, L. E. G. (1993). A clinical typology of interparental violence in disputed-custody divorces. *American Orthopsychiatric Association, 63,* 190–193.

Johnston, J. R., & Roseby, V. (1997). *In the name of the child: A developmental approach to understanding and helping children of conflicted and violent divorces.* New York: Free Press.

Jones, M. (1962). *Beyond the therapeutic community: Social learning and social psychiatry.* New Haven, CT: Yale University Press.

Jordan, C. E., Quinn, K., Jordan, B., & Daileader, C. R. (2000). Stalking: Cultural, clinical and legal considerations. *University of Louisville Brandeis Law Journal, 38,* 313–579.

Judd, T. (1999). *Neuropsychotherapy and community integration: Brain illness, emotions, and behavior.* New York: Kluwer Academic/Plenum.

Judd, T., & Fordyce, D. (1996). Personality tests. In R. Sbordone & D. Long (Eds.), *Ecological validity of neuropsychological tests.* Winter Park, FL: GP Press.

Jurado, C., Gimenez, M. P., Soriano, T., Menendez, M., & Repetto, M. (2000). Rapid analysis of amphetamine, methamphetamine, MDA, and MDMA in urine using solid-phase microextraction, direct on-fiber derivatization, and analysis by GC-MS. *Journal of Analytical Toxicology, 42,* 11–16.

Kail, R. (1990). *The development of memory in children* (3rd ed.). New York: W. H. Freeman.

Kapardis, A. (1992). Killed by a stranger in Victoria, January 1990–April 1992: Locations, victims' age and risk. In H. Strang & S. Gerull (Eds.), *Homicides: Patterns, prevention and control: Proceedings of a conference held 12–14 May 1992.* Canberra: Australian Institute of Criminology.

Karmen, A. (2001). *Crime victims: An introduction to victimology* (4th ed.). Belmont, CA: Wadsworth.

Kassin, S. M., Goldstein, C. C., & Savitsky, K. (2003, April). Behavioral confirmation in the interrogation room: On the dangers of presuming guilt. *Law and Human Behavior, 27,* 187–203.

Kassin, S. M., & Neumann, K. (1997). On the power of confession evidence: An experimental test of the fundamental difference hypothesis. *Law and Human Behavior, 21,* 469–484.

Kazdin, A. E. (2002). Psychosocial treatments for conduct disorder in children and adolescents. In P. E. Nathan & J. M. Gorman (Eds.), *A guide to treatments that work* (2nd ed.). New York: Oxford University Press.

Keeling, J. A., & Rose, J. L. (2005). Relapse prevention with intellectually disabled sexual offenders. *Sexual Abuse: A Journal of Research and Treatment, 17,* 407–423.

Keenan, K., & Shaw, D. (2003). Starting at the beginning: Exploring the etiology of antisocial behavior in the first years of life. In B. B. Lahey, T. E. Moffitt, & A. Caspi (Eds.), *Causes of conduct disorder and juvenile delinquency.* New York: Guilford Press.

Kelling, G., & Coles, C. M. (1996). *Fixing broken windows: Restoring order and reducing crime in our communities.* New York: Touchstone.

Kendall-Tackett, K. A., & Watson, M. W. (1992). Use of anatomical dolls by Boston-area professionals. *Child Abuse and Neglect, 16,* 423–428.

Kendig, N. E. (2004). Correctional health care systems and collaboration with academic medicine. *Journal of the American Medical Association, 292,* 501–503.

Kent v. U.S., 383 U.S. 541 (1966).

Keppel, R. D., & Weis, J. G. (1993). *Improving the investigation of violent crime: The homicide investigation and tracking system.* Washington, DC: National Institute of Justice.

Kernberg, O. F. (1984). *Severe personality disorders: Psychotherapeutic strategies.* New York: Jason Aronson.

Kilburg, R. R. (1984). Psychologists in management: The unseen career path in psychology. *Professional Psychology: Research and Practice, 15,* 613–625.

Kilpatrick, D. G., Edmunds, C., & Seymour, A. (1992). *Rape in America: A report to the nation.* Arlington, VA: National Victim Center.

Kilpatrick, D. G., Saunders, B. E., Amick-McMullan, A., & Best, C. L. (1989). Victim and crime factors associated with the development of crime-related post-traumatic stress disorder. *Behavior Therapy, 20,* 199–214.

Kimble, G. A. (1994). *How to use (and misuse) statistics.* New York: Prentice Hall.

King, R., & Norgard, K. (1999, Summer). What about our families? Using the impact of death row defendants' family members as a mitigating factor in death penalty sentencing. *Florida State Law Review,* 1121–1141.

Klecan-Aker, J. S., & Swank, P. R. (1988). The use of a pragmatic protocol with normal preschool children. *Journal of Communication Disorders, 21,* 85–102.

Kleck, G., & Sayles, S. (1990). Rape and resistance. *Social Problems, 37,* 149–162.

Knight, K., Simpson, D. D., & Hiller, M. L. (1999). Three-year reincarceration outcomes for in-prison therapeutic community treatment in Texas. *The Prison Journal, 79,* 337–351.

Knight, R. A. (1989). An assessment of the concurrent validity of child molester typology. *Journal of Interpersonal Violence, 4,* 131–150.

Knight, R. A. (1992). The generation and corroboration of a taxonomic model for child molesters. In W. O'Donohue & J. H. Geer (Eds.), *The sexual abuse of children: Theory, research, and therapy.* Hillsdale, NJ: Erlbaum.

Knight, R. A. (1999). Validation of a typology for rapists. *Journal of Interpersonal Violence, 14,* 303–330.

Knight, R. A., Carter, D. L., & Prentky, R. A. (1989). A system for the classification of child molesters: Reliability and application. *Journal of Interpersonal Violence, 4,* 3–23.

Knopp, F. H., Rosenberg, J., & Stevenson, W. (1986). *Report on nationwide survey of juvenile and adult sex-offender treatment programs and providers.* Syracuse, NY: Safer Society Press.

Kochanska, G. (1998). Mother–child relationship, child fearfulness, and emerging attachment: A short-term longitudinal study. *Developmental Psychology, 34,* 480–490.

Kochanska, G., Murray, K., & Coy, K. (1997). Inhibitory control as a contributor to conscience in childhood: From toddler to early school age. *Child Development, 68,* 263–277.

Kocsis, R. N. (2004). Psychological profiling of serial arson offenses: An assessment of skills and accuracy. *Criminal Justice and Behavior, 31,* 341–361.

Kocsis, R. N., Irwin, H. J., Hayes, A. F., & Nunn, R. (2000). Expertise in psychological profiling. *Journal of Interpersonal Violence, 15,* 311–331.

Kohout, J., & Wicherski, M. (1999). *1997 Doctorate employment survey.* Washington, DC: American Psychological Association, Research Office.

Koocher, G. P., Goodman, G. S., White, C. S., Friedrich, W. N., Sivan, A. B., & Reynolds, C. R. (1995). Psychological science and the use of anatomically detailed dolls in child sexual abuse assessments. *Psychological Bulletin, 118,* 199–222.

Koss, M. P. (1984). Hidden rape: Sexual aggression and victimization in a national sample of students in higher education. In A. Burgess (Ed.), *Rape and sexual assault II.* New York: Garland.

Koss, M. P. (1985). The hidden rape victim: Personality, attitudinal, and situational characteristics. *Psychology of Women Quarterly, 9,* 192–212.

Koss, M. P., & Cleveland, H. (1996). Athletic participation, fraternity membership, and date rape. *Violence Against Women, 2,* 180–190.

Koss, M. P., & Dinero, T. E. (1988). Predictors of sexual aggression among male college students. *Annals of the New York Academy of Sciences, 528,* 133–147.

Koss, M. P., & Dinero, T. E. (1989). Discriminant analysis of risk factors for sexual victimization among a national sample of college women. *Journal of Consulting Clinical Psychology, 57,* 242.

Koss, M. P., & Gaines, J. A. (1993). The prediction of sexual aggression by alcohol use, athletic participation, and fraternity affiliation. *Journal of Interpersonal Violence, 8,* 84–108.

Koss, M. P., Gidycz, C. A., & Wisniewski, N. (1987). The scope of rape: Incidence and prevalence of sexual aggression and victimization in a national sample of higher education students. *Journal of Counseling and Clinical Psychology, 55,* 162–170.

Koss, M. P., & Heslet, L. (1992). Somatic consequences of violence against women. *Archives of Family Medicine, 1,* 53–59.

Kosson, D. S., Smith, S. S., & Newman, J. P. (1990). Evaluating the construct validity of psychopathy in black and white male inmates: Three preliminary studies. *Journal of Abnormal Psychology, 99,* 250–259

Kroes, W. H., Margolis, L., & Hurrell, J. J. (1974). Job stress in policemen. *Journal of Police Science and Administration, 2,* 145–155.

Kropp, P. R., Hart, S. D., Webster, C. D., & Eaves, D. (1999). *Spousal assault risk assessment guide.* North Tonawanda, NY: Multi-Health Systems.

Kurki, L. (1999). Incorporating restorative and community justice into American sentencing and corrections: Sentencing and corrections 3. *Papers from the Executive Sessions on Sentencing and Corrections.* Washington, DC: U.S. Department of Justice.

Lagattuta, K. H., & Wellman, H. M. (2002). Differences in early parent–child conversations among negative versus positive emotions: Implications for the development of psychological understanding. *Developmental Psychology, 38,* 564–580.

Lahey, B. B., & Kazdin, A. (Eds.). (1990). *Advances in clinical child psychology* (Vol. 13). New York: Plenum.

Lahey, B. B., & Waldman, I. D. (2003). A developmental propensity model of the origins of conduct problems during childhood and adolescence. In B. B. Lahey, T. E. Moffitt, & A. Caspi (Eds.), *Causes of conduct disorder and juvenile delinquency.* New York: Guilford Press.

Laird, R. D., Jordan, K., Dodge, K. A., Pettit, G. S., & Bates, J. E. (2001). Peer rejection in childhood, involvement with antisocial peers in early adolescence, and the development of externalizing problems. *Development and Psychopathology, 13,* 337–354.

Lamb, M.E. (1994). The investigation of child sexual abuse: An interdisciplinary consensus statement. *Child Abuse & Neglect, 18,* 1021–1028.

Lambrick, F., & Glaser, W. (2004). Sex offenders with an intellectual disability. *Sexual Abuse: A Journal of Research and Treatment, 16,* 381–392.

Landenberger, N. A., & Lipsey, M. W. (2005). The positive effects of cognitive behavioral programs for offenders: A meta-analysis of factors associated with effective treatment. *Journal of Experimental Criminology, 1,* 451–476.

Langan, N. P., & Pelissier, B. M. M. (2001). The effect of drug treatment on inmate misconduct in federal prisons. *Journal of Offender Rehabilitation, 34,* 21–30.

Langan, P. A., & Levin, D. J. (2002). *Recidivism of prisoners released in 1994.* Washington, DC: Bureau of Justice Statistics, U.S. Department of Justice.

Langevin, R., Hucker, S. J., Handy, L., Hook, H. J., Purins, J. E., & Russon, A. E. (1985) Erotic preference and aggression in pedophilia: A comparison of heterosexual, homosexual, and bisexual types. In R. Langevin (Ed.), *Erotic preference, gender identity, and aggression in men: New research studies.* Hillsdale, NJ: Erlbaum.

Lapierre, D., Braun, M. J., & Hodgins, S. (1995). Ventral frontal deficits in psychopathy: Neuropsychological test findings. *Neuropsychologia, 11,* 139–151.

Larbig, W., Veit, R., Rau, H., Schlottke, P., & Birbaumer, N. (1992, October). *Cerebral and peripheral correlates of psychopaths during anticipation of aversive stimulation.* Paper presented at the Annual Meeting of the Society for Psychophysiological Research, San Diego, CA.

Latessa, E. J. (2004). The challenge of change: Correctional programs and evidence-based practices. *Criminology and Public Policy, 3,* 547–559.

Latessa, E. J., Cullen, F. T., & Gendreau, P. (2002). Beyond correctional quackery: Professionalism and the possibility of effective treatment. *Federal Probation, 66,* 43–49.

Laub, J. H. (1981). Ecological considerations in victim reporting to the police. *Journal of Criminal Justice, 9,* 419–430.

Laub, J. H. (1997). Patterns of criminal victimization in the United States. In R. C. Davis, A. J. Lurigio, & W. G. Skogan (Eds.), *Victims of crime* (2nd ed.). Thousand Oaks, CA: Sage.

Launay, G., & Murray, P. (1989). Victim/offender groups. In M. Wright & B. Galaway (Eds.), *Mediation and criminal justice (pp. 113–131).* Newbury Park, CA: Sage.

Lawrence, R. A. (1983). The role of legal counsel in juveniles' understanding of their rights. *Juvenile and Family Court Journal, 34,* 49–58.

LeBeau, M., Andollo, W., Hearn, W. L., Baselt, R., Cone, E., Finkle, B., et al. (1999). Recommendations for toxicological investigations of drug-facilitated sexual assaults. *Journal of Forensic Sciences, 44,* 227–230.

Lefkowitz, J. (1975). Psychological attributes of policemen: A review of research and opinion. *Journal of Social Issues, 31,* 3–26.

Lemon, N. K. D. (1999). The legal system's response to children exposed to domestic violence. *Domestic Violence and Children, 9,* 67–83.

Lemon, N. K. D. (2000). Custody and visitation trends in the United States in domestic violence cases. *Journal of Aggression, Maltreatment, & Trauma, 3,* 329–343.

Leschied, A. W., & Cunningham, A. (2001). *Clinical trials of multisystemic therapy, 1977 to 2001: Evaluation update report.* London, Ont., Canada: Centre for Children and Families in the Justice System.

Lester, D. (1983). The selection of police officers: An argument for simplicity. *Police Journal, 56,* 53–55.

Letourneau, E. J., Cunningham, P. B., & Henggeler, S. W. (2002). Multisystemic treatment of antisocial behavior in adolescents. In S. G. Hofmann & M. C. Tompson (Eds.), *Treating chronic and severe mental disorders: A handbook of empirically supported interventions.* New York: Guilford Press.

Levinson, R. B. (1985). The psychologist in the correctional system. *The American Journal of Forensic Psychology, 3,* 41–43.

Lezak, M. D. (1995). *Neuropsychological assessment* (3rd ed.). New York: Oxford University Press.

Li, J. (1999). The new "Mickey Finn Specials"— Should GHB and Ketamine be banned? *Journal of the American Pharmaceutical Association, 39,* 442–443.

Lipton, D. S. (1995). *The effectiveness of treatment for drug abusers under criminal justice supervision.* Washington, DC: National Institute of Justice.

Lipton, D. S., Pearson, F. S., Cleland, C. M., & Yee, D. (2002). The effects of therapeutic communities and milieu therapy on recidivism. In J. McGuire (Ed.), *Offender rehabilitation and treatment: Effective programmes and policies to reduce reoffending.* Etobicoke, Ont., Canada: Wiley.

Liska, A., & Baccaglini, W. (1990). Feeling safe by comparison: Crime in the newspapers. *Social Problems, 37,* 360–374.

Littell, J. H., Popa, M., & Forsythe, B. (2006). Multisystemic therapy for social, emotional, and behavioral problems in youth aged 10–17 (Review). *The Cochrane Database of Systematic Reviews, Issue 1.* New York: Wiley. Retrieved April 12, 2007, from htpp://www.mrw.inter science.wiley.com/cochrane/clsysrev/articles/CD004797/pdf_fs.html.

Livesley, W. J., Jackson, D. N., & Schroeder, M. (1992). Factorial structure of traits delineating personality disorders in clinical and general population samples. *Journal of Abnormal Psychology, 101,* 432–440.

Livesley, W. J., & Schroeder, M. (1991). Dimension of personality disorder: The DSM-III-R Cluster B diagnoses. *Journal of Nervous and Mental Disease, 179,* 320–328.

Liwag, M. D., & Stein, N. L. (1995). Children's memory for emotional events: The importance of emotion-related retrieval cues. *Journal of Experimental Child Psychology, 60,* 2–31.

Lizotte, A. (1985). The uniqueness of rape: Reporting assaultive violence to the police. *Crime & Delinquency, 31,* 169–190.

Locke, B. D., & Mahalik, J. R. (2005). Examining masculinity norms, problem drinking, and athletic involvement as predictors of sexual aggression in college men. *Journal of Counseling Psychology, 52,* 279–283.

Loeb, P. A. (1996). *Independent living scales.* Itasca, IL: Riverside.

London, K. (2001). Investigative interviews of children: A review of psychological research and implications for police practices. *Police Quarterly, 4,* 123–144.

London, K., & Nunez, N. (2002, October). Examining the efficacy of various truth/lie discussions in increasing the veracity of children's reports. *Journal of Experimental Child Psychology, 83*(2), 131–147.

Longo, R. F. S., Bird, S., Stevenson, W. F., & Fiske, J. A. (1995). *1994 Nationwide survey of treatment programs and models.* Brandon, VT: Safer Society Press.

Lonner, W., & Malpass, R. (1994). *Psychology and culture.* Boston: Allyn & Bacon.

Lonsway, K. A. (1996). Preventing acquaintance rape through education: What do we know? *Psychology of Women Quarterly, 20,* 229–265.

Lösel, F. (2001). Evaluating the effectiveness of correctional programs: Bridging the gap between research and practice. In G. A. Bernfeld, D. P. Farrington, & A. W. Leschied (Eds.), *Offender rehabilitation in practice* (pp. 67–92). New York: Wiley.

Lösel, F., & Bender, D. (2003). Protective factors and resilience. In D. P. Farrington & J. W. Coid (Eds.), *Early prevention of adult antisocial behaviour.* Cambridge, UK: Cambridge University Press.

Lösel, F., & Schmucker, M. (2005). The effectiveness of treatment for sexual offenders: A comprehensive

meta-analysis. *Journal of Experimental Criminology, 1,* 117–146.

Low, J., & Durkin, K. (2000). Event knowledge and children's recall of television-based narratives. *British Journal of Developmental Psychology, 18,* 247–267.

Lowenkamp, C. T. (2004). *Correctional program integrity and treatment effectiveness: A multi-site, program-level analysis.* Unpublished doctoral dissertation, University of Cincinnati, OH.

Lurigio, A. J., Rollins, A., & Fallon, J. (2004). The effects of serious mental illness on offender reentry. *Federal Probation, 68,* 45–53.

Luthar, S. S., Cicchetti, D., & Becker, B. (2000). The construct of resilience: A critical evaluation and guidelines for future work. *Child Development, 71,* 543–562.

Lykken, D. T. (1981). *A tremor in the blood: Uses and abuses of the lie detector.* New York: McGraw-Hill.

Lykken, D. T. (1995). *The antisocial personalities.* Hillsdale, NJ: Erlbaum.

MacDonald, S., & Hayne, H. (1996). Child-initiated conversations about the past and memory performance by preschoolers. *Cognitive Development, 11,* 421–442.

Macklin, C. (1994). The effects of advertising retrieval cue on young children's memory and brand evaluation. *Psychology and Marketing, 11,* 291–311.

Macy, R. J., Nurius, P., & Norris, J. (2006). Responding in their best interests: Contextualizing women's coping with acquaintance sexual aggression. *Violence Against Women, 12,* 478–500.

Madigan, L., & Gamble, N. C. (1991). *The second rape: Society's continued betrayal of rape victims.* New York: Lexington Books.

Magaletta, P. R., Ax, R. K., Patry, M., & Dietz, E. F. (2005, February). Clinical practice in segregation: The crucial role of psychologists. *Corrections Today,* 34–36.

Magaletta, P. R., & Boothby, J. L. (2003). Correctional mental health professionals. In T. J. Fagan & R. K. Ax. (Eds.), *Correctional mental health handbook* (pp. 21–38). Thousand Oaks, CA: Sage.

Magaletta, P. R., Fagan, T. J., & Ax, R. K. (1998). Advancing psychology services through Telehealth in the Federal Bureau of Prisons. *Professional Psychology Research and Practice, 29,* 543–548.

Magaletta, P. R., Patry, M. W., Dietz, E. F., Ax, R. K. (2007). *Criminal Justice and Behavior, 34,* 7–21.

Magaletta, P. R., & Verdeyen, V. (2005). Clinical practice in corrections: A conceptual framework. *Professional Psychology: Research and Practice, 36,* 37–43.

Mahoney, P., & Williams, L. M. (1998). Sexual assault in marriage: Prevalence, consequences, and treatment of wife rape. In J. L. Jasinski & L. M. Williams (Eds.), *Partner violence: A comprehensive review of 20 years of research* (pp. 113–162). Thousand Oaks, CA: Sage.

Malloy v. Hogan, 378 U.S. 1 (1964).

Manning, P. K. (1994). Economic rhetoric and policing reform. *Police Forum, 4,* 1–8.

Marlowe, D. B. (2003). Integrating substance abuse treatment and criminal justice supervision. *Science & Practice Perspectives, 2,* 4–14.

Marques, J. K. (1999). How to answer the question: "Does sexual offender treatment work?" *Journal of Interpersonal Violence, 14,* 437–451.

Marques, J. K., Day, D. M., Nelson, C., West, M. A., & Hall, M. A. (1993). Findings and recommendation from California's experimental treatment program. In G. C. Nagayama, R. Hirschman, J. R. Graham, & M. S. Zaragoza (Eds.), *Sexual aggression: Issues in etiology, assessment, and treatment.* Philadelphia: Taylor & Francis.

Marques, J. K., Wiederanders, M., Day, D. M., Nelson, C., & van Ommeren, A. (2005). Effects of a relapse prevention program on sexual recidivism: Final results from California's Sex Offender Treatment and Evaluation Project (SOTEP). *Sexual Abuse: A Journal of Research and Treatment, 17,* 79–107.

Marshall, W. L. (2005). Therapist style in sexual offender treatment: Influences on indices of change. *Sexual Abuse: A Journal of Research and Treatment, 17,* 109–116.

Marshall, W. L., Barbaree, H. E., & Fernandez, M. (1995). Some aspects of social competence in sexual offenders. *Sexual Abuse: A Journal of Research and Treatment, 7,* 113–127.

Marshall, W. L., & Serran, G. A. (2000). Improving the effectiveness of sex offender treatment. *Trauma, Violence, & Abuse, 1,* 203–222.

Marshall, W. L., Ward, T., Mann, R. E., Moulden, H., Fernandez, Y. M., Serran, G., et al. (2005). Working positively with sexual offenders: Maximizing the effectiveness of treatment. *Journal of Interpersonal Violence, 20,* 1096–1114.

Martens, W. H. J. (1997). *Psychopathy and remission.* Maastricht, The Netherlands: Shaker Publishing.

Martens, W. H. J. (2000a). Antisocial and psychopathic personality disorders: Causes, course, and remission: A review article. *International Journal of Offender Therapy and Comparative Criminology, 44,* 406–430.

Martens, W. H. J. (2000b). What shall we do with untreatable forensic psychiatric patients? *Medicine and Law, 19,* 389–395.

Martens, W. H. J. (2001a). Agitation therapy for antisocial and psychopathic personalities: An outline. *American Journal of Psychotherapy, 55,* 234–250.

Martens, W. H. J. (2001b). Effects of antisocial and social attitudes on neurobiological functioning. *Medical Hypotheses, 56,* 664–771.

Martens, W. H. J. (2001c). Physical and mental illness in homeless persons: An overview. *Public Health Reviews, 29,* 13–33.

Martens, W. H. J. (2001d). A theoretical framework for ethics therapy as a distinctive forensic therapeutic discipline. *International Journal of Offender Therapy and Comparative Criminology, 45,* 383–394.

Martens, W. H. J. (2001/2002). Homelessness and mental disorders: A comparison between homeless populations from different Western countries: A review. *International Journal of Mental Health, 30,* 79–96.

Martens, W. H. J. (2002a). Criminality and moral dysfunctions: Neurologic, biochemical, and genetic dimensions. *International Journal of Offender Therapy and Comparative Criminology, 46,* 170–182.

Martens, W. H. J. (2003a). *A new model of treatment community for antisocial and psychopathic personalities.* Manuscript submitted for publication.

Martens, W. H. J. (2003b). Theoretical building-blocks of spiritual psychotherapy for non-religious patients. *Journal of Contemporary Psychotherapy, 33,* 205–218.

Martin, S. (1990). *Progress in policing.* Washington, DC: Police Foundation.

Martin, S., & Bachman, R. (1998). The contribution of alcohol to the likelihood of completion and severity of injury in rape incidents. *Violence Against Women, 4,* 694–712.

Martin, S. S., Butzin, C. A., Saum, C. A., & Inciardi, J. A. (1999). Three-year outcomes of therapeutic community treatment for drug-involved offenders in Delaware: From prison to work release and aftercare. *The Prison Journal, 79,* 294–317.

Martinson, R. (1974). What works? Questions and answers about prison reform. *The Public Interest, 35,* 22–54.

Marx, B. P., Calhoun, K. S., Wilson, A. E., & Meyerson, L. A. (2001). Sexual revictimization prevention: An outcome evaluation. *Journal of Consulting and Clinical Psychology, 69,* 25–32.

Masten, A. S. (1994). Resilience in individual development: Successful adaptation despite risk and adversity. In M. C. Wang & E. W. Gordon (Eds.), *Educational resilience in inner-city America: Challenges and prospects.* Hillsdale, NJ: Erlbaum.

Masten, A. S. (2001). Ordinary magic: Resilience processes in development. *American Psychologist, 56,* 227–238.

Masten, A. S., & Coatsworth, J. D. (1998). The development of competence in favorable and unfavorable environments. *American Psychologist, 53,* 205–220.

Matilla, M. A. K., & Larni, H. M. (1980). Flunitrazepam: A review of its pharmaceutical properties and therapeutic use. *Drugs, 20,* 353–374.

Matlin, M. W. (1998). *Cognition* (4th ed.). Fort Worth, TX: Harcourt Brace.

Mawby, R. I., & Walklate, S. (1995). *Critical victimology.* Thousand Oaks, CA: Sage.

Maxfield, M. (1989). Circumstances in supplementary homicide reports: Variety and validity. *Criminology, 27,* 671–695.

McCaffrey, R. J., Williams, A. D., Fisher, J. M., & Laing, L. C. (Eds.). (1997). *The practice of forensic Neuropsychology: Meeting challenges in the courtroom.* New York: Plenum.

McCaughey, M. (1997). *Real knockouts: The physical feminism of women's self-defense.* New York: New York University Press.

McConaghy, N. (1999). Methodological issues concerning evaluation of treatment for sexual offenders: Randomization, treatment dropouts, untreated controls, and within-treatment studies. *Sexual Abuse: A Journal of Research and Treatment, 11,* 183–194.

McDaniel, M. A., & Frei, R. L. (1994). *Validity of customer service measures in personnel selection: A review of criterion and construct evidence.* Unpublished manuscript.

McGough, L. S. (1994). *Child witnesses: Fragile voices in the American legal system.* New Haven, CT: Yale University Press.

McGrath, R. J., Cumming, G. F., & Burchard, B. L. (2003). *Current practices and trends in sexual abuser management: The Safer Society 2002 nationwide survey.* Brandon, VT: Safer Society Press.

McGuire, J. (2002, November). *Evidence-based programming today.* Paper presented at the International Community Corrections Association Annual Conference, Boston.

McGuire, J. (2005). *Meta-analytic reviews of offender treatment, 1985–2005.* Unpublished report. Liverpool, UK: University of Liverpool.

McKenzie, J. D. (1986). Preface. In J. T. Reese & H. A. Goldstein (Eds.), *Psychological services for law enforcement.* Washington, DC: Government Printing Office.

McKnight, L. R., & Loper, A. B. (2002). The effect of risk and resilience factors on the prediction of delinquency in adolescent girls. *School Psychology International, 23,* 186–198.

Mealey, L. (1995). The sociobiology of sociopathy: An integrated evolutionary model. *Behavioral and Brain Sciences, 18,* 523–599.

Meier, R. D., Farmer, R. E., & Maxwell, D. (1987). Psychological screening of police candidates: Current perspectives. *Journal of Police Science and Administration, 15,* 210–216.

Meier, R. F., & Miethe, T. D. (1993). Understanding theories of criminal victimization. In M. Tonry (Ed.), *Crime and justice: A review of research* (Vol. 17, pp. 459–499). Chicago: University of Chicago Press.

Meloy, J. R. (1992). *Violent attachments.* Northvale, NJ: Jason Aronson.

Merrington, S., & Stanley, S. (2004). "What works?": Revisiting the evidence in England and Wales. *Probation Journal, 5,* 7–20.

Mesiarik, C., Goldstein, N. E., & Thomson, M. (2002, March). *Validity of the Miranda Rights Comprehension Instruments–II scoring criteria and attorneys' perceptions of adequate Miranda comprehension.* Symposium conducted at the Biennial Conference of the American Psychology-Law Society (Division 41 of the American Psychological Association), Austin, TX.

Milan, M. A., Chin, C. E., & Nguyen, Q. X. (1999). Practicing psychology in correctional settings: Assessment, treatment, and substance abuse programs. In A. K. Hess & I. B. Weiner (Eds.), *The handbook of forensic psychology* (2nd ed.). New York: Wiley.

Milan, M. A., & Long, C. K. (1980). Crime and Delinquency: The last frontier? In D. Glenwick & L. Jason (Eds.), *Behavioral community psychology: Progress and prospects.* New York: Praeger.

Milan, M. A., Montgomery, R.W., & Rogers, E. C. (1994). Theoretical orientation revolution in clinical psychology: Fact or fiction? *Professional Psychology: Research and Practice, 25,* 398–402.

Miller, W. R., & Rollnick, S. (1991). *Motivational interviewing: Preparing people to change addictive behavior.* New York: Guilford Press.

Miller, W. R., & Rollnick, S. (Eds.). (2002). *Motivational interviewing: Preparing people for change* (2nd ed.). New York: Guilford Press.

Millon, T. (1994). *Millon Clinical Multiaxial Inventory—III manual.* Minneapolis: National Computer Systems.

Ministry of Justice. (2002). *Residential forensic treatment of children and adolescents.* The Hague, The Netherlands: Author.

Minuchin, S., Montalvo, B., Guerney, B., Rosman, B., & Schumer, F. (1967). *Families of the slums: An exploration of their structure and treatment.* New York: Basic Books.

Miranda v. Arizona, 384 U.S. 436 (1966).

Mitrushina, M. N., Boone, K. B., & D'Elia, L. F. (1999). *Handbook of normative data for neuropsychological assessment.* New York: Oxford University Press.

Moffitt, T. E., Caspi, A., Dickson, N., Silva, P., & Stanton, W. (1996). Childhood-onset versus adolescent-onset antisocial conduct problems in males: Natural history from ages 3 to 18. *Development and Psychopathology, 8,* 399–424.

Mohandie, K., Hatcher, C., & Raymond, D. (1996). False victimization syndromes in stalking. In J. R. Meloy (Ed.), *The psychology of stalking: Clinical and forensic perspectives.* San Diego, CA: Academic Press.

Monahan, J., Steadman, H., Silver, E., Appelbaum, P., Robbins, P. C., Mulvey, E., et al. (2001). *Rethinking risk assessment: The MacArthur Study of Mental Disorder and Violence.* NewYork: Oxford University Press.

Moore, M., & Trojanowicz, R. (1988). *Corporate strategies for policing: Perspectives on policing.* Washington, DC: Government Printing Office.

Morey, L. C. (1991). *The Personality Assessment Inventory professional manual.* Odessa, FL: Psychological Assessment Resources.

Morgan, A. B., & Lilienfeld, S. O. (2000). A meta-analytic review of the relation between antisocial behavior and neuropsychological measures of executive functions. *Clinical Psychology Review, 20,* 113–136.

Morgan, R. D. (2003). Basic mental health services: Services and issues. In T. J. Fagan & R. K. Ax. (Eds.), *Correctional mental health handbook* (pp. 59–72). Thousand Oaks, CA: Sage.

Morgan, R. D., Beer, A. M., Fitzgerald, K. L., & Mandracchia, J. T. (2007). Graduate student's experiences, interests and attitudes towards correctional/forensic psychology. *Criminal Justice and Behavior, 34,* 96–107.

Morgan, R. D., Winterowd, C. L., & Ferrel, S. W. (1999). A national survey of group psychotherapy services in correctional facilities. *Professional Psychology: Research and Practice, 30,* 600–606.

Morgen, K., & Grossman, J. (1988). *The prevalence of anti-gay/lesbian victimization in Baltimore.* Unpublished manuscript, available from Dr. Morgen, 28 Allegheny Avenue, Suite 1304, Townsend, MD.

Moriarty, L. J., Jerin, R. A., & Pelfrey, W. V. (1998). Evaluating victim services: A comparative analysis of North Carolina and Virginia Victim Witness Assistance Programs. In L. J. Moriarty & R. A. Jerin (Eds.), *Current issues in victimology research.* Durham, NC: Carolina Academic Press.

Morland, J. (2000). Toxicity of drug abuse—Amphetamine designer drugs (ecstasy): Mental effects and consequences of single dose use. *Toxicology Letter, 112–113,* 147–152.

Morris, E. F. (2001). Clinical practices with African Americans: Juxtaposition of standard clinical practices and Africentricism. *Professional Psychology: Research and Practice, 32,* 563–572.

Morrissey, E., Wandersman, A., Seybolt, D., Nation, M., Crusto, C., & Davino, K. (1997). Toward a famework. for bridging the gap between science and practice in prevention: A focus on evaluator and practitioner perspectives. *Evaluation and Program Planning, 20,* 367–377.

Moston, S. (1990). How children interpret and respond to questions: Situational sources of suggestibility in eyewitness interviews. *Social Behaviour, 5,* 155–167.

Moston, S., Stephenson, G. M., & Williamson, T. M. (1992). The effects of case characteristics on suspect behavior during police questioning. *British Journal of Criminology, 32,* 23–40.

Motiuk, L. L. (1999, August). Role of psychology in applied correctional research. In C. B. Clements

(Chair), *Correctional psychology in North America: New roles, new challenges.* Symposium conducted at the Annual Meeting of the American Psychological Association, Boston.

Mpofu, E. (2002). Indigenization of the psychology of human intelligence in sub-Saharan Africa. In W. J. Lonner, D. L. Dinnel, S. A. Hayes, & D. N. Sattler (Eds.), *Online readings in psychology and culture* (Unit 5, Chapter 2; http://www.wwu .edu/~culture). Bellingham, WA: Center for Cross-Cultural Research, Western Washington University.

Muehlenhard, C. L., & Linton, M. A. (1987). Date rape and sexual aggression in dating situations: Incidence and risk factors. *Journal of Counseling Psychology, 34,* 186–196.

Mullen, P. E., Pathé, M., & Purcell, R. (2000). *Stalkers and their victims.* Cambridge, UK: Cambridge University Press.

Muller, D. A. (2000). Criminal profiling: Real science or just wishful thinking? *Homicide Studies, 4,* 234–264.

Mumola, C. J. (1999). *Substance abuse and treatment, state and federal prisoners.* Washington, DC: National Institute of Justice.

Murphy, J. J. (1972). Current practices in the use of psychological testing by police agencies. *The Journal of Criminal Law, Criminology, and Police Science, 63,* 570–576.

Murrey, G. J. (Ed.). (2000). *The forensic evaluation of traumatic brain injury: A handbook for clinicians and attorneys.* Boca Raton, FL: CRC Press.

Myers, D. G. (1996). *Social psychology* (6th ed.). Boston: McGraw-Hill.

Myers, J., Gramzow, E., Ornstein, P. A., Wagner, L., Gordon, B. N., & Baker-Ward, L. (2003). Children's memory of a physical examination: A comparison of recall and recognition assessment protocol. *International Journal of Behavioral Development, 27,* 66–73.

Myers, N. A., & Perlmutter, M. (1978). Memory in the years from two to five. In P. A. Ornstein (Ed.), *Memory development in children* (pp. 191–218). Hillsdale, NJ: Erlbaum.

Nadeau, J. W. (1998). *Families making sense of death.* Thousand Oaks, CA: Sage.

Narrol, H. G., & Levitt, E. E. (1963). Formal assessment procedures in police selection. *Psychological Reports, 12,* 691–694.

Nasby, W., Hayden, B., & DePaulo, B. M. (1979). Attributional bias among aggressive boys to interpret unambiguous social stimuli as displays of hostility. *Journal of Abnormal Psychology, 89,* 459–468.

Nation, M., Crusto, C., Wandersman, A., Kumpfer, K. I., Seybolt, D., Morrissey-Kane, E., et al. (2003). What works in prevention: Principles of effective prevention programs. *American Psychologist, 58,* 449–456.

National Advisory Commission on Criminal Justice Standards and Goals. (1973). *Task force on police.* Washington, DC: Government Printing Office.

National Police Chiefs and Sheriffs Information Bureau. (1996). *The national directory of law enforcement administrators and correctional agencies.* Milwaukee, WI: Author.

National Victim Center and Crime Victims Research and Treatment Center. (1992). *Rape in America: A report to the nation.* Arlington, VA: National Victim Center.

Nell, V. (2000). *Cross-cultural neuropsychological assessment: Theory and practice.* Mahwah, NJ: Erlbaum.

Newman, J. P., & Wallace, J. F. (1993). Psychopathy and cognition. In P. Kendall & K. Dobson (Eds.), *Psychopathology and cognition.* New York: Academic.

Newmark, L., Hartell, A., & Salem, P. (1995). Domestic violence and empowerment in custody and visitation cases. *Family and Conciliation Courts Review, 33,* 30–62.

New York Criminal Procedure Law, Section § 120.45 (1999).

Nicholaichuk, T., Gordon, A., Gu, D., & Wong, S. (2000). Outcome of an institutional sexual offender treatment program: A comparison between treated and matched untreated offenders. *Sexual Abuse: A Journal of Research and Treatment, 12,* 139–153.

Nigg, J. T., & Huang-Pollock, C. L. (2003). An early-onset model of the role of executive functions and intelligence in conduct disorder/delinquency. In B. B. Lahey, T. E. Moffitt, & A. Caspi (Eds.), *Causes of conduct disorder and juvenile delinquency.* New York: Guilford Press.

Nigg, J. T., Quamma, J. P., Greenberg, M. T., & Kusche, C. A. (1999). A two-year longitudinal study of neuropsychological and cognitive performance in relation to behavioral problems and competencies in elementary school children. *Journal of Abnormal Child Psychology, 27,* 51–63.

Nix, R. L., Pinderhughes, E. E., Dodge, K. A., Bates, J. E., Pettit, G. S., & McFadyen-Ketchum, S. A.

(1999). The relation between mothers' hostile attribution tendencies and children's externalizing behavior problems: The mediating role of mothers' harsh discipline practices. *Child Development, 70,* 896–909.

Norris, F. H., & Kaniasty, K. (1994). Psychological distress following criminal victimization in the general population: Cross-sectional, longitudinal, and prospective analysis. *Journal of Consulting and Clinical Psychology, 62,* 111–123.

Norris, F. H., Kaniasty, K., & Scheer, D. A. (1990). Use of mental health services among victims of crime: Frequency, correlates, and subsequent recovery. *Journal of Consulting and Clinical Psychology, 58,* 538–547.

Norris, J., Nurius, P. S., & Dimeff, L. A. (1996). Through her eyes: Factors affecting women's perception of and resistance to acquaintance sexual aggression threat. *Psychology of Women Quarterly, 20,* 123–145.

Northey, W. (1994). Restorative justice: Rebirth of an ancient practice. *New Perspectives on Crime and Justice, 14,* 1–39.

Norton, S. (1990). Supervision needs of correctional mental health counselors. *Journal of Addictions and Offender Counseling, 11,* 13–19.

Nowikowski, F. (1995). Psychological offender profiling: An overview. *Criminologist, 19,* 225–226.

Nurius, P. S. (2000). Risk perception of acquaintance sexual aggression: A social-cognitive perspective. *Aggression and Violent Behavior, 5,* 63–79.

Nurius, P. S., Norris, J., Macy, R. J., & Huang, B. (2004). Women's situational coping with acquaintance sexual assault. *Violence Against Women, 10,* 450–478.

Nurius, P. S., Norris, J., Young, D. S., Graham, T. L., & Gaylord, J. (2000). Interpreting and defensively responding to threats: Examining appraisals and coping with acquaintance sexual aggression. *Violence and Victims, 15,* 187–208.

Oberlander, L. B., & Goldstein, N. E. (2001). A review and update on the practice of evaluating Miranda comprehension. *Behavioral Sciences & the Law, 19,* 453–471.

Oberlander, L. B., Goldstein, N. E., & Ho, C. N. (2001). Preadolescent adjudicative competence: Methodological consideration and recommendations for practice standards. *Behavioral Sciences & the Law, 19,* 545–563.

Office of Justice Programs. (2004). *Reentry.* Retrieved March 27, 2006, from http://www.ojp.usdoj.gov/reentry/learn.html.

Oglesby, T. M. (1957). Use of emotional screening in the selection of police applicants. *Public Personnel Review, 18,* 228–231.

Ogloff, J. R., Wong, S., & Greenwood, A., (1990). Treating adult psychopaths in a therapeutic community program within a correctional setting. *Behavioral Sciences & the Law, 8,* 81–90.

Olsson, C. A., Bond, L., Burns, J. M., Vella-Broderick, D. A., & Sawyer, S. M. (2003). Adolescence resilience: A concept analysis. *Journal of Adolescence, 26,* 1–11.

Orcutt, J. D., & Faison, R. (1988). Sex-role attitude change and reporting of rape victimization, 1973–1985. *Sociological Quarterly, 29,* 589–604.

Ornstein, P. A., Merritt, K. A., Baker-Ward, L., Furtado, E., Gordon, B. N., & Principe, G. (1998). Children's knowledge, expectation, and long-term retention. *Applied Cognitive Psychology, 12,* 387–405.

O'Shaughnessy, R., Hare, R. D., Gretton, H., & McBride, M. (1994). *Psychopathy and adolescent sex offending.* Unpublished raw data.

Ostrosky, F., Ardila, A., Rosselli, M., López-Arango, G., & Uriel-Mendoza, V. (1998). Neuropsychological test performance in illiterates. *Archives of Clinical Neuropsychology, 13,* 645–660.

Ostrosky-Solis, F., López-Arango, G., & Ardila, A. (2000). Sensitivity and specificity of the Mini-Mental State Examination in a Spanish-speaking population. *Applied Neuropsychology, 7,* 25–31.

Otero, R. F., McNally, D., & Powitzky, R. (1981). Mental health services in adult correctional systems. *Corrections Today, 43*(1), 8–18.

Otto, R. K., & Heilbrun, K. (2002). The practice of forensic psychology: A look toward the future in light of the past. *American Psychologist, 57,* 5–18.

Ozer, E. J. (2005). The impact of violence on urban adolescents: Longitudinal effects of perceived school connection and family support. *Journal of Adolescent Research, 20,* 167–192.

Ozer, E. M., & Bandura, A. (1990). Mechanisms governing empowerment effects: A self-efficacy analysis. *Journal of Personality and Social Psychology, 58,* 472–486.

Pagelow, M. D. (1993). Justice for victims of spouse abuse in divorce and child custody cases. *Violence and Victims, 8,* 69–83.

Pappas, D. (2000). Stopping New Yorkers' stalkers: An anti-stalking law for the new millennium. *Fordham Urban Law Journal, 27,* 945–952.

Parker, J. G., & Asher, S. R. (1987). Peer relations and later personal adjustment: Are low-accepted children at risk? *Psychological Bulletin, 102,* 357–389.

Parks, K. A., & Miller, B. A. (1997). Bar victimization of women. *Psychology of Women Quarterly, 21,* 509–525.

Parks, K. A., & Zetes-Zanatta, L. (1999). Women's bar-related victimization: Refining and testing a conceptual model. *Aggressive Behavior, 25,* 349–364.

Pasternack, S. A. (1995). Homicide bereavement: Diagnostic assessment and psychoanalytic psychotherapy. *Psychoanalysis and Psychotherapy, 12,* 163–182.

Pathé, M., Mullen, P. E., & Purcell, R. (1999). Stalking: False claims of victimization. *British Journal of Psychiatry, 174,* 170–172.

Patrick, C. J. (1994). Emotion and psychopathy: Some startling new insights. *Psychophysiology, 31,* 319–330.

Pattavina, A. (2004). The emerging role of information technology in prison reentry initiatives. *Federal Probation, 68,* 40–44.

Patterson, G. R., DeGarmo, D., & Knutson, N. (2000). Hyperactive and antisocial behaviors: Comorbid or two points in the same process? *Developmental and Psychopathology, 12,* 91–106.

Pearson, F. S., & Lipton, D. S. (1999). A meta-analytic review of the effectiveness of corrections-based treatment for drug abuse. *The Prison Journal, 79,* 384–410.

Pelissier, B., Rhodes, W., Saylor, W., Gaes, G., Camp, S., Vanyur, S. D., et al. (2000). *TRIAD drug treatment evaluation project: Final report of three-year outcomes.* Washington, DC: Federal Bureau of Prisons.

People v. Lara, 432 P.2d 202 (1967).

Pepler, D. J., Byrd, W., & King, G. (1991). A social-cognitively based social skills training program for aggressive children. In D. J. Pepler & K. H. Rubin (Eds.), *The development and treatment of childhood aggression.* Hillsdale, NJ: Erlbaum.

Perkins, D., & Taylor, R. (1996). Ecological assessments of community disorder: Their relationship to fear of crime and theoretical implications. *American Journal of Community Psychology, 24,* 63–107.

Petersilia, J. (2004). What works in prisoner reentry? *Federal Probation, 68,* 4–8.

Peterson, C. (2002). Children's long-term memory for autobiographical events. *Developmental Review, 22,* 370–402.

Peterson, C., & Biggs, M. (1997). Interviewing children about trauma: Problems with "specific" questions. *Journal of Traumatic Stress, 10,* 279–290.

Peterson, C., Dowden, C., & Tobin, J. (1999). Interviewing preschoolers: Comparisons of yes/no and wh- questions. *Law and Human Behavior, 23,* 539–555.

Pinizzotto, A. J. (1984). Forensic psychology: Criminal personality profiling. *Journal of Police Science and Administration, 12,* 32–40.

Pinizzotto, A. J., & Finkel, N. J. (1990). Criminal personality profiling: An outcome and process study. *Law and Human Behavior, 14,* 215–233.

Pino, R., & Meier, F. (1999). Gender differences in rape reporting. *Sex Roles: A Journal of Research, 40,* 979–990.

Pipe, M. E., & Wilson, J. C. (1994). Cues and secrets: Influences on children's event reports. *Developmental Psychology, 30,* 515–525.

Pithers, W. D. (1990). Relapse prevention with sexual aggressors: A method for maintaining therapeutic gain and enhancing external supervision. In W. L. Marshall, D. R. Laws, & H. E. Barbaree (Eds.), *Handbook of sexual assault: Issues, theories, and treatment of the offender.* New York: Plenum.

Pithers, W. D., & Cumming, G. F. (1989). Can relapse be prevented? Initial outcome data from the Vermont treatment program for sex offenders. In D. R. Laws (Ed.), *Relapse Prevention With sex offenders.* New York: Guilford Press.

Pithers, W. D., Martin, G. R., & Cumming, G. F. (1989). Vermont treatment program for sexual aggressors. In D. R. Laws (Ed.), *Relapse prevention with sex offenders.* New York: Guilford Press.

Pitts, V. L., & Schwartz, M. D. (1993). Promoting self-blame in hidden rape cases. *Humanity and Society, 17,* 383–398.

Polk, K. (1994). *When men kill: Scenarios of masculine violence.* Melbourne, Australia: University of Cambridge Press.

Poole, D. A., & Lamb, M. E. (1998). *Investigative interviews of children: A guide for helping professionals.* Washington, DC: American Psychological Association.

Poole, D. A., & Lindsay, D. S. (1995). Interviewing preschoolers: Effects of nonsuggestive techniques, parental coaching, and leading questions on reports of nonexperienced events. *Journal of Experimental Child Psychology, 60,* 129–154.

Porter, S., Fairweather, D., Drugge, J., Hervé, H., Birt, A., & Boer, D. P. (2000). Profiles of psychopathy in incarcerated sexual offenders. *Criminal Justice and Behavior, 27,* 216–233.

Prendergast, M. L., Hall, E. A., Wexler, H. K., Melnick, G., & Cao, Y. (2004). Amity prison–based therapeutic community: 5-year outcomes. *The Prison Journal, 84,* 36–60.

Prentky, R. A., Burgess, A. W., & Carter, D. (1986). Victim response by rapist type: An empirical and clinical analysis. *Journal of Interpersonal Violence, 1,* 688–695.

Prentky, R. A., & Knight, R. A. (1991). Identifying critical dimensions for discriminating among rapists. *Journal of Consulting and Clinical Psychology, 59,* 643–661.

Prentky, R. A., & Knight, R. A. (1993). Age of onset of sexual assault: Criminal and life history correlates. In G. C. M. Hall, R. Hirschamn, J. R. Graham, & M. S. Zaragoza (Eds.), *Sexual aggression: Issues in etiology, assessment, and treatment.* Washington, DC: Taylor & Francis.

Prentky, R. A., & Knight, R. A., Lee, A. F. S. (1997). Risk factors associated with recidivism among extrafamilial child molesters. *Journal of Consulting and Clinical Psychology, 65,* 141–149.

Prentky, R. A., & Quinsey, V. L. (Eds.). (1988). *Human sexual aggression: Current perspectives.* Annals of the New York Academy of Sciences, 528. New York: New York Academy of Sciences.

President's Commission on Law Enforcement and the Administration of Justice. (1967). *Task force report: The police.* Washington, DC: Government Printing Office.

Psychological Corporation. (1992). *Wechsler Individual Achievement Test Manual.* San Antonio, TX: Author.

Purcell, R., Pathé, M., & Mullen, P. E. (2001). A study of women who stalk. *American Journal of Psychiatry, 158,* 2056–2060.

Quas, J. A., Goodman, G. S., Ghetti, S., & Redlich, A. D. (2000). Questioning the child witness: What can we conclude from the research thus far? *Trauma Violence and Abuse, 1,* 223–249.

Quas, J. A., Schaaf, J. M., Alexander, K. W., & Goodman, G. S. (2000). Do you really remember it happening or do you only remember being asked about it happening? Children's source monitoring in forensic contexts. In K. P. Roberts & M. Blades (Eds.), *Children's source monitoring* (pp. 197–226). Mahwah, NJ: Erlbaum.

Quigley, P. (1989). *Armed and female.* New York: St. Martin's Press.

Quinnell, F. A., & Bow, J. N. (2001). Psychological tests used in child custody evaluations. *Behavioral Sciences & the Law, 19,* 491–501.

Quinsey, V. L., & Chaplin, T. C. (1988). Penile responses of child molesters and normals to descriptions of encounters with children involving sex and violence. *Journal of Interpersonal Violence, 3,* 259–274.

Quinsey, V. L., Harris, G. E., Rice, M. E., & Lalumiere, M. L. (1993). Assessing treatment efficacy in outcome studies of sex offenders. *Journal of Interpersonal Violence, 8,* 512–523.

Quinsey, V. L., Rice, M. E., & Harris, G. T. (1995). Actuarial prediction of sexual recidivism. *Journal of Interpersonal Violence, 10,* 85–105.

Quinsey, V. L., & Upfold, D. (1985). Rape completion and victim injury as a function of female resistance strategy. *Canadian Journal of Behavioral Science, 17,* 40–50.

Radelet, M., & Borg, M. (2000). Comment on Umbreit and Vos. *Homicide Studies, 4,* 88–92.

Radelet, M., & Vandiver, M. (1983). The Florida Supreme Court and death penalty appeals. *Journal of Criminal Law and Criminology, 74,* 913–926.

Rafilson, F. M., & Sison, R. (1996). Seven criterion-related validity studies conducted with the National Police Officer Selection Test. *Psychological Reports, 78,* 163–176.

Raine, A., Venables, P. H., & Williams, M. (1996). Better autonomic conditioning and faster electro-dermal half-recovery time at age 15 as possible protective factors against crime at age 19. *Developmental Psychology, 32,* 624–630.

Rakis, J. (2005). Improving the employment rates of ex-prisoners under parole. *Federal Probation, 69,* 7–14.

Raskin, D. C., & Yuille, J. C. (1989). Problems in evaluating interviews of children in sexual abuse cases. In S. J. Ceci, D. F. Ross, & M. P. Toglia (Eds.), *Perspectives on children's testimony.* New York: Springer-Verlag.

Rasmussen, K., & Levander, S. (1994). *Symptoms and personality characteristics of patients in a maximum security psychiatric unit.* Manuscript submitted for publication.

Realmuto, G., Jensen, J., & Wescoe, S. (1990). Specificity and sensitivity of sexually anatomically correct dolls in substantiating abuse: A pilot study. *Journal of the Academy of Child and Adolescent Psychiatry, 29,* 743–746.

Redmond, L. M. (1996). Sudden violent death. In K. J. Doka (Ed.), *Living with grief after sudden loss* (pp. 53–71). Washington, DC: Hospice Foundation of America.

Reese, J. T. (1986). Forward. In J. T. Reese & H. A. Goldstein (Eds.), *Psychological services for law enforcement.* Washington, DC: Government Printing Office.

Reese, J. T. (1987). *A history of police psychological services.* Washington, DC: Government Printing Office.

Reese, J. T., & Goldstein, H. A. (Eds.). (1986). *Psychological services for law enforcement.* Washington, DC: Government Printing Office.

Reich, P. A. (1986). *Language development.* Englewood Cliffs, NJ: Prentice Hall.

Reiser, M. (1972). *The police psychologist.* Springfield, IL. C. C. Thomas.

Reiser, M. (1982). *Police psychology: Collected papers.* Los Angeles: LEHI.

Reiss, A. D., Ones, D. S., & Viswesvaran, C. (1996, August). *Big Five personality dimensions and expatriate completion of overseas assignments.* Paper presented at the annual conference of the American Psychological Association, Toronto, Ont., Canada.

Reitzel, L. R. (2006, April). Sexual offender update: Public policy. *The Correctional Psychologist, 38,* 1–4.

Rennison, C. (1999). *Criminal victimization 1998: Changes 1997–98 with trends 1993–98.* Washington, DC: US Department of Justice, Bureau of Justice Statistics.

Ressler, R. K., & Burgess, A. W. (1985, August). Violent crime. *FBI Law Enforcement Bulletin,* pp. 1–32.

Ressler, R. K., Burgess A. W., & Douglas, J. E. (1988). *Sexual homicide: Patterns and motives.* Lexington, MA: Lexington Books.

Ressler, R. K., Burgess, A. W., Douglas, J. E., Hartman, C. R., & D'Agostino, R. B. (1986). Sexual killers and their victims: Identifying patterns through crime scene analysis. *Journal of Interpersonal Violence, 1,* 288–308.

Ressler, R. K., & Schachtman, T. (1992). *Whoever fights monsters: My twenty years tracking serial killers for the FBI.* New York: St. Martin's Press.

Reynolds, C. R. (Ed.). (1998). *Detection of malingering during head injury litigation.* New York: Kluwer/Plenum.

Rhodes, L. A. (2004). *Total confinement.* Berkeley: University of California Press.

Rice, M. E., & Harris, G. T. (1997). The treatment of adult offenders. In D. M. Stoff, J. Breiling, & J. D. Maser (Eds.), *Handbook of antisocial behavior.* New York: Wiley.

Rice, M. E., & Harris, G. T. (2003). The size and sign of treatment effects in sex offender therapy. *Annals of the New York Academy of Sciences, 989,* 428–440.

Rice, M. E., & Harris, G. T., & Cormier, C. A. (1992). An evaluation of a maximum security therapeutic community for psychopaths and other mentally disordered offenders. *Law and Human Behavior, 16,* 399–412.

Rice, M. E., Harris, G. T., & Quinsey, V. L. (1990). A follow-up of rapists assessed in a maximum security psychiatric facility. *Journal of Interpersonal Violence, 4,* 435–448.

Richardson, G., Gudjonsson, G. H., & Kelly, T. P. (1995). Interrogative suggestibility in an adolescent forensic population. *Journal of Adolescence, 18,* 211–216.

Rickert, V. I., & Wiemann, C. M. (1998). Date rape among adolescents and young adults. *Journal of Pediatric and Adolescent Gynecology, 11,* 167–175.

Roberts, T. (1995). *Evaluation of the victim offender mediation program in Langley, B.C.* Victoria, Canada: Focus Consultants.

Robins, L. N. (1966). *Deviant children grown up: A sociological and psychiatric study of sociopathic personality.* Baltimore: Williams & Wilkins.

Robins, L. N., & Rutter, M. R. (Eds.). (1990). *Straight and devious pathways from childhood to adulthood.* New York: Cambridge University Press.

Rock, P. (1998). *After homicide: Practical and political responses to bereavement.* Oxford, UK: Clarendon Press.

Rodenhauser, P., & Fornal, R. E. (1991). How important is the mental status examination? *Psychiatric Hospital, 22,* 21–24.

Roiphe, K. (1993). *The morning after: Sex, fear, and feminism on campus.* Boston: Little, Brown.

Rokach, A. (1987). Anger and aggression control training: Replacing attack with interaction. *Psychotherapy, 24,* 353–362.

Rosenfeld, B. (2003). When stalking turns violent: Developments in the assessment of stalking risks.

In M. Brewster (Ed.), *Stalking victims and offenders: Treatment, intervention, and research.* Kingston, NJ: Civic Research Institute.

Rosenfeld, B., & Harmon, R. (2002). Factors associated with violence in stalking and obsessional harassment cases. *Criminal Justice and Behavior, 29,* 671–691.

Rotenberg, M., & Diamond, B. L. (1971). The biblical conception of the psychopath: The law of the stubborn and rebellious son. *Journal of History of Behavioral Sciences, 7,* 29–38.

Rotundo, M., Nguyen, D. H., & Sackett, P. R. (2001). A meta-analytic review of gender differences in perceptions of sexual harassment. *Journal of Applied Psychology, 86,* 914–922.

Rowland, M. D., Henggeler, S.W., Gordon, A. M., Pickrel, S. G., Cunningham, P. B., & Edwards, J. E. (2000). Adapting multisystemic therapy to serve youth presenting psychiatric emergencies: Two case studies. *Child Psychology and Psychiatry Review, 5,* 30–43.

Rozee, P., & Koss, M. P. (2001). Rape: A century of resistance. *Psychology of Women Quarterly, 25,* 295–311.

Ruback, R. B., Menard, K. S., Outlaw, M. C., & Shaffer, J. N. (1999). Normative advice to campus crime victims: Effects of gender, age, and alcohol. *Violence and Victims, 14,* 381–396.

Russell, D. E. H. (1975). *The politics of rape: The victim's perspective.* New York: Stein & Day.

Rutter, M. L. (1999). Psychosocial adversity and child psychopathology. *The British Journal of Psychiatry, 174,* 480–493.

Rutter, M. L., & the English and Romanian Adoptees (ERA) Study Team. (1998). Developmental catch-up and deficit following adoption after severe global early privation. *Journal of Child Psychology and Psychiatry, 39,* 465–476.

Salekin, R., & Lochman, J. (Eds.). (2008). Child and adolescent psychopathy: The search for protective factors [Special issue]. *Criminal Justice and Behavior, 35.*

Salfati, C. G. (2000). The nature of expressiveness and instrumentality in homicide: Implications for offender profiling. *Homicide Studies, 4,* 265–293.

Sampson, R., & Laub, J. (1993). *Crime in the making: Pathways and turning points through life.* Cambridge, MA: Harvard University Press.

Santrock, J. W. (2005). *Children* (8th ed.). Boston: McGraw-Hill.

Saxe, L. (1994). Detection of deception: Polygraph and integrity tests. *Current Directions, 3,* 69–73.

Saylor, W. G., & Gaes, G. G. (1997). Training inmates through industrial work participation and apprenticeship instruction. *Corrections Management Quarterly, 1,* 32–43.

Saywitz, K. J., Geiselman, R. E., & Bornstein, G. K. (1992). Effects of cognitive interviewing and practice on children's recall performance. *Journal of Applied Psychology, 77,* 744–756.

Saywitz, K. J., Goodman, G. S., & Lyon, T. D. (2002). Interviewing children in and out of court: Current research and practice implications. In J. E. B. Myers & L. Berliner (Eds.), *The APSAC handbook on child maltreatment* (2nd ed., pp. 349–377). Thousand Oaks, CA: Sage.

Saywitz, K. J., & Lyon, T. D. (2002). Coming to grips with children's suggestibility. In M. L. Eisen (Ed.), *Memory and suggestibility in the forensic interview* (pp. 85–113). Mahwah, NJ: Erlbaum.

Sbordone, R. J., Strickland, T. L., & Purisch, A. D. (2000). Neuropsychological assessment of the criminal defendant: The significance of cultural factors. In E. Flechter-Janzen, T. L. Strickland, & C. R. Reynolds (Eds.), *Handbook of cross-cultural neuropsychology.* New York: Kluwer/Plenum.

Schiff, M. (1998). Restorative justice interventions for juvenile offenders: A research agenda for the next decade. *Western Criminology Review, 1,* 1–16.

Schmidt, F. L., Hunter, J. E., McKenzie, R. C., & Muldrow, T.W. (1979). Impact of valid selection procedures on work-force productivity. *Journal of Applied Psychology, 64,* 609–626.

Schwartz, I. L. (1991). Sexual violence against women: Prevalence, consequences, societal factors, and prevention. *American Journal of Preventive Medicine, 7,* 363–373.

Scogin, F., Schumacher, J., Howland, K., & McGee, J. (1989, August). *The predictive validity of psychological testing and peer evaluation in law enforcement settings.* Paper presented at the American Psychological Association Convention, New Orleans, LA.

Scott, H., & Beaman, R. (2004). Demographic and situational factors affecting injury, resistance, completion, and charges brought in sexual assault cases: What is best for arrest? *Violence and Victims, 19,* 479–494.

Scrivner, E. M. (1994). *The role of police psychology in controlling excessive force.* Washington, DC: National Institute of Justice.

Séguin, J., Tremblay, R. E., Boulerice, B., Pihl, R. O., & Harden, P. (1999). Executive functions and physical aggression after controlling for attention deficit hyperactivity disorder, general memory, and IQ. *Journal of Child Psychology and Psychiatry, 40,* 1197–1208.

Seligman, M. E. P. (2002). Positive psychology, positive prevention, and positive therapy. In C. R. Snyder & S. J. Lopez (Eds.), *Handbook of positive psychology.* New York: Oxford University Press.

Seligman, M. E. P. (2004). *Positive psychology network concept paper.* Retrieved October 4, 2004, from http://www.psych.upenn.edu/seligman/ppgrant.htm.

Seligman, M. E. P., Linley, P. A., & Joseph, S. (2004). *Positive psychology in practice.* Hoboken, NJ: Wiley.

Sell, D. E. (Ed.). (1955). *Manual of applied correctional psychology.* Columbus: Ohio Department of Mental Hygiene and Correction.

Serin, R. C. (1991). Psychopathy and violence in criminals. *Journal of Interpersonal Violence, 6,* 423–431.

Seto, M. C., & Barbaree, H. E. (1995). The role of alcohol in sexual aggression. *Clinical Psychology Review, 15,* 545–566.

Sheldon, K. M., Williams, G., & Joiner, T. E. (2003). *Self-determination theory in the clinic: Motivating physical and mental health.* New Haven, CT: Yale University Press.

Shepherd, R. E., Jr., & Zaremba, B. A. (1995). When a disabled juvenile confesses to a crime: Should it be admissible? *Criminal Justice, 9,* 31–35.

Sheridan, L. P., & Blaauw, E. (2004). Characteristics of false stalking reports. *Criminal Justice and Behavior. 31,* 55–72.

Shusman, E. J., Inwald, R. E., & Landa, B. (1984). Correction officer job performance as predicted by the IPI and MMPI. *Criminal Justice and Behavior, 11,* 309–329.

Siegal, M., & Peterson, C. C. (1996). Breaking the mold: A fresh look at children's understanding of questions about lies and mistakes. *Developmental Psychology, 32,* 322–334.

Siegal, M., & Peterson, C. C. (1998). Preschoolers' understanding of lies and innocent and negligent mistakes. *Developmental Psychology, 34,* 332–341.

Siegel, J. M., Sorenson, S. B., Golding, J. M., Burnham, M. A., & Stein, J. A. (1987). The prevalence of childhood sexual assault: The Los Angeles epidemiologic catchment area. *American Journal of Epidemiology, 126,* 1141–1164.

Silber, D. E. (1974). Controversy concerning the criminal justice system and its implications for the role of mental health workers. *American Psychologist, 29,* 239–244.

Simcock, G., & Hayne, H. (2002). Breaking the barrier? Children fail to translate their preverbal memories into language. *Psychological Science, 13,* 225–231.

Simcock, G., & Hayne, H. (2003). Age-related changes in verbal and nonverbal memory during early childhood. *Developmental Psychology, 39,* 805–814.

Simmons, M. M., & Cupp, M. (1998). Use and abuse of flunitrazepam. *Annals of Pharmacotherapy, 32,* 117–119.

Simpson, D. D. (2004). A conceptual framework for drug treatment process and outcomes. *Journal of Substance Abuse Treatment, 27,* 99–121.

Sinclair, H. C., & Frieze, I. H. (2000). Initial courtship behavior and stalking: How should we draw the line? *Violence and Victims, 15,* 23–40.

Skogan, W. G. (1984). Reporting crimes to the police: The status of world research. *Journal of Research in Crime and Delinquency, 21,* 113–138.

Smith, G. (1999). Resilience concepts and findings: Implications for family therapy. *Journal of Family Therapy, 21,* 154–158.

Smith, K. M. (1999). Drugs used in acquaintance rape. *Journal of the American Pharmaceutical Association, 39,* 519–525.

Smith, R. R., & Sabatino, D. A. (1990). Roles and functions of psychologists in American correctional institutions. *Journal of Offender Rehabilitation, 16,* 163–174.

Smykla, J. O. (1987). The human impact of capital punishment: Interviews with families of persons on death row. *Journal of Criminal Justice, 15,* 331–347.

Snyder, C. R., & Lopez, S. J. (2001). *Handbook of positive psychology.* New York: Oxford University Press.

Snyder, J., Cramer, A., Afrank, J., & Patterson, G. R. (2005). The contributions of ineffective discipline and parental hostile attributions of child misbehavior to the development of conduct problems at home and school. *Developmental Psychology, 41,* 30–41.

Sochting, I., Fairbrother, N., & Koch, W. J. (2004). Sexual assault of women: Prevention efforts and risk factors. *Violence Against Women, 10,* 73–93.

Society for Industrial and Organizational Psychology. (1987). *Principles for validation and use of personnel selection procedures.* Washington, DC: American Psychological Association.

Solomon, S. D., & Johnson, D. M. (2002). Psychosocial treatment of posttraumatic stress disorder: A practice-friendly review of outcome research. *Journal of Clinical Psychology, 58,* 947–959.

Sorensen, E., Goldman, J., Ward, M., Albanese, I., Graves, L., & Chamberlain, C. (1995). Judicial decision-making in contested custody cases: The influence of reported child abuse, spouse abuse, and parental substance abuse. *Child Abuse & Neglect, 19,* 251–260.

Soroka et al. v. Dayton Hudson Corporation, 91 Daily Journal D. A. R. 13204 (1991).

Speltz, M. L., DeKlyen, M., Calderon, R., Greenberg, M. T., & Fisher, P. A. (1999). Neuropsychological characteristics and test behaviors of boys with early onset conduct problems. *Journal of Abnormal Psychology, 108,* 315–325.

Spielberger, C. D. (1979). *Police selection and evaluation: Issues and techniques.* Washington, DC: Hemisphere.

Spielberger, C. D., Ward, J. C., & Spaulding, H. C. (1979). A model for the selection of law enforcement officers. In C. D. Spielberger (Ed.), *Police selection and evaluation: Issues and techniques.* Washington, DC: Hemisphere.

Spreen, O., & Strauss, E. (1998). *A compendium of neuropsychological tests* (2nd ed.). New York: Oxford University Press.

Spungen, D. (1998). *Homicide: The hidden victims: A resource for professionals.* Thousand Oaks, CA: Sage.

Stahl, P. M. (1994). *Conducting child custody evaluations: A comprehensive guide.* Thousand Oaks, CA: Sage.

Stahl, P. M. (1999). *Complex issues in child custody evaluations.* Thousand Oaks, CA: Sage.

Standards Committee, American Association for Correctional Psychology. (2000). Standards for psychology services in jails, prisons, correctional facilities, and agencies. *Criminal Justice and Behavior, 27,* 433–494.

State v. Michaels, 625 A2d 489 (N.J. App. 1993), aff'd, 1994WL278424 (N.J. Spu. 1994).

Stattin, H., & Klackenberg-Larsson, I. (1993). Early language and intelligence development and their relationship to future criminal behavior. *Journal of Abnormal Psychology, 102,* 369–378.

Steadman, H. J. (2001). *Jail diversion: Creating alternatives for persons with mental illnesses.* Washington, DC: U.S. Department of Health and Human Services, National Institute of Mental Health and Policy Research Associates.

Sternberg, K. J., Lamb, M. E., Hershkowitz, I., Esplin, P. W., Redlich, A., & Sunshine, N. (1996). The relation between investigative utterance types and the informativeness of child witnesses. *Journal of Applied Developmental Psychology, 17,* 439–451.

Sternberg, K. J., Lamb, M. E., Hershkowitz, I., Yudilevitch, L., Orbach, Y., Esplin, P. W., et al. (1997). Effects of introductory style on children's abilities to describe experiences of sexual abuse. *Child Abuse & Neglect, 21,* 1133–1146.

Stockdale, M. S., O'Connor, M., Gutek, B. A., & Geer, T. (2002). The relationship between prior sexual victimization and sensitivity to social sexual behavior in the workplace and education: Literature review and empirical study. *Psychology, Public Policy, and Law, 8,* 64–95.

Stoolmiller, M. (2001). Synergistic interaction of child manageability problems and parent-discipline tactics in predicting future growth in externalizing behavior for boys. *Developmental Psychology, 37,* 814–825.

Storaska, F. (1975). *How to say no to a rapist and survive.* New York: Random House.

Stouthamer-Loeber, M., Loeber, R., Farrington, D. P., Zhang, Q., van Kammen, W., & Maguin, E. (1993). The double edge of protective and risk factors for delinquency: Interrelations and developmental patterns. *Development and Psychopathology, 5,* 683–701.

Stowe, R. M., Arnold, D. H., & Ortiz, C. (2000). Gender differences in the relationship of language development to disruptive behavior and peer relationships in preschoolers. *Journal of Applied Developmental Psychology, 20,* 521–536.

Strachan, C. (1994). *Assessment of psychopathy in female offenders.* Unpublished doctoral dissertation, University of British Columbia, Vancouver, Canada.

Strang, H. (1993). *Homicides in Australia 1991–92.* Canberra: Australian Institute of Criminology.

Straus, M. A. (1979). Measuring intrafamily conflict and violence: The Conflict Tactics (CT) Scales. *Journal of Marriage and the Family, 41,* 75–88.

Straus, M. A. (1990). Injury and frequency of assault and the "Representative Sample Fallacy" in measuring wife beating and child abuse. In M. A. Straus & R. J. Gelles (Eds.), *Physical violence in American families: Risk factors and adaptations to violence in 8,145 families.* New Brunswick, NJ: Transaction.

Straus, M. A. (1993). Physical assaults by wives: A major social problem. In R. J. Gelles & D. R. Loseke (Eds.), *Current controversies on family violence.* Thousand Oaks, CA: Sage.

Straus, M. A., & Gelles, R. J. (1988). How violent are American families? Estimates from the National Family Violence Resurvey and other studies. In G. Hotaling, D. Finkelhor, J. T. Kirkpatrick, & M. A. Straus (Eds.), *Family abuse and its consequences: New directions in research.* Thousand Oaks, CA: Sage.

Straus, M. A., Hamby, S. L., Boney-McCoy, S., & Sugarman, D. B. (1996). The revised Conflict Tactics Scales (CTS2): Development and preliminary psychometric data. *Journal of Family Issues, 17,* 283–316.

Strauss, A., & Corbin, J. (1990). *Basics of qualitative theory procedures and techniques.* Newbury Park, CA: Sage.

Strickland, T. L., & Gray, G. (2000). Neurobehavioral disorders and pharmacologic intervention: The significance of ethnobiological variation in drug responsivity. In E. Fletcher-Janzen, T. L. Strickland, & C. R. Reynolds (Eds.), *Handbook of cross-cultural neuropsychology.* New York: Kluwer/Plenum.

Sweet, J. (Ed.). (1999). *Forensic neuropsychology: Fundamentals and practice.* Royersford, PA: Swets & Zeitlinger.

Sweet, J., Dawes, R., & Monahan, J. (2000). Psychological science can improve diagnostic decisions. *Psychological Science in the Public Interest, 1,* 1–26.

Tancredi, L. R. (1987). The Mental Status Examination. *Generations: Journal of the American Society on Aging, 11,* 24–31.

Tang, M., Zou, X., Han, H., Wang, Y., Zhang, L., Tang, M., et al. (1999). Application of the Chinese version of the Mini-Mental State Exam (MMSE) in 55-year-olds and above from the districts of Chengdu City, China. *Chinese Mental Health Journal, 13,* 200–202.

Taxman, F. S., & Bouffard, J. A. (2002). Assessing therapeutic integrity in modified therapeutic communities for drug-involved offenders. *The Prison Journal, 82,* 189–212.

Taylor, M., Esbensen, B. M., & Bennett, R. T. (1994). Children's understanding of knowledge acquisition: The tendency for children to report they have always known what they have just learned. *Child Development, 65,* 1581–1604.

Taylor, M. J., & Heaton, R. K. (2001). Sensitivity and specificity of WAIS-III/WMS-III demographically corrected factors in neuropsychological assessment. *Journal of the International Neuropsychological Society, 7,* 867–874.

Telford, F., & Moss, F. A. (1924). Suggested tests for patrolmen. *Public Personnel Studies, 2,* 112–144.

Terman, L. M. (1917). A trial of mental and pedagogical tests in a civil service examination for policemen and firemen. *Journal of Applied Psychology, 1,* 17–29.

Terman, L. M., & Oden, M. (1947). *The gifted child grows up: Twenty-five years' follow-up of a superior group.* Stanford, CA: Stanford University Press.

Terr, L.C. (1991). Childhood traumas: An outline and overview. *American Journal of Psychiatry, 148,* 10–20.

Tett, R. P., Jackson, D. N., & Rothstein, M. (1991). Personality measures as predictors of job performance: A meta-analytic review. *Personnel Psychology, 44,* 703–740.

Thierry, K. L., & Spence, M. J. (2002). Source-monitoring training facilitates preschoolers' eyewitness memory performance. *Developmental Psychology, 38,* 428–437.

Thomas, A., & Chess, S. (1977). *Temperament and development.* New York: Brunner/Mazel.

Thompson, M. D., Reuland, M., & Souweine, D. (2003). Criminal justice/mental health consensus: Improving responses to people with mental illness. *Crime and Delinquency, 49,* 30–52.

Thurstone, L. L (1922). The intelligence of policemen. *Journal of Personnel Research, 2,* 64–74.

Thurstone, L. L. (1924). The civil service tests for patrolmen in Philadelphia. *Public Personnel Studies, 2,* 1–5.

Tiẽt, Q. Q., & Huizinga, D. (2002). Dimensions of the construct of resilience and adaptation among inner-city youth. *Journal of Adolescent Research, 17,* 260–276.

Tims, F. M., De Leon, G., & Jainchill, N. (Eds.). (1994). *Therapeutic community: Advances in research and application* (Research Monograph No. 144). Rockville, MD: National Institute on Drug Abuse.

Tjaden, P., & Thoennes, N. (1998). *Stalking in America: Findings from the National Violence Against Women Survey.* Washington, DC: U.S. Department of Justice, National Institute of Justice.

Tjaden, P., & Thoennes, N. (2000a). *Extent, nature, and consequences of intimate partner violence: Findings from the National Violence Against*

Women Survey. Washington, DC: National Institute of Justice and Centers for Disease Control and Prevention.

Tjaden, P., & Thoennes, N. (2000b). *Full report of the prevalence, incidence, and consequences of intimate partner violence against women: Findings from the National Violence Against Women Survey.* Washington, DC: National Institute of Justice and Centers for Disease Control and Prevention.

Toch, H. (Ed.). (1980). *Therapeutic communities in corrections.* New York. Praeger.

Toglia, M. P., Ross, D. F., Ceci, S. J., & Hembrooke, H. (1992). The suggestibility of children's memory: Asocial-psychological and cognitive interpretation. In M. L. Howe, C. J. Brainard, & V. F. Reyna (Eds.), *Development of long-term memory.* New York: Springer-Verlag.

Tolan, P. H., & Thomas, P. (1995). The implications of age of onset for delinquency II: Longitudinal data. *Journal of Abnormal Child Psychology, 23,* 157–169.

Tomz, J. E., & McGillis, D. (1997). *Serving crime victims and witnesses* (2nd ed.). Washington, DC: U.S. Department of Justice.

Tremblay, R. E. (2003). Why socialization fails: The case of chronic physical aggression. In B. B. Lahey, T. E. Moffitt, & A. Caspi (Eds.), *Causes of conduct disorder and juvenile delinquency.* New York: Guilford Press.

Tucillo, J. A., DeFilippis, N. A., Denny, R. L., & Dsurney, J. (2002). Licensure requirements for interjurisdictional forensic evaluations. *Professional Psychology: Research and Practice, 33,* 377–383.

Tugade, M. M., & Fredrickson, B. L. (2004). Resilient individuals use positive emotions to bounce back from negative emotional expressions. *Journal of Personality and Social Psychology, 86,* 320–333.

Turvey, B. (1999). *Criminal profiling: An introduction to behavioral evidence analysis.* San Diego, CA: Academic Press.

Tutu, D. (1999). *No future without forgiveness.* New York: Image Doubleday.

Ullman, S. E. (1997). Review and critique of empirical studies of rape avoidance. *Criminal Justice and Behavior, 24,* 177–204.

Ullman, S. E. (1998). Does offender violence escalate when rape victims fight back? *Journal of Interpersonal Violence, 13,* 179–192.

Ullman, S. E. (1999a). Social support and recovery from sexual assault: A review. *Aggression and Violent Behavior: A Review Journal, 4,* 343–358.

Ullman, S. E. (1999b). A comparison of gang and individual rape incidents. *Violence and Victims, 14,* 1–11.

Ullman, S. E. (2002). Rape avoidance: Self-protection strategies for women. In P. A. Schewe (Ed.), *Preventing violence in relationships: Interventions across the life span* (pp. 137–162). Washington, DC: American Psychological Association.

Ullman, S. E. (2003). A critical review of field studies on the link of alcohol and adult sexual assault in women. *Aggression and Violent Behavior: A Review Journal, 8,* 471–486.

Ullman, S. E. (2007). Comparing gang and individual rapes in a community sample of urban women. *Violence and Victims.*

Ullman, S. E., & Brecklin, L. R. (2000). Alcohol and adult sexual assault in a national sample of women. *Journal of Substance Abuse, 12,* 1–16.

Ullman, S. E., & Brecklin, L. (2002). Sexual assault and suicidal behavior in the National Comorbidity Survey. *Suicide and Life-Threatening Behavior, 32,* 117–130.

Ullman, S. E., & Brecklin, L. (2003). Sexual assault history and health-related outcomes in a national sample of women. *Psychology of Women Quarterly, 27,* 46–57.

Ullman, S. E., Filipas, H. H., Townsend, S. M., & Starzynski, L. L. (2006). The role of victim–offender relationship in women's sexual assault experiences. *Journal of Interpersonal Violence, 21,* 798–819.

Ullman, S. E., Karabatsos, G., & Koss, M. P. (1999). Alcohol and sexual assault in a national sample of college women. *Journal of Interpersonal Violence, 14,* 603–625.

Ullman, S. E., & Knight, R. A. (1991). A multivariate model for predicting rape and physical injury outcomes during sexual assaults. *Journal of Consulting and Clinical Psychology, 59,* 724–731.

Ullman, S. E., & Knight, R. A. (1992). Fighting back: Women's resistance to rape. *Journal of Interpersonal Violence, 7,* 31–43.

Ullman, S. E., & Knight, R. A. (1995). Women's resistance strategies to different rapist types. *Criminal Justice and Behavior, 22,* 263–283.

Ullman, S. E., & Siegel, J. M. (1993). Victim–offender relationship and sexual assault. *Violence and Victims, 8,* 121–134.

Ullman, S. E., & Siegel, J. M. (1995). Sexual assault, social reactions, and physical health. *Women's Health: Research on Gender, Behavior, and Policy, 1,* 289–308.

Ullman, S. E., Townsend, S. M., Filipas, H. H., & Starzynski, L. L. (2007). Structural models of the relations of assault severity, social support, avoidance coping, self-blame, and PTSD among sexual assault survivors. *Psychology of Women Quarterly, 31,* 23–37.

Umbreit, M. (1989). Violent offenders and their victims. In M. Wright & B. Galaway (Eds.), *Mediation and criminal justice* (pp. 337–352). London: Sage.

Umbreit, M. (1994). *Victim meets offender: The impact of restorative justice and mediation.* Monsey, NY: Criminal Justice Press.

Umbreit, M. (1998). Restorative justice through victim–offender mediation: A multi-site assessment. *Western Criminology Review, 1,* 1–27.

Umbreit, M., & Vos, B. (2000). Homicide survivors meet the offender prior to execution. *Homicide Studies, 4,* 63–87.

U.S. Department of Education. (1993). *Fall enrollment statistics, 1991.* Washington, DC: Government Printing Office.

U.S. Department of Justice. (1996). *Bureau of justice statistics: Local police departments.* Washington, DC: Office of Justice Programs.

U.S. Department of Justice. (2006). *Criminal offenders statistics.* Washington, DC: Bureau of Justice Statistics. Retrieved on March 25, 2006, from http://www.ojp.usdoj.gov.bjs.crimoff.htm.

Vaillant, G. (1977). *Adaptation to life.* Boston: Little, Brown.

Vaillant, G. (1993). *The wisdom of the ego.* Cambridge, MA: Harvard University Press.

Valciukas, J. A. (1995). *Forensic neuropsychology: Conceptual foundations and clinical practice.* New York: Haworth Press.

Vandiver, M. (1989). Coping with death: Families of the terminally ill, homicide victims, and condemned prisoners. In M. L. Radelet (Ed.), *Facing the death penalty: Essays on a cruel and unusual punishment* (pp. 123–138). Philadelphia: Temple University Press.

Vandiver, M. (1998). The impact of the death penalty on the families of homicide victims and of condemned prisoners. In J. R. Acker, R. M. Bohm, & C. S. Lanier (Eds.), *America's experiment with capital punishment: Reflections on the past, present, and future of the ultimate penal sanction* (pp. 385–415). Durham, NC: Carolina Academic Press.

van Marle, H. J. C. (1995). *A closed system: A psychoanalytical framework for forensic therapeutic communities.* Arnhem, The Netherlands: Gouda Quint.

Van Ness, D., & Strong, K. (2002). *Restoring justice.* Cincinnati, OH: Anderson.

Viteles, M. S. (1929). Psychological methods in the selection of patrolmen in Europe. *Annals of the American Academy, 146,* 160–165.

Waaktaar, T., Christie, H. J., Borge, A. I. H., & Torgerson, S. (2004). How can young people's resilience be enhanced? Experiences from a clinical intervention project. *Clinical Child Psychology and Psychiatry, 9,* 167–183.

Walker, A. G. (1994). *Handbook on questioning children: A linguistic perspective.* Washington, DC: American Bar Association Center on Children and the Law.

Walker, L. E., & Edwall, G. E. (1987). Domestic violence and determination of visitation and custody in divorce. In D. J. Sonkin (Ed.), *Domestic violence on trial: Psychological and legal dimensions of family violence.* New York: Springer.

Walker-Perry, N., & Wrightsman, L. S. (1991). *The child witness: Legal issues and dilemmas.* Thousand Oaks, CA: Sage.

Wall, S., & Furlong, M. (1985). Comprehension of Miranda rights by urban adolescents with law-related education. *Psychological Reports, 56,* 359–372.

Waller, M. A. (2001). Resilience in ecosystemic context: Evolution of the concept. *American Journal of Orthopsychiatry, 71,* 290–297.

Walters, G. D. (2002). *Criminal belief systems: An integrated-interactive theory of lifestyle.* Westport, CT: Praeger.

Wandersman, A., & Nation, M. (1998). Urban neighborhoods and mental health: Psychological contributions to understanding toxicity, resilience, and interventions. *American Psychologist, 53,* 647–656.

Ward, T., & Hudson, S. M. (1998). A model of the relapse process in sexual offenders. *Journal of Interpersonal Violence, 13,* 400–425.

Ward, T., & Stewart, C. A. (2003). The treatment of sexual offenders: Risk management and good lives. *Professional Psychology: Research and Practice, 34,* 353–360.

Warren, A. R. (1992, May). *Interviewing child witnesses: Some linguistic considerations.* Paper presented at the Child Witness in Context North Atlantic Treaty Organization Advanced Study Institute, Lucca, Italy.

Warren, A. R., Hulse-Trotter, K., & Tubbs, E. C. (1991). Inducing resistance to suggestibility in children. *Law and Human Behavior, 15,* 273–285.

Warren, A. R., & McCloskey, L. A. (1997). Language in social contexts. In J. B. Gleason (Ed.), *The development of language* (4th ed.). New York: Allyn & Bacon.

Warren, A. R., Woodall, C. E., Hunt, J. S., & Perry, N.W. (1996). "It sounds good in theory, but . . ." Do investigative interviewers follow guidelines based on memory research? *Child Maltreatment, 1,* 231–245.

Webster, S. D. (2005). Pathways to sexual offense recidivism following treatment. *Journal of Interpersonal Violence, 20,* 1175–1196.

Wechsler, D. (1997). *Wechsler Adult Intelligence Scale* (3rd ed.). San Antonio, TX: Psychological Corporation.

Welch-Ross, M. (2000). A mental-state reasoning model of suggestibility and memory source monitoring. In K. P. Roberts & M. Blades (Eds.), *Children's source monitoring* (pp. 227–255). Mahwah, NJ: Erlbaum.

Wells-Parker, E., Bangert-Drowns, R., McMillen, R., & Williams, M. (1995). Final results from a meta-analysis of remedial interventions with drink/drive offenders. *Addiction, 9,* 907–926.

Werner, E. E. (1987). Vulnerability and resiliency in children at risk for delinquency: A longitudinal study from birth to young adulthood. In J. D. Burchard & S. N. Burchard (Eds.), *Prevention of delinquency.* Thousand Oaks, CA: Sage.

Werner, E. E. (1993). Risk, resilience, and recovery: Perspectives from the Kauai longitudinal study. *Development and Psychopathology, 5,* 503–515.

Werner, E. E. (1995). Resilience in development. *Current Directions in Psychological Science, 4,* 81–85.

Werner, E. E., Bierman, J. M., & French, F. E. (1971). *The children of Kauai: A longitudinal study from the prenatal period to age ten.* Honolulu: University of Hawaii Press.

Werner, E. E., & Smith, R. S. (1977). *Kauai's children come of age.* Honolulu: University of Hawaii Press.

Werner, E. E., & Smith, R. S. (1982). *Vulnerable, but invincible: A longitudinal study of resilient children and youth.* New York: McGraw-Hill.

Werner, E., & Smith, R. S. (1992). *Overcoming the odds: High-risk children from birth to adulthood.* Ithaca, NY: Cornell University Press.

West, A. (2000). Clinical assessment of homicide offenders: The significance of crime scene in offense and offender analysis. *Homicide Studies, 4,* 219–233.

Wexler, H. K., Melnick, G., Lowe, L., & Peters, J. (1999). Three-year reincarceration outcomes for Amity in-prison therapeutic community and aftercare in California. *The Prison Journal, 79,* 321–336.

Wexler, H. K., Prendergast, M. L., & Melnick, G. (2004). Introduction to a special issue: Correctional drug treatment outcomes—focus on California. *The Prison Journal, 84,* 3–7.

What is investigative psychology? (1997). Liverpool, UK: Center for Investigative Psychology. Available at http://www.liv.ac.uk/Investigative Psychology/explained/explain.html.

Widiger, R. A., & Corbitt, E. (1995). The DSM-IV antisocial personality disorder. In W. J. Livesley (Ed.), *The DSM-IV personality disorders.* New York: Guilford Press.

Widiger, T. A., Cadoret, R., Hare, R. D., Robins, L., Rutherford, M., Zanarini, M., et al. (1996). DSM-IV Antisocial Personality Disorder Field Trial. *Journal of Abnormal Psychology, 105,* 3–16.

Wiener, R. L., & Hurt, L. E. (1999). An interdisciplinary approach to understanding social sexual conduct at work. *Psychology, Public Policy, and Law, 5,* 556–595.

Wilkinson, J. (2005). Evaluating evidence for the effectiveness of the Reasoning and Rehabilitation Programme. *The Howard Journal, 44,* 70–85.

Williams, J. E. (1984). Secondary victimization: Confronting public attitudes about rape. *Victimology, 9,* 66–81.

Williams, P., & Dickinson, J. (1993). Fear of crime: Read all about it? *British Journal of Criminology, 33,* 33–56.

Williamson, S. E., Hare, R. D., & Wong, S. (1987). Violence: Criminal psychopaths and their victims. *Canadian Journal of Behavioral Science, 19,* 454–462.

Williamson, S. E., Harpur, T. J., & Hare, R. D. (1991). Abnormal processing of affective words by psychopaths. *Psychophysiology, 28,* 260–273.

Wilson, D. B., Bouffard, L. A., & Mackenzie, D. L. (2005). A quantitative review of structured, group-oriented, cognitive-behavioral programs for offenders. *Criminal Justice and Behavior, 32,* 172–204.

Wilson, J. C., & Pipe, M. E. (1995). Children's disclosure of secrets: Implications for interviewing. In G. Davis, S. Lloyd-Bostock, M. McMurran, &

C. Wilson (Eds.), *Psychology, law, and criminal justice: International developments in research and practice.* Berlin, Germany: Walter de Gruyter.

Wilson, J. Q. (1968). *Varieties of police behavior.* Cambridge, MA: Harvard University Press.

Wilson, J. Q., & Herrnstein, R. J. (1985). *Crime and human nature.* New York: Simon & Schuster.

Wilson, P., Lincoln, R., & Kocsis, R. N. (1997). Validity, utility and ethics of profiling for serial violent and sexual offenders. *Psychiatry, Psychology and Law, 4,* 1–12.

Wilson, P. & Soothill, K. (1996, January). Psychological profiling: Red, green, or amber? *Police Journal, 69,* 12–20.

Wilson, R. J., & Prinzo, M. (2001). Circles of Support: A restorative justice initiative. *Journal of Psychology and Human Sexuality, 13,* 59–77.

Wilson, R. J., Picheca, J. E., & Prinzo, M. (2005). *Circles of support and accountability: An evaluation of the pilot project in South-Central Ontario* (No. R-168). Ottawa: Correctional Services of Canada.

Wimmer, H., Hogrefe, G. J., & Perner, J. (1988). Children's understanding of informational access as source of knowledge. *Child Development, 59,* 386–396.

Wiseman, R., & West, D. (1997, January). An experimental test of psychic detection. *Police Journal, 70,* 19–25.

Witkin, G. (1996, April 22). How the FBI paints portraits of the nation's most wanted. *U.S. News and World Report, 120,* 32.

Wolff, N. (2005). Community reintegration of prisoners with mental illness: A social investment perspective. *International Journal of Law and Psychiatry, 28,* 43–58.

Wolff, N., & Pogorzelski, W. (2005). Measuring the effectiveness of mental health courts: Challenges and recommendations. *Psychology, Public Policy, and Law, 11,* 539–569.

Wong, S. (1984). *Criminal and institutional behaviors of psychopaths* (Program branch users report). Ottawa: Ministry of the Solicitor-General of Canada.

World Health Organization. (1990). *International classification of diseases and related health problems* (10th ed.). Geneva, Switzerland: Author.

Wormith, J. S., & Olver, M. E. (2002). Offender treatment attrition and its relationship with risk, need, responsivity, and recidivism. *Criminal Justice and Behavior, 29,* 447–471.

Yarmey, A. D. (1990). *Understanding police and police work: Psychosocial issues.* New York: New York University Press.

Yates, P. M. (2005). Pathways to treatment of sexual offenders: Rethinking intervention. *Forum on Corrections Research, 17,* 1–9.

Yehuda, R. (2002). Clinical relevance of biological findings in PTSD. *Psychiatric Quarterly, 73,* 123–133.

Yochelson, S., & Samenow, S. (1976). *The criminal personality. Vol. 1: A profile for change.* New York: Jason Aronson.

Yochelson, S., & Samenow, W. (1977). *The criminal personality, Vol. 2: The change process.* New York: Jason Aronson.

Yuille, J. C., Hunter, R., Jeffe, R., & Zaparniuk, J. (1993). Interviewing children in sexual abuse cases. In G. S. Goodman & B. L. Bottoms (Eds.), *Child victims, child witnesses: Understanding and improving testimony.* New York: Guilford Press.

Zehr, H. (1985). Retributive justice, restorative justice. New perspectives on crime and justice. *Occasional Papers of the MCC Canada Victim Offender Ministries Program and the MCC U.S. Office on Crime and Justice, 4,* 1–20.

Zelazo, P. D., Carter, A., Resnick, J. S., & Frye, D. (1997). Early development of executive functions: A problem-solving framework. *Review of General Psychology, 1,* 198–226.

Zoucha-Jensen, J. M., & Coyne, A. (1993). The effects of resistance strategies on rape. *American Journal of Public Health, 83,* 1633–1634.

Zuckerman, M. (1994). *Behavioral expressions and biosocial basis of sensation seeking.* New York: Cambridge University Press.

INDEX

ABOUT THE EDITORS

Curt R. Bartol, who earned a PhD in Social Psychology from Northern Illinois University, was a college professor for more than 30 years. He taught a wide variety of both undergraduate and graduate courses, including biopsychology, criminal behavior, juvenile delinquency, introduction to forensic psychology, social psychology, and psychology and law. As a licensed clinical psychologist, he has been a consulting police psychologist to local, municipal, state, and federal law enforcement agencies for nearly 25 years. He is also the Editor of *Criminal Justice and Behavior,* the international journal of the American Association for Correctional Psychologists, published by Sage Publications. In addition to editing *Current Perspectives in Forensic Psychology and Criminal Behavior,* he has coauthored, with Anne Bartol, *Introduction to Forensic Psychology,* second edition (2008); *Criminal Behavior: A Psychosocial Approach,*

now in its eighth edition; *Juvenile Delinquency,* third edition (2008); and *Psychology and Law: Theory, Research, and Application,* third edition. He has published extensively in the field of forensic psychology.

Anne M. Bartol earned an MA and a PhD in Criminal Justice from the State University of New York at Albany. She also holds an MA in journalism from the University of Wisconsin–Madison. She taught criminal justice, sociology, and journalism courses over a 20-year college teaching career and has worked as a journalist and as a social worker in child and adolescent protective services. She is Managing Editor of *Criminal Justice and Behavior.* In addition to *Current Perspectives,* she has coauthored the above books with Curt Bartol and has published articles on women and criminal justice, rural courts, and the history of forensic psychology.